James Love

Scottish Church Music

Its composers and sources

James Love

Scottish Church Music
Its composers and sources

ISBN/EAN: 9783337087661

Printed in Europe, USA, Canada, Australia, Japan

Cover: Foto ©Lupo / pixelio.de

More available books at **www.hansebooks.com**

SCOTTISH CHURCH MUSIC

SCOTTISH CHURCH MUSIC

ITS COMPOSERS AND SOURCES

BY

JAMES LOVE

WILLIAM BLACKWOOD AND SONS
EDINBURGH AND LONDON
MDCCCXCI

PREFACE.

IN this book will be found an account of the source and history —so far as is known to me—of upwards of ONE THOUSAND PSALM AND HYMN TUNES; THREE HUNDRED CHANTS, DOXOLOGIES, AND SCRIPTURE SENTENCES OR ANTHEMS,—being those contained in the following works:—

    'The United Presbyterian Hymnal, with Accompanying Tunes,' 1877;

    'The United Presbyterian Psalter, with Accompanying Tunes,' 1878;

    'The Presbyterian Hymnal Scripture Sentences and Chants,' 1886,

—all published by the authority of the Synod of the United Presbyterian Church:

    'The Free Church Hymn Book, with Tunes,' 1882;

    'The Scottish Psalter, . . . with Appropriate Tunes and Chants,' 1883,

—both published by authority of the General Assembly of the Free Church of Scotland:

    'The Scottish Hymnal (Appendix Incorporated), with Tunes, for Use in Churches,' 1885;

'The Book of Psalms and Paraphrases (in Metre), with Tunes, for Use in Churches,' 1886,

—both published by authority of the General Assembly of the Church of Scotland.

There are also about FIVE HUNDRED BIOGRAPHICAL NOTICES OF THE COMPOSERS, AND AN APPENDIX CONTAINING SOME PARTICULARS REGARDING THE PRINCIPAL COLLECTIONS OF PSALMODY ISSUED IN SCOTLAND SINCE 1700.

A deep interest in the Biography of our psalm and hymn tune writers, and the tracing of our Church music to its original sources, led me, during my spare moments within the last ten years, to compile this work. I was also actuated by the idea that, as a leader of Praise, I ought to have some knowledge of the sources of our Church music, and of the leading facts of the composers' lives. To publish the results of my investigations was not my intention, as I lay no claim to literary ability; but it was pointed out to me that a work of this kind had never been issued in Scotland, although much had been written regarding hymns and their writers: and it is a fact well known to all experts, that Scottish Psalmodies have been notoriously untrustworthy as regards the source and authorship of their contents. The apparent inclination of editors to accept current testimony without question, has led to much confusion, and it is not uncommon to find tunes assigned to composers who were not born when the tunes were published, and composers bearing the same surnames hopelessly mixed. Though I make no claim to rank with those whose researches have disclosed facts of paramount national importance, I may surely claim to have approached a subject on which a great deal of uncertainty exists, and I am persuaded that additional light will be acceptable. To those who know anything of the subject, it will, I hope, be evident that considerable trouble has been taken to ensure accuracy regarding dates and facts, but it would be idle to suppose that errors have not crept into the work; these I shall be glad to have pointed out to me.

In the compilation of the work, I have had much valuable assistance and many kind suggestions from the following gentlemen, to whom I accord my warmest thanks: J. O. Anderson, Esq., Edinburgh; John Montgomerie Bell, Esq., W.S., Edinburgh; William Carnie, Esq., Aberdeen; Major George Arthur Crawford, Sevenoaks, Kent; John Spencer Curwen, Esq., London; F. G. Edwards, Esq., London; J. Cuthbert Hadden, Esq., Edinburgh; Walter Hately, Esq., Edinburgh; Rev. Dr Andrew Henderson, Paisley; Hubert P. Main, Esq., New York; Rev. Dr Andrew Melville, Glasgow; Rev. Henry Parr, Vicar of Yoxford, Suffolk; Ebenezer Prout, Esq., B.A., London; Gregg Wilson, Esq., B.D., Falkirk.

Nor can I forget the many kindnesses shown me by the late John Dobson, Esq., of Richmond, Surrey, whose great knowledge of the subject was the means of settling many doubtful points. I have also to acknowledge the help given to me by the Librarians of the British Museum, London; Euing Library, Glasgow; Advocates' and Signet Libraries, Edinburgh.

In a special measure I have to thank my friend Miss C. L. Gair, The Kilns, Falkirk, for much valuable aid, generously extended to me during the years I have been engaged on this work.

That the book may be of use to all who are interested in Church music is my earnest wish.

JAMES LOVE.

Arnothill Gardens, Falkirk,
    May 1891.

CONTENTS.

	PAGE
ALPHABETICAL INDEX OF TUNES, WITH THEIR NUMBERS, COMPOSERS OR SOURCES,	1
ALPHABETICAL INDEX OF COMPOSERS WHOSE CHANTS APPEAR IN THE U.P.H., U.P.P., S.H., S.P., AND F.C.H., WITH THEIR NUMBERS,	43
DOXOLOGIES IN U.P.H.,	46
ALPHABETICAL INDEX OF SCRIPTURE SENTENCES IN FREE CHURCH HYMNAL, AND UNITED PRESBYTERIAN HYMNAL, WITH THEIR NUMBERS, COMPOSERS OR SOURCES,	47
BIOGRAPHICAL SKETCHES OF COMPOSERS, WITH NOTES AND ILLUSTRATIVE EXAMPLES,	55
APPENDIX, CONTAINING A LIST OF THE PRINCIPAL COLLECTIONS OF PSALMODY ISSUED IN SCOTLAND FROM THE YEAR 1700 TO THE PRESENT TIME,	313

ABBREVIATIONS.

Mus. Bac.,	Bachelor of Music.
Mus. Doc.,	Doctor of Music.
Ph. Doc.,	Doctor of Philosophy.
U.P.H.,	United Presbyterian Hymnal, with accompanying Tunes, published 1877.
U.P.H.,	The Presbyterian Hymnal Scripture Sentences and Chants, published 1886.[1]
U.P.P.,	United Presbyterian Psalter, with accompanying Tunes, published 1878.
F.C.H.,	Free Church Hymnal, with Tunes, published 1882.
S.P.,	Scottish Psalter, with Tunes and Chants, published 1883.
S.H.,	Scottish Hymnal, with Tunes, published 1885.
P. & P.,	Psalms and Paraphrases, with Tunes, published 1886.
S.S.,	Scripture Sentence (Anthem).

[1] The first twenty-four Scripture Sentences in this work also appear in the United Presbyterian Hymnal of 1877, under corresponding numbers.

ADDITIONS AND CORRECTIONS.

BREMNER, ROBERT, p. 83—for additional matter regarding the tune "St Paul," see James Chalmers in Appendix, page 318.

CASE, B., p. 92, *for* "London, 1872," *read* "London, 1827."

CLARK, JEREMIAH, p. 95, l. 6, *for* "1708," *read* "1709."

DEARLE, EDWARD, Mus. Doc., p. 111, *add*, that he died April 1891.

HENDERSON, Rev. Dr ANDREW, p. 168, *add*, Elected Moderator of the United Presbyterian Synod, May 4, 1891.

OAKELEY, Sir HERBERT STANLEY, Mus. Doc., p. 222, *add*, that he received from the University of Edinburgh the degree of LL.D., together with the title of "Emeritus" Professor of Music, on his retirement from that Chair of Music in 1891.

SCOTTISH CHURCH MUSIC.

ALPHABETICAL INDEX OF TUNES, WITH THEIR NUMBERS, COMPOSERS OR SOURCES.

Tunes.	Numbers.	Composers or Sources.
Abbey . . .	87 F.C.H., 20 U.P.H., 58 U.P.P., 29 S.P., 45 P. & P.	Scottish Psalter, 1615.
Abbey Close .	25 U.P.P.	Bartholomäus Gesius' Collection, 1605.
Abends . . .	291 S.H., 23 F.C.H., 303 U.P.H.	Sir Herbert Stanley Oakeley, Mus. Doc.
Aber	44 S.H., 135 F.C.H.	William Henry Monk, Mus. Doc., 1823-1889.
Aberdeen . .	219 S.P.	Rev. R. Brown-Borthwick.
Aberfeldy . .	219 P. & P.	Scottish Psalter, 1635.
Abraham . .	235 S.H.	John Hill, 1797-1846.
Ad Inferos . .	46 S.H.	Walter Hay Sangster, Mus. Doc.
Adeste Fideles .	28 S.H., 33 U.P.H.	John Reading, 1677-1764 (?).
Adoration . .	67 S.H.	Sir George Job Elvey, Mus. Doc.
Adoration . .	224 F.C.H.	Richard Redhead.
Advent . . .	87 S.H.	William Henry Monk, Mus. Doc., 1823-1889.
Agatha . . .	174 U.P.H.	Walter Cecil Macfarren.
Alexandria . .	100 & 217 S.H., 178 P. & P.	Henry John Gauntlett, Mus. Doc., 1805-1876.

Tunes.	Numbers.	Composers or Sources.
Alford . . .	219 F.C.H.	Rev. John Bacchus Dykes, Mus. Doc., 1823-1875.
Alla Trinita .	8 S.H., 252 F.C.H.	Laudi Spirituali.
All Hallows .	118 F.C.H.	Arthur Henry Brown.
Alleluia . . .	67 S.H.	Samuel Sebastian Wesley, Mus. Doc., 1810-1876.
All Saints . .	11 & 65 S.H.	Darmstädter Gesangbuch, 1698, and Johann Georg Christian Störl's Würtemberger Gesangbuch, 1711.
All Things Bright	410 S.H.	Rev. Sir F. A. Gore Ouseley, Bart., Mus. Doc., 1825-1889.
Almsgiving . .	127 S.H., 281 F.C.H., 18 U.P.H.	Rev. J. B. Dykes, Mus. Doc., 1823-1875.
Alstone . . .	425 S.H., 336 F.C.H.	Christopher Edwin Willing.
Altenburg . .	4 F.C.H.	Gotha Cantional, 1651.
Altenburg . .	28 U.P.H.	Justin Heinrich Knecht, 1752-1817.
Altona . . .	43 S.H.	Kocher's Zionsharfe.
Amberg . . .	221, 277 S.H.	French Melody.
Angelic Songs .	247 S.H.	Thomas Hewlett, Mus. Bac., 1845-1874.
Angels . . .	378 S.H.	Albert Lister Peace, Mus. Doc.
Angels' Hymn, or Song	130 S.H., 140 U.P.H., 16 F.C.H., 1 S.P., 162 U.P.P., 1 P. & P.	Orlando Gibbons, Mus. Doc., 1583-1625.
Angelus . . .	288 S.H., 32 F.C.H., 304 U.P.H.	Georg Josephi.
Apostles' Tune .	220 P. & P.	From Christopher Tye, Mus. Doc., ob. 1572.
Argyle . . .	322 S.H.	Edmund Hart Turpin, Mus. Doc.
Arms of Jesus .	419 S.H.	Wm. Howard Doane, Mus. Doc.
Arnold . . .	46 P. & P., 30 S.P., 63 U.P.P.	Samuel Arnold, Mus. Doc., 1740-1802.
Arnsberg . .	270 U.P.H., 327 F.C.H.	Joachim Neander, 1640(?)-1680.
Arran . . .	222 S.H.	Samuel Sebastian Wesley, Mus. Doc., 1810-1876.
Artaxerxes . .	31 S.P.	From Thos. Augustine Arne, Mus. Doc., 1710-1778.
Arundel . . .	16 U.P.P.	Rev. John Chetham's Collection, 1718.
Ascension . .	57 U.P.H.	Henry John Gauntlett, Mus. Doc., 1805-1876.
Ashgrove . .	206 U.P.H.	Henry Smart, 1813-1879.
Aspiration . .	418 S.H.	Albert Lister Peace, Mus. Doc.
Aspurg . . .	47 P. & P., 179 U.P.P., 201 S.H.	Johann Georg Frech, 1790-1864.

INDEX TO TUNES.

Tunes.	Numbers.	Composers or Sources.
Assisi	43 S.H.	Francis Henry Champneys, M.D.
Atlantic	22 S.H., 42 F.C.H.	James Merrylees.
Augsburg	27 U.P.H.	German.
Augustine	133 F.C.H., 179 P. & P.	From Johann Sebastian Bach's Vierstimmige Choralgesänge, vol. ii., 1769.
Augustine	317 & 357 U.P.H.	From Samuel Webbe's Collection, 1792.
Aurelia	198, 272, & 330 S.H., 217 F.C.H., 95, 218, & 260 U.P.H.	Samuel Sebastian Wesley, Mus. Doc., 1810-1876.
Austria, or Austrian Hymn	243 U.P.H., 234 F.C.H.	Franz Joseph Haydn, 1732-1809.
Ave Maris Stella	408 S.H.	Adapted by Rev. Alexander Galloway, B.D.
Aventine	32 S.P.	Adapted by Lowell Mason, Mus. Doc., 1792-1872.
Aynhoe	180 P. & P.	James Nares, Mus. Doc., 1715-1783 (?).
Babylon's Streams	2 P. & P., 21 U.P.P.	Thomas Campion or Campian, M.D., *ob.* 1619.
Baca	260 F.C.H.	Rev. William Henry Havergal, M.A., 1793-1870.
Bach	138 F.C.H.	German.
Bach's Passion Chorale	50 S.H.	Hans Leo Hassler, 1564-1612.
Baden	121 F.C.H., 187 S.P., 74 U.P.P.	German.
Baden	216 S.H., 173 U.P.H.	Severus Gastorius, or Johann Pachelbel, 1690.
Ballerma	33 S.P., 38 & 57 U.P.P., 48 P. & P.	Adapted by Robert Simpson, *ob.* 1832.
Bangor	5 U.P.P., 34 S.P.	William Tans'ur's Collection, 1736.
Barnby	360 U.P.H.	Joseph Barnby.
Barnet	49 P. & P.	Nathaniel Gawthorn's Harmonia Perfecta, 1730.
Barossa	2 S.P., 31 F.C.H.	Ebenezer John Wallis, 1831-1879.
Barrow	35 S.P.	Lowell Mason, Mus. Doc., 1792-1872.
Basil	347 U.P.H.	Friedrich Filitz, Ph. Doc., 1804-1876.
Battishill	415 S.H., 333 U.P.H.	Jonathan Battishill, 1738-1801.
Batty or Turnau	185 & 331 S.H.	Johann Thommen's Choralbuch, 1745.

TUNES.	NUMBERS.	COMPOSERS OR SOURCES.
Bavaria . . .	3 P. & P.	Darmstädter Gesangbuch, 1698.
Beaminster . .	263 & 266 U.P.H.	Henry John Gauntlett, Mus. Doc., 1805-1876.
Beatitude . .	270 S.H.	Albert Lister Peace, Mus. Doc.
Beaufort . . .	359 S.H.	David Weyman's Sequel to Melodia Sacra.
Beautiful River	440 S.H.	Rev. Robert Lowry, D.D.
Bedford . . .	195 S.H., 50 P. & P., 152 & 155 U.P.H., 36 S.P., 143 U.P.P.	William Weale or Wheal, Mus. Bac., *ob.* 1727.
Beethoven . .	220 F.C.H.	From Ludwig van Beethoven, 1770-1827.
Belgrave . . .	37 S.P., 145 U.P.P.	William Horsley, 1774-1858.
Belmont . . .	38 S.P., 275 & 328 U.P.H., 106 U.P.P., 126 S.H., 83 & 339 F.C.H.	Anonymous. Samuel Webbe, jun., 1770-1843 (?).
Benediction .	293 S.H.	Edward John Hopkins, Mus. Doc.
Benevento . .	164 & 187 F.C.H.	Samuel Webbe, 1740-1816.
Benison . . .	300 U.P.H.	Bamberg Gesangbuch, 1707.
Bentley . . .	240 S.H., 198 F.C.H.	John Pyke Hullah, LL.D., 1812-1884.
Berlin . . .	325 S.H.	Johann Crüger's Praxis Pietatis Melica, 1656.
Berlin . . .	169 F.C.H.	Freylinghausen's Geistreiches Gesangbuch, 1704.
Bethabara . .	131 U.P.H.	Rev. William Henry Havergal, M.A., 1793-1870.
Bethany . . .	61 F.C.H.	Gregorian.
Bethany . . .	56 S.H.	Henry Smart, 1813-1879.
Bethany . . .	201 U.P.H.	Lowell Mason, Mus. Doc., 1792-1872.
Bethesda . .	359 U.P.H.	Henry Smart, 1813-1879.
Bethlehem . .	156, 206, & 282 S.H.	Samuel Wesley, 1766-1837.
Bethlehem . .	27 S.H., 195 F.C.H., 31 U.P.H.	Adapted from Felix Mendelssohn Bartholdy, Ph. Doc., 1809-1847, by W. H. Cummings.
Better World .	433 S.H.	Adapted by Hubert Platt Main.
Bevan . . .	4 U.P.H., 121 & 251 S.H.	Sir John Goss, Mus. Doc., 1800-1880.
Beverley . . .	7 & 269 S.H.	Thomas Greatorex's Parochial Psalmody, 1823.
Bickleigh . .	215 S.P.	Samuel Reay, Mus. Bac.
Bishopthorpe .	51 P. & P.	Jeremiah Clark, 1670-1707.

INDEX TO TUNES.

Tunes.	Numbers.	Composers or Sources.
Blackburn	10 U.P.P.	Ascribed to J. Fish.
Blenheim	52 P. & P.	John Arnold's Compleat Psalmodist, 1749.
Bloxham	39 S.P.	Aaron Williams's Psalmody in Miniature, 1778.
Bohemia	185 U.P.H., 10 S.H.	German.
Bohemia	256 F.C.H.	German.
Bon - Accord (Aberdeen)	221 P. & P., 40 S.P.	Scottish Psalter, 1635.
Bonar	136 F.C.H.	Charles Steggall, Mus. Doc.
Bonn	329 U.P.H.	Johann Rosenmüller, ob. 1686.
Borlan	65 S.H., 231 F.C.H.	Dr Conrad Kocher's Zionsharfe.
Boston	276 U.P.H., 11 F.C.H.	Arranged by Lowell Mason, Mus. Doc., 1792-1872.
Boswell	95 U.P.P.	Adapted from Christoph Willibald Ritter von Gluck, 1714-1787.
Bowden	181 P. & P.	Dr Samuel Sebastian Wesley's European Psalmist, 1872.
Bowdler	404 S.H.	Cyril Bowdler, Mus. Bac.
Boylston	188 S.P., 75 U.P.P., 140 & 342 F.C.H.	Lowell Mason, Mus. Doc., 1792-1872.
Bozrah	56 U.P.H.	Cornelius Heinrich Dretzell's Choralbuch, 1731.
Brandenburg	364 U.P.H.	German.
Braun	227 S.H.	Johann Georg Braun's Echo Hymnodiæ Cœlestis, 1675.
Braylesford	215 U.P.H.	Henry John Gauntlett, Mus. Doc., 1805-1876.
Bredon	43 U.P.P., 104 & 258 U.P.H.	Henry John Gauntlett, Mus. Doc., 1805-1876.
Bremen	197 F.C.H., 85, 118, & 337 S.H.	Melchior Vulpius.
Breslau	39, 88, & 168 U.P.H., 184, 332 S.H., 6 F.C.H., 71 U.P.P., 4 P. & P.	Joseph Clauder's Psalmodia Sacra, Leipzig, 1630.
Brierley	64 S.H.	Augustus Grant Jamieson, 1844-1888.
Brighton	41 S.P.	Lowell Mason, Mus. Doc., 1792-1872.
Bristol	42 S.P., 53 P. & P., 60 U.P.P.	Thomas Ravenscroft's Psalter, 1621.
Broadlands	172 U.P.H., 209 P. & P.	Cantiques Sacrez, &c., Cassel, 1740.
Brockham	337 F.C.H.	Jeremiah Clark, 1670-1707.
Brünn	171 S.H., 182 P. & P.	German.

Tunes.	Numbers.	Composers or Sources.
Bucer	211 & 243 S.H., 183 P. & P., 140 F.C.H.	From Robert Alexander Schumann, Ph. Doc., 1810-1856 (?).
Buckland	415 S.H.	Rev. Leighton George Hayne, Mus. Doc., 1836-1883.
Bunyan	43 S.P., 72 S.H., 68 F.C.H.	From Felix Mendelssohn Bartholdy, Ph. Doc., 1809-1847.
Burford	44 S.P., 54 P. & P., 14 U.P.P.	Henry Purcell, 1658-1695 (?).
Caerleon	72 & 240 U.P.H.	Henry John Gauntlett, Mus. Doc., 1805-1876.
Caithness	219 & 318 S.H., 45 S.P., 121 U.P.P., 55 P. & P.	Scottish Psalter, 1635.
Caius College	112 U.P.H.	Henry John Gauntlett, Mus. Doc., 1805-1876.
Callcott	40 S.H.	Adapted from John Wall Callcott, Mus. Doc., 1766-1821.
Calm	272 F.C.H.	Anonymous.
Calvary	56 P. & P.	Charles Steggall, Mus. Doc.
Calvin	222 U.P.P., 47 & 256 U.P.H.	Genevan Psalter, 1549.
Calwood	360 S.H.	Adapted by Thomas Legerwood Hately, 1815-1867.
Cambridge	189 S.P.	Rev. Ralph Harrison, 1748-1810.
Cambridge New	57 P. & P.	John Randall, Mus. Doc., *ob.* 1799.
Camden	119 F.C.H.	Edward John Hopkins, Mus. Doc.
Cannons	182 U.P.H., 7 P. & P.	Georg Friedrich Händel, 1685-1759.
Canterbury or Paston	58 P. & P., 104 U.P.P.	Thomas Este's Psalter, 1592.
Capernaum	281 U.P.H.	Rev. William Henry Havergal, M.A., 1793-1870.
Capetown	289 S.H., 280 F.C.H.	Friedrich Filitz, Ph. Doc., 1804-1876.
Carey's (or Surrey)	5 P. & P., 161 U.P.P.	Henry Carey, *ob.* 1743.
Carinthia	35 U.P.H.	Freylinghausen's Geistreiches Gesangbuch, 1704.
Caritas	337 U.P.H.	Richard William Beaty, *ob.* 1883.
Carlisle	126 F.C.H., 184 P. & P., 190 S.P.	Charles Lockhart, *ob.* 1815.
Carmel	6 P. & P.	Genevan Psalter, 1551.

Tunes.	Numbers.	Composers or Sources.
Carmel	277 U.P.H.	Sir John Goss, Mus. Doc., 1800-1880.
Carrow	305 F.C.H.	Sir Arthur Seymour Sullivan, Mus. Doc.
Cassel	195 & 316 U.P.H., 17 & 303 S.H., 185 F.C.H.	Johann Thommen's Choralbuch, 1745.
Casterton	155 F.C.H., 92 U.P.H.	Adapted from Franz Joseph Haydn, 1732-1809.
Castleford	59 P. & P.	Dr Samuel Sebastian Wesley's European Psalmist, 1872.
Castle Rising	97 F.C.H.	Rev. Frederick Alfred John Hervey, M.A.
Caswall	411 S.H.	Friedrich Filitz, Ph. Doc., 1804-1876.
Caterham	46 S.P.	Arthur Cottman, ob. 1879.
Cecil	10 U.P.H.	Lowell Mason, Mus. Doc., 1792-1872.
Certa Clarum Certamen	166 U.P.H.	Henry John Gauntlett, Mus. Doc., 1805-1876.
Chadwick	225 U.P.H.	—— Oliver.
Chalvey	248 S.H.	Rev. Leighton George Hayne, Mus. Doc., 1836-1883.
Chandos or Cannons	7 P. & P.	Georg Friedrich Händel, 1685-1759.
Chant — Benedictus. Prose	352 S.H.	Rev. Robert Philip Goodenough, 1775-1826.
Chants — Gloria in Excelsis. Prose	355 S.H.	Sir George Alexander Macfarren, Mus. Doc., 1813-1887.
Chants — Magnificat. Prose	353 S.H.	1. Thomas Sanders Dupuis, Mus. Doc., 1730-1796. 2. William Russell, Mus. Bac., 1777-1813.
Chants — Nunc Dimittis. Prose	354 S.H.	1. Edwin George Monk, Mus. Doc. 2. John Jones, ob. 1796.
Chants — Te Deum. Prose	356 S.H.	1. Sir John Goss, Mus. Doc., 1800-1880, and A. L. Peace, Mus. Doc. 2. William Crotch, Mus. Doc., 1775-1847, and William Croft, Mus. Doc., 1678-1727 (?).
Chapel Royal	309 F.C.H.	William Boyce, Mus. Doc., 1710-1779.
Charity	289 S.H.	Sir John Stainer, M.A., Mus. Doc.

TUNES.	NUMBERS.	COMPOSERS OR SOURCES.
Charmouth	36 F.C.H.	Adapted by Edward Bowles Fripp, 1787-1870.
Chenies	274, 308, & 363 S.H.	Rev. Timothy Richard Matthews, B.A.
Chesalon	183 U.P.P.	Rev. William Henry Havergal, M.A., 1793-1870.
Cheshire or Chester	47 S.P., 60 P. & P. 52 U.P.P., 180 U.P.H.	Thomas Este's Psalter, 1592.
Chichester	136 U.P.P., 61 P. & P.	Thomas Ravenscroft's Psalter, 1621.
Childhood's Years	420 S.H.	Albert Lister Peace, Mus. Doc.
Children's Voices	363 F.C.H.	Edward John Hopkins, Mus. Doc.
Children of Jerusalem	371 S.H.	Anonymous.
Child's Song	349 F.C.H.	Sabbath School Union Hymnal, 1876.
Christchurch	152 F.C.H.	Charles Steggall, Mus. Doc.
Christchurch	188 S.H.	Samuel Wesley, 1766-1837.
Christ's Crown	381 F.C.H.	George Frederick Root, Mus. Doc.
Claremont	48 S.P.	James Foster, 1807-1885.
Clarence	304 S.H., 313 U.P.H., 172 F.C.H.	Sir Arthur Seymour Sullivan, Mus. Doc.
Clarewood	345 U.P.H., 344 F.C.H.	Sir John Goss, Mus. Doc., 1800-1880.
Cloisters	49 S.P.	James Turle, 1802-1882.
Coblentz	97 S.H., 102 U.P.H.	French Melody.
Coburg	63 S.H.	His Royal Highness the Prince Consort, 1819-1861.
Cœli enarrant	315 S.H.	Sir Robert Prescott Stewart, Mus. Doc.
Cœna Domini	226 S.H.	Sir Arthur Seymour Sullivan, Mus. Doc.
Colchester	50 S.P., 62 P. & P., 146 U.P.P.	William Tans'ur's Collection, 1736.
Coleshill	20 & 195 U.P.P., 324 U.P.H., 63 P. & P., 51 S.P.	William Barton's Psalms.
Cologne	15 & 51 U.P.P.	German.
Columba	103 U.P.P.	Henry Smart, 1813-1879.
Come unto Me	208 F.C.H.	Rev. John Bacchus Dykes, Mus. Doc., 1823-1875.
Comfort	93 U.P.P.	Mrs Patrick Gibson, ob. 1838.
Commandments	33 F.C.H., 8 P. & P., 6, 20, 284, & 311 S.H., 3 S.P.	Genevan Psalter, 1549.

INDEX TO TUNES. 9

TUNES.	NUMBERS.	COMPOSERS OR SOURCES.
Commendatio	45 S.H.	Rev. John Bacchus Dykes, Mus. Doc., 1823-1875.
Communion or Rockingham	35 F.C.H., 9 P. & P., 47 & 319 S.H., 4 S.P., 228 U.P.P.	Adapted by Edward Miller, Mus. Doc., 1731-1807.
Compline	45 F.C.H. & 79 U.P.H.	Rev. Leighton George Hayne, Mus. Doc., 1836-1883.
Confidence	10 P. & P., 205 S.H.	Jeremiah Clark, 1670-1707.
Consolation	94 U.P.P.	From Ludwig van Beethoven, 1770-1827.
Constance	49 U.P.H.	Friedrich Filitz, Ph. Doc., 1804-1876.
Contemplation	110 S.H., 292 U.P.H.	Felix Mendelssohn Bartholdy, Ph. Doc., 1809-1847.
Conway	207 P. & P.	Albert Lister Peace, Mus. Doc.
Corinth	241 F.C.H., 8 & 83 S.H., 137 U.P.H.	Samuel Webbe's Collection, 1792.
Corona	96 F.C.H., 192 U.P.P., 55 U.P.H.	Mrs Elizabeth Raymond Barker.
Cotfield	64 P. & P.	Anonymous.
Coventry	65 P. & P.	Samuel Howard, Mus. Doc., 1710-1782.
Cowper	76 F.C.H., 52 S.P.	From Johann Michael Haydn, 1737-1806.
Crasselius	36 S.H., 192 U.P.H., 11 P. & P.	Hamburger Musikalisches Handbuch, 1690.
Crayford	361 F.C.H.	Edward John Hopkins, Mus. Doc.
Crediton	71 S.H., 66 P. & P., 149 U.P.P., 53 S.P.	Thomas Clark, 1775-1859.
Credo	73 S.H.	Sir John Stainer, M.A., Mus. Doc.
Croft's 148th	212 P. & P.	William Croft, Mus. Doc., 1678-1727.
Cromarty	137 U.P.P.	Scottish Psalter, 1565.
Crowle	13 U.P.P.	James Green's Collection, 1724.
Croyland	81 & 196 U.P.H.	Henry John Gauntlett, Mus. Doc., 1805-1876.
Crucifer	230 F.C.H.	Henry Smart, 1813-1879.
Crucifixion	390 S.H.	John Montgomerie Bell, W.S.
Crux Crudelis	390 S.H.	Albert Lister Peace, Mus. Doc.
Cry of Faith	40 S.H.	Henry John Gauntlett, Mus. Doc., 1805-1876.
Cui habet dabitur	406 S.H.	George Herbert Gregory, Mus. Bac.
Culbach	234 S.H., 268 U.P.H.	Johann Scheffler's Hirtenlieder.

SCOTTISH CHURCH MUSIC.

TUNES.	NUMBERS.	COMPOSERS OR SOURCES.
Culford	187 F.C.H.	Edward John Hopkins, Mus. Doc.
Culm	12 P. & P.	German.
Culross	67 P. & P., 8 U.P.P.	Scottish Psalter, 1635.
Cyprus	177 F.C.H., 101 U.P.H.	Johann Crüger's Collection.
Dalkeith	168 S.H.	Thomas Hewlett, Mus. Bac., 1845-1874.
Damascus	184 U.P.H.	Mrs Elizabeth Raymond Barker.
Darmstadt	301 F.C.H.	Adam Drese, 1620-1701.
Darwall's	154 F.C.H., 216 S.P., 204 U.P.P., 65 U.P.H., 129 S.H., 213 P. & P.	Rev. John Darwall, 1731-1789.
David	338 F.C.H.	From Georg Friedrich Händel, 1685-1759.
Day	47 F.C.H., 54 S.P.	John Day's Psalter, 1562.
Day-star	173 F.C.H.	From Franz Joseph Haydn, 1732-1809.
Day by Day	407 S.H.	Rev. Edmund Sardinson Carter, M.A.
Day of Rest	315 & 341 S.H.	James William Elliott.
Dedham	58 F.C.H., 55 S.P.	Alfred Lister Sutcliffe.
Deerhurst	112 S.H., 235 F.C.H.	James Langran, Mus. Bac.
Delhi	143 U.P.H.	Edward Francis Rimbault, LL.D., 1816-1876.
Denbigh	40 & 229 U.P.H.	Henry John Gauntlett, Mus. Doc., 1805-1876.
Denfield	362 F.C.H., 56 S.P., 357 S.H.	From Carl Gotthelf Gläser, 1784-1829.
Denham or Southwell	185 P. & P.	Henrie Denham's Psalter, 1588.
Dennis	144 F.C.H., 191 S.P.	From Johann Georg Nageli, 1768-1836.
Deptford	286 F.C.H.	Orlando Gibbons, Mus. Doc., 1583-1625.
Dessau	313 S.H.	Johann Rudolph Ahle, 1625-1673.
Dettingen	66 U.P.H.	German.
Devonport	269 U.P.H.	Henry John Gauntlett, Mus. Doc., 1805-1876.
Diademata	70 S.H.	Sir George Job Elvey, Mus. Doc.
Dies Iræ	89 S.H.	Rev. John Bacchus Dykes, Mus. Doc., 1823-1875.
Dies Iræ	356 U.P.H.	Anonymous.
Dijon	347 F.C.H,, 341 U.P.H., 416 S.H.	German.

INDEX TO TUNES.

Tunes.	Numbers.	Composers or Sources.
Dilherr	2 F.C.H.	Sigmund Gottlieb Stade, 1607-1655.
Diligence	387 F.C.H., 431 S.H.	Lowell Mason, Mus. Doc., 1792-1872.
Dismission	347 S.H.	William Henry Monk, Mus. Doc., 1823-1889.
Dismission	251 F.C.H.	Samuel Webbe's Collection, 1792.
Dismission	362 U.P.H.	Thomas Legerwood Hately, 1815-1867.
Dix	31 & 280 S.H., 36 U.P.H., 180 F.C.H.	Conrad Kocher, Ph. Doc., 1786-1872.
Doncaster	192 S.P., 146 U.P.H.	Samuel Wesley, 1766-1837.
Dortmund	116 & 162 S.H.	Johann Wolff's Gesangbuch, 1569.
Doversdale	160 U.P.P., 5 S.P.	Samuel Stanley, *ob.* 1822.
Dresden	326 & 351 F.C.H., 297 & 364 S.H., 309 U.P.H.	Johann Abraham Peter Schulz, 1747-1800.
Duke Street	13 P. & P., 197 U.P.P., 284 U.P.H., 6 S.P.	John Hatton, *ob.* 1793.
Duke's Tune	68 P. & P.	Scottish Psalter, 1615.
Dunblane	18 U.P.P.	Arnold & Callcott's Psalms of David, 1791.
Dundee	1 U.P.P., 69 P. & P., 57 S.P.	Adapted from Christopher Tye, Mus. Doc., *ob.* 1572. Este's Psalter, 1592.
Dunfermline	298 S.H., 12 & 247 U.P.H., 58 S.P., 152 U.P.P., 70 P. & P.	Scottish Psalter, 1615.
Dunstan	80 U.P.H., 166 F.C.H.	Richard Redhead.
Dura	100 & 312 U.P.H.	Henry John Gauntlett, Mus. Doc., 1805-1876.
Durham	210 U.P.H., 181 U.P.P., 71 P. & P., 59 S.P.	Thomas Ravenscroft's Psalter, 1621.
Easter Hymn	169 F.C.H., 54 S.H., First Tune.	Lyra Davidica, 1708.
Easter Hymn	54 S.H., Second Tune.	William Henry Monk, Mus. Doc., 1823-1889.
Eastgate	182 S.P.	Robert Bennett, 1788-1819.
Eastham	276 S.H.	Rev. Sir F. A. Gore Ouseley, Bart., Mus. Doc., 1825-1889.
Eastnor	186 P. & P., 188 S.H.	Alfred King, Mus. Doc.
Eatington	72 P. & P., 126 U.P.P.	William Croft, Mus. Doc., 1678-1727.

SCOTTISH CHURCH MUSIC.

Tunes.	Numbers.	Composers or Sources.
Eaton	38 F.C.H., Doxology, 12 U.P.H., 92 S.H.	Zerubbabel Wyvill, 1763-1837.
Eber	189 U.P.H.	Rev. Caspar Ulenberg's Psalms of David, 1582.
Ebford	187 P. & P.	Anonymous.
Ecclesia	146 F.C.H.	Sir Arthur Seymour Sullivan, Mus. Doc.
Eden	74 F.C.H., 60 S.P., 88 U.P.P.	Rev. William Henry Havergal, M.A., 1793-1870.
Eden	435 S.H.	Tyrolean.
Edina	66 S.H.	Sir Herbert Stanley Oakeley, Mus. Doc.
Edinburgh	438 S.H., 73 P. & P.	Henry Smart, 1813-1879.
Edom	61 & 399 S.H.	Albert Lister Peace, Mus. Doc.
Effingham	56 F.C.H., 61 S.P.	Hamburger Musikalisches Handbuch, 1690.
Egham	188 P. & P.	William Turner, Mus. Doc., 1652-1740 (?).
Eilenburg	324 S.H.	Johann Schop.
Ein' feste Burg	182 S.H.	Martin Luther, D.D., 1483-1546.
Eirene	45 S.H.	Frances Ridley Havergal, 1836-1879.
Eisenach	14 P. & P., 77 S.H.	Johann Hermann Schein, 1586-1630.
Eisfeld	7 S.P.	George Rhaw's Lieder, 1544.
Elah	255 F.C.H.	From Franz Joseph Haydn, 1732-1809.
Elgin	6 U.P.P., 74 P. & P., 62 S.P.	Scottish Psalter, 1635.
Ellacombe	350 F.C.H., 400 S.H., 344 U.P.H.	Dr Conrad Kocher's Zionsharfe.
Ellers	291 F.C.H., 279 U.P.H.	Edward John Hopkins, Mus. Doc.
Elliot	148 S.H.	Lowell Mason, Mus. Doc., 1792-1872.
Elmham	374 F.C.H.	Adapted by Thomas Legerwood Hately, 1815-1867.
Ellon	335 U.P.H.	George Frederick Root, Mus. Doc.
Elvet	97 U.P.P.	Rev. John Bacchus Dykes, Mus. Doc., 1823-1875.
Elvey	303 F.C.H., 64 S.H.	Sir George Job Elvey, Mus. Doc.
Ely	25 F.C.H., 8 S.P., 223 U.P.P., 6, 224, 361 U.P.H., 3, 34, & 334 S.H.	Rev. Thomas Turton, D.D., Bishop of Ely, *ob.* 1864.

INDEX TO TUNES.

Tunes.	Numbers.	Composers or Sources.
Emmanuel	71 & 340 F.C.H., 63 S.P.	From Ludwig van Beethoven, 1770-1827.
Endsleigh	212 & 354 F.C.H.	S. Salvatori.
Ephesus	101 U.P.H.	Arranged by Sir John Goss, Mus. Doc., 1800-1880.
Ephratah	226 F.C.H., 30 U.P.H.	Latin.
Epiphany	383 F.C.H.	From Felix Mendelssohn Bartholdy, Ph. Doc., 1809-1847.
Epsom College	409 S.H.	Rev. Samuel James Rowton, M.A., Mus. Bac.
Epworth	113 F.C.H., 75 P. & P.	Charles Wesley, 1757-1834.
Erfurt	199 U.P.P., 290 U.P.H.	Attributed to Dr Martin Luther, 1483-1546.
Erk	324 F.C.H.	Wittenberger Liedersammlung, 1524.
Erlangen	323 S.H.	German. Adapted by Walter Hately.
Ernan	9 S.P.	Lowell Mason, Mus. Doc., 1792-1872.
Erskine	188 U.P.P.	Henry Smart, 1813-1879.
Eudoxia	371 F.C.H., 361 S.H.	Rev. Sabine Baring-Gould, M.A.
Evan	76 F.C.H., 64 S.P., 36 U.P.P., 105, 187, & 203 U.P.H., 24 & 218 S.H., 76 P. & P.	Adapted from the Rev. William Henry Havergal, M.A., 1793-1870, by Lowell Mason, Mus. Doc.
Evangel	356 F.C.H., 174 & 369 S.H.	William Howard Doane, Mus. Doc.
Evangel	156 U.P.P.	Arranged by Sir Arthur Seymour Sullivan, Mus. Doc.
Evelyn	106 S.H.	Sir Arthur Seymour Sullivan, Mus. Doc.
Evening Hymn	22 F.C.H., 10 S.P., 302 U.P.H, 285 S.H.	Thomas Tallis, *ob.* 1585.
Even Me	222 F.C.H., 322 U.P.H., 165 S.H.	William Batchelder Bradbury, 1816-1868.
Evensong	320 F.C.H.	Thomas Bishop Southgate, 1814-1868.
Eventide	285 F.C.H., 234 U.P.H., 245 S.H.	William Henry Monk, Mus. Doc., 1823-1889.
Evermore	316 S.H.	Henry John Gauntlett, Mus. Doc., 1805-1876.
Everton	60 & 366 U.P.H.	Henry Smart, 1813-1879.
Ewing	212 F.C.H., 251 U.P.H., 275 S.H.	Lieut.-Colonel Alexander Ewing.
Exeter	77 P. & P.	Dr Crotch's Collection, 1836.
Eynsham	340 S.H.	Edmund Hart Turpin, Mus. Doc.

Tunes.	Numbers.	Composers or Sources.
Fabian	269 F.C.H., 278 U.P.H.	From the Rev. William Felton, *ob.* 1769.
Fairfield	123 F.C.H., 206 P. & P.	Rev. Peter La Trobe, 1795-1863.
Faith	90 U.P.P., 65 S.P.	Rev. John Bacchus Dykes, Mus. Doc., 1823-1875.
Faith	216 F.C.H.	William Howard Doane, Mus. Doc.
Fareham	342 S.H.	Sir John Goss, Mus. Doc., 1800-1880.
Farningham	66 S.P.	Charles Edward Kettle.
Farrant	89 F.C.H., 67 S.P., 43, 82, 157, & 272 U.P.H., 35 U.P.P., 99 & 231 S.H., 78 P. & P.	Richard Farrant, *ob.* 1580, or John Hilton, Mus. Bac., *ob.* 1657.
Felix	101 F.C.H., 151 U.P.H., 54 U.P.P., 68 S.P., 24 S.H., 79 P. & P.	Adapted from Felix Mendelssohn Bartholdy, Ph. Doc., 1809-1847, by Lowell Mason, Mus. Doc.
Feniton Court	147 S.H.	Edward John Hopkins, Mus. Doc.
Ferrier	348 F.C.H., 367 S.H.	Rev. John Bacchus Dykes, Mus. Doc., 1823-1875.
Fides	2 S.H.	Rev. Clement Cotterill Scholefield, M.A.
Fiducia	183 U.P.H.	Samuel Sebastian Wesley, Mus. Doc., 1810-1876.
Fight of Faith	180 S.H.	Albert Lister Peace, Mus. Doc.
Filitz	256 F.C.H.	Friedrich Filitz, Ph. Doc., 1804-1876.
Fingal	317 S.H.	James Smith Anderson, Mus. Bac.
Flensburg	82 F.C.H., 114 U.P.H.	From Louis Spohr, Mus. Doc., 1784-1859.
Formosa	175 F.C.H.	James Merrylees.
Fortitude	386 F.C.H.	Horatio Richmond Palmer, Mus. Doc.
Franconia	127 F.C.H., 193 S.P., 25 & 198 U.P.H., 113 U.P.P., 100, 156, 252 S.H., 189 P. & P.	From John Daniel Müller's Choralbuch, 1754.
Frankfort	373 S.H.	Arranged by Johann Christoph Bach, 1643-1703.
Freiburg	110 U.P.H.	Conrad Kocher, Ph. Doc., 1786-1872.
Freiburg	159 S.H.	From Tochter Sion.

INDEX TO TUNES.

Tunes.	Numbers.	Composers or Sources.
French	112 F.C.H., 69 S.P., 207 S.H., 80 P. & P., 218 U.P.P.	Scottish Psalter, 1615.
Freshwater	362 S.H.	T. B.
Gauntlett	202 U.P.H.	Henry John Gauntlett, Mus. Doc., 1805-1876.
Geneva	220 F.C.H.	Johann Thommen's Choralbuch, 1745.
Germania	253 S.H.	German.
Gerontius	49 S.H.	Rev. John Bacchus Dykes, Mus. Doc., 1823-1875.
Gerum	115 S.H.	August Gerum, 1818-1885.
Gethsemane	179 F.C.H., 41 U.P.H.	From Christopher Tye, Mus. Doc., ob. 1572.
Gethsemane	37 & 42 S.H.	Rev. Sir F. A. Gore Ouseley, Bart., Mus. Doc., 1825-1889.
Ghent	157 F.C.H., 217 S.P.	Congregational Psalmist, 1861.
Gibbons	163 F.C.H., 159 & 363 U.P.H., 161 S.H.	Orlando Gibbons, Mus. Doc., 1583-1625.
Giessen	44 F.C.H., 74 & 164 S.H.	Adapted by Edwin Moss.
Gillespie	101 U.P.P.	Henry Smart, 1813-1879.
Glasgow	70 S.P., 81 P. & P.	Thomas Moore's Psalm-Singers' Pocket Companion, Glasgow, 1756.
Glencairn	71 S.P.	Thomas Legerwood Hately, 1815-1867.
Gloria in Excelsis	334 F.C.H.	Edward John Hopkins, Mus. Doc.
Gloria in Excelsis	353 U.P.H.	Henry John Gauntlett, Mus. Doc., 1805-1876.
Glory	343 F.C.H., 331 U.P.H., 436 S.H.	Anonymous.
Gloucester	11 & 219 U.P.H., 153 U.P.P., 72 S.P., 82 P. & P.	Thomas Ravenscroft's Psalter, 1621, and Playford's Psalter, 1671.
Godesberg	117 U.P.H., 187 S.H.	Heinrich Albert, 1604-1651.
Goldel	9 S.H., 220 S.P., 15 P. & P.	Johann Hermann Schein, 1586-1630.
Good Shepherd	377 F.C.H., 414 S.H.	Radcliffe Boorman Lockwood.
Gopsal	150 F.C.H., 251 S.H.	Georg Friedrich Händel, 1685-1759.
Goshen	376 F.C.H.	Anonymous.
Goss	241 S.H.	Adapted from Händel by Sir John Goss.
Gotha	223 F.C.H., 7 U.P.H., 144 S.H.	His Royal Highness the Prince Consort, 1819-1861.

Tunes.	Numbers.	Composers or Sources.
Gounod	243 F.C.H.	Charles François Gounod.
Gräfenberg	73 S.P., 108 & 150 U.P.H., 68 U.P.P., 18 & 104 S.H., 83 P. & P.	From Johann Crüger, 1598-1662.
Grafton	84 P. & P.	Lowell Mason, Mus. Doc., 1792-1872.
Grange	171 S.H.	John Montgomerie Bell, W.S.
Green Hill	389 S.H.	Albert Lister Peace, Mus. Doc.
Greenland	108 S.H., 209 F.C.H.	From Johann Michael Haydn, 1737-1806.
Greenwich	85 P. & P., 74 S.P., 140 U.P.P.	William Richardson's Pious Recreation, 1729.
Grimma	86 P. & P.	From Johann Michael Haydn, 1737-1806.
Grosvenor	30 S.H.	Charles Steggall, Mus. Doc.
Guilton	34 S.H.	John Harrison, *ob.* 1871.
Haarlem	236 S.H.	Adam Drese, 1620-1701.
Haddo	317 F.C.H.	Edward John Hopkins, Mus. Doc.
Hagar	194 S.P.	American.
Hall	16 P. & P.	Johann Georg Bernhard Beutler's Choralbuch, 1799.
Halle	325 S.H.	Freylinghausen's Neues Geistreiches Gesangbuch, 1714.
Hampton	217 S.H., 190 P. & P., 289 U.P.H., 195 S.P.	Aaron Williams's Psalmody in Miniature.
Hanover	16 S.H., 207 U.P.H., 289 F.C.H.	William Croft, Mus. Doc., 1678-1727 (?)
Happy Land	432 S.H., 352 U.P.H., 367 F.C.H.	Indian Air.
Harington	244 U.P.H., 109 U.P.P., 87 P. & P., 76 S.P.	Henry Harington, M.D., 1727-1816.
Harnal	75 S.P., 98 U.P.P.	Frank Cuisset.
Harts	15 & 53 S.H., 159 F.C.H.	Benjamin Milgrove, 1731-1810.
Harwich	401 & 420 S.H.	John Whitaker, *ob.* 1848.
Hastings	412 S.H.	Thomas Hastings, Mus. Doc., 1784-1872.
Havergal	278 U.P.H.	Rev. William Henry Havergal, M.A., 1793-1870.
Havergal	29 F.C.H.	Bamberg Gesangbuch, 1707.
Havilah	Dox., 9 U.P.H.	Rev. William Henry Havergal, M.A., 1793-1870.
Hawarden	265 S.H.	Samuel Sebastian Wesley, Mus. Doc., 1810-1876.

INDEX TO TUNES.

TUNES.	NUMBERS.	COMPOSERS OR SOURCES.
Haydn's Hymn	191 S.H.	Franz Joseph Haydn, 1732-1809.
Hayne	77 S.P.	From Louis Spohr, Mus. Doc., 1784-1859.
Heathlands	178 S.H., Part I., 141 U.P.H., 183 F.C.H.	Henry Smart, 1813-1879.
Heavenly Land	434 S.H.	William Batchelder Bradbury, 1816-1868.
Heber	108 S.H., 204 F.C.H.	Lowell Mason, Mus. Doc., 1792-1872.
Hebron	78 & 175 U.P.H.	Melchior Vulpius, 1560-1621.
Heidelberg	164 & 286 U.P.H.	Melchior Vulpius, 1560-1621.
Heinlen	33 S.H., 166 F.C.H.	Nürnberg Hymn-book, 1677.
Herbert	277 S.H.	Rev. Richard Robert Chope.
Hereford	162 S.H.	Samuel Sebastian Wesley, Mus. Doc., 1810-1876.
Hereford	78 S.P.	William Hayes, Mus. Doc., 1706-1777.
Heriot's Tune	88 P. & P.	Alexander M'Donald's Collection, Edinburgh, 1807.
Hermas	393 S.H., 96 U.P.H., 365 F.C.H.	Frances Ridley Havergal, 1836-1879.
Hermon	314 F.C.H.	Johann Georg Braun's Echo Hymnodiæ Cœlestis, 1675.
Hermon	89 P. & P.	Jeremiah Clark, 1670-1707.
Herr Jesu	258 S.H.	Nürnberg Hymn-book, 1677.
Hesperus	34 F.C.H.	Henry Baker, Mus. Bac.
Hilary	253 U.P.H., 232 F.C.H.	Ganther.
Holland	90 P. & P.	Evangelische Gezangen, 1806.
Holley	426 S.H.	George Hews, 1806-1873.
Hollingside	192 S.H., 133 U.P.H., 186 F.C.H.	Rev. John Bacchus Dykes, Mus. Doc., 1823-1875.
Holstein	226 U.P.H.	Arranged by Johann Christoph Bach, 1643-1703.
Holy Cross	79 S.P.	Adapted by James Clifft Wade.
Holyrood	84, 157, & 422 S.H., 267 U.P.H., 134 & 346 F.C.H.	James Watson, 1816-1880.
Holy Trinity	80 S.P.	Joseph Barnby.
Holywood	82 & 347 S.H.	From Samuel Webbe's Collection, 1792.
Horbury	241 S.H.	Rev. John Bacchus Dykes, Mus. Doc., 1823-1875.
Horsley	91 P. & P., 341 F.C.H.	William Horsley, Mus. Bac., 1774-1858.
Hosanna	139 S.H.	From Justin Heinrich Knecht, 1752-1817.

B

Tunes.	Numbers.	Composers or Sources.
Houghton	16 S.H., 8 U.P.H., 288 F.C.H.	Henry John Gauntlett, Mus. Doc., 1805-1876.
Howard	158 U.P.H., 108 U.P.P., 81 S.P., 92 P. & P.	John Wilson's Collection, Edinburgh, 1825. Sir John Andrew Stevenson, Mus. Doc. (?).
Howard's 148th	214 P. & P.	Samuel Howard, Mus. Doc., 1710-1782.
Huddersfield	82 S.P., 93 P. & P., 130 U.P.P.	Rev. Martin Madan, 1729-1790.
Hull	311 F.C.H.	S. Chandler.
Humility	383 S.H.	Sir John Goss, Mus. Doc., 1800-1880.
Hursley	23 F.C.H.	Peter Ritter, 1760-1846.
Iconium	94 P. & P., 83 S.P., 65 U.P.P.	James Nares, Mus. Doc., 1715-1783 (?).
Idumea	Dox., 13 U.P.H.	Rev. William Henry Havergal, M.A., 1793-1870.
Ilfracombe	335 F.C.H., 158 U.P.P., 11 S.P.	Lowell Mason, Mus. Doc., 1792-1872.
Immanuel	29 U.P.H.	Henry John Gauntlett, Mus. Doc., 1805-1876.
Immanuel	402 S.H.	From Ludwig van Beethoven, 1770-1827.
Immortality	37 S.H.	Latin.
Inchcolm	283 F.C.H.	Walter Hately.
In Excelsis Gloria	387 S.H.	Albert Lister Peace, Mus. Doc.
Infant Praises	364 F.C.H., 423 S.H., 340 U.P.H.	Friedrich Silcher, Ph. Doc., 1789-1860.
Infants' Prayer	364 F.C.H.	German.
Infants' Prayer	362 S.H.	Albert Lister Peace, Mus. Doc.
Innocents	162 F.C.H., 84 U.P.H., 25 & 232 S.H.	Anonymous.
Innsbrück, or Innspruck	280 U.P.H., 193 S.H.	Heinrich Isaac.
Intercession	330 F.C.H., 273 U.P.H.	William Hutchins Callcott, 1807-1882, and Felix Mendelssohn Bartholdy, Ph. Doc., 1809-1847.
Intercession	344 S.H., 17 P. & P.	Latin.
Inverness	95 P. & P.	Scottish Psalter, 1635.
Invitation	369 F.C.H.	George Frederick Root, Mus. Doc.
Invitation	223 U.P.H.	Johann Thommen's Choralbuch, 1745.
Invitation	158 S.H.	Thomas Hastings, Mus. Doc., 1784-1872.

INDEX TO TUNES.

Tunes.	Numbers.	Composers or Sources.
Invocation	222 P. & P., 102 U.P.P., 183 S.P.	Robert Archibald Smith, 1780-1829.
Iona	39 U.P.P.	Ancient.
Irby	385 F.C.H., 384 S.H.	Henry John Gauntlett, Mus. Doc., 1805-1876.
Irene	266 F.C.H., 236 U.P.H.	Rev. Clement Cotterill Scholefield, M.A.
Irish	131 U.P.P., 96 P. & P., 84 S.P.	Dublin Hymn Book, 1749
Israel	206 F.C.H.	German.
Italian Chorale	227 F.C.H.	Anonymous.
Iver	273 F.C.H.	James Clifft Wade.
Jackson	97 P. & P., 242 U.P.H., 69 U.P.P., 85 S.P.	Thomas Jackson, *ob.* 1781.
Jam Lucis	80 S.H.	John Bishop, *ob.* 1737.
Jehovah	293 F.C.H.	Edward John Hopkins, Mus. Doc.
Jerusalem	352 F.C.H.	From Jacques Arcadelt (?).
Jesus Loves Me	405 S.H.	William Batchelder Bradbury, 1816-1868.
Jesus Saviour	374 S.H.	From Sacred Melodies, 1872.
Joyful	437 S.H., 350 U.P.H., 379 F.C.H.	Thomas Bilby, 1794-1872.
Kedron	86 S.P.	T. A. A.
Kelham	3 U.P.P.	Edward Dearle, Mus. Doc., 1806-1891.
Kent	18 P. & P., 77 & 179 S.H.	Johann Friedrich Lampe, 1703-1751.
Kiel	164 F.C.H.	Andreas Jacob Romberg, Ph. Doc., Mus. Doc., 1767-1821.
Kilmarnock	87 S.P., 98 P. & P., 96 U.P.P.	Neil Dougall, 1776-1862.
Kilsyth	318 S.H., 99 P. & P.	German.
Kindly Light	216 U.P.H.	Henry John Gauntlett, Mus. Doc., 1805-1876.
King's Norton	100 P. & P.	Jeremiah Clark, 1670-1707.
Kingston	101 P. & P.	Jeremiah Clark, 1670-1707.
Kingston	355 F.C.H., 343 U.P.H.	William Litton Viner, *ob.* 1867.
Kirkmay	102 P. & P.	Friedrich Filitz, Ph. Doc., 1804-1876.
Knecht	207 F.C.H., 237 & 338 S.H.	Justin Heinrich Knecht, 1752-1817.
Kornthal	52 F.C.H., 88 S.P.	Johann Georg Frech, 1790-1864.
Kreuznach	335 S.H.	German.

Tunes.	Numbers.	Composers or Sources.
Lacrymæ . .	137 & 169 S.H.	Sir Arthur Seymour Sullivan, Mus. Doc.
Ladbroke . .	89 S.P.	Rev. Wm. Hayes, 1741-1790.
Lancashire . .	55 S.H., 26 & 294 U.P.H., 203 F.C.H.	Henry Smart, 1813-1879.
Lancaster . .	90 S.P., 60 & 301 S.H., 122 U.P.P., 103 P. & P.	Samuel Howard, Mus. Doc., 1710-1782.
Landskron . .	276 F.C.H.	Bohemian Hymnal, 1531.
Langdon . .	91 S.P.	George Frederick Root, Mus. Doc.
Langholm . .	104 P. & P.	Arnold & Callcott's Psalms of David, 1791.
Laud	21 F.C.H.	Ancient.
Lauder . . .	7 U.P.P.	Israel Holdroyd's Spiritual Man's Companion, 1753.
Laudes Domini	261 F.C.H.	Joseph Barnby.
Lausanne . .	281 U.P.H.	Genevan Psalter, 1543.
Lavington . .	177 U.P.H.	Congregational Church Music.
Leamington .	92 S.P.	Frederick Marshall, ob. 1857.
Lebanon . .	14 U.P.H.	Johann Friedrich Naue's Choralbuch, 1829.
Lebanon . . .	93 S.P.	John Dobson, ob. 1888.
Lebbæus . .	372 F.C.H.	From Children's Worship, 1879.
Leeds . . .	191 P. & P.	William Roger's New and Easie Method, 1686.
Leicester . .	317 S.H.	William Hurst.
Leipzig . . .	192 P. & P.	Felix Mendelssohn-Bartholdy, Ph. Doc., 1809-1847.
Leominster . .	147 F.C.H., 248 S.H., 318 U.P.H.	George William Martin, 1828-1881.
Leoni . . .	322 F.C.H., 235 S.H. Part I., 210 P. & P., 23 U.P.H.	Hebrew Melody (?).
Leuchars . .	45 U.P.P., 210 S.P., 208 P. & P.	Thomas Legerwood Hately, 1815-1867.
Lichfield . .	105 P. & P.	Philip Hart, ob. 1749 (?).
Liguria . . .	181 & 194 U.P.H.	Ancient.
Linden . . .	48 S.H., 40 F.C.H., 19 P. & P.	Dr Conrad Kocher's Zionsharfe.
Lintz	196 F.C.H.	Strasburg Psalter.
Litany . . .	136 & 271 U.P.H.	Walter Newport.
Litany (No. 1) .	167 & 381 S.H.	Arranged by Sir Arthur Seymour Sullivan, Mus. Doc.
Litany (No. 2) .	167 S.H.	Sir Arthur Seymour Sullivan, Mus. Doc.
Litany . . .	327 S.H.	William Henry Monk, Mus. Doc., 1823-1889.

INDEX TO TUNES. 21

Tunes.	Numbers.	Composers or Sources.
Litany . . .	333 S.H.	Frederic Clay, 1838-1889.
Litany . . .	382 S.H.	Albert Lister Peace, Mus. Doc.
Little Children	388 S.H.	Sir George Job Elvey, Mus. Doc.
Little Pilgrim .	368 F.C.H.	William Batchelder Bradbury, 1816-1868 (?).
Liverpool . .	106 P. & P.	Robert Wainwright, Mus. Doc., *ob*. 1782.
Llandaff . . .	20 P. & P.	Robert Hudson, Mus. Bac., 1732-1815 (?).
London . . .	2 F.C.H.	Henry Smart, 1813-1879.
London New .	19 S.H., 94 S.P., 107 P. & P., 216 U.P.P., 274 U.P.H.	Scottish Psalter, 1635, and Playford's Psalter, 1677.
Louisberg . .	298 F.C.H.	Friedrich Silcher, Ph. Doc., 1789-1860.
Lowliness . .	380 F.C.H.	Rev. Benjamin Russell Hanby, 1833-1867.
Lübeck . . .	200 & 234 S.H.	Freylinghausen's Geistreiches Gesangbuch, 1704.
Lucca . . .	249 S.H.	Adapted by Bartholomäus Gesius.
Lucerne . . .	240 F.C.H.	Johann Georg Christian Störl, 1676-1743.
Lucerne, or Cassel	195 & 316 U.P.H.	Johann Thommen's Choralbuch, 1745.
Ludborough .	336 S.H., 27 F.C.H.	Rev. Timothy Richard Matthews, B.A.
Ludlow . . .	24 U.P.P.	Thomas Ravenscroft's Psalter, 1621.
Lugano . . .	295 S.H., 305 U.P.H.	Anonymous.
Luneburg . .	21 P. & P.	Gotha Cantional, 1651.
Lusatia . . .	359 F.C.H., 229 S.H.	Melchior Vulpius, 1560-1621.
Luther's Hymn	155 S.H., 318 F.C.H., 71 U.P.H.	Martin Luther, D.D., 1483-1546 (?).
Luther's 130th	125 U.P.H.	Probably Martin Luther, D.D., 1483-1546.
Lutzen . . .	15 & 35 U.P.H.	German.
Lux Alma . .	200 U.P.P., 12 S.P., 74, 139, 197, 230 U.P.H.	Henry John Gauntlett, Mus. Doc., 1805-1876.
Lux Beata . .	246 S.H.	Albert Lister Peace, Mus. Doc.
Lux Benigna .	246 S.H., 310 F.C.H.	Rev. John Bacchus Dykes, Mus. Doc., 1823-1875.
Lux Eoi . . .	229 F.C.H., 329 S.H.	Sir Arthur Seymour Sullivan, Mus. Doc.
Lux Mundi . .	75 S.H.	Sir Arthur Seymour Sullivan, Mus. Doc.

Tunes.	Numbers.	Composers or Sources.
Lyra	95 S.P.	George Frederick Root, Mus. Doc.
Lyra	243 S.H.	Albert Lister Peace, Mus. Doc.
Lyte	228 S.H., 137 F.C.H.	John Wilkes.
Madrid . . .	182 F.C.H., 339 U.P.H., 372 S.H.	B. Case, 1834 (?).
Magdala . . .	57 S.H.	Joseph Barnby.
Magdeburg . .	68 & 83 S.H.	Joachim Neander, 1640 (or 1650)-1680.
Maidstone . .	193 F.C.H., 349 U.P.H., 128 S.H.	Walter Bond Gilbert, Mus. Doc.
Mainzer . . .	17 F.C.H., 59, 163, 213, & 319 U.P.H., 6, 94, & 135 S.H., 22 P. & P., 201 U.P.P., 13 S.P.	Joseph Mainzer's Standard Psalmody of Scotland, 1845.
Makerstoun .	292 S.H.	Thomas Legerwood Hately, 1815-1867.
Mamre . . .	244 S.H.	From Georg Friedrich Händel, 1685-1759.
Mamre . . .	346 U.P.H.	—— Scholinus.
Manchester . .	108 P. & P., 127 U.P.P., 96 S.P.	Robert Wainwright, Mus. Doc., ob. 1782.
Mannheim . .	214 U.P.H., 247 F.C.H., 229 & 348 S.H.	Friedrich Filitz, Ph. Doc., 1804-1876.
Manningtree .	108 F.C.H.	Alfred Lister Sutcliffe.
Margaret . .	385 S.H.	Rev. Timothy Richard Matthews, B.A.
Margaretha . .	376 S.H.	German.
Marienberg . .	308 F.C.H.	Michael Gotthardt Fischer's Choralbuch, 1820.
Mariners . . .	360 F.C.H.	Sicilian Melody.
Martyrdom . .	124, 160, 208 U.P.H., 109 P. & P., 34 U.P.P., 97 S.P.	Hugh Wilson, 1764-1824.
Martyrs . . .	19 & 194 U.P.P., 98 & 99 S.P., 110 P. & P.	Scottish Psalter, 1615.
Mason . . .	10 F.C.H.	Timothy Battle Mason, 1801-1861.
Meinau . . .	138 S.H.	Johann Georg Braun's Echo Hymnodiæ Cœlestis, 1675.
Meinhold . .	260 S.H.	From Johann Sebastian Bach's Vierstimmige Choralgesänge, vol. ii. 1769.

INDEX TO TUNES.

TUNES.	NUMBERS.	COMPOSERS OR SOURCES.
Meiningen	193 P. & P.	Michael Frank, 1609-1677.
Melanchthon	170 F.C.H.	German.
Melanchthon	119 U.P.H.	Joachim Neander, 1640 (or 1650)-1680.
Melcombe	93 & 279 S.H., 45, 107, 212, 257 U.P.H., 23 P. & P., 227 U.P.P., 14 S.P.	Samuel Webbe, 1740-1816.
Melita	327 U.P.H., 21 S.H., 41 F.C.H.	Rev. John Bacchus Dykes, Mus. Doc., 1823-1875.
Melrose	59 U.P.P., 100 S.P., 111 P. & P.	Scottish Psalter, 1635.
Memoria	321 S.H.	Samuel Sebastian Wesley, Mus. Doc., 1810-1876.
Metzler's Redhead (No. 66)	101 S.P., 170 S.H. (Part II.)	Richard Redhead.
Middleton	128 U.P.H.	Henry John Gauntlett, Mus. Doc., 1805-1876.
Midian	116 U.P.H.	Rev. William Henry Havergal, M.A., 1793-1870.
Milan	Doxology, 15 U.P.H.	Samuel Webbe's Collection, 1792.
Milan	165 F.C.H.	Ancient.
Miles Lane	55 F.C.H.	William Shrubsole, 1760-1806.
Milton	172 S.H.	—— Scholinus.
Milton	102 S.P.	American.
Minto	85 S.H.	Conrad Kocher, Ph. Doc., 1786-1872.
Miserere	166 S.H.	William Henry Monk, Mus. Doc., 1823-1889.
Misericordia	131 U.P.H., 278 F.C.H.	Henry Smart, 1813-1879.
Missionary	134 & 294 U.P.H.	Lowell Mason, Mus. Doc., 1792-1872.
Mistley	313 F.C.H.	Rev. Leighton George Hayne, Mus. Doc., 1836-1883.
Monica	91 U.P.H.	From Samuel P. Warren.
Monkland	160 F.C.H., 13 S.H.	German.
Monsell	142 U.P.H.	Rev. Jacob Gottfried Hegler, 1794-1877.
Montgomery	252 U.P.H., 132 F.C.H.	Isaac Baker Woodbury, 1819-1858.
Montrose	191 & 221 U.P.P.	Robert Gilmour's Psalm-Singer's Assistant, Paisley, 1793.
Moravia	112 P. & P., 17 U.P.H., 103 S.P., 67 U.P.P., 151, 264, 421 S.H.	German.

Tunes.	Numbers.	Composers or Sources.
Moredun	264 U.P.H., 296 F.C.H., 132 S.H.	Henry Smart, 1813-1879.
Morning	181 F.C.H., 345 S.H.	William Henry Monk, Mus. Doc., 1823-1889.
Morning Hymn	20 F.C.H., 297 U.P.H., 278 S.H.	François Hippolite Barthélémon, 1741-1808.
Morning Hymn	278 & 283 S.H.	William Boyce, Mus. Doc., 1710-1779 (?).
Morning Light	215 F.C.H., 403 S.H.	George James Webb, 1803-1887.
Morning Star	328 F.C.H.	Adapted by Philipp Nicolai, 1556-1608.
Morven	104 S.P.	Robert Archibald Smith, 1780-1829 (?).
Moscow	315 F.C.H., 107 S.H.	Felice de Giardini, 1716-1796.
Mount Vernon	357 F.C.H., 359 S.H.	Lowell Mason, Mus. Doc., 1792-1872.
Mount Zion	176 F.C.H.	Sir Arthur Seymour Sullivan, Mus. Doc.
Mozart	167 F.C.H.	From Johann Chrysostomus Wolfgang Amadeus Mozart, 1756-1791.
Munich	274 S.H., 211 F.C.H., 21 & 250 U.P.H.	Würtemberg Gesangbuch. 1711.
Nain	268 F.C.H.	Lowell Mason, Mus. Doc., 1792-1872.
Naomi	110 U.P.P., 105 S.P.	From Johann Georg Nageli, 1768-1836.
Narenza	179 U.P.H., 129 F.C.H., 194 P. & P., 211 S.H., 164 U.P.P., 196 S.P.	Cologne Gesangbuch.
Nassau	323 F.C.H.	Johann Rosenmüller, *ob.* 1686 (?).
Nativity	106 S.P.	Henry Lahee.
Nativity	34 U.P.H., 167 U.P.P.	Dr Conrad Kocher's Zionsharfe.
Nazareth	73 S.H.	Rev. Henri Abraham Cæsar Malan, D.D., 1787-1864.
Neander	239 F.C.H., 62 U.P.H.	Joachim Neander, 1640 (or 1650)-1680.
Neander	107 S.P.	Friedrich Filitz, Ph. Doc., 1804-1876.
Nenthorn	241 S.H., 312 F.C.H.	Thomas Legerwood Hately, 1815-1867.
Neumark	209 S.H.	Georg Neumarck, 1621-1681.
Newark	113 P. & P.	Nathaniel Gawthorn's Harmonia Perfecta, 1730.

INDEX TO TUNES.

Tunes.	Numbers.	Composers or Sources.
Newcastle	108 S.P.	American.
Newcastle	297 F.C.H.	Henry L. Morley.
Newington	114 F.C.H., 114 P. & P., 90 S.H., 142 U.P.P., 109 S.P.	Rev. William Jones, 1726-1800.
Newland	44 & 157 S.H.	Henry John Gauntlett, Mus. Doc., 1805-1876.
New London	216 U.P.P., 274 U.P.H., 94 S.P., 107 P. & P., 19 S.H.	Scottish Psalter, 1635.
New St Ann	129 U.P.P., 177 S.P.	Sir George Thomas Smart, 1776-1867.
New 136th	216 P. & P.	Albert Lister Peace, Mus. Doc.
New 137th	168 P. & P.	Albert Lister Peace, Mus. Doc.
New 143d	211 P. & P.	John Montgomerie Bell, W.S.
Nicea	1 U.P.H., 1 S.H., 295 F.C.H.	Rev. John Bacchus Dykes, Mus. Doc., 1823-1875.
Nicolai	86 S.H., 67 U.P.H., 329 F.C.H.	Philip Nicolai, 1556-1608, or Jacob Practorius.
Nicomedia	298 U.P.H., 344 S.H., 24 P. & P.	Ancient.
Nina	4 S.H.	Würtemberg Melody, 1760.
Ninety-and-Nine	378 F.C.H.	M. C. Wilson.
Noel	32 U.P.H., 60 F.C.H., 169 P. & P., 29 S.H.	Arranged by Sir Arthur Seymour Sullivan, Mus. Doc.
Norfolk	299 & Doxology, 4 U.P.H., 12 F.C.H., 25 P. & P.	Samuel Howard, Mus. Doc., 1710-1782.
Norman	233 S.H.	Johann Gottlob Werner's Choralbuch, 1815.
Northampton	115 P. & P.	William Croft, Mus. Doc., 1678-1727.
Northumberland	187 U.P.P., 94 F.C.H.	Henry Smart, 1813-1879.
Norwich	116 P. & P.	Thomas Ravenscroft's Psalter 1621.
Norwood	117 P. & P.	Anonymous.
Notting Hill	110 S.P.	Charles Henry Purday, 1799-1885.
Nox Præcessit	95 F.C.H.	John Baptiste Calkin.
Nun Danket	141 S.H.	Johann Crüger, 1598-1662.
Nürnberg	Doxology, 11 U.P.H.	German.
Nürnberg	200 F.C.H., 215 S.H.	Johann Crüger, 1598-1662.
Nutfield	292 S.H.	William Henry Monk, Mus. Doc. 1823-1889.

Tunes.	Numbers.	Composers or Sources.
Oberlin	87 & 295 U.P.H.	Johann Gottlob Werner's Choralbuch, 1815.
Oberlin	300 F.C.H.	German.
O Come let us Sing	377 S.H.	Adapted by Rev. James Gall.
Old 1st	111 S.P.	Scottish Psalter, 1565.
Old 8th	213 U.P.P.	Scottish Psalter, 1565.
Old 9th	40 U.P.P.	Scottish Psalter, 1565.
Old 21st	196 U.P.P.	Scottish Psalter, 1565.
Old 22d or Hurstbourne	170 P. & P.	Thomas Ravenscroft's Psalter, 1621.
Old 29th	214 U.P.P., 112 S.P., 171 P. & P.	Scottish Psalter, 1565.
Old 42d	236 F.C.H.	French Melody.
Old 44th	182 U.P.P., 59 F.C.H. 97 & 200 U.P.H., 172 P. & P., 113 S.P.	John Day's Psalter, 1563.
Old 49th	53 U.P.P.	Scottish Psalter, 1565.
Old 61st	41 U.P.P.	John Day's Psalter, 1562.
Old 68th	185 U.P.P., 173 P. & P.	John Day's Psalter, 1562.
Old 78th	56 U.P.P.	Scottish Psalter, 1565.
Old 81st	186 U.P.P., 174 P. & P., 124 S.H.	John Day's Psalter, 1562.
Old 100th	224 U.P.P., 26 P. & P., 20 & 22 F.C.H., Doxology 3 U.P.H., 15 & 16 S.P., 135 S.H.	Genevan Psalter, 1551.
Old 113th	Doxology 10 U.P.H.	Strasburg Psalter, 1539.
Old 117th	43 F.C.H.	Genevan Psalter, 1551.
Old 124th	203 U.P.P., 217 P. & P., 214 S.P.	Genevan Psalter, 1551.
Old 132d	66 U.P.P.	John Day's Psalter, 1562.
Old 134th	202 U.P.P., 125 F.C.H., 162 U.P.H., 197 S.P.	John Day's Psalter, 1562.
Old 137th	175 P. & P., 215 U.P.P., 81 F.C.H., 114 S.P., 37 & 254 U.P.H.	John Day's Psalter, 1562.
Old 143d	44 U.P.P.	Anonymous.
Old Carlisle	42 U.P.P.	Thomas Ravenscroft's Psalter, 1621.
Old Glasgow	180 U.P.P.	Scottish Psalter, 1615.
Old Saxony	230 U.P.P., 68 U.P.H., 24 F.C.H., 17 S.P.	German.
Old Winchester	178 U.P.P., 291 & Doxology 2 U.P.H.	Christopher Tye, Mus. Doc., and Thomas Este's Psalter, 1592.
Olivet	115 S.P.	Joseph Virgo Watts.

INDEX TO TUNES.

Tunes.	Numbers.	Composers or Sources.
Olivet . . .	227 S.H., 314 F.C.H.	Lowell Mason, Mus. Doc., 1792-1872.
Olmütz . . .	116 S.P.	Arranged by Lowell Mason, Mus. Doc., 1792-1872.
Oriel	26, 115 & 328 S.H., 118 & 323 U.P.H.	Dr Conrad Kocher's Zionsharfe.
Orlestrand . .	379 S.H.	Frederic Weber.
Orton . . .	299 F.C.H.	Thomas Hastings, Mus. Doc., 1784-1872.
O Sanctissima .	199 S.H.	Sicilian Melody.
Otterbourne .	18 S.P.	From Franz Joseph Hadyn, 1732-1809.
Oxford . . .	117 S.P.	William Coombs, of Bristol, about 1770.
Oxford . . .	27 P. & P.	Thomas Wood, Organist of St Giles-in-the-Fields, London, 1762.
Paddington . .	195 P. & P.	Rev. Basil Woodd, 1760-1831.
Palestrina . .	126 U.P.H., 278 F.C.H., 118 S.P.	From Giovanni Pierluigi da Palestrina, ob. 1594.
Palmyra . . .	330 U.P.H.	Felice de Giardini, 1716-1796.
Paraclete . .	370 F.C.H.	Charles Crozat Converse.
Paradise . . .	270 S.H.	Henry Smart, 1813-1879.
Paran . . .	37 F.C.H.	Johann Abraham Peter Schulz, 1747-1800.
Pascal or Hursley	178 F.C.H., 132 U.P.H., 291 S.H.	Peter Ritter, 1760-1846.
Paston . . .	207 S.H., 58 P. & P.	Thomas Este's Psalter, 1592, and Playford Psalter, 1671.
Patmos . . .	177 S.H.	Rev. William Henry Havergal, M.A., 1793-1870.
Pax Dei . . .	293 S.H.	Rev. John Bacchus Dykes, Mus. Doc., 1823-1875.
Pax Tecum . .	292 F.C.H., 226 S.H.	G. T. Caldbeck.
Pearsall . . .	353 F.C.H., 109 & 335 S.H., 63 U.P.H.	St Gall Katholisches Gesangbuch, 1863.
Penitence . .	299 F.C.H., 158 S.H.	William Henry Monk, Mus. Doc., 1823-1889.
Penitentia . .	168 S.H.	Edward Dearle, Mus. Doc., 1806-1891.
Pentecost . .	106 U.P.H., 120 F.C.H.	German.
Penuel . . .	205 U.P.H.	Leipzig Melody.
Peterborough .	13 & 326 U.P.H., 226 U.P.P.	Sir John Goss, Mus. Doc., 1800-1880.
Peterborough .	151 S.H., 118 P. & P., 119 S.P.	Rev. Ralph Harrison's Sacred Harmony, vol. ii. (1791).
Petra	132 & 149 U.P.H., 178 F.C.H., 78 & 149 S.H.	Richard Redhead.

Tunes.	Numbers.	Composers or Sources.
Philadelphia	19 S.P.	William Batchelder Bradbury, 1816-1868.
Philippi	120 S.P., 92 U.P.P.	Samuel Wesley, 1766-1837.
Pilgrimage	246 F.C.H.	Sir George Job Elvey, Mus. Doc.
Pilgrims	247 S.H., 233 U.P.H.	Henry Smart, 1813-1879.
Pilgrim Song	232 U.P.H.	Hymn Music. Rev. Henri Abraham Cæsar Malan, D.D., 1787-1864.
Playford	28 P. & P.	John Playford's Psalter, 1671.
Pleyel	167 F.C.H.	From Ignatius Josef Pleyel, 1757-1831.
Pleyel	73 U.P.H.	From Ignatius Josef Pleyel, 1757-1831.
Portuguese Hymn	306 F.C.H.	John Reading, 1677-1764 (?).
Potsdam	198 S.P., 73 U.P.P., 147 U.P.H., 62 & 152 S.H., 196 P. & P.	From Johann Sebastian Bach, 1685-1750.
Prætorius	246 U.P.H., 119 P. & P., 77 F.C.H., 394 S.H., 121 S.P., 151 U.P.P.	Michael Prætorius, Musæ Sioniæ, 1609.
Prague	199 S.P., 163 U.P.P., 197 P. & P., 113, 221, & Doxology 5 U.P.H.	Rev. Lewis Renatus West, 1753-1826.
Prescot or Old 132d	66 U.P.P.	John Day's Psalter, 1562.
Preston	225 P. & P.	John Day's Psalter, 1563.
Princethorpe	66 S.H., 253 F.C.H.	William Pitts.
Proclamation	429 S.H.	Albert Lister Peace, Mus. Doc.
Rabenlei	408 S.H.	Johann Christian Heinrich Rinck, 1770-1846.
Radford	346 S.H.	Samuel Sebastian Wesley, Mus. Doc., 1810-1876.
Raleigh	20 S.P.	David Grant.
Ramoth	365 U.P.H.	John Baptiste Calkin.
Randegger	373 S.H.	Alberto Randegger.
Ratisbon	174 F.C.H., 86 & 111 U.P.H.	From Johann Gottlob Werner's Choralbuch, 1815.
Ravenna	165 F.C.H., 228 U.P.H.	Justin Heinrich Knecht, 1752-1817.
Ravensburg	120 P. & P., 139 U.P.P., 122 S.P.	Friedrich Silcher, Ph. Doc., 1789-1860.
Ravenshaw	257 F.C.H.	Bohemian Hymnal, 1531.
Redemption	184 S.P., 223 P. & P.	Rev. Andrew Mitchell Thomson, D.D., 1778-1831.

INDEX TO TUNES.

TUNES.	NUMBERS.	COMPOSERS OR SOURCES.
Redemption	26 S.H.	Charles François Gounod.
Redhead (No. 45)	25 S.H.	French Melody, adapted by Richard Redhead.
Refuge	261 S.H.	Joseph Summers, Mus. Doc.
Regent Square	237 F.C.H., 82 S.H., 293 U.P.H.	Henry Smart, 1813-1879.
Renfrew	281 S.H.	John Montgomerie Bell, W.S.
Requiem	123 S.H.	Wilhelm Schulthes, 1816-1879.
Requiem	259 S.H.	Joseph Barnby.
Requiescat	257 S.H.	Rev. John Bacchus Dykes, Mus. Doc., 1823-1875.
Rescue	146 S.H.	William Howard Doane, Mus. Doc.
Resignation	106 F.C.H., 123 S.P.	From Giovanni Pierluigi da Palestrina, *ob*. 1594.
Resignation	221 S.H.	Anonymous.
Rest	96 F.C.H., 124 S.P.	American.
Rest	237 U.P.H.	Henry John Gauntlett, Mus. Doc., 1805-1876.
Resurrection	153 F.C.H.	William Henry Monk, Mus. Doc., 1823-1889.
Retreat	30 F.C.H., 241 U.P.H., 21 S.P.	Thomas Hastings, Mus. Doc., 1784-1872.
Ridley	198 P. & P.	Rev. Ralph Harrison's Sacred Harmony, vol. i. (1784).
Ringwood	121 P. & P.	John Playford's Psalter, 1671.
Riseholme	123 U.P.H.	Henry John Gauntlett, Mus. Doc., 1805-1876.
Rochester	29 P. & P., 94, 98, & 190 S.H.	John Day's Psalter, 1562.
Rock of Ages	149 & 178 S.H. (Part II.)	Rev. John Bacchus Dykes, Mus. Doc., 1823-1875.
Romsdal	204 U.P.H.	Lindeman (Norwegian).
Rousseau	358 F.C.H., 370 S.H., 332 U.P.H.	Jean Jacques Rousseau, 1712-1778.
Ruth	254 F.C.H., 299 S.H., 310 U.P.H.	Samuel Smith.
Ruth	91 U.P.P.	American.
Rutherford	213 F.C.H., 235 U.P.H., 266 S.H.	From Chrétien Urhan, 1790-1845.
Ruthwell	201 & 365 S.H.	John Montgomerie Bell, W.S.
St Aelred	225 S.H., 271 F.C.H.	Rev. John Bacchus Dykes, Mus. Doc., 1823-1875.
St Agatha	52 S.H.	Rev. Frederic Southgate, 1824-1885.

Tunes.	Numbers.	Composers or Sources.
St Agnes	279 U.P.H., 320 S.H., 287 F.C.H.	James Langran, Mus. Bac.
St Agnes	48 S.H., 30 P. & P.	Augusta Amherst Austen, 1827-1877.
St Agnes, Durham	170 S.H. (Part I.), 75 U.P.H., 69 F.C.H., 125 S.P.	Rev. John Bacchus Dykes, Mus. Doc., 1823-1875.
St Albans	122 P. & P.	Rev. John Chetham's Psalmody, 1718.
St Albinus	58 U.P.H., 59 S.H.	Henry John Gauntlett, Mus. Doc., 1805-1876.
St Alphege	153 & 249 U.P.H., 273 & 338 S.H., 210 F.C.H.	Henry John Gauntlett, Mus. Doc., 1805-1876.
St Ambrose or Treves	76 S.H.	Ancient.
St Ambrose	22 S.P.	Latin.
St Ambrose	164 S.P.	Charles Steggall, Mus. Doc.
St Anatolius	304 F.C.H., 294 S.H.	Arthur Henry Brown.
St Anatolius	294 S.H.	Rev. John Bacchus Dykes, Mus. Doc., 1823-1875.
St Andrew	144 S.H.	Edward Henry Thorne.
St Andrew	128 U.P.P., 123 P. & P., 126 S.P.	William Tans'ur's Collection, 1746.
St Anne	128 S.P., 110 F.C.H., 19, 167, & 315 U.P.H., 309 S.H., 124 P. & P., 219 U.P.P.	William Croft, Mus. Doc., 1678-1727 (?).
St Anselm	31 P. & P., 18 F.C.H.	Ancient.
St Asaph	73 F.C.H., 127 S.P., 250 S.H., 176 P. & P., 157 U.P.P.	Giovanni Maria Giornovichj, 1745-1804.
St Audoën	131 S.H.	Sir Robert Prescott Stewart, Mus. Doc.
St Augustine	199 P. & P.	Lowell Mason, Mus. Doc., 1792-1872.
St Austin	307 S.H.	Anonymous.
St Baldred	376 S.H.	John Montgomerie Bell, W.S.
St Bartholomew	23 S.P.	John Bishop, ob. 1737.
St Beatrice	302 S.H.	John Fred. Bridge, Mus. Doc.
St Bede	288 U.P.H.	Richard Redhead.
St Bees	164 F.C.H., 161 S.H.	Rev. John Bacchus Dykes, Mus. Doc., 1823-1875.
St Benet	118, 140, & 172 S.H.	Ancient.
St Bernard	88 F.C.H., 129 S.P., 38 & 77 U.P.H., 194, 264, 351 S.H., 125 P. & P. 84 U.P.P.	John Richardson, 1816-1879.

Tunes.	Numbers.	Composers or Sources.
St Bernard	179 S.H.	William Henry Monk, Mus. Doc., 1823-1889.
St Bride	200 S.P., 200 P. & P., 22 U.P.P.	Samuel Howard, Mus. Doc., 1710-1782.
St Bruno	303 S.H.	John Pyke Hullah, LL.D., 1812-1884.
St Catharine	276 S.H.	John Montgomerie Bell, W.S.
St Catharine	205 F.C.H.	Rev. Reginald Francis Dale, M.A., Mus. Bac.
St Cecilia	211 S.P., 222 S.H., 259 F.C.H.	Rev. Leighton George Hayne, Mus. Doc., 1836-1883.
St Chad	17 U.P.P.	James Nares, Mus. Doc., 1715-1783.
St Clement	199 U.P.H.	Charles Steggall, Mus. Doc.
St Colm	48 U.P.H.	Henry John Gauntlett, Mus. Doc., 1805-1876.
St Columba	270 F.C.H., 287 S.H.	Herbert Stephen Irons.
St Columba or Erin	351 S.H.	Ancient.
St Crispin	148 S.H.	Sir George Job Elvey, Mus. Doc.
St Cross	26 F.C.H., 38 S.H.	Rev. John Bacchus Dykes, Mus. Doc., 1823-1875.
St Cuthbert	96 S.H., 274 F.C.H., 98 U.P.H.	Rev. John Bacchus Dykes, Mus. Doc., 1823-1875.
St Cyriac	107 U.P.P.	Rev. Thomas Turton, D.D., Bishop of Ely, ob. 1864.
St Cyril	411 S.H.	Philip Paul Bliss, 1838-1876.
St David	130 S.P., 16 U.P.H., 108 F.C.H., 126 P. & P., 124 U.P.P.	Thomas Ravenscroft's Psalter, 1621, and Playford's Psalter, 1677.
St Dunstan	255 S.H.	Richard Redhead.
St Ebbe	255 U.P.H.	Richard Redhead.
St Ethelreda	153 S.H., 131 S.P., 100 U.P.P., 127 P. & P., 102 F.C.H.	Rev. Thomas Turton, D.D., Bishop of Ely, ob. 1864.
St Ethelwald	181 S.H.	William Henry Monk, Mus. Doc., 1823-1889.
St Fillan	265 F.C.H.	Joseph Barnby.
St Flavian	12 S.H., 128 P. & P.	John Day's Psalter, 1562.
St Frances	132 S.P., 62 F.C.H., 129 P. & P., 83 U.P.P., 79, 213, & 219 S.H., 186 & 282 U.P.H.	George Augustus Löhr.
St Francis	314 S.H.	Sir Arthur Seymour Sullivan, Mus. Doc.
St Francis Xavier	194 S.H.	Sir John Stainer, M.A., Mus. Doc.

TUNES.	NUMBERS.	COMPOSERS OR SOURCES.
St Fulbert	86 U.P.P., 50 & 109 U.P.H., 126 S.H., 133 S.P., 130 P. & P.	Henry John Gauntlett, Mus. Doc., 1805-1876.
St Gabriel	286 S.H.	Rev. Sir F. A. Gore Ouseley, Bart., Mus. Doc., 1825-1889.
St George	112 U.P.P., 245 U.P.H.	Henry John Gauntlett, Mus. Doc., 1805-1876.
St George	71 S.H., 131 P. & P., 150 U.P.P., 115 F.C.H., 134 S.P.	Nicolaus Hermann, ob. 1561.
St George's, Edinburgh	224 P. & P., 185 S.P., 189 U.P.P.	Rev. Andrew Mitchell Thomson, D.D., 1778-1831.
St George's, Windsor	5 & 300 S.H., 52, 64, & 311 U.P.H., 192 F.C.H.	Sir George Job Elvey, Mus. Doc.
St Gertrude	255 F.C.H., 142 S.H.	Sir Arthur Seymour Sullivan, Mus. Doc.
St Giles	125 S.H.	John Montgomerie Bell, W.S.
St Godric	320 U.P.H., 151 F.C.H., 392 S.H.	Rev. John Bacchus Dykes, Mus. Doc., 1823-1875.
St Gregory	190 & 283 S.H., 32 P. & P.	Adapted from Darmstädter Gesangbuch, 1698.
St Gregory	132 P. & P., 135 S.P., 135 U.P.P.	Robert Wainwright, Mus. Doc., ob. 1782.
St Helen	212 S.H.	Walter Hately.
St Helena	263 S.H., 128 F.C.H.	Anonymous.
St Helen's	163 S.H.	Sir Robert Prescott Stewart, Mus. Doc.
St Hilda	366 F.C.H.	Richard Tomlinson.
St Hugh	49 F.C.H., 136 S.P.	Edward John Hopkins, Mus. Doc.
St Ignatius	368 S.H.	Joseph Barnby.
St James	22 & 85 U.P.H., 137 S.P., 133 P. & P., 125 U.P.P.	Raphael Courteville, ob. 1772.
St Jerome	129 & 191 U.P.H.	Henry John Gauntlett, Mus. Doc., 1805-1876.
St John	259 & Doxology 8 U.P.H., 204, 269, & 392 S.H., 158 F.C.H., 218 S.P., 215 P. & P., 166 U.P.P.	Congregational Church Music. Rev. William Henry Havergal, M.A., 1793-1870 (?).
St John Baptist	208 S.H.	Rev. Oswald Mosley Feilden, M.A.
St John, Damascene	271 S.H.	Mrs Elizabeth Raymond Barker.
St John, Westminster	65 F.C.H.	James Turle, 1802-1882.

Tunes.	Numbers.	Composers or Sources.
St Kilda	92 F.C.H., 138 S.P., 4 U.P.P.	William Robert Broomfield, 1826-1888.
St Lawrence	139 S.P., 134 P. & P., 64 U.P.P.	Robert Archibald Smith, 1780-1829.
St Lawrence, New	145 U.P.H.	Edward Henry Thorne.
St Lawrence	312 S.H.	Rev. Leighton George Hayne, Mus. Doc., 1836-1883.
St Leonard	99 F.C.H., 210 S.H., 140 S.P.	Henry Smart, 1813-1879.
St Lucy	417 S.H.	J.
St Luke	33 P. & P.	Jeremiah Clark, 1670-1707.
St Luke	93 F.C.H.	Johann Hermann Schein's Cantional, 1627.
St Magnus	135 P. & P., 51 F.C.H., 69 S.H., 141 S.P., 51, 93, & Doxology 1 U.P.H., 184 U.P.P.	Jeremiah Clark, 1670-1707.
St Malo	156 U.P.H.	Henry John Gauntlett, Mus. Doc., 1805-1876.
St Margaret	176 S.H.	Albert Lister Peace, Mus. Doc.
St Margaret	39 S.H.	Rev. William Statham, Mus. Doc.
St Margaret	209 U.P.H., 87 U.P.P., 142 S.P.	Rev. Leighton George Hayne, Mus. Doc., 1836-1883.
St Mark	282 F.C.H.	Dr Conrad Kocher's Zionsharfe.
St Martin's	305 S.H.	Albert Lister Peace, Mus. Doc.
St Mary	136 P. & P., 2 U.P.P., 122 U.P.H., 143 S.P., 91 F.C.H., 153 S.H.	Playford's Psalter, 1677, and Pry's Psalter, 1621.
St Mary Abbotts	201 S.P.	William Horsley, Mus. Bac., 1774-1858.
St Matthew	144 S.P., 325 U.P.H., 124 S.H., 55 U.P.P., 177 P. & P.	William Croft, Mus. Doc., 1678-1727.
St Matthias	211 U.P.H., 145 S.P., 105 U.P.P., 137 P. & P.	Orlando Gibbons, Mus. Doc., 1583-1625.
St Matthias	46 F.C.H., 350 S.H.	William Henry Monk, Mus. Doc., 1823-1889.
St Methodius	121 U.P.H.	Henry John Gauntlett, Mus. Doc., 1805-1876.
St Michael	201 P. & P., 58 & 239 S.H.	Genevan Psalter, 1543, and John Day's Psalter, 1563.
St Minver	146 S.P.	Simeon Grosvenor, Mus. Bac., 1816-1866.

Tunes.	Numbers.	Composers or Sources.
St Mirren	147 S.P., 138 P. & P., 220 U.P.P.	Robert Archibald Smith, 1780-1829.
St Mungo	139 P. & P.	Albert Lister Peace, Mus. Doc.
St Neot	140 P. & P., 12 U.P.P., 148 S.P.	John & James Green's Collection, 1715.
St Nicholas	141 P. & P., 193 U.P.P., 149 S.P.	Israel Holdroyd's Collection, 1753.
St Nicolas	154 S.H.	Richard Redhead.
St Ninian's	3 U.P.H.	Dr Conrad Kocher's Zionsharfe.
St Olave or Olaf	112 U.P.P., 202 P. & P., 202 S.P., 245 U.P.H., 130 F.C.H., 102, 206, 339 S.H.	Henry John Gauntlett, Mus. Doc., 1805-1876.
St Oswald	228 F.C.H., 143, 407 S.H.	Rev. John Bacchus Dykes, Mus. Doc., 1823-1875.
St Pancras	34 P. & P.	Jonathan Battishill, 1738-1801.
St Paul	142 P. & P., 61 U.P.P., 150 S.P., 130 U.P.H., 85 F.C.H.	Robert Bremner's Collection, Edinburgh, 1756. See Jas. Chalmers, in Appendix.
St Peter	76, 83, 170, 283 U.P.H., 151 S.P., 63 F.C.H., 85 U.P.P., 143 P. & P., 160 & 186 S.H.	Alexander Robert Reinagle, 1799-1877.
St Peter (Westminster)	70 U.P.H., 245 F.C.H.	James Turle, 1802-1882.
St Petersburg	175 S.H.	Dimitri Bortnianski, 1751-1828.
St Philip	284 F.C.H., 262 S.H.	Joseph Barnby.
St Philip	95 & 169 S.H.	William Henry Monk, Mus. Doc., 1823-1889.
St Raphael	242 F.C.H.	Edward John Hopkins, Mus. Doc.
St Saviour	375 S.H.	John Montgomerie Bell, W.S.
St Saviour	152 S.P.	Frederick George Baker.
St Sebastian	150 & 326 S.H.	Samuel Sebastian Wesley, Mus. Doc., 1820-1876.
St Sepulchre	35 P. & P., 122, 343 S.H.	George Cooper, 1810-1876.
St Silvester	145 S.H.	Joseph Barnby.
St Stephen (Abridge)	153 S.P., 144 U.P.P., 144 P. & P., 296 U.P.H.	Isaac Smith, *ob.* about 1800.
St Sulpice	306 S.H.	Augustus Grant Jamieson, 1844-1888.

INDEX TO TUNES.

Tunes.	Numbers.	Composers or Sources.
St Sylvester	310 S.H.	Rev. John Bacchus Dykes, Mus. Doc., 1823-1875.
St Theodulph	35, 109, 240 S.H.	Melchior Teschner.
St Thomas	62 U.P.P., 145 P. & P., 154 S.P., 222 U.P.H.	Charles Ashworth's Collection, about 1760.
St Timothy	109 F.C.H.	Rev. Sir Henry Williams Baker, Bart., 1821-1877.
St Ulrich	199 F.C.H.	Charles Henry Purday, 1799-1885.
St Ursula	57 F.C.H.	Frederick Westlake.
St Victor	337 & 358 S.H.	Richard Redhead.
St Wolstan	302 F.C.H.	Edward John Hopkins, Mus. Doc.
Salamis	338 U.P.H., 384 F.C.H., 396 S.H.	Greek Air.
Salem	66 F.C.H.	Arranged by Sir Arthur Seymour Sullivan, Mus. Doc.
Sâles	105 S.H., 275 F.C.H.	Francis Henry Champneys, M.A., M.D.
Salisbury	138 U.P.P., 146 P. & P., 155 S.P.	Thomas Ravenscroft's Psalter, 1621.
Salzburg	147 P. & P., 37 U.P.P., 156 S.P., 178 U.P.H., 98 F.C.H.	From Johann Michael Haydn, 1737-1806.
Samson	14 F.C.H., 24 S.P.	From Georg Friedrich Händel, 1685-1759.
Samuel	413 S.H., 345 F.C.H., 342 U.P.H.	Sir Arthur Seymour Sullivan, Mus. Doc.
Sanctuary	119 S.H.	Rev. John Bacchus Dykes, Mus. Doc., 1823-1875.
Sandon	310 F.C.H.	Charles Henry Purday, 1799-1885.
Sardis	231 F.C.H.	From Ludwig van Beethoven, 1770-1827.
Sarum	5 U.P.H.	Ancient.
Sarum Hymnal (No. 46)	36 P. & P.	Theodore Edward Aylward.
Saul	237 U.P.H.	From Georg Friedrich Händel, 1685-1759.
Sawley	157 S.P., 80 F.C.H.	James Walch.
Saxony	186 S.P.	From Georg Friedrich Händel, 1685-1759.
Saxony	81 & 254 S.H., 37 P. & P.	German.
Scarborough	158 S.P.	Altered from William Shrubsole, 1760-1806.
Scheffler	163 F.C.H.	Johann Scheffler's Hirtenlieder.
Schönberg	186 F.C.H.	Johann Rosenmüller, 1686.

Tunes.	Numbers.	Composers or Sources.
Scott	111 U.P.P.	From Johann Georg Nageli, 1768-1836.
Sebaste	290 S.H., 332 F.C.H.	Sir John Stainer, M.A., Mus. Doc.
Selma	72 U.P.P., 203 S.P., 203 P. & P.	Robert Archibald Smith's Collection, 1825.
Selville	148 P. & P.	John Montgomerie Bell, W.S.
Sepulchre	49 U.P.H.	Edward Henry Thorne.
Serenity	204 S.P., 204 P. & P.	Cornelius Bryan, *ob.* 1845.
Shalem	19 F.C.H.	Ancient.
Sharon	14 S.H., 221 F.C.H., 220 U.P.H.	William Boyce, Mus. Doc., 1710-1779.
Sheba	248 U.P.H.	Rev. William Henry Havergal, M.A., 1793-1870.
Sheffield	134 U.P.P., 159 S.P., 149 P. & P.	William Mather, *ob.* 1808.
Shirland	205 S.P.	Samuel Stanley, *ob.* 1822.
Shropshire	1 F.C.H.	Edward John Hopkins, Mus. Doc.
Sicilian	348 U.P.H.	Sicilian Melody.
Sigillus	171 U.P.H., 258 F.C.H., 212 S.P.	Michael Siegel or Sigillus.
Sigismund	46 U.P.H., 225 F.C.H.	Gotha Cantional, 1715.
Silchester	124 F.C.H., 165 U.P.P., 206 S.P.	From the Rev. Henri Abraham Cæsar Malan, 1787-1864.
Silesia	11 U.P.P.	Adam Krieger, *ob.* 1666.
Siloam	430 S.H.	Albert Lister Peace, Mus. Doc.
Slingsby	117 F.C.H.	Rev. John Bacchus Dykes, Mus. Doc., 1823-1875.
Smart	238 S.H.	Henry Smart, 1813-1879.
Soldau	103 S.H., 25 S.P., 229 U.P.P., 13 F.C.H., 38 P. & P., 169, 188, & 193 U.P.H.	Adapted by H. E. Dibdin from Martin Luther, D.D., 1483-1546.
Solitude	366 S.H.	Harriet Anne Callow, 1817-1883.
Solomon	160 S.P., 150 P. & P.	From Georg Friedrich Händel, 1685-1759.
Sonning	238 U.P.H.	Henry John Gauntlett, Mus. Doc., 1805-1876.
Southwark	94 U.P.H., 154 U.P.P., 151 P. & P., 161 S.P., 53 F.C.H.	From Christopher Tye, Mus. Doc., *ob.* 1572.
Southwell	207 S.P.	Henrie Denham's Psalter, 1588.
Southwell	268 S.H.	Herbert Stephen Irons.

INDEX TO TUNES.

Tunes.	Numbers.	Composers or Sources.
Southwold	162 S.P., 99 U.P.P., 220 S.H., 152 P. & P., 190 U.P.H.	Henry John Gauntlett, Mus. Doc., 1805-1876.
Spires	231 U.P.P.	Martin Luther, D.D., 1483-1546.
Spohr	163 S.P., 136 S.H., 90 F.C.H., 153 P. & P., 42 U.P.H.	From Louis Spohr, Mus. Doc., 1784-1859.
Springfield	32 S.H.	From the Rev. Dr Peter Maurice's Choral Harmony, 1854.
Springtide	296 S.H.	Edward John Hopkins, Mus. Doc.
Springtime	375 F.C.H.	German.
Stabat Mater	41 S.H.	Rev. John Bacchus Dykes, Mus. Doc., 1823-1875.
Steggall's	301 U.P.H.	Charles Steggall, Mus. Doc.
Steggall (St Ambrose)	164 S.P.	Charles Steggall, Mus. Doc.
Stella	397 S.H., 46 F.C.H., 358 U.P.H.	Henri Fred. Hemy's Crown of Jesus Music.
Stephanos	163 S.H., 267 F.C.H., 120 U.P.H.	Rev. Sir Henry Williams Baker, Bart., 1821-1877.
Stettin	155 S.H., 24 U.P.H.	Adapted by Nicolaus Decius, ob. 1541.
Stiastny	117 S.H.	From Johann Stiastny.
Stobel	107 S.H., 135 U.P.H.	German.
Stockton	165 S.P., 230 S.H., 154 P. & P.	Thomas Wright, 1763-1829.
Strasburg	53 U.P.H.	German.
Strasburg	41 F.C.H.	Strasburg Psalter.
Strattner	171 F.C.H., 316 S.H.	Georg Christoph Strattner, 1650-1705.
Stroudwater	166 S.P., 190 U.P.P., 155 P. & P., 55 U.P.H.	Matthew Wilkins's Collection, about 1730.
Stuttgart	11 & 380 S.H.	Gotha Cantional, 1715.
Stuttgart	214 F.C.H., 44 & 127 U.P.H.	Hans Leo Hassler, 1564-1612.
Suavitas	438 S.H.	George Herbert Gregory, Mus. Bac.
Submission No. I.	214 S.H.	George Lomas, Mus. Bac., 1834-1884.
Submission No. II.	214 S.H.	Albert Lister Peace, Mus. Doc.
Submission	276 F.C.H.	Anonymous.
Sudeley	167 S.P.	Sir John Stainer, M.A., Mus. Doc.
Sunshine	224 S.H.	Philip Paul Bliss, 1838-1876.

Tunes.	Numbers.	Composers or Sources.
Swabia	133 & 282 S.H., 208 S.P., 232 U.P.P., 139 F.C.H., 103, 161 U.P.H.	Adapted from Johann Crüger's Praxis Pietatis Melica, 1698.
Tabor	351 U.P.H.	Charles Steggall, Mus. Doc.
Tallis (Ordinal)	308 U.P.H., 70 & 123 U.P.P., 67 F.C.H., 168 S.P., 101 & 189 S.H., 156 P. & P.	Thomas Tallis, ob. 1585.
Te Deum	354 U.P.H.	William Jackson, 1730-1803 (?).
Te Deum	333 F.C.H., Anthem Music	Edward John Hopkins, Mus. Doc.
Temple	292 S.H., 331 F.C.H.	Edward John Hopkins, Mus. Doc.
Temple Bar	141 F.C.H.	Edward John Hopkins, Mus. Doc.
Tenderness	398 S.H., 382 F.C.H.	Richard William Beaty, ob. 1883.
Thanksgiving	441 S.H., 54 U.P.H.	Walter Bond Gilbert, Mus. Doc.
The Blessed Home	265 S.H., 262 F.C.H.	Sir John Stainer, M.A., Mus. Doc.
Theodora	173 S.H.	Georg Friedrich Händel, 1685-1759.
Theodore	154 U.P.H.	Henry Smart, 1813-1879.
Theodulph	177 U.P.P., 336 U.P.H.	Melchior Teschner.
Thetford	205 P. & P.	Frederick Cook Atkinson, Mus. Bac.
The Three Kings	32 S.H.	Francis Henry Champneys, M.A., M.D.
Tichfield	189 F.C.H., 5 & 349 S.H.	John Richardson, 1816-1879.
Tiverton	113 & 267 S.H., 148 U.P.P., 157 P. & P., 169 S.P., 84 F.C.H.	Grigg. From the Rev. John Rippon's Collection, 1806.
Toplady	89 U.P.P., 227 & 239 U.P.H.	Henry John Gauntlett, Mus. Doc., 1805-1876.
Tottenham	155 U.P.P., 170 S.P.	Thomas Greatorex's Collections, 1823 and 1829.
Tours	395 S.H.	Berthold Tours.
Treves	263 F.C.H.	Ancient.
Trinity	287 U.P.H.	Felice de Giardini, 1716-1796.
Trinity	1 S.H.	Samuel Sebastian Wesley, Mus. Doc., 1810-1876.
Triumph	61 & 111 S.H., 61 & Doxology 7 U.P.H., 249 F.C.H.	Henry John Gauntlett, Mus. Doc., 1805-1876.

INDEX TO TUNES.

Tunes.	Numbers.	Composers or Sources.
Troyte's Chant (No. 1)	245 S.H., 271 S.P., 174, 234 U.P.H., 50 U.P.P., 276 F.C.H.	Arthur Henry Dyke Troyte, 1811-1857.
Troyte's Chant (No. 2)	334 & 355 U.P.H., 262 & 386 S.H., 284 & 373 F.C.H., 272 S.P.	William Hayes, Mus. Doc., 1706-1777. Abridged by A. H. D. Troyte.
Truro . . .	117 S.H.	Charles Burney, Mus. Doc., 1726-1814 (?).
Trust . . .	250 F.C.H.	German.
Trust . . .	171 S.P.	Henry Temple Leslie (Mus. Doc.?) ob. 1876.
Turle . . .	265 U.P.H.	James Turle, 1802-1882.
Ulm	158 P. & P.	Adam Krieger, ob. 1666.
Ulpha . . .	248 F.C.H.	Edwin Moss.
University . .	172 S.P., 132 U.P.P.	John Randall, Mus. Doc., ob. 1799 (?).
University College	161 F.C.H., 232 S.H., 165 U.P.H.	Henry John Gauntlett, Mus. Doc., 1805-1876.
Urswicke . .	10 S.H.	Sir George Job Elvey, Mus. Doc.
Uxbridge . .	159 P. & P.	Henry Edward Dibdin's Standard Psalm Tune Book.
Valley of Blessing	428 S.H.	William Gustavus Fischer.
Veni Cito . .	88 S.H.	Rev. John Bacchus Dykes, Mus. Doc., 1823-1875.
Veni Creator .	91 S.H., 39 F.C.H., 99, 115, & 321 U.P.H.	Latin Melody.
Veni Immanuel	29 U.P.H.	Latin Melody.
Vesper Hymn (or Vespers)	244 F.C.H., 295 S.H.	Arranged by Sir John Andrew Stevenson, Mus. Doc., ob. 1833.
Vespers . . .	287 S.H.	Sir Robert Prescott Stewart, Mus. Doc.
Vevay . . .	278 F.C.H.	James Allan, 1842-1885.
Vexillum . .	424 S.H.	Henry Smart, 1813-1879.
Victory . . .	57 S.H.	From Giovanni Pierluigi da Palestrina, ob. 1594.
Vienna . . .	201 F.C.H.	Melchior Teschner.
Vienna or Ravenna	173, 223, & 349 S.H.	Justin Heinrich Knecht, 1752-1817.
Vigilate . . .	277 F.C.H., 183 S.H.	William Henry Monk, Mus. Doc., 1823-1889.

Tunes.	Numbers.	Composers or Sources.
Vox Dilecti	81 F.C.H., 197 S.H.	Rev. John Bacchus Dykes, Mus. Doc., 1823-1875.
Vulpius	5 F.C.H.	Melchior Vulpius, 1560-1616, or 1621.
Währing	256 S.H.	Samuel Webbe, 1740-1816.
Wainwright	196 S.H.	Richard Wainwright, ob. 1825.
Waldeck	160 P. & P., 147 U.P.P.	Justin Heinrich Knecht, 1752-1817.
Waldeck	15 F.C.H.	Johann Christian Heinrich Rinck, 1770-1846.
Waldheim	76 S.H.	From Johann Gottfried Schicht's Choralbuch, 1819.
Walsal	9 U.P.P., 173 S.P.	Matthew Wilkins's Psalmody, about 1730.
Walton	26 S.P., 39 P. & P., 7 F.C.H.	From Ludwig van Beethoven, 1770-1827 (?).
Warburton	174 S.P.	Rev. George Wharton, M.A., 1803-1867.
Wareham	40 P. & P., 159 U.P.P., 294 F.C.H., 307 & 314 U.P.H.	William Knapp, 1698-1768.
Warfare	427 S.H.	Laura Josephine Hutton.
Warrington	41 P. & P., 114 & 130 S.H., 198 U.P.P., 3 F.C.H., 27 S.P.	Rev. Ralph Harrison, 1748-1810.
Warwick	175 S.P., 133 U.P.P.	Samuel Stanley, ob. 1822.
Waterstock	156 F.C.H., 202 S.H.	Sir John Goss, Mus. Doc., 1800-1880.
Weimar	191 F.C.H., 51 & 166 S.H.	Melchior Vulpius, 1560-1616, or 1621.
Weimar	262 U.P.H.	Carl Philipp Emanuel Bach, 1714-1788.
Wellesley	273 & 308 S.H.	Sir George Job Elvey, Mus. Doc.
Wells	176 & 306 U.P.H.	Dimitri Bortnianski, 1751-1828.
Westenhanger	142 F.C.H.	Clement William Poole.
Westminster	161 P. & P., 54 F.C.H., 217 U.P.P., 9 & 89 U.P.H., 176 S.P.	James Turle, 1802-1882.
Westmoreland	53 U.P.H.	Charles Steggall, Mus. Doc.
Westover	261 U.P.H.	Henry John Gauntlett, Mus. Doc., 1805-1876.
Wetherby	162 P. & P.	Samuel Sebastian Wesley, Mus. Doc., 1810-1876.

INDEX TO TUNES.

TUNES.	NUMBERS.	COMPOSERS OR SOURCES.
When He Cometh	442 S.H.	George Frederick Root, Mus. Doc.
Whiteford	312 F.C.H.	Edward John Hopkins, Mus. Doc.
Whither, Pilgrims?	439 S.H.	William Batchelder Bradbury, 1816-1868.
Who is He?	391 S.H.	Rev. Benjamin Russell Hanby, 1833-1867.
Wigton	163 P. & P.	Scottish Psalter, 1635.
Wiltshire	164 P. & P., 177 S.P., 129 U.P.P.	Sir George Thomas Smart, 1776-1867.
Wimbledon	90 U.P.H., 286 S.H.	Samuel Sebastian Wesley, Mus. Doc., 1810-1876.
Winchester	165 P. & P., 178 S.P., 23 & 203 S.H.	From Christopher Tye, Mus. Doc., and Thomas Este's Psalter, 1592.
Winchester (or Crasselius)	225 U.P.P., 192 U.P.H.	From Hamburger Musikalisches Handbuch, 1690.
Windsor (or Dundee)	57 S.P.	From Christopher Tye, Mus. Doc., and Thomas Este's Psalter, 1592.
Winter	138 U.P.H.	From Peter von Winter, 1754-1825.
Winthorpe	296 S.H.	Rev. Timothy Richard Matthews, B.A.
Wirksworth	218 P. & P., 23 U.P.P.	James Green's Collection, 1724.
Wittemberg or Wittenberg	148 U.P.H. 321 F.C.H.	Johann Crüger, 1598-1662.
Wittemberg	23 S.P., 42 P. & P.	Martin Luther, D.D., 1483-1546.
Wix	86 F.C.H.	Rev. Leighton George Hayne, Mus. Doc., 1836-1883.
Woburn	166 P. & P.	From Henry Edward Dibdin's Standard Psalm Tune Book.
Worcester	44 P. & P.	Sir John Goss, Mus. Doc., 1800-1880.
Wordsworth	341 S.H.	William Henry Monk, Mus. Doc., 1823-1889.
Worgan	43 P. & P.	John Worgan, Mus. Doc., 1724-1790.
Worms	325 F.C.H., 144 U.P.H.	Martin Luther, D.D., 1483-1546.
York	167 P. & P., 141 U.P.P., 179 S.P., 105 F.C.H., 120 S.H.	Scottish Psalter, 1615.

Tunes.	Numbers.	Composers or Sources.
Zinzendorf	217 U.P.H.	Adam Drese, 1620-1701.
Zion	180 S.P.	William Robert Broomfield, 1826-1888.
Zoan	285 U.P.H.	Rev. William Henry Havergal, M.A., 1793-1870.
Zuingle	181 S.P.	Thomas Legerwood Hately, 1815-1867.
Zurich	2 U.P.H., 134 & 242 S.H.	From Wolfgang Carl Briegel's Darmstädter Cantional, 1687.
Zurich	209 S.P., 148 F.C.H.	Johann Georg Nageli, 1768-1836.

ALPHABETICAL INDEX OF COMPOSERS WHOSE CHANTS APPEAR IN THE U.P.H., U.P.P., S.H., S.P., AND F.C.H., WITH THEIR NUMBERS.

Composers or Sources.	Date.	Numbers.
Alcock, John, Mus. Doc.	1715-1806	Chant I., set to Hymn 334 F.C.H.
Ancient		270 S.P.
Bacon, Rev. Robert, B.A.	ob. 1759	231 S.P.
Barrow, Thomas	ob. 1789	168 U.P.P. and Chant I. to Hymn 353 U.P.H.
Battishill, Jonathan	1738-1801	221 S.P., 354 U.P.H., 205 U.P.P., 255 S.P., 261 S.P., 30 U.P.P., 333 F.C.H. (Chant I.)
Beckwith, John (Christmas?), Mus. Doc.	1750-1809	212 U.P.P.
Blow, John, Mus. Doc.	1648-1708	223 S.P.
Boyce, William, Mus. Doc.	1710-1799	211 U.P.P., 218 S.P., 233 S.P.
Cooke, Robert	ob. 1814	235 U.P.P.
Croft, William, Mus. Doc.	1678-1727	356 S.H., 222 S.P., 354 U.P.H., 26 U.P.P.
Crotch, William, Mus. Doc.	1775-1847	234 S.P., 250 S.P., 209 U.P.P., 262 S.P., 118 U.P.P., 356 S.H. (Chant II.)
Cummings, William Hayman		Chants III. set to Hymn 333 F.C.H.
Dolomite Chant		213 S.P.
Dupuis, Thomas Sanders, Mus. Doc.	1730-1796	78 U.P.P., 235 S.P., 355 S.H. (A minor), 353 S.H. (Chant I.), 254 S.P., 333 F.C.H.

Composers or Sources.	Date.	Numbers.
Farrant, Richard	ob. 1580	224 S.P. and 77 U.P.P.
Finch, Hon. and Rev. Edward	ob. 1738	333 F.C.H.
Flintoft, Rev. Luke	ob. 1727	236 S.P., 29 U.P.P.
Gibbons, Christopher	1615-1676	115 U.P.P.
Goodenough, Rev. Robert Philip	1775-1826	352 S.H.
Goss, Sir John, Mus. Doc.	1800-1880	81 U.P.P., 356 S.H.
Gregorian		237 S.P., 234 U.P.P.
Händel, Georg Friedrich	1685-1759	238 S.P., 171 U.P.P.
Harrison, Rev. Ralph	1748-1810	268 S.P.
Hately, Thomas Legerwood	1815-1867	225 & 269 S.P.
Havergal, Frances Ridley	1836-1879	49 U.P.P. (Sardis chant).
Havergal, Rev. William Henry	1793-1870	266 S.P., 119 U.P.P.
Hayes, William, Mus. Doc.	ob. 1777	175 U.P.P., 239 S.P., 334 & 355 U.P.H., 272 S.P., 262 & 386 S.H., 284 & 373 F.C.H.
Heathcote, Rev. Gilbert, M.A.	ob. 1829	120 U.P.P., 258 S.P.
Hine, William	1687-1730	334 F.C.H.
Hopkins, Edward John, Mus. Doc.		333 F.C.H., 259 & 260 S.P.
Houldsworth, John	ob. 18—	169 U.P.P., 353 U.P.H.
Humfrey, Pelham	ob. 1674	233 U.P.P., 229 S.P.
Jackson, Thomas	ob. 1781	242 S.P., 82 U.P.P., 267 S.P., 207 U.P.P.
Jackson, William	1730-1803	227 & 240 S.P.
Jones, John	1728-1796	354 S.H., 249 S.P., 176 U.P.P.
Lambeth, Henry Albert		48 U.P.P.
Langdon, Richard, Mus. Bac.	ob. 1803	241 S.P., 79 U.P.P.
Lawes, Henry	ob. 1662	256 S.P.
Lemon, John	1754-1814	116 U.P.P.
Macfarren, Sir George Alexander, Mus. Doc.	1813-1887	355 S.H.
Monk, Edwin George, Mus. Doc.		354 S.H. (Chant I.)
Morley, William, Mus. Bac.	ob. 1721	243 S.P., 31 U.P.P.
Mornington, Earl of	1735-1781	257 S.P., 172 U.P.P., 244 S.P., 173 U.P.P.
Nares, James, Mus. Doc.	1715-1783	114 U.P.P.
Norris, Thomas, Mus. Doc.	1741-1790	174 U.P.P., 245 S.P.
Parr, Rev. Henry		33 U.P.P.

Composers or Sources.	Date.	Numbers.
Peace, Albert Lister, Mus. Doc.		356 S. H.
Peregrine Tone		27 U.P.P.
Purcell, Thomas	*ob.* 1682	Chant in G, 230 S.P., 334 F.C.H.
		Chant II. in G Minor, 333 F.C.H.
		Chant I. in G Minor, 334 F.C.H., 353 U.P.H., 46 U.P.P.
Randall, John, Mus. Doc.	*ob.* 1799	246 S.P.
Robinson, John	1682-1762	247 S.P., 170 U.P.P.
Russell, William, Mus. Bac.	1777-1813	353 S.H., 210 U.P.P.
Scotch Chant		333 F.C.H.
Smith, John Stafford	1750-1836	251, 252 S.P.
Soaper, John	*ob.* 1794	80 U.P.P., 263 S.P.
Tallis, Thomas	*ob.* 1585	226 S.P., 76 U.P.P.
Troyte, Arthur Henry Dyke	1811-1857	245 S.H., 271 S.P., 174 & 234 U.P.H., 50 U.P.P., 276 F.C.H., 334 & 355 U.P.H., 262 & 386 S.H., 284 & 373 F.C.H., 272 S.P.
Turle, James	1802-1882	28 U.P.P., 253 S.P.
Weldon, John	*ob.* 1736	232 S.P., 17 U.P.P., 353 U.P.H. (Chant III.)
Wesley, Samuel	1766-1837	231 U.P.H., 117 U.P.P., 265 S.P., 32 U.P.P.
Woodward, Richard	*ob.* 1777	228 S.P., 206 U.P.P., 264 S.P., 208 U.P.P.

DOXOLOGIES IN U.P.H.

Title.	No.	Composers or Sources.
Blessed, blessed be Jehovah	15	Samuel Webbe's Collection, 1792.
From all that dwell below the skies	6	Henry Smart, 1813-1879.
Glory be to God, the Father	13	Rev. William Henry Havergal, M.A., 1793-1870.
Glory be to Him who gave us	11	German.
Glory be to the Father, and to the Son	18	William Jackson, 1730-1803 (?).
Glory, glory everlasting	9	Rev. William Henry Havergal, M.A., 1793-1879.
Hallelujah! for the Lord God Omnipotent reigneth	16	Henry Smart, 1813-1879.
Hark! how the adoring hosts	5	Rev. Lewis Renatus West, 1753-1826.
Holy, holy, holy. Sanctus I.	17	John Camidge, Mus. Doc., 1790-1859.
Holy, holy, holy. Sanctus II.	17	Thomas Ebdon, 1738-1811.
Holy, holy, holy. Sanctus III.	17	Samuel Arnold, Mus. Doc., 1740-1802.
I'll praise my Maker with my breath	10	Strasburg Psalter, 1539.
Immortal honour, endless fame	12	Zerubbabel Wyvill, 1763-1837.
Lord, bless us still	14	Robert Archibald Smith, 1780-1829.
Now to Him who loved us, gave us	7	Henry John Gauntlett, Mus. Doc., 1805-1876.
Now to the King of Heaven	8	Rev. William Henry Havergal, M.A., 1793-1879 (?), Congregational Church Music.
Praise God from whom all blessings flow	3	Genevan Psalter.
To Father, Son, and Holy Ghost	1	Jeremiah Clark, 1670-1707.
To Him who sits upon the throne	2	From Christopher Tye, Mus. Doc., and Thomas Este's Psalter, 1592.
Unto the Father, God of Heaven	4	Samuel Howard, Mus. Doc., 1710-1782.

ALPHABETICAL INDEX OF SCRIPTURE SENTENCES IN FREE CHURCH HYMNAL, AND UNITED PRESBYTERIAN HYMNAL, WITH THEIR NUMBERS, COMPOSERS, OR SOURCES.

Sentences marked thus (*) have Chant Music.

Scripture Sentences.	Numbers.	Composers or Sources.
Arise, O Lord, into Thy rest	11 U.P.H.	Sir George Alexander Macfarren, Mus. Doc., 1813-1887.
Arise, shine, for thy light is come	84 U.P.H.	Sir George Job Elvey, Mus. Doc.
Arise, shine, for thy light is come	17 F.C.H.	Edward John Hopkins, Mus. Doc.
*Arise, shine, for thy light is come	123 U.P.H.	William Russell, Mus. Bac., 1777-1813.
Awake, put on strength	83 U.P.H.	John Wall Callcott, Mus. Doc., 1766-1821.
Behold, a Virgin shall conceive	77 U.P.H.	Thomas Smith.
*Behold, happy is the man	109 U.P.H.	Gregorian.
Behold, how good and joyful	68 U.P.H.	John Clarke-Whitfeld, Mus. Doc., 1770-1836.
Behold, I bring you good tidings	95 U.P.H.	Sir John Goss, Mus. Doc., 1800-1880.
Behold my servant, whom I uphold	120 U.P.H.	Sir John Goss, Mus. Doc., 1800-1880.
Behold the Lamb of God	96 U.P.H.	From August Edward Grell, 1800-1886.
Behold, the Lord is my salvation	79 U.P.H.	Rev. John Chetham's Psalmody, 1718. Maurice Greene, Mus. Doc., 1696-1755 (?).
Blessed are the dead	106 U.P.H.	Nicolo Zingarelli, 1752-1837.
*Blessed are the poor in spirit	124 U.P.H.	Gregorian.

SCOTTISH CHURCH MUSIC.

SCRIPTURE SENTENCES.	NUMBERS.	COMPOSERS OR SOURCES.
Blessed be the Lord God of Israel	8 U.P.H.	Robert Archibald Smith, 1780-1829.
Blessed be the Lord God of Israel	93 U.P.H.	Sir John Goss, Mus. Doc., 1800-1880.
*Blessed be the Lord God of Israel	127 U.P.H.	William Russell, Mus. Bac., 1777-1813.
Blessed be Thou, Lord God of Israel	28 U.P.H.	James Kent, 1700-1776.
Blessed, blessed be Jehovah	7 F.C.H.	Samuel Webbe's Collection, 1792.
Blessed is He who cometh	90 U.P.H.	From Charles François Gounod.
Blessed is the man that endureth	100 U.P.H.	Sir John Stainer, Mus. Doc.
Blessed is the people	6 U.P.H.	Lowell Mason, Mus. Doc., 1792-1872.
Blessing and honour, glory and power	101 U.P.H.	From Mozart, 1756-1791.
Blessing, glory, wisdom, and thanks	102 U.P.H.	Johann Sebastian Bach, 1685-1750 (?).
Bless the Lord, O my soul	58 U.P.H.	From George James Webb, 1803-1887.
Both riches and honour	29 U.P.H.	From James Kent, 1700-1776.
Bow down Thine ear	53 U.P.H.	From August Edward Grell, 1800-1886.
*But now is Christ risen	129 U.P.H.	Robert Cooke, ob. 1814.
Cast thy burden on the Lord	48 U.P.H., 6 F.C.H.	William Batchelder Bradbury, 1816-1868.
Christ is risen, . . . blessing and honour	98 U.P.H.	Sir John Goss, Mus. Doc., 1800-1880.
Christ is risen, . . . for since by man	97 U.P.H.	Thomas Smith.
Come, and let us return	86 U.P.H.	William Jackson (of Masham), 1815-1866.
Come unto me, all ye that labour	14 U.P.H.	Sir Herbert Stanley Oakeley Mus. Doc.
Come unto me, all ye that labour	88 U.P.H.	From Charles François Gounod.
Come unto me, all ye that labour	23 F.C.H.	John Stafford Smith, Mus. Doc., 1750-1836.
*Comfort ye, comfort ye	119 U.P.H.	From Händel, 1685-1759.
Create in me a clean heart	45 U.P.H.	Ebenezer Prout, B.A.
*Doth not wisdom cry	113 U.P.H.	William Crotch, Mus. Doc., 1775-1847.
Enter not into judgment	72 U.P.H.	Sir John Goss, Mus. Doc., 1800-1880.

INDEX TO SCRIPTURE SENTENCES. 49

Scripture Sentences.	Numbers.	Composers or Sources.
For the eyes of the Lord	3 F.C.H.	James Merrylees.
Give ear to my prayer	47 U.P.H.	Jacques Arcadelt (?).
Glory be to God on high	334 F.C.H.	Edward John Hopkins, Mus. Doc.
Glory to God in the highest	15 U.P.H.	Ebenezer Prout, B.A.
God is a Spirit	17 U.P.H., 26 F.C.H.	Henry Smart, 1813-1879.
Great and marvellous	24 U.P.H.	Henry Smart, 1813-1879.
Great is the Lord	4 U.P.H.	Henry Smart, 1813-1879.
Hallelujah! for unto us a child is born	78 U.P.H.	William Henry Monk, Mus. Doc., 1823-1889.
Hallelujah! salvation, and glory	132 U.P.H.	Henry John Gauntlett, Mus. Doc., 1805-1876.
Hallelujah! what are these	103 U.P.H.	Sir John Stainer, Mus. Doc.
Have mercy upon me	42 U.P.H.	Sir George Alexander Macfarren, Mus. Doc., 1813-1887.
Hear my pray'r	71 U.P.H.	From Peter von Winter, 1775-1825.
He knoweth the way that I take	4 F.C.H.	Rev. Robert Riach Thom.
He shall feed His flock	16 F.C.H.	Allan Macbeth.
*Ho, every one that thirsteth	122 U.P.H.	John Lemon, 1754-1814.
Holiness becometh Thine house	7 U.P.H.	Lowell Mason, Mus. Doc., 1792-1872.
*Holy, holy, holy, Lord God Almighty	130 U.P.H.	Henry John Gauntlett, Mus. Doc., 1805-1876.
Holy, holy, holy, Lord God of hosts	14 F.C.H.	John Camidge, Mus. Doc., 1790-1859.
Holy, holy, holy, Lord God of hosts	14 F.C.H.	Thomas Ebdon, 1738-1811.
Holy, holy, holy, Lord God of hosts	14 F.C.H.	Orlando Gibbons, Mus. Doc., 1583-1625.
How beautiful upon the mountains	12 U.P.H.	Robert Archibald Smith, 1780-1829.
I acknowledge my transgressions	44 U.P.H.	Rev. Joseph Muenscher's Church Choir, 1839.
I heard a voice	104 U.P.H.	Sir John Goss, Mus. Doc., 1800-1880.
I heard a voice	105 U.P.H., 30 F.C.H.	John Harrison Tenney.
I know whom I have believed	99 U.P.H.	Sir George Alexander Macfarren, Mus. Doc., 1813-1887.
I love them that love me	13 F.C.H.	Lowell Mason, Mus. Doc., 1792-1872.

D

Scripture Sentences.	Numbers.	Composers or Sources.
In all their affliction	19 F.C.H.	William Jonas Hutchins.
Incline Thine ear	37 U.P.H.	Friedrich Heinrich Himmel, 1765-1814.
*In that day shall this song	117 U.P.H.	Richard Woodward, Mus. Doc., ob. 1777.
I was glad when they said	67 U.P.H.	John Wall Callcott, Mus. Doc., 1766-1821.
I will arise	25 F.C.H., 16 U.P.H.	Rev. Richard Cecil, M.A., 1748-1810.
I will lift up mine eyes	66 U.P.H.	John Clarke-Whitfeld, Mus. Doc., 1770-1836.
Let the people praise Thee	52 U.P.H.	Thomas Hastings, Mus. Doc., 1784-1872.
Like as the hart	41 U.P.H.	Vincent Novello, 1781-1861.
Lord, for Thy tender mercies' sake	87 U.P.H.	Richard Farrant, ob. 1580, or John Hilton, Mus. Bac., ob. 1657.
Lord, now lettest Thou	94 U.P.H.	Samuel Sebastian Wesley, Mus. Doc., 1810-1876.
*Lord, now lettest Thou	128 U.P.H.	Thomas Tallis, ob. 1585.
Lord, we cry unto Thee	70 U.P.H.	Rev. William Henry Havergal, M.A., 1793-1870.
*Man that is born of a woman	110 U.P.H.	Gregorian.
My God, look upon me	32 U.P.H.	John Reynolds, ob. 1770 (?).
*My heart rejoiceth	108 U.P.H.	Samuel Wesley, 1766-1837.
My song shall be of mercy	57 U.P.H.	Jeremiah Clark, ob. 1707.
My soul doth magnify the Lord	91 U.P.H.	Sir John Stainer, Mus. Doc.
My soul doth magnify the Lord	92 U.P.H.	Samuel Sebastian Wesley, Mus. Doc., 1810-1876.
*My soul doth magnify the Lord	126 U.P.H.	Richard Woodward, Mus. Doc., ob. 1777.
My voice shalt Thou hear	30 U.P.H.	Sir John Goss, Mus. Doc., 1800-1880.
Not unto us, O Lord	9 U.P.H.	Dr Lowell Mason's Hallelujah, 1854.
Now unto Him that is able	20 U.P.H.	Dr Lowell Mason's Hallelujah, 1854.
Now unto Him that is able	28 F.C.H.	From Andreas Jacob Romberg, Mus. Doc., Ph. Doc., 1767-1821.
Now unto the King eternal	19 U.P.H.	Sir Herbert Stanley Oakeley, Mus. Doc.
O, be joyful in the Lord	56 U.P.H.	Sir John Goss, Mus. Doc., 1800-1880.

INDEX TO SCRIPTURE SENTENCES. 51

Scripture Sentences.	Numbers.	Composers or Sources.
O death, where is thy sting?	27 F.C.H.	Arthur Henry Brown.
O Lord, how manifold	59 U.P.H.	Joseph Barnby.
*O Lord, I will praise Thee	115 U.P.H.	Sir George Alexander Macfarren, Mus. Doc., 1813-1887.
O Lord, my God	26 U.P.H.	Rev. Henri Abraham Cæsar Malan, D.D., 1787-1864.
O Lord, my God	27 U.P.H.	Samuel Sebastian Wesley, Mus. Doc., 1810-1876.
*O Lord, Thou art my God	116 U.P.H.	Rev. William Henry Havergal, M.A., 1793-1870.
O love the Lord	38 U.P.H.	Sir Arthur Seymour Sullivan, Mus. Doc.
One thing have I desired	35 U.P.H.	Sir George Alexander Macfarren, Mus. Doc., 1813-1887.
O praise God in His holiness	75 U.P.H.	John Weldon, *ob.* 1736.
O praise the Lord	9 F.C.H.	Edward John Hopkins, Mus. Doc.
O praise the Lord, all ye heathen	62 U.P.H.	Earl of Wilton, 1799-1882.
O praise the Lord, for it is a good thing	74 U.P.H.	John Weldon, *ob.* 1736.
O taste and see	39 U.P.H.	Sir John Goss, Mus. Doc., 1800-1880.
O that thou hadst hearkened	31 U.P.H.	From Charles François Gounod.
O that Thou wouldst bless me indeed	2 F.C.H.	Allan Macbeth.
O the Hope of Israel	85 U.P.H.	Rev. Andrew Henderson, LL.D.
O Thou that hearest prayer	50 U.P.H.	Thomas Hastings, Mus. Doc., 1784-1872.
*Our Father which art in heaven	125 U.P.H.	Thomas Tallis, *ob.* 1585.
Our soul waiteth for the Lord	3 U.P.H.	Lowell Mason, Mus. Doc., 1792-1872.
O worship the Lord	55 U.P.H.	Thomas Smith.
Praise waiteth for Thee	49 U.P.H.	Sir John Goss, Mus. Doc., 1800-1880.
Praise ye the Lord	61 U.P.H.	Maximilian Stadler, 1748-1833.
Pray for the peace of Jerusalem	10 U.P.H., 10 F.C.H.	Lowell Mason, Mus. Doc., 1792-1872.
Remember me, O Lord	60 U.P.H.	Sir George Alexander Macfarren, Mus. Doc., 1813-1887.

Scripture Sentences.	Numbers.	Composers or Sources.
Remember now thy Creator	76 U.P.H.	Ebenezer Prout, B.A.
*Remember now thy Creator	114 U.P.H.	Thomas Tallis, ob. 1585.
*Salvation and glory	132 U.P.H.	Henry John Gauntlett, Mus. Doc., 1805-1876.
Salvation to our God	23 U.P.H.	Sir George Alexander Macfarren, Mus. Doc., 1813-1887.
Search me, O God	69 U.P.H., 11 F.C.H.	Lowell Mason, Mus. Doc., 1792-1872.
Shew me Thy ways	34 U.P.H.	Rev. James Lamb.
Sing, O heavens	82 U.P.H.	James Kent, 1700-1776.
Sing unto the Lord	36 U.P.H.	Ebenezer Prout, B.A.
Suffer the little children	89 U.P.H.	Ebenezer Prout, B.A.
Suffer the little children	24 F.C.H.	Henry Gadsby.
Teach me, O Lord, the way	65 U.P.H.	George William Martin, 1828-1881.
The grace of the Lord Jesus Christ	18 U.P.H.	Dr Lowell Mason's Hallelujah, 1854.
The Lord bless thee, and keep thee	1 U.P.H., 1 F.C.H.	Hebrew Melody (?).
The Lord is gracious	73 U.P.H.	August Edward Grell, 1800-1886.
The Lord is in His holy temple	13 U.P.H.	Adapted by Lowell Mason, Mus. Doc., 1792-1872.
The Lord is my shepherd	33 U.P.H.	Sir George Alexander Macfarren, Mus. Doc., 1813-1887.
The Lord is my portion	20 F.C.H.	Edward John Hopkins, Mus. Doc.
The Lord loveth the gates of Zion	54 U.P.H.	Vincent Novello, 1781-1861.
The Lord redeemeth	40 U.P.H.	Sir George Alexander Macfarren, Mus. Doc., 1813-1887.
The Lord will be a refuge	31 U.P.H.	George James Webb, 1803-1887.
The path of the just	12 F.C.H.	William Smallwood.
The righteous shall be glad	5 U.P.H.	From August Edward Grell, 1800-1886.
The sacrifices of God	46 U.P.H.	Anonymous.
The Spirit and the Bride	107 U.P.H.	Ebenezer Prout, B.A.
The sun shall be no more	18 F.C.H.	Walter Strang.
*The wilderness and the solitary place	118 U.P.H.	From Henry Lawes, ob. 1662.
They that be wise shall shine	21 F.C.H.	John Montgomerie Bell, W.S.
Thine, O Lord, is the greatness	2 U.P.H.	From James Kent, 1700-1776.
This is the day	63 U.P.H.	John Sewell.

Scripture Sentences.	Numbers.	Composers or Sources.
Thou crownest the year	51 U.P.H.	Thomas Smith.
Thou wilt keep him in perfect peace	80 U.P.H.	Henry John Gauntlett, Mus. Doc., 1805-1876.
Thou wilt keep him in perfect peace	15 F.C.H.	Walter Hately.
*Trust in the Lord	112 U.P.H.	William Crotch, Mus. Doc., 1775-1847.
Turn Thy face from my sins	43 U.P.H.	From Thomas Attwood, 1765-1838.
Unto Him that loved us	21 U.P.H., 29 F.C.H.	Congregational Church Music.
Wait on the Lord	5 F.C.H.	Johann Christian Heinrich Rinck, Ph. Doc., 1770-1840.
*We give Thee thanks, O Lord	131 U.P.H.	Henry John Gauntlett, Mus. Doc., 1805-1876.
We praise Thee, O God	133 U.P.H.	Samuel Sebastian Wesley, Mus. Doc., 1810-1876.
We praise Thee, O God	333 F.C.H., Anthem Music.	Edward John Hopkins, Mus. Doc.
What shall I render	8 F.C.H.	Arthur Henry Brown.
*Where shall wisdom be found	111 U.P.H.	Richard Woodward, Mus. Doc., *ob.* 1777.
Wherewithal shall a young man	64 U.P.H.	Sir John Goss, Mus. Doc., 1800-1880.
*Who hath believed our report	121 U.P.H.	William Croft, Mus. Doc., 1678-1727.
Who is a God like unto Thee	22 F.C.H.	Walter Hately.
Will God in very deed	25 U.P.H.	Sir John Goss, Mus. Doc., 1800-1880.
Worthy is the Lamb	22 U.P.H.	Henry Smart, 1813-1879.

BIOGRAPHICAL SKETCHES
OF COMPOSERS.

WITH NOTES AND ILLUSTRATIVE EXAMPLES.

BIOGRAPHICAL SKETCHES.

A. T. A. are the initials of a student who attended Dr Root's Normal Musical Institute, at New York, in 1855, and who composed

KEDRON, No. 86 S.P. It was published the following year in Dr Root's 'Sabbath Bell' under the name of "Carolina." It is wrongly assigned to Dr Root in the S.P. As the great fire at Chicago in 1871 destroyed the Doctor's record-book of dates and memoranda, the full name of this composer cannot now be ascertained. From the name he gave to his tune Dr Root thinks he was probably a Southerner.

Ahle, Johann Rudolph, born at Mühlhausen in Thuringia, December 24, 1625; educated at the Universities of Göttingen and Erfurt; appointed organist and burgomaster at Mühlhausen, where he died in 1673.

DESSAU, No. 313 S.H., was composed in 1664 to Burmeister's hymn "Ja, er ist's das Heil der Welt," and was transferred in the 'Altdorfer Gesangbuch' of 1671 to Clausnitzer's hymn "Liebster Jesu, wir sind hier."

Albert (or Alberti) Heinrich, born at Lobenstein, Voigtland, June 28, 1604. He intended to study law at Leipzig, but devoted himself entirely to music, and in 1631 was appointed organist of the Cathedral at Königsberg in Prussia, where he died, October 6, 1651. He composed many sacred songs.

GODESBERG, No. 187 S.H. and 117 U.P.H., "Gott des Himmels und der Erden," was published in the fifth part of Albert's 'Arien,' 1643.

Albert (Prince) Francis Charles Augustus Albert Emmanuel, Prince Consort of Queen Victoria; born at the Rosenau, near Coburg, August 26, 1819; a skilful and enthusiastic musician; died at Windsor Castle, December 14, 1861. His compositions include a Choral Service and an Anthem for the Church, many German songs, and a piece entitled "L' Invocazione all' Armonia," which was performed with success at the Birmingham Musical Festivals of 1849 and 1855.

GOTHA, No. 144 (Second Tune) S.H., 233 F.C.H., and 7 U.P.H., appears in 'Songs and Ballads written and set to Music by their Royal Highnesses Albert and Ernest, Princes of Saxe-Coburg Gotha, . . . London, 1840,' and is there set to a poem by Eichendorff, beginning—

"O wunderbares tiefes Schwingen!
Wie einsam ist's noch auf der Welt!"

It is found as a long-metre tune, under the name of "Greatness," in E. J. Westrop's 'Universal Psalmodist,' which was not published before 1840, although dated 1837 in Major's 'Tunes for the Family and Congregation.' It is named "Albert's" in 'The Sacred Choir,' edited by the Rev. Wm. Anderson, D.D., Glasgow (1841), that being perhaps its first appearance in a Scotch Collection. It is first found as an 8787 tune in Dr Lowell Mason's Psaltery, 1847. In the autumn of 1852 it was submitted to the Royal composer, who approved it by giving his permission for its publication in 'Congregational Church Music,' London, 1853. The tune is introduced by Sir John Goss in his anthem "The Lord is my strength," composed for her Majesty's Thanksgiving at St Paul's Cathedral, for the recovery of the Prince of Wales, 1872; also in an anthem composed by Dr Bridge for the Queen's Jubilee. "A Song of Praise," composed by Joseph Bradley, Mus. Bac., for performance by the Glasgow Choral Union on the visit of her Majesty the Queen to the Glasgow International Exhibition, 22d August 1888, is founded on "Gotha." During one of the early visits of her Majesty the Queen and Prince Albert to Balmoral, the late Mr Peacock, music-master at Perth, was commanded to form a small choir to assist in leading the praise at Crathie Church. "Gotha" was one of the tunes then sung. (See Boyack, George, in Appendix.)

COBURG, No. 63 S.H., was composed for the words to which it is set, and seems to have been first printed in 'Congregational Church Music,' London, 1853. A copy of the tune was "forwarded by command from Buckingham Palace, March 1853, to the Rev. Dr Maurice," and published by him in his 'Choral Harmony,' 1854.

Alcock, John, Mus. Doc., was born in London, April 11, 1715; chorister in St Paul's Cathedral under Charles King, Mus. Bac.; afterwards a pupil of John Stanley, the blind organist; graduated Mus. Bac. Oxford 1755, Mus. Doc. 1761; organist of St Andrew's, Plymouth, in 1737; of St Lawrence's, Reading, 1741; organist, master of the choristers, and lay vicar of Lichfield Cathedral, 1749 to 1760; organist of Sutton Coldfield, 1761 to 1786; and of Tamworth, 1766 to 1790; retaining the place of vicar at Lichfield until his decease; died at Lichfield, February 1806.

CHANT, No. 1, set to Hymn No. 334 in F.C.H., is from his 'Divine Harmony; or, a Collection of Fifty-five Double and Single Chants, for Four Voices, as they are sung at the Cathedral of Lichfield.' Printed for the Author, and in Birmingham: 1752. It is wrongly assigned to Dr Aldrich.

Allan, James, son of Richard Allan; born in the parish of Polmont, Stirlingshire, July 27, 1842; in 1850 removed to Glasgow, where he served his apprenticeship as a lithographic printer; appointed Conductor of Psalmody in Sydney Place U.P. Church 1870; in 1872 conductor in Kelvinside Free Church, Glasgow; Conductor of the Glasgow Select Choir (of which he was a prominent member) in succession to Mr Frederick Archer in 1880; died at Glasgow, August 10, 1885. A conductor of much ability, and an excellent baritone vocalist.

His tune VEVAY, No. 278 (Third Tune) F.C.H., was first published in that work.

American.

HAGAR, No. 194 S.P., appears in Mason & Webb's 'National Psalmist,' Boston, 1849, and is there anonymous.

MILTON, No. 102 S.P., appears in Dr Mason's 'Hallelujah,' 1854, under the name of "Kinlock," and is there anonymous.

NEWCASTLE, No. 108 S.P., appears in Dr Mason's 'Sabbath Hymn and Tune Book,' 1859, and is there named "Otto."

REST, No. 124 S.P., 96 (Second Tune) F.C.H., 91 U.P.P., there named "Ruth," is wrongly referred in these works to the 'Carmina Sacra.' It was adapted by Mr Carnie of Aberdeen from an anonymous tune named "Millbury" in Dr Mason's 'Hallelujah,' 1854, where it was published for the first time. To Mr Carnie belongs the credit of introducing the above tunes, and many others, into Scotland. In the Free Church collections about thirty of these tunes have been published, but, strange to say, Mr Carnie has never received a word of acknowledgment.

Ancient.

CHANT, No. 270 S.P., from a melody of the seventh century.

BETHANY, No. 61 F.C.H. In the 'Psalmist,' edited by Vincent Novello, this tune is marked "Gregorian Melody, adapted for this work by S. Wesley, 1836."

IONA, No. 39 U.P.P. One of the tunes collected by the late Dr George Petrie in the remote parts of Ireland; believed by him to be a hymn of the ancient Irish Church. The form of melody in the above collection and S.H. differs in the first two strains from the reading published by Dr Petrie.

Laud, No. 21 F.C.H.

Liguria, No. 181 and 194 U.P.H.

Milan, No. 165 F.C.H.

St Ambrose or Treves, No. 76 S.H.

St Anselm, No. 31 P. and P., 18 F.C.H. Wrongly assigned in F.C.H. to Dr Hayne, who only arranged the melody for his 'Merton Tune Book.'

St Benet, No. 118, 140, and 172 S.H. Arranged by Henry John Gauntlett, Mus. Doc.

St Columba or Erin, No. 351 S.H. See "Iona," which is the same tune.

Sarum, No. 5 U.P.H., same as—

Shalem, No. 19 F.C.H., is said to be a melody of the fourth century.

Treves, No. 263 F.C.H., is the same as St Ambrose.

Anderson, James Smith, son of Mr William Anderson, Town Treasurer of the Royal Burgh of Crail, Fifeshire; born at Crail, June 30, 1853; received his musical education at Edinburgh under Mr (now Dr) G. C. Martin, then organist to the Duke of Buccleuch at Dalkeith, from his successor, Mr G. F. Tendall, Mus. Bac., and afterwards at Glasgow under Dr A. L. Peace; graduated Mus. Bac., Oxford, 1878; Fellow of the College of Organists, London, 1878; organist and choirmaster of Nicolson Square Chapel, Edinburgh, 1872 to 1877; Abbey Parish Church, 1877 to 1879; St Thomas's Episcopal Chapel, 1879; since 1881 has held the important position of organist and choirmaster at St Andrew's Parish Church, George Street, where he frequently gives recitals on an organ built by Messrs Peter Conacher & Co. of Huddersfield, and placed in the church in 1880 at a cost of about £1000.

Mr Anderson has contributed to many Hymnals, amongst which may be mentioned 'Songs of Zion,' Chant portion of 'Hymnal Companion,' Sunday-school Supplement to 'Blackburn Tune Book,' and 'National Tune Book.' He revised the harmonies of the 'Blackburn Tune Book' already mentioned, and the present 'U.P. Children's Hymnal.' He has published some pianoforte music, but the bulk of his compositions for the voice, organ, and pianoforte remain in MS.

Fingal, No. 317 (Second Tune) S.H., was composed for that work.

Anonymous.

Belmont, No. 38 S.P., 83 F.C.H., 126 S.H., 106 U.P.P., 275, 328 U.P.H. This tune has been assigned to Samuel Webbe, sen., and Samuel Webbe, jun., but it is not found in the collections of psalmody they issued, nor is it at all in the style of Webbe the elder. It has also been assigned to Mozart, without, it is feared, good grounds. The statement that it is adapted from his opera of the "Seraglio" is unfounded, for although there is a character in that work named "Belmonte," there is nothing in the music resembling the hymn tune. A writer in 'Notes and Queries' (August 1876) says: "It has been stated that this tune (Belmont) is by Samuel Webbe, jun., and was adapted from, or rather suggested by, Haydn's canzonet 'My mother bids me bind my hair.'" This would be adapting with a vengeance. The facts regarding this tune are as follows: It is found in Purday's 'Psalm and Hymn Tunes,' 1860; in Routledge's 'Church and Home Metrical Psalter and Hymnal,' 1860; in Aviolet's 'Tunes and Chants,' 1862. In all these works "Belmont" is anonymous. In 1862 the Rev. W. Windle rearranged Routledge's work mentioned above, and there "Belmont" is assigned to "S. Webbe." In 1863 the 'Bristol Tune Book' was issued, and the tune ascribed to the same composer. Doubtless the editor of the "Bristol" book followed Routledge, and since that time we invariably find Webbe's name attached to "Belmont." The late Mr John Dobson, the well-known psalmody collector, knew of no earlier copy than that given in the 'Bristol Tune Book.' Below will be found a double form of the tune, which appears in a small collection published for use at Tonbridge School Chapel about 1861:—

BIOGRAPHICAL SKETCHES.

Key G.

```
{ :s₁  | m  :—  :r   | d  :—  :t₁  | t₁  :l₁  :d   | s₁  :—  }
{ :m₁  | d  :—  :t₁  | s₁ :—  :s₁  | f₁  :—   :l₁  | s₁  :—  }
{ :d   | s  :—  :f   | m  :—  :m   | f   :—   :f   | m   :—  }
{ :d   | d  :—  :d   | d  :—  :d   | d   :—   :d   | d   :—  }

{ :s   | s  :f   :m  | m  :r   :d  | d  :—  :—  | t₁  :—  }
{ :m   | m  :r   :d  | d  :—  :l₁  | s₁ :—  :—  | —   :—  }
{ :s   | s  :—  :s   | l  :—  :r   | m  :—  :—  | r   :—  }
{ :d   | d₁ :r₁  :m  | f₁ :—  :fe₁ | s₁ :—  :—  | —   :—  }
```

:S:

```
{ :s₁  | m  :—  :r   | d  :—  :t₁  | t₁  :l₁  :d   | s₁  :—  }
{ :m₁  | d  :—  :t₁  | s₁ :—  :s₁  | f₁  :—   :l₁  | s₁  :—  }
{ :d   | s  :—  :f   | m  :—  :m   | f   :—   :f   | m   :—  }
{ :d   | d  :—  :d   | d  :—  :d   | d   :—   :d   | d   :—  }
```

Fine.

```
{ :s   | s  :f   :r  | d  :m   :r  | d  :—  :—  | —  :—  }
{ :s₁  | r  :—  :l₁  | d  :—  :t₁  | s₁ :—  :—  | —  :—  }
{ :s   | l  :—  :l   | s  :—  :f   | m  :—  :—  | —  :—  }
{ :m   | r  :—  :f   | s₁ :—  :s₁  | d  :—  :—  | —  :—  }
```

Key D t.

```
{ :ᵗm.f | s   :—  :d¹  | m¹ :—  :d¹  | m¹ :r¹  :d¹  | d¹  :t   }
{ :ˢd.r | m   :—  :m   | s  :—  :m   | s  :f   :m   | m   :r   }
{ :ʳs   | s   :—  :s   | s  :—  :s   | s  :—   :s   | s   :—   }
{ :ˢd   | d   :—  :d   | d  :—  :d   | d  :t₁  :d   | s₁  :—   }
```

f. Key G.   D.S.

```
{ :l   | s   :d   :f   | m  :—  :r   | ᵈs₁ :—  :—  | —  :—  }
{ :r   | s   :—  :d    | d  :—  :t₁  | ᵈs₁ :—  :—  | —  :—  }
{ :t   | d¹  :—  :l    | s  :—  :f   | ᵐt₁ :—  :—  | —  :—  }
{ :f   | m   :—  :f    | s  :—  :s₁  | ᵈs₁ :—  :—  | —  :—  }
```

If "Belmont" be an adaptation, it seems to the writer that it is from the melody given below. This is found in William Gardiner's 'Sacred Melodies from Haydn, Mozart, and Beethoven, adapted to the best English Poets,' vol. i., 1812, and although anonymous there, it is understood to be Gardiner's composition :—

CALM, No. 272 F.C.H. Seems to have been first published in the 'Leeds Tune Book,' 1868, where it is anonymous.

CHILDREN OF JERUSALEM, No. 371 S.H. Appears in the 'Wesleyan Sunday-school Tune Book,' 1858, set to the hymn with which it is now associated. The harmony in S.H. is by Dr W. H. Monk.

COTFIELD, No. 64 P. and P.

DIES IRÆ, No. 356 U.P.H. From a Roman Gradual of 1599.

EBFORD, No. 187 P. and P., appears in 'The Psalmist,' by Vincent Novello, Part IV., 1842; is there named "Saltsburgh," and arranged by Dr Gauntlett.

GLORY, No. 343 F.C.H., 331 U.P.H., and 436 S.H. Appears in the 'Wesleyan Sunday-school Tune Book,' 1858. Associated with the hymn "Around the Throne of God in Heaven," written by Anne Shepherd (Houlditch) in 1847.

GOSHEN, No. 376 F.C.H., assigned by some to one Yardley, and by others to a Mrs Davis, is said to be adapted from an old ballad, "Hours of Happy Childhood."

INNOCENTS, No. 162 F.C.H., 84 U.P.H., 25 and 232 S.H. A tune much used during the last forty years. Nothing definite seems to be known of its origin. The earliest copy the writer has seen is in 'The Parish Choir,' vol. iii., 1851. It is there set to the hymn beginning "Little flowers of martyrdom," named "Innocents," and described as an "Ancient Litany." It seems to be an altered copy of Thomas Walker's tune "Stoel," which is found in the Rev. John Rippon's collection, 1806, in the preparation of which Walker assisted.

ITALIAN CHORALE, No. 227 F.C.H., or

LUGANO, No. 295 S.H., 305 U.P.H. This tune is now associated with James Edmeston's hymn, "Saviour, breathe an evening blessing." It is of Italian origin, but this seems to be all that is known regarding it.

NORWOOD, No. 117 P. and P. Probably a tune of last century.

OLD 143D, No. 44 U.P.P. An English melody.

RESIGNATION, No. 221 (Second Tune) S.H. This tune is assigned by some to Lady E. Osborne, but the writer is unable to corroborate this. It is associated with the hymn "My God and Father, while I stray," written by Miss Elliott in 1834, to whom also the tune has been assigned.

ST AUSTIN, No. 307 S.H. Appears in the 2d edition of 'The Temple Tune Book,' edited by E. J. Hopkins, Mus. Doc., 1869.

ST HELENA, No. 263 S.H., 128 F.C.H.

SUBMISSION, No. 276 F.C.H. See "Resignation," which is the same tune.

S.S., No. 46 U.P.H., "The sacrifices of God."

Arcadelt, Jacques, a native of Brabant, in the Netherlands; born about the end of the fifteenth century; master of the children of the choir in St Peter's, Rome, in 1539; about 1555 became chapelmaster to the Cardinal of Lorraine, and accompanied him to Paris; died in Paris. He is known as the composer of many madrigals.

S.S., No. 47 U.P.H., "Give ear to my prayer," is an adaptation from an "Ave Maria" said to have been composed by Arcadelt.

JERUSALEM, No. 352 F.C.H., is also from the same work.

Arne, Thomas Augustine, son of Mr Thomas Arne, an upholsterer; born in London, 1710; studied the violin under Festing; created Mus. Doc. of Oxford University, July 6, 1759. He composed the oratorios "Abel" and "Judith," and many operas; his songs "Where the bee sucks" and "Rule Britannia" are universally known; died March 5, 1778, and was buried in St Paul's, Covent Garden.

ARTAXERXES, No. 31 S.P., is an adaptation from a minuet at the close of the overture to the opera of "Artaxerxes," composed by Arne in 1762. The Rev. R. Harrison, who adapted it, published it in vol. i. of his 'Sacred Harmony' (1784). It is in Henry Boyd's collection, Glasgow, 1793, which is the first time the writer finds it in a Scotch Psalmody. In the first part of 'The Sacred Harmony, for the use of St George's Church, Edinburgh,' dated 1820, edited by Dr Andrew Thomson, the minuet, in nearly its original form, appears as a L.M. tune, with a repeat of the last two lines, under the name of "Princes Street."

Arnold, John, "Philo Musicæ," of Great Warley, Essex; author of several collections of vocal music; died 1792, buried February 14. Edited 'The Compleat Psalmodist,' in Four Books, 1741. Preface dated Great Warley, October 29, 1739. It went through many editions, the contents of which vary considerably. One issued in 1749 contains

BLENHEIM, No. 52 P. and P.

Arnold, Samuel, Mus. Doc., son of Mr Thomas Arnold, was born in London, August 10, 1740. He studied in the Chapel Royal under Bernard Gates and Dr Nares, and obtained the degree of Doctor of Music at Oxford in 1773. In 1783 he was appointed organist and composer to the Chapel Royal, and in 1793 organist of Westminster Abbey. He died October 22, 1802, and was buried in Westminster Abbey. Arnold composed upwards of forty operas, and a number of oratorios, besides many pieces for the Church. In 1791 he edited, in conjunction with Dr Callcott, 'The Psalms of David, for the Use of Parish Churches.' In that collection his tune

ARNOLD, No. 46 P. and P., 30 S.P., and 63 in U.P.P., appears on page 18 set to Psalm xv., and so arranged that the first two lines are sung as a duet by first and second trebles, the same lines are then taken up by bass and tenor (also as a duet), the whole parts joining in chorus to sing the last two lines. It was early introduced into Scotland, and is found in the form we now use in Robert Gilmour's 'Psalm Singer's Assistant,' Glasgow. No date; but issued before 1793.

LANGHOLM, No. 104 P. and P., is on page 97 of the above work, and is there set to Psalm 90, and named "Lancaster."

DUNBLANE, No. 18 U.P.P., on page 45 set to Psalm 39, and named "Funeral."

DOXOLOGY, No. 17 U.P.H. (Sanctus III.), is assigned to Arnold, but where it was first published the writer is unable to state.

Ashworth, Charles, edited 'A Collection of Tunes suited to the several Metres commonly used in Public Worship, set in Four Parts.'

ST THOMAS, No. 222 U.P.H., 62 U.P.P., 154 S.P., and 145 P. and P., is in the 3d edition of the above Collection, 1766, also in another without date printed from the same plates, and probably the first (about 1760), and is in them named "Walney Tune." It appears under its present name in Thomas Moore's 'The Psalm Singer's Delightful Pocket Companion,' Glasgow (1762). This seems to be its first appearance in a Scottish Psalmody. To assign it to Henry Purcell is erroneous.

Atkinson, Frederick Cook, born at Norwich, August 21, 1841; between the years 1849 and 1860 chorister and assistant-organist in the Cathedral of Norwich; graduated Mus. Bac. at Cambridge, 1867; organist and choirmaster of St Paul's and St John's Churches, Bradford, for a number of years; organist of Norwich Cathedral from 1881 to 1885.

THETFORD, No. 205 in P and P., is a prize tune, and first appeared in the 'Bristol Tune Book,' 1863.

Attwood, Thomas, was born in London in 1765, not 1767 as sometimes stated. When nine years of age he became a chorister in the Chapel Royal, studying successively under Dr Nares and Dr Ayrton. In 1783 he was sent by the Prince of Wales, afterwards George IV., to study under the celebrated masters of Italy. He afterwards removed to Vienna, where he studied under Mozart, who said that he had the sincerest affection for him, and that he considered him to have imbibed more of his style than any scholar he ever had. In 1796 he was appointed organist of St Paul's Cathedral and composer to the Chapel Royal, and in 1821 organist of King George IV.'s private chapel at Brighton, and organist of the Chapel Royal in 1836. Attwood died at Chelsea, March 24, 1838, and was buried in St Paul's Cathedral under the organ.

S. S., No. 43 U.P.H., "Turn Thy face from my sins," was composed for and first published in a work entitled 'Sacred Minstrelsy; a Collection of Sacred Music by the Great Masters of all ages and nations, consisting of

Anthems, Solos, Duets, Trios, &c., with Accompaniment for Piano or Organ,' vol. i., 1834. Vol. ii. of the above work, published in 1835, contains his anthem, "Enter not into judgment."

Austen, Augusta Amherst, was born in London, August 2, 1827. She received her musical education at the Royal Academy of Music, and studied the pianoforte under Mrs G. F. Anderson (*née* Lucy Phillpot), teacher to her Majesty Queen Victoria. She was organist at Ealing Church from 1844 till 1848, when she became organist at Paddington Chapel. This post she resigned in 1857. She afterwards married Mr Thomas Anstey Guthrie. One of her sons is well known as the author of 'Vice Versâ,' &c. She died at Glasgow, August 5, 1877.

St Agnes, No. 48 S.H. and 30 in P. and P., was composed in 1848, and published in Dr Steggall's 'Church Psalmody,' 1849.

Aylward, Theodore Edward, son of Mr W. P. Aylward, and great-great-nephew of Theodore Aylward, Mus. Doc.; born at Salisbury, February 28, 1844; pupil of C. J. Read of Salisbury, Dr S. S. Wesley, and Sir G. A. Macfarren; successively organist of the Temporary Parish Church, Cheltenham — St Columba College, Ireland — St Mary's, Spring Grove — Llandaff Cathedral (in 1870), and (in 1876) Chichester Cathedral; since 1886 organist of St Andrew's Church, Cardiff, and of the Park Hall. His tune

Sarum Hymnal, No. 36 P. and P., was composed in 1868, and published the following year in the 'Sarum[1] Hymnal,' of which he was musical editor.

B. T.

Freshwater, No. 362 (First Tune) in S.H., was written for the 'Children's Hymn Book' (1881) by a composer bearing the above initials who courts anonymity.

Bach, Johann Christoph, one of the most distinguished organists of his time; a first cousin of the father of Johann Sebastian Bach; born at Arnstadt in 1643; Court organist at Eisenach in 1665; died March 31, 1703.

Holstein, No. 226 U.P.H. and 373 in S.H. (there named "Frankfort"), is an old melody which he harmonised in 1680. It is wrongly assigned in the S.H. Joseph's name may have become associated with the tune from the fact that in North Germany it is mostly set to a pastoral by Scheffler, "Liebe die du mich zum Bilde." It seems to have been introduced into England by the Rev. John Wesley, who published it in 'A Collection of

---

[1] Ecclesiastical name for Salisbury.

Tunes, set to Music, as they are commonly sung at the Foundery,' 1742. It is there named Frankfort Tune.

Bach, Johann Sebastian, son of Johann Ambrosius Bach; born at Eisenach, March 21, 1685; one of the greatest composers and organists the world has ever seen; devoted the major part of his life to perfecting the music of the Church; died at Leipzig, July 28, 1750.

POTSDAM, No. 152 S.H., 196 P. and P., 198 S.P., 147 U.P.H., and 73 U.P.P., is from the subject of a fugue in E in his "Wohltemperirte Klavier."

AUGUSTINE, No. 133 F.C.H., and 179 in P. and P., is adapted from the following tune, which appears in vol. ii. of his 'Vierstimmige Choralgesänge,' edited by P. E. Bach, 1769, where it stands No. 163, and is set to the words "Als der gütige Gott":—

MEINHOLD, No. 260 in S.H., is No. 155 in the same vol., and is the chorale "Meinen Jesum lass ich nicht."

The harmony of BACH, No. 138 F.C.H., is his.

S. S., No. 102 U.P.H., "Blessing and Glory," is from a motett, "Lob und Ehre und Weisheit," originally written for two choirs of eight voices. Spitta, in his 'Life of Bach,' throws doubt on Bach's authorship. He says: "Some of these motetts for two choirs are certainly spurious, or at least doubtful. At any rate, the score published in 1819, by Breitkopf and Härtel, of the motett 'Lob und Ehre,' is not genuine, though it afterwards was republished as No. 3 in the new edition of 'Schicht's Collection,' after the motett 'Ich lasse dicht Nicht' had been rejected as being by Johann Christoph Bach. The fact that it bears Bach's name in a MS. copy in Gotthold Library at Königsberg (No. 13569.2) proves little, since the copies of Bach's motetts in this collection appear to have been made by Schicht. The motett 'Lob und Ehre' is full of the grossest musical blunders, and it is difficult to imagine how it can so long have passed for Bach's work. In the collection of Herr Hauser (Kammersänger), of Carlsruhe, the same motett is to be found in score and two parts, as a composition by Georg Gottfried Wagner, whom we may more readily suppose to be the author. Wagner, born in 1698, was a St Thomas Scholar from 1712 to 1719, studied theology till 1726, and was still a performer in Bach's Choir from 1723 to 1726; he then became Cantor at Plauen. It is easy to understand from this that the work should frequently remind us of Bach, whom Wagner evidently took as his model."

Bach, Carl Philipp Emanuel, third son of the above; born at Weimar, March 14, 1714; studied at the Thomas School, Leipzig, and at Leipzig University and Frankfort-on-the-Oder, for the Law; chamber musician and accompanist to the Court at Berlin, 1746; went to Hamburg as choirmaster, 1751; director of music in succession to Telemann at the Court, Hamburg, 1767; died at Hamburg, December 14, 1788. Composer of vocal and instrumental music.

WEIMAR, No. 262 U.P.H., is assigned to him by Dr Layriz, but it seems doubtful if he composed it.

Bacon, (Rev.) Robert; B.A. Oxford, 1738; there is no record of his proceeding M.A. as generally stated; Priest Vicar of Salisbury Cathedral in 1753; died 1759.

His CHANT, No. 231 in S.P., was published by John Marsh in one of his excellent collections.

Baker, Frederick George, born in the Isle of Wight, May 19, 1840; chorister in Winchester Cathedral for seven years, part of which time Dr S. S. Wesley was organist; studied harmony under Dr Iliffe—otherwise self-taught; organist of Christ Church, Sandown, Isle of Wight, from 1864 to 1872; since then organist of St Saviour's, Shanklin, Isle of Wight; a watchmaker and jeweller by trade. His tune

ST SAVIOUR, No. 152 S.P., was composed in 1872, and was first published in the 'Bristol Tune Book.'

Baker, Henry, Mus. Bac., son of the Rev. James Baker, Chancellor of the diocese of Durham; born at Nuneham, Oxfordshire; educated at Winchester School; graduated Bachelor in Music at the University of Oxford in 1867; is a civil engineer. His tune

HESPERUS, No. 34 F.C.H., was composed in 1854, and appeared in 'A Hymnal for Use in the English Church,' with accompanying Tunes by the Hon. and Rev. John Grey, 1866. It is there named "Whitburn."

Baker, Rev. Sir Henry Williams, son of Vice-Admiral Sir Henry Loraine Baker, C.B.; born in London, May 27, 1821; after completing his university education at Trinity College, Cambridge, took his B.A. degree in 1844, and proceeded to the degree of M.A. in 1847; in 1851 presented to the vicarage of Monkland, near Leominster; on the death of his father, November 2, 1859, succeeded him as third baronet; died at the vicarage of Monkland, February 12, 1877, and was buried in the churchyard of the parish. Author of 'Daily Prayers for the Use of those who have to Work Hard,' as well as of a 'Daily Text-book,' for the same class, and other works. He was the originator in 1858 of 'Hymns Ancient and Modern,' as well as one of the principal compilers.

STEPHANOS, No. 163 S.H., 267 F.C.H., and 120 U.P.H., was first published in the Appendix to 'Hymns Ancient and Modern,' 1868. ST TIMOTHY, No. 109 F.C.H. in the Revised and Enlarged Edition of the same work, 1875. The harmonies of both tunes are by Dr W. H. Monk.

Bamberg Gesangbuch. A Catholic book for the Bishopric of Bamberg in Bavaria. It contains songs for Sundays, Feast Days, and Holidays, by the Rev. Johann Leisentritt, and was published at Dilingen in 1575. According to Kocher's 'Zionsharfe,'

BENISON, No. 300 U.P.H., 29 F.C.H., there named "Havergal," is from an edition issued in 1707.

Baring-Gould, Rev. Sabine, M.A., eldest son of Mr Edward Baring-Gould of Lew-Trenchard, Devon; born at Exeter, January 28, 1834; educated at Clare College, Cambridge, where he graduated in 1854; took holy orders in 1864; Rector of East Mersea, Essex, 1871 to 1881; now of Lew-Trenchard, Lew Down, North Devon.

EUDOXIA, No. 361 in S.H. and 371 in F.C.H., was first published in the Appendix to 'Hymns Ancient and Modern,' 1868. The hymn to which it is set is also his, and was written in 1865.

Barker, Elizabeth (not Baker, as in the U.P. Hymnal), daughter of Mr William Hacket of Aylestone Hall, Leicestershire; born at Leicester, 1829; pupil of G. A. Löhr; married in 1853 to the Rev. Frederic Mills Raymond Barker, M.A., of Oriel College, Oxford; joined the Catholic Church in 1867, when she took the additional names of Mary Agnes; composer of much beautiful music. Mrs Barker composed, at the request of Dr Neale, tunes to his 'Hymns of the Eastern Church.' The first series, published in 1864, contains six hymns which were set to music at Bisley, Gloucestershire, in 1863. One of these is the tune

ST JOHN DAMASCENE. This occurs as No. 271 in S.H., No. 184 in U.P.H. (where it is named "Damascus"), but the form of the melody in both of these Hymnals is a corrupt one. The tune was a favourite with Dr Neale, who had it sung to him while on his death-bed.

CORONA, No. 96 F.C.H. and 55 (Second Tune) U.P.H., 192 U.P.P., was also composed by Mrs Barker, and was published in the fourth series, which bears the title of 'Catholic Hymns,' 1868.

Barnby, Joseph, born at York, August 12, 1838; in 1846 became a chorister in York Minster, where he remained till 1852; studied at the Royal Academy of Music, London; organist of St Andrew's Church, Wells Street, London, from 1863 till 1871; of St Anne's, Soho, from 1871 to 1886; since 1875 organist and precentor of Eton College; appointed conductor at the Royal Academy of Music 1886; resigned 1888; conductor of the Royal Choral Society, &c. Of his larger compositions, the best known are the cantata "Rebekah"; a psalm, "The Lord is King," which was performed with success at the Leeds Festival of 1883, and other works. The following tunes were composed by him, the first five being taken from 'The Hymnary,' which he edited in 1872:—

MAGDALA, No. 57 S.H.
BARNBY, No. 360 U.P.H.
HOLY TRINITY, No. 80 S.P.
ST IGNATIUS, No. 368 S.H., 265 in F.C.H. (there named "St Fillan").
REQUIEM, No. 259 in S.H.
ST PHILIP, No. 262 S.H. (First Tune), 284 (Second Tune) F.C.H.—first appeared in 'The Sarum Hymnal,' 1869.
ST SILVESTER, No. 145 in S.H.—first in 'Christmas Carols,' edited by Dr Stainer, 1867.
LAUDES DOMINI, No. 261 F.C.H.—first published in the Appendix to 'Hymns Ancient and Modern,' 1868.
S. S., No. 59 U.P.H., "O Lord, how manifold," was published for the first time in 'The Musical Times,' July 1866.

Barrow, Thomas, chorister, and afterwards gentleman and copyist of the Chapel Royal; had a high counter-tenor voice, and led that part in Händel's oratorios on account of his power and steadiness; composer of sacred music; died August 13, 1789.

CHANT, No. 168 U.P.P. and Chant I. to Hymn 353 U.P.H., is his composition, and not J. Stafford Smith's. It appears in Bennett and Marshall's collection, 1829.

Barthélémon, François Hippolite, one of the most distinguished violinists of his time, was born at Bordeaux, July 27, 1741. His father, Emanuel Barthélémon, held during many years a respectable situation under the French Government in one of their colonial departments; and his mother, an Irish lady, was of a wealthy family in Queen's County. Young Barthélémon was for some time an officer in Berwick's Regiment in the Irish Brigade. "His gentlemanly manners and polite accomplishments, especially those of music and fencing, together with a knowledge of most of the modern languages, and no mean proficiency in the ancient Hebrew, Greek, and Celtic, acquired for him the admiration and esteem of all who knew him." He became the friend of the Earl of Kellie, who being himself passionately fond of music, soon became attached to him, and succeeded in inducing him to change his profession for that of music. He settled in England in 1765 under the protection and patronage of the Earl of Kellie, and his success as a violinist was pronounced; indeed, wherever he performed, he was greeted with the greatest enthusiasm. In the same year he became leader of the Opera band, and in 1770 leader at Marylebone Gardens. In 1766 he married Miss Mary Young (died 1799), niece of Mrs Arne and Mrs Lampe, and in 1776 began a professional tour through Germany, Italy, and France. While at Florence he composed, at the request of the Grand Duke of Tuscany, an oratorio, "Jefte in Masfa." He also visited Dublin in 1784. Barthélémon died in London, July 20, 1808. "As a player he was distinguished by the firmness of his hand, the purity of his tone, and his admirable manner of executing an adagio." His compositions include operas, string quartets, concertos, songs, organ preludes, &c.

MORNING HYMN, No. 278 S.H. (Second Tune), 297 U.P.H., 20 F.C.H., was composed by Barthélémon about 1780 for the hymn "Awake, my soul," at the request of the Rev. Jacob Duché, Chaplain to the Female Orphan Asylum, London. He also composed many hymn tunes and anthems for the same charity, and was awarded with a Governorship for life. Benjamin Jacob's 'National Psalmody' (1819) contains the earliest copy the writer has seen. It is there described as "Morning Hymn as usually sung."

Barton, William, "hymnologist," supposed to have been born about 1598; probably the same William Barton who was vicar of Mayfield, Staffordshire, at the opening of the civil wars, afterwards vicar of St Martin's in Leicester, where he died May 1678, aged eighty. His verse-translation of the Psalms was first published in 1644. It was reprinted and altered in 1645, 1646, 1651, 1654, and later. The text was revised by Barton for "the last time," and was posthumously republished in 1682.

COLESHILL, No. 324 U.P.H., 51 S.P., 63 P. and P., 20 and 195 U.P.P. This tune was at one time much used in Scotland, and especially on Communion Sundays, when it was sung to Psalm 103; but it is now rarely heard. Of late, however, interest in it has been reviving, from the fact that it is introduced by Mr Hamish M'Cunn into his setting of James Hyslop's poem, "The Cameronian's Dream." Some time ago a correspondence appeared in one of our leading newspapers regarding its origin and the length of time it had been in use in Scotland, but nothing satisfactory was elicited; and so far as the writer knows, the history of the tune has not yet been fully ascertained. In our Psalters it is usually marked "Author Unknown," and indeed there is no testimony to its origin and past history, save the tradition that it has been in use in Scotland for centuries; yet it may be traced to its source.

We start with the fact that "Coleshill" is not an original tune, but is simply an altered copy of the tune "Dundee" or "Windsor." This will be abundantly evident to all who compare the melodies of these tunes.

The question now naturally arises, What is the source of "Dundee" or "Windsor"? This we are able to answer. (See Tye, Christopher.)

Of this altered form of "Dundee" or "Windsor" we have various examples. It occurs in William Barton's 'The Book of Psalms in Metre Close and Proper to the Hebrew, Smooth and Pleasant for the Metre; Plain and Easie for the Tune, with Musical Notes, Arguments, Annotations, and Index. Fitted for the ready use and understanding of all good Christians. . . . London: Printed by Matthew Simmons, for the Companie of Stationers, 1644.' It is there described as "London, long tune, proper for Solemn ditties, and used everywhere," and appears in the following form:—

* Doubtless a misprint for E, or in Sol-fa **m**.

KEY C.
{| 1 :— :l :s :d¹ :— :t :d¹ :— :l :m :— | d¹ :m¹ :r¹ :d¹ }

{:— :s :d¹ :— | d¹ :— :m¹ :r¹ :d¹ :— :t :d¹ :t :f* :— }

{| 1 :d¹ :— :t :d¹ :r¹ :l :— :— :— :— ||

According to H. E. Dibdin it appears under the name of "Mepsell" in Edmund Ireland's 'Tunes of the Psalms, in Two Parts,' York, 1699,[1] thus:—

---

[1] The writer has not seen this work.

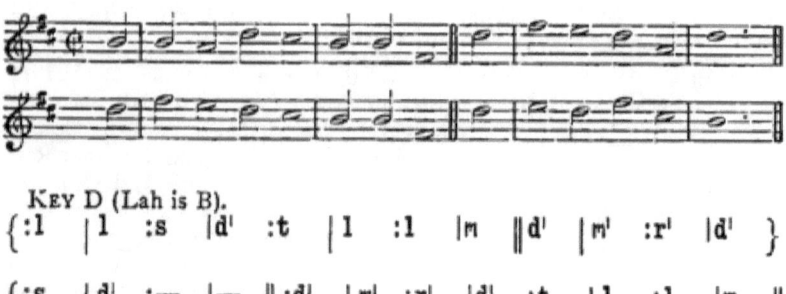

KEY D (Lah is B).

{ :l | l :s | d¹ :t | l :l | m ‖ d¹ | m¹ :r¹ | d¹ }

{ :s | d¹ :— | — ‖ :d¹ | m¹ :r¹ | d¹ :t | l :l | m ‖

{ :d¹ | r¹ :d¹ | m¹ :t | l :— :— ‖

In 'The Most Useful Tunes of the Psalms,' &c., by Edmund Ireland, second edition, 1713, it is named " Hull Tune," and is in the following form :—

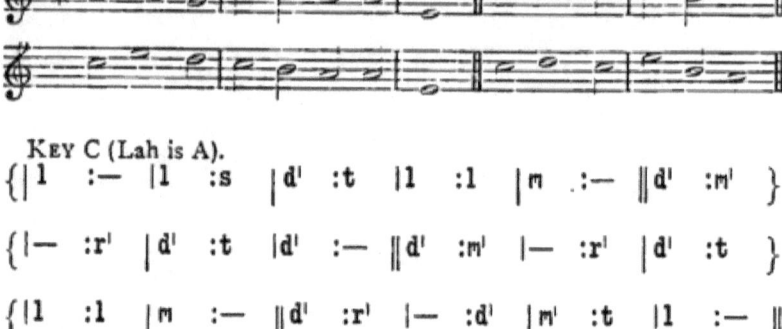

KEY C (Lah is A).

{ | l :— | l :s | d¹ :t | l :l | m :— ‖ d¹ :m¹ }

{ | — :r¹ | d¹ :t | d¹ :— ‖ d¹ :m¹ | — :r¹ | d¹ :t }

{ | l :l | m :— ‖ d¹ :r¹ | — :d¹ | m¹ :t | l :— ‖

Again, in 'The Psalms of David in Metre, newly Translated, with Amendments, by William Barton, M.A., and set to the best Psalm Tunes, in Two Parts — viz., Treble and Bass,' &c. — the Second Edition, Corrected and Amended, with the Basses, by Thomas Smith: Dublin, 1706, — it is named "Dublin Tune," the melody being identical with the form used in Scotland :—

DUBLIN TUNE (in Barton's Psalms, Dublin, 1706).

Key C (Lah is A).

{| l :l | s :d' | s :l | l :m | d' :m' | r' :d' | s :d' }

{| d' :m' | r' :d' | s :l | l :m | d' :s | l :r' | t :l ||

The earliest copy of this tune the writer can find bearing the name of "Coleshill," is in 'The Psalm Singer's Divine Companion,' published at Manchester in 1750, by Thomas Moore. (See that name.) To Moore perhaps belongs the credit of introducing the tune into Scotland; at all events he seems to have been the first to publish it, for it is found in his 'Psalm Singer's Delightful Pocket Companion,' Glasgow (1762), under the name "Coleshill," and with the following directions: "Sing 'Dundee' Bass and Counter to this Tune." It is not found in any of the Scottish Psalmodies published before Moore's book (so far as the writer knows), but after 1762 editors seem to have been of the opinion that their collections were not complete without it. It is set to Psalm 103 in 'The Psalms of David in Metre. . . . Allowed by the Authority of the General Assembly of the Kirk of Scotland, and appointed to be sung in Congregations and Families. With Twenty-three Select Psalm-Tunes. Particularly adapted to the subject of the Psalms to which they are set.' Printed by Alexander Adam, Glasgow, 1773.

For what reasons were the alterations made on "Dundee" or "Windsor"? The late Mr John Dobson of Richmond was of the opinion that the substitution of the dominant for the sharp seventh at the close of the first and third strains, and the second for the same at the close of the last strain, was made to adapt the tune to chimes. Is it not probable that the alterations at the close of the first and third strains were made to avoid the interval G sharp to C, which is neither melodious nor easy to sing? At all events, congregations in last century seem to have had difficulty in singing the G sharp, for Robert Bremner in his 'Treatise on Music' (Edinburgh, 1756), says: "The 'Dundee' tune . . . has been laid aside by such precentors or church clerks as have been regularly taught, because they found it was impossible to bring their congregations to fall the half-note, they having been in use for many years past to fall a whole note—that is, to sing G natural instead of G sharp." To get over the difficulty, Bremner recommended that B natural should be used, and the G sharp transferred to an inner part.

It is a matter for regret that "Coleshill," with its hallowed associations, should fall into disuse in our Scottish churches. Probably one reason why it is so seldom heard is, that praise leaders have got hold of the idea that it can only be used with such a psalm as "Jehovah hear thee in the day"; let them adapt it, however, to "God is our refuge and our strength," sing it quickly and boldly, and we feel sure they will admit its suitability to that psalm and to others of a similar character.

Battishill, Jonathan, son of Mr Jonathan Battishill, solicitor, and Mary Leverton of Great Torrington; born in London, May 1738; chorister in St Paul's Cathedral under William Savage, 1748; organist of the united parishes of St Clement, Eastcheap, and St Martin, Orgar, London; afterwards of Christ Church, Newgate Street, 1767; died at Islington, December 10, 1801, and was buried in St Paul's Cathedral.

ST PANCRAS, No. 34 P. and P., was first published in William Riley's 'Parochial Harmony; consisting of a Collection of Psalm Tunes, in Three and Four Parts,' London, 1762.

BATTISHILL, No. 415 S.H. (Second Tune) and 333 in U.P.H., is a much altered copy of the following tune, which appears in 'Twelve Hymns; the Words by the Rev. Charles Wesley, M.A., late student at Christ Church, Oxford: set to Musick by Jonathan Battishill.'

{| d :m .,r | r   :f .,m | m .,f s:f .m | m   :r |}
{| Ev'...ry | stum..bling | block   re. | move; |}

{| s :f .,m |"r :d | r^mrdr :m .,f | f   :m |}
{| Each to | e:ch u.... | nite,   en- | dear; |}

{| 1 :— .s | f .,s:m .,'f | m   :r .,d | d   :— ||}
{| Come, and | spread Thy | ban.....ner | here. |}

CHANTS No. 221 S.P., 354 U.P.H., 205 U.P.P.; No. 255 S.P.; No. 261 S.P., 30 U.P.P.; No. 333 F.C.H. (Second Chant), were published in 'Divine Harmony, being a Collection of Two Hundred and Seven Double and Single Chants, in Score, ... Sung at his Majesty's Chapels Royal': February 1770, which was edited by Thomas Vandernan, a Gentleman of the Chapel Royal. Dr Crotch has made chant in D, No. 255 S.P., and chant in A minor, No. 261 S.P. and 30 U.P.P., the subjects of two cleverly constructed fugues.

Beaty, Richard William, born in Dublin about 1799; educated in Christ Church Cathedral, Dublin; appointed about 1824 organist and musical instructor at the Molyneux Asylum for Blind Women; organist of the Free Church, Great Charles Street, 1828 to 1877; master of the choristers in Christ Church Cathedral from 1830 to 1872; composer of songs and other works; died in Dublin, 1883. Beaty composed the tune

TENDERNESS, No. 398 S.H., 382 F.C.H., 337 U.P.H. (there named "Caritas"), for the children of Lady Harberton's School, Dublin, in 1830. It is, however, seldom assigned to him.

Beckwith, John (Christmas ?), born at Norwich on Christmas Day, 1750; pupil and assistant successively to Dr William Hayes and Dr Philip Hayes at Magdalen College, Oxford; appointed organist of St Peter's, Mancrofts, Norwich, January 16, 1794; graduated Mus. Bac. and Doc. at Oxford in 1803, and in 1808 succeeded Thomas Garland as organist of Norwich Cathedral, retaining his office at St Peter's; died in consequence of a paralytic stroke, June 3, 1809; buried at St Peter's, Mancrofts. Of his organ-playing Professor Taylor said: "I have never heard Dr Beckwith's equal upon the organ either in this country or in Germany.... Neither is this my opinion only, but that of every competent judge who has heard him." He had a remarkable power of extemporising, and would frequently play four extempore organ fugues at one Sunday's services. There is some doubt as to whether Dr Beckwith was christened John Christmas, or whether his second name was only a nickname. In the works he published he is described as John Beckwith, but in the register of his burial the name is stated as "John Christmas Beckwith, married man, an organist of this parish," and it is by this name he is generally known. Some years ago the writer endeavoured to find in what parish he was born, but without success.

CHANT in D, No. 212 U.P.P., is from 'The First Verse of every Psalm of David, with an Ancient or Modern Chant in Score,' published by Dr Beckwith in 1808.

Beethoven, Ludwig van, born at Bonn, December 16, 1770; one of the greatest of modern musicians; resided chiefly at Vienna, where he died March 26, 1827; interred in Währing Cemetery; re-interred in the Central Cemetery, Vienna, June 22, 1888. The tunes bearing his name are adaptations from his works.

EMMANUEL or IMMANUEL, No. 402 S.H., 63 in S.P., 71 in F.C.H., and 94 in U.P.P. (there named "Consolation"), is a ridiculous perversion of the Theme of the Finale of his Quintett, Op. 16.

BEETHOVEN, No. 220 F.C.H. (Second Tune), is an adaptation from his Sonata in A flat, Op. 26; and SARDIS, No. 231 F.C.H. (First Tune), is from a Romance for Violin, Op. 40.

WALTON, No. 39 P. and P., 26 in S.P., and 7 in F.C.H., appears in this form in Cotterill's 'Christian Psalmody, for Congregational or Family Use,' 1831. It had been published before that time as a Psalm Tune in a slightly different form by William Gardiner in his 'Sacred Melodies from Haydn, Mozart, and Beethoven, adapted to the best English Poets,' vol. ii. (1815), and is headed "Subject from Beethoven." Although it is generally assigned to Beethoven, Sir George Grove, Mr Ernst Pauer, Mr Ebenezer Prout, and Mr August Manns are of the opinion that it is not from any of his works. Mr Manns thinks it "is rather more in sympathy with the German Volkslied than the spirit of Beethoven's 'Song Melodies.'" It may be noted here that the opening line is identical with the commencing symphony in Mozart's air *Possenti Numi* in the opera of the "Magic Flute."

Bell, John Montgomerie, Writer to the Signet; son of Mr Alexander Montgomerie Bell, Writer to the Signet and Professor of Conveyancing in the University of Edinburgh; born in Edinburgh, May 28, 1837, and educated there; studied music under Professor Donaldson at the University; amateur composer of many fine hymn tunes, anthems, &c.

GRANGE, No. 171, and RUTHWELL, No. 201 (First Tune) in S.H., were first published in 'The National Book of Hymn Tunes, Chants, and Kyries,' by W. A. Jefferson, Leeds, 1885.

ST GILES, No. 125; RENFREW, No. 281; ST CATHARINE, No. 276 (Second Tune); ST SAVIOUR, No. 375; ST BALDRED, No. 376 (Second Tune); and

CRUCIFIXION, No. 390, were first published in the S.H., the last-named being composed for that work.

SELVILLE, No. 148 in P. and P., was composed in 1869, and first published in a tentative collection issued by the Free Church in 1870; NEW 143D, No. 211 in P. and P., was partly composed for and first published there.

S.S., No. 21 F.C.H., "They that be wise," was composed for that work.

Bennett, Robert, sixth son of John Bennett, was born at Bakewell, Derbyshire, and was baptised in Bakewell Church, February 6, 1788. His father removed to Cambridge in 1791, on being appointed Lay-Clerk in the united choir of King's, Trinity, and St John's Colleges, a post he held for thirty-six years, and then retired on his full pension. Robert Bennett was a chorister in King's College, and on leaving the choir, June 24, 1804, was articled to Dr Clarke-Whitfeld, then organist of Trinity College, and afterwards Professor of Music in the University. After serving his apprenticeship, Robert Bennett remained with Dr Clarke-Whitfeld for four years as a pupil in composition and assistant-organist. On June 10, 1811, he was appointed organist to the Parish Church, Sheffield; and in the following year (May 12, 1812) he married Elizabeth, daughter of James Donn, a botanist of some mark, and the first curator of the Botanical Gardens at Cambridge. As a teacher Bennett took a prominent place in Sheffield and the neighbourhood. He became an adherent of the Logierian system, and was so far valued by its founder as to be intrusted with the education of his son, Henry Logier, who went to Sheffield as an articled pupil. He published six songs (dedicated to the Duke of Devonshire) to words furnished by his friend Mr William Sterndale, after whom he named his only son, a notice of whose career is given below. Robert Bennett died November 3, 1819, and was buried in Ecclesall churchyard, near Sheffield.

EASTGATE, No. 182 in S.P., was composed by him, and was for many years indelibly associated in Scotland with Psalm 133. The second edition of R. A. Smith's 'Sacred Music . . . Sung in St George's Church, Edinburgh' (1828), contains the earliest copy the writer has seen in a Scottish psalmody. The tune is known by the name of "Bennett's" in England. Cotterill's 'Christian Psalmody' (1831) contains three tunes by Bennett, but "Eastgate" is not there.

Bennett, Sir William Sterndale, MUS. DOC., M.A., D.C.L., "the only English musical composer since Purcell who has attained a distinct style and individuality of his own, and whose works can be reckoned among the models or 'classics' of the art";

born at Sheffield, April 13, 1816; pupil of Dr Crotch, W. H. Holmes, and Cipriani Potter; studied also at Leipzig; Principal of the Royal Academy of Music; Musical Professor at the University of Cambridge; knighted in 1871; died February 1, 1875; buried in Westminster Abbey. Composer of the cantata the "May Queen," the oratorio the "Woman of Samaria," and also some beautiful instrumental music and songs.

Beutler,[1] **Johann Georg Bernhard,** born May 17, 1762, at Mühlhausen in Thuringia; organist of the principal church at Mühlhausen, where he died, April 14, 1814. He published, under the *nom de plume* of H. G. Demme, 'Neue Christliche Lieder,' Gotha, 1799. The work contains 51 tunes, of which 32 are by J. R. Ahle; the others, except a few by Beutler himself, are composed by Joachim Von Burgk, and Johann Eccard, arranged by Beutler.

HALL, No. 16 in P. and P., is his, and stands No. 51 in the above work, set to the words—

"Geweihter Ort wo Saat, von Gott."

By repeating the first two lines, the tune will appear as composed by Beutler.

Bilby, Thomas, son of Mr John Bilby, born at Southampton, April 18, 1794; served eight years in the army; then studied the infant-school system under a Mr Buchanan, who is said to have founded the first Infant School in England; in 1825 took charge of the Training School at Chelsea; in 1835 went to the West Indies, and introduced his system of teaching there; founded in connection with Mr J. S. Reynolds the Home and Colonial School Society for training infant-school teachers; held the post of parish clerk in St Mary's, Islington, for twenty-eight years; died there September 24, 1872, and was buried in Finchley cemetery. The tune

JOYFUL (associated with Bilby's Hymn "Here we suffer grief and pain"), No. 350 U.P.H., 437 S.H., 379 F.C.H., was composed by him for a school treat. It is doubted by some if Bilby composed it, but his son, Mr Henry Bilby, Parish Clerk of St Mary's, Islington, claims for his father both the tune and the hymn.

Bishop, John, born about 1665; pupil of Daniel Roseingrave; Lay-Vicar of King's College, Cambridge; organist of Winchester

---

[1] Not Z. B. Beutler, as in S.H. and other works.

College,[1] 1695 ; of Winchester Cathedral in succession to Vaughan Richardson, 1729 ; died December 1737, and was succeeded by James Kent. His tune

JAM LUCIS, No. 80 S.H., and 23 in S.P. (there named "St Bartholomew"), appears in his work 'A Sett of New Psalm Tunes, in Four Parts' (1700), set to Psalm 100, and named "Illsley Tune."

Bliss, Philip Paul, son of Isaac Bliss; born at Clearfield, Clearfield County, Pennsylvania, July 19, 1838; composer of many hymns and tunes which have become popular in this country. While travelling to undertake some revival work at Chicago, he and his wife were burned to death in a railway accident at Ashtabula, Ohio, U.S., December 29, 1876.

SUNSHINE, No. 224, and ST CYRIL, No. 411 (Second Tune) in S.H., were first published in 'The Charm: A Collection of Sunday School Music,' Cincinnati, 1871. The words are also by Bliss.

Blow, John, Mus. Doc., by faculty from the Dean and Chapter of Canterbury; born at North Collingham, Nottinghamshire, 1648 [2]; chorister in the Chapel Royal, 1660; organist of Westminster Abbey, 1669 to 1680, and 1695 to 1708; Gentleman of the Chapel Royal 1673-74, Master of the Choristers 1674, and one of the organists there about 1676; Almoner and Master of the Choristers of St Paul's Cathedral, London, 1687 to 1693; composer to the Chapel Royal, 1699; died in London, October 1, 1708.

CHANT, No. 223 in S.P., appears at the end of the seventh edition of John Playford's 'A Brief Introduction to the Skill of Music,' 1674.

Bohemian Hymnal, 1531.

The above contained a German version of some of the old Bohemian hymns already printed in Czech in 1505, and even earlier. The translation was made by Michael Weisse, pastor of a German congregation at Landskron, for the use of his own flock. The old Bohemian hymns and melodies were in great part preserved. This book is cited as the earliest known source of

[1] This is probable, though the books of the College contain no reference to his having held the office of organist there. He was buried at the College, as will be seen by the following extract from the Winchester Cathedral Register of 1737 — "Mr John Bishop (organist), bury'd at the College, Decemr. 22."

[2] The Records of North Collingham contain no entry of the birth or baptism of Blow, although they were searched at the writer's instigation, May 5, 1889. A MS. note of Anthony à Wood's, in his 'Athenæ Oxoniensis,' shows that Dr Rogers told Wood that Blow was born in London.

LANDSKRON, No. 276 F.C.H. (Third Tune), which may, however, have been known in Bohemia much earlier.

RAVENSHAW, No. 257 F.C.H. This ancient church melody, assigned to the twelfth century, is set to Weisse's hymn, "Menschenkind merk eben," and styled "Ave Hierarchia." The version in the F.C.H. is considerably reduced.

Bortnianski, Dimitri, was born in 1751 in the village of Gloutroff in the Ukraine. He became a chorister in the Imperial Chapel at St Petersburg, and there he studied music under Galuppi. In 1768 he removed to Italy to pursue his studies. Shortly after his return to Russia (in 1779) he was appointed Director of the Imperial Choir at St Petersburg, where he died October 28, 1828. He was a distinguished composer of sacred music, and has been styled by some the Russian Palestrina.

ST PETERSBURG, No. 175 in S.H. and 176 in U.P.H. (there named "Wells," the title by which it is commonly known), is adapted from a hymn tune sung in the Chapel of the British Embassy at St Petersburg.

Bowdler, Cyril, Mus. Bac. This is the *nom de plume* of an amateur, holding an important position in the War Office, and who has composed some excellent hymn tunes, but courts anonymity. He has published several collections of hymn tunes.

BOWDLER, No. 404 in S.H., is his.

Boyce, William, Mus. Doc., was born in London, 1710. As a chorister of St Paul's Cathedral he received his first instruction in music from Charles King, and afterwards became an articled pupil of Dr Maurice Greene. In 1734 he became organist of Oxford Chapel, Vere Street, London; in 1736 organist of St Michael's, Cornhill, and one of the composers and joint organists to the Chapel Royal; and in 1749 organist of All-hallows, Thames Street. In the same year he received the degrees of Bachelor and Doctor in Music from the University of Cambridge. He died February 7, 1779, and was buried in St Paul's Cathedral. Charles Wesley wrote a hymn on his death beginning "Father of heroes, farewell."

SHARON, No. 14 S.H., 220 U.P.H., and 221 F.C.H., appears without a name in 'A Collection of Melodies for the Psalms of David, according to the Version of Christopher Smart, A.M. By the most Eminent Composers of Church Music' (1765), and is there set in two parts to Psalm 4.

CHAPEL ROYAL, No. 309 in F.C.H., is also from the same work, where it bears no name and is set to Psalm 1.

Morning Hymn, No. 278 (First Tune) in S.H., is assigned by Dibdin to Dr Boyce, but it does not appear in the collections to which he contributed. It may be an adaptation from one of his anthems or songs.

Chant in D, No. 211 U.P.P. and 248 S.P., appears in Vandernan's Collection, 1770 (the title of which is quoted under Battishill), where it is assigned to a Mr Davis. As Dr Boyce and Vandernan were both connected with the Chapel Royal when the Chant was published, it is very probable that Davis and not Dr Boyce is composer. No. 233 S.P., is found in Harrison's 'Sacred Harmony,' vol. ii. (1791).

Bradbury, William Batchelder, was born at York, Maine, U.S.A., January 16, 1816. In 1830 he went to Boston, and became an organist; and in 1836 he settled at New York as a teacher. In 1847 he studied under Hauptmann and others at Leipzig. His compositions are very numerous, and many of his hymn tunes are exceedingly popular in this country. Bradbury died at Montclair, New Jersey, January 7, 1868. His tune

Even Me, No. 165 S.H., 322 U.P.H., 222 F.C.H., was first published in 'The Golden Shower,' which he edited, in 1862.

Jesus Loves Me, No. 405; Heavenly Land, No. 434; and Whither, Pilgrims? No. 439, all in S.H., were first published in 'The Golden Chain' (also edited by him), 1861.

Philadelphia, No. 19 S.P., was composed in 1843, and published in 'The Psalmodist,' which Bradbury edited in conjunction with Dr Thomas Hastings. Its original name is "Zephyr."

Little Pilgrim, No. 368 F.C.H. It is doubtful if this is the composition of Bradbury. It is, however, American.

S. S., No. 6 F.C.H. and 48 U.P.H., "Cast thy burden on the Lord," was published for the first time in the 'New York Choralist,' 1847.

Braun, Johann Georg, precentor in Eger, Bohemia, in the latter half of the seventeenth century.

Hermon, No. 314 (Second Tune) F.C.H., and 227 in S.H. (First Tune), (there named "Braun"), and Meinau, No. 138 S.H., are from his 'Echo Hymnodæ Cœlestis,' 1675.

Bremner, Robert, born (according to Dr Rimbault) in Scotland about 1720; pupil of Geminiani; teacher of singing in Edinburgh; about 1748 commenced business as a musicseller in the High Street there, under the sign of the "Harp and Hautboy"; afterwards settled in London, and began business with the same sign, opposite Somerset House in the Strand; published many collections of Scotch music; died at Kensington Gore, May 12, 1789. He published at Edinburgh in 1756 'The Rudiments of

Music; or, A Short and Easy Treatise on that Subject, to which is added, A Collection of the best Church Tunes, Canons, and Anthems.'

ST PAUL, No. 142 in P. and P., 61 in U.P.P., 130 U.P.H., 85 F.C.H., 150 S.P., is first found by the writer in Bremner's work, set in two parts, and bearing its present name. It seems to be of Scotch origin, as it is not found in the English Psalmodies published before Bremner's work. It was certainly in use in Aberdeen in 1755, if not earlier; and in the second edition of Bremner's work, with considerable additions, and "A Plan for Teaching a Croud," 1762, it is set in four parts, and named "Aberdeen or St Paul's."

Dr Mainzer and others ascribed the tune to a William Tate, but little weight can be attached to the ascription. To ascribe it to Nahum Tate is erroneous in the extreme. He died in 1715, and if he composed it, it is singular that no earlier copy than that mentioned above has been found.

Bremner's book of 1756 contains among others the following tunes, which is perhaps their first appearance in a Scotch collection :—ST MATTHEW'S, ST ANN'S, HANOVER, ST MARY, ST JAMES'S (Courteville). See Moore, Thomas.

Bridge, John Frederick, born at Oldbury, Worcestershire, December 5, 1844; chorister at Rochester Cathedral under John L. Hopkins and John Hopkins, successive organists there; pupil of Sir John Goss and Sir George J. Elvey; organist (first) of a Parish Church in Kent, 1862 to 1865; Trinity Church, Windsor, 1865 to 1869; Mus. Bac. Oxford, 1868; organist and master of the children, Manchester Cathedral, 1869 to 1875; Mus. Doc. Oxford, 1874, for which he composed as an exercise the oratorio "Mount Moriah"; deputy-organist and master of the children, Westminster Abbey, 1875; promoted to the full offices on the death of James Turle, 1882. For the celebration of the Queen's Jubilee in Westminster Abbey (21st June 1887), he arranged all the music and composed a special anthem, for which he received the thanks of her Majesty, and the Silver Jubilee Medal. His compositions include a setting of Mr Gladstone's Latin translation of Toplady's hymn, "Rock of Ages," which was performed at the Birmingham Festival of 1885; also a cantata, "Callirhoe," produced at the Birmingham Festival of 1888; an oratorio, "The Repentance of Nineveh," composed for and performed at the Worcester Musical Festival, September 1890. Elected Gresham Professor of Music in succession to Dr Henry Wylde, May 1, 1890.

ST BEATRICE, No. 302 in S.H., was first published in the Revised and Enlarged Edition of 'Hymns Ancient and Modern,' 1875.

Briegel, Wolfgang Carl, born May 21, 1626; educated in Nürnberg, where he was a treble singer in the chapel; organist at

Stettin; after 1650 Court precentor at Gotha in the service of Duke Ernst the Pious, when he first made himself publicly known by his sacred arias and concertos published at Erfurt in 1652. He is designed as "Music Director to the princely house of Friedenstein." He left Gotha probably after the death of Duke Ernst in 1675, and betook himself to Darmstadt as Court Chapel Master in the service of Landgrave Ludwig VI. of Hesse-Darmstadt, an office he retained till his death in November 1712. In 1687 Briegel issued an important collection of chorales, which is known as the Darmstadt Cantional, and in which will be found, beginning on page 537,

ZURICH, No. 2 U.P.H., 134 and 242 S.H., set to the words, "Alle Menschen müssen sterben," &c. The composer is unknown.

Broomfield, William Robert, son of Mr William Broomfield; born at Inverary, Argyleshire, October 14, 1826; baptised November 22; studied music under John Turnbull at Glasgow, where he resided for some time; settled in Aberdeen about 1850, and died there October 16, 1888; buried in the "Strangers' Ground," but reinterred in Allanvale Cemetery, July 1889; author of 'The Principles of Ancient and Modern Music,' Aberdeen, 1863; composer of many psalm and hymn tunes, two of which (never published) are in the possession of J. Cuthbert Hadden, Esq., Edinburgh.

ST KILDA, No. 4 U.P.P., 138 S.P., 92 F.C.H., was originally named "Strathpeffer," and first published on single slips about 1850. It is cut on a handsome monument erected over his grave by public subscription.

ZION, No. 180 S.P., was published in the 'Scottish Psalmist,' Aberdeen, 1876, but was circulated in MS. before that time.

Brown, Arthur Henry, born at Brentwood, Essex, July 24, 1830; organist of the church of St Thomas the Martyr, Brentwood, 1842 to 1853; of the church of St Edward the Confessor, Romford, Essex, till 1858; and since that time again organist of Brentwood, and a professor of music there; organist also of St Peter's Church, South Weald.

ST ANATOLIUS, No. 294 (First Tune) in S.H., and 304 in F.C.H., was composed for the hymn to which it is set on February 8, 1862, and published in November following along with a few others.

ALLHALLOWS, No. 118 F.C.H., was composed October 2, 1862, and first published in the 'Bristol Tune Book,' 1863.

S. S., No. 8, "What shall I render?" and 27, "O death, where is thy sting?" in F.C.H., were composed for and first published in that collection.

Brown-Borthwick, Rev. Robert, son of Mr Robert Brown of H.M. Civil Service; Scottish divine and amateur musician; born at Aberdeen, May 18, 1840; educated at St Mary's Hall, Oxford, which he left without graduating; afterwards, in 1865, took holy orders; curate of Sudeley Manor, Gloucestershire, and chaplain to the Winchcomb Union; curate of Evesham, Worcestershire, and assistant minister of Quebec Chapel, London; incumbent of Holy Trinity, Grange-in-Borrowdale, Cumberland, 1869 to 1872; since 1872 vicar of All Saints, Scarborough. Mr Brown assumed the additional name of Borthwick in 1868, on his marriage with Grace (died 1884), the only surviving daughter of the late Mr John Borthwick of Borthwick Castle. His tune

ABERDEEN, No. 219 in S.P., was composed about 1866 for Psalm 136, and first published in the 'Supplemental Hymn and Tune Book,' which he edited.

Bryan, Cornelius, was born at Bristol about the year 1775, but all the writer's attempts to find the exact year of his birth have proved unsuccessful. He became organist of St Mark's (the Mayor's Chapel), Bristol, and afterwards of St Mary Redcliffe Church, both of which appointments he held at the same time. While conducting his operetta of "Lundy" (never published) at the Theatre Royal, Bristol, he fell down a trap-door on the stage, which was not properly fastened, and so injured his spine that he died, March 18, 1840, a few days after the accident. Bryan was considered a good organist; and he was an excellent musician, as his compositions testify.

About 1830 [1] he published 'A Collection of the most esteemed Psalm Tunes, Ancient and Modern, Selected and Harmonized for Four Voices, and interspersed with a few original Compositions.'

SERENITY, No. 204 P. and P., and 204 S.P., appears there as shown below, set to Psalm 25th, and is nameless.

[1] Reviewed in the 'Harmonicon' for March 1831.

BURNEY.   87

[Musical notation in staff notation with lyrics: "In bring-ing wand'r-ing sin-ners home, And teach-ing them His ways."]

[Tonic sol-fa notation follows, Key G, Key D t., f. Key G.]

'Effusions for the organ, containing eight voluntaries, one hundred interludes, and three psalms by Cornelius Bryan, organist of the Mayor's Chapel, Bristol,' contains another Short Metre tune, "St Mary Redcliffe," which will be found in the Bristol Tune Book (No. 15).

Burney,[1] **Charles,** Mus. Doc., son of James and Anne Macburney; born at Shrewsbury, April 7, 1726; pupil of his half-brother, James Burney, and of Dr Arne; appointed organist of St Dionis Back-church, London, 1749; of King's Lynn Church,

[1] The following is the entry of his baptism in the records of St Mary's Church, Shrewsbury, where his father was organist—

"May 1726.
Charles and Susannah, son and daughter of
James and Anne Macburney, bapt the 5th Day."

The prefix Mac was dropped by the children as they grew into active life. This fact does not seem to have been noticed by musical writers.

1751; Mus. Bac., and Mus. Doc., Oxford, 1769; organist of Chelsea College from 1783 till he died, April 12, 1814. Author of 'A General History of Music,' 4 volumes, and other works. Madame d'Arblay, the author of the celebrated 'Diary,' 'Evelina,' 'Cecilia,' &c., was his daughter.

TRURO, No. 117 in S.H., commonly assigned to Burney, appears on page 65 of Thomas Williams's 'Psalmodia Evangelica, A Complete Set of Psalm and Hymn Tunes for Public Worship,' 1789. It is there anonymous, but Burney's tunes have his name attached to them. The writer can find no authority for assigning "Truro" to Burney. As he was alive and eminent as a musician and author when Williams published the above work, his name would certainly have been given as composer there.

In Isaac Smith's 'Collection of Psalm Tunes,' the fifth edition, with great additions by S. Major—published after 1787—the tune is also found, but is anonymous.

Dr Burney contributed eight tunes to 'The Lock Collection,' 1769.

Caldbeck, G. T. (not Caldeck), an amateur; for some time a missionary in China.

PAX TECUM, No. 226 S.H. (Second Tune), and 292 F.C.H. When in China he became deeply impressed with the beauty of the hymn, "Peace, perfect peace," and although by no means skilled in music, he composed as best he could a tune for it, the MS. of which he sent to the author of the hymn, the Rev. E. H. Bickersteth (now the Bishop of Exeter). After undergoing some alterations, it was published in its present form in the 'Revised and Enlarged Edition of the Hymnal Companion to the Book of Common Prayer,' 1878.

Calkin, John Baptiste, was born in London, March 16, 1827; studied under his father; organist of St Columba College, Ireland, from 1846 to 1853; organist and choir-master of Woburn Chapel, 1853 to 1857; organist and choir-master of Camden Road Chapel, 1863 to 1868; of St Thomas's Church, Camden, New Town, London, 1870 to 1884; Professor at the Guildhall School of Music and Croydon Conservatoire; Member of Council, Trinity College; Fellow of College of Organists; author of many published works, including services, anthems, part-songs, glees, songs, original organ music, hymn tunes, &c.

RAMOTH, No. 365 in U.P.H., was composed for the Rev. R. Brown-Borthwick's 'Supplemental Hymn and Tune Book.'

NOX PRÆCESSIT, No. 95 in F.C.H., was first published in the 'Christian Hymnal,' 1873.

Callcott, John Wall, son of Thomas Callcott, a bricklayer and builder, born at Kensington, November 20, 1766; a self-taught musician; appointed assistant-organist of St George's

Church, Hanover Square, London, 1783; afterwards organist of the Asylum for Female Orphans, and of St Paul's, Covent Garden; graduated Mus. Bac., Oxford, 1785; Mus. Doc. 1800; died near Bristol, May 15, 1821; buried at Kensington; one of the greatest of English glee composers.

CALLCOTT, No. 40 (Second Tune) S.H., is adapted from the music he set about the year 1794 to the following words, which will be found on a tombstone in Brading Churchyard, Isle of Wight, erected by one Robert Berry in memory of his wife, who died August 24, 1790, aged twenty-five years:—

I.

" Forgive, blest shade, the tributary tear
That mourns thy exit from a world like this;
Forgive the wish that would have kept thee here,
And stayed thy progress to the seats of bliss.

II.

No more confined to grov'ling scenes of night,
No more a tenant pent in mortal clay;
We rather now should hail thy glorious flight,
And trace thy progress to the realms of day."

In 1791 Dr Callcott edited, in conjunction with Dr Samuel Arnold, 'The Psalms of David, for the Use of Parish Churches.'

LANGHOLM, No. 104 P. and P., is on page 97 of the above work, and is there set to Psalm 90, and named " Lancaster."

DUNBLANE, No. 18 U.P.P., on page 45 set to Psalm 39, and named " Funeral."

S. S., No. 67 U.P.H., "I was glad," and No. 83, " Awake, awake," appear in 'Anthems, Hymns, Psalms, and Sentences sung at the Asylum Chapel.' Music chiefly composed by Dr J. W. Callcott. No date.

Callcott, William Hutchins, son of the preceding, was born at Kensington Gravel Pits, London, September 28, 1807; studied music under his brother-in-law, Mr William Horsley, Mus. Bac.; was organist of Ely Chapel, Holborn, London, and afterwards, for sixteen years, of St Barnabas's Church, Kensington; died August 5, 1882, and was buried at Kensal Green.

INTERCESSION, No. 330 F.C.H., and 273 U.P.H., was composed in 1865 for 'Psalms and Hymns for Divine Worship,' for the use of the Presbyterian Church in England, 1867 (Nisbet & Co.).

The last two lines are taken from "Look down on us," an air and chorus in Mendelssohn's oratorio "Elijah," composed for and performed at the Birmingham Musical Festival, 1846.

Callow, Harriet Anne, born in London, October 20, 1817, was the younger of the two daughters of the late Henry Smart the elder (a skilful violinist in London in the early part of the present century), also niece of Sir George Smart. She was one of a musical family, her mother being a clever teacher of vocal and instrumental music, and her brother the celebrated composer and organist, Henry Smart (see that name). She herself, though inheriting the tastes and talents of the family, never took part in professional life, being early married to Mr William Callow, "Member of the Royal Society of Painters in Water Colours," of Great Missenden, Bucks, where the greater portion of her married life was spent. She was singularly gifted (being a clever linguist), and highly intellectual. She died in London, June 30, 1883. Her tune

SOLITUDE, No. 366 in S.H., was specially composed for 'The Children's Hymn Book' (1881).

Camidge, John, the younger, organist and composer; grandson of John Camidge the elder, born in York 1790; pupil of his father Matthew Camidge; graduated as Mus. Bac., at Cambridge, 1812; Mus. Doc., 1819; assistant to his father; succeeded him 15th October 1842, and held the post till his death, which took place at York, September 29, 1859; on 28th November 1848 he became paralysed while playing the evening service, and never again touched the organ.

DOXOLOGY, No. 17 (Sanctus I.) in U.P.H. and S.S., 14 F.C.H., was composed by Camidge for 'Sacred Harmony, for Use in St George's Church, Edinburgh,' edited by the Rev. Dr Andrew Thomson, in 1820. The work also contains another original Sanctus by Camidge, and a Long Metre Tune by his father. A perusal of the following notices will show that the Camidges held the office of organist at York Minster for upwards of a hundred years.

Camidge, John, the elder, born at York, 1735; chorister in York Minster under Dr Nares, to whom he was articled for seven years, after which he studied in London under Dr Greene, and received some lessons from Handel; on his return to Yorkshire, Camidge became a candidate for the post of organist at Doncaster Parish Church, but the Dean of York hearing him play, offered him the appointment of organist to York Minster, where he entered upon his duties on 31st January 1756; famous as a brilliant and extempore organ-player; resigned his office as organist November 11, 1799; died April 25, 1803.

Camidge, Matthew, son of John Camidge the elder, born at York, 1758 (not 1764 as commonly stated); chorister of the Chapel

Royal under Dr Nares; on returning to York became assistant to his father, on whose resignation in 1799 he was appointed his successor, retiring 8th October 1842; died October 23, 1844, aged eighty-six years.

Campion, or Campian, Thomas, M.D., a physician by profession, was a poet, dramatist, composer, and writer on music in the early part of the seventeenth century; died in London, 1619; buried in the Church of St Dunstan in the West, Fleet Street, March 1st of that year. He published about 1613 'Two Bookes of Ayres, the First contayning Diuine and Morall Songs.' No. 14 in Book First is the tune

BABYLON STREAMS, No. 2 P. & P., and 21 U.P.P., set to the following:—

"As by the streames of Babilon,
Farre from our natiue soyle we sat,
Sweet Sion thee we thought vpon,
And ew'ry thought a tear begat," &c.

It is wrongly assigned by some to Thomas Ravenscroft. It appears in Moore's 'Delightful Pocket Companion,' Glasgow (1762), which is the first time the writer finds it in a Scotch Psalmody.

Cantiques sacrez pour les principales Solemnitez des Chrétiens, &c., Cassel, 1740, contains the tune

BROADLANDS, No. 172 U.P.H., 209 P. and P. It is set to Cantique 34 on page 190, and the second cadence reads thus—

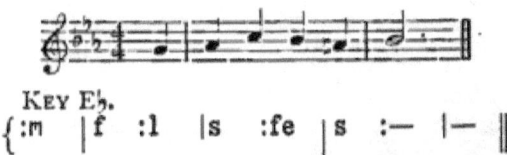

KEY E♭.
{ :m | f :l | s :fe | s :— |— ‖

It was altered to its present form by Dr Rimbault, and published in 'Psalms and Hymns for Divine Worship,' London, Nisbet & Co., 1867, where it bears its present name.

Carey, Henry, a reputed natural son of George Saville, Marquis of Halifax, was a popular composer and dramatist in the beginning of the eighteenth century. He composed largely for the theatre. Of all his compositions, the most popular, and that which will transmit his name to posterity, is his ballad of "Sally in our Alley," one of the most striking melodies ever composed. Carey died in London, October 4, 1743. His tune

CAREYS, No. 5 P. and P., and 161 U.P.P., was composed for Addison's

Paraphrase of Psalm 23, and appears in 'John Church's Psalmody,' 1723. It seems to have been first published in Scotland in 'Henry Boyd's Collection,' Glasgow, 1793.

EASTER HYMN, No. 169 (Second Tune) F.C.H., is assigned to Carey, but without sufficient authority. See Lyra Davidica.

Carter, Rev. Edmund Sardinson, M.A., son of the late Rev. William Carter, Rector of Shirgsby, Yorkshire; born at New Malton, Yorkshire, February 3, 1845; educated at Durham Grammar School—elected "King's Scholar" 1858—and Worcester College, Oxford—elected "Eaton Scholar" 1864; graduated B.A. and M.A. June 1871; curate of Christ Church, Ealing, Middlesex, 1871 to 1875; vicar-choral of York Minster from 1875 to the present time; rector of St Martin-cum-Gregory, York, 1877; vicar of St Michael-le-Belfrey, York, 1882; a self-taught musician. His tune

DAY BY DAY, No. 407 S.H., was composed about 1865, and first published in 'Church Hymns with Tunes,' edited by Sir Arthur S. Sullivan, 1874.

Case, B.

MADRID, No. 372 S.H., 182 F.C.H., 339 U.P.H., is assigned to a composer of the above name in the 'Washington Harmony,' by T. B. White, 2d edition, 1833, and is there named "Ascription." In later publications it is also ascribed to Case. Mason and Webb in their 'National Psalmist' call it a "Spanish Melody," but it is questionable if it is like Spanish music of any kind. It appears in the following form in 'A Collection of Metrical Versions, with Sixty Psalms and Fifty Hymns, by the most approved Authors.' By Montagu Burgoyne, Esq. The Music newly harmonized and arranged for One, Two, or Three Voices, by J. Macdonald Harris: London, 1872:—

SPANISH CHANT.

KEY B♭.   D.C.

{ :d | t, :-.d|1, :-.t,| s, :— |m :-.d| f :r |d :t, |d :— |— ||

{| m :— |r :-.m| f :m |r :— | m :— |r :m | f :m |s :d }

{| t, :-.d|1, :-.t,| s, :— |m :d | f :r |d :t, |d :— |— ||

Cecil, Rev. Richard, M.A., Oxford, was born in London, November 8, 1748; appointed minister of St John's Chapel, Bedford Row, London, 1780; Lecturer at Christ Church, Spitalfields, 1787; Rector of Bisley, and Vicar of Chobham, Surrey, 1800; died August 15, 1810.

S. S., No. 16 U.P.H., 25 F.C.H., "I will arise," was published in 'The Psalm and Hymn Tunes used at St John's Chapel, Bedford Row,' edited in 1814 by the composer's daughter, Theophania Cecil (died November 15, 1879, aged ninety-seven years and six months), who was for many years organist of that chapel.

Champneys, Francis Henry, born in London, March 25, 1848; educated at Winchester College, and Brasenose College, Oxford, where he graduated M.A. and M.B. 1875; Fellow of the Royal College of Physicians, London, 1882; pupil of Sir John Goss, and amateur composer. Wrongly described as Mus. Doc., in S.H. His tunes

Sâles, No. 105 S.H. and 275 F.C.H., and Assisi, No. 43 S.H., were composed for, and first published in, the Revised and Enlarged Edition of 'Hymns Ancient and Modern,' 1875.

The Three Kings, No. 32 (Second Tune) S.H., was composed at Oxford about 1866.

Chandler, S., an American musician who flourished during the close of the last and the beginning of the present centuries, and was resident in or near Troy, New York. His biography is obscure.

Hull, No. 311 F.C.H., is assigned in several American collections to Chandler. The earliest copy the writer has seen is in John Wyeth's 'Repository of Sacred Music,' 1812, where it is named "Ganges." In 'A Small Collection of Sacred Music,' printed by A. Davisson for Stephen D. Puller, July 1825, the tune is named "Indian Philosopher," and set to a hymn written by an Indian preacher, the Rev. Samson Occum (1723-1792). In Andrew Law's 'Christian Harmony,' 1792, there are three tunes by Chandler, and five in the 'New York and Vermont Collection of Sacred Music,' by F. Atwill, second edition, 1804.

Chetham, Rev. John, appointed Master of the Clerk's School, Skipton, Yorkshire, March 1737; Curate of Skipton in June 1739; died August 1763;[1] buried on the 29th of that month at Skipton.

[1] Chetham is generally stated to have died before 1761, as he is spoken of in the 'Compleat Psalmodist,' by J. Arnold, fifth edition, 1761, as "the late Reverend Mr John Chetham." This must be an error, as the facts given above were brought to light by the writer from the Skipton Church Records.

He edited 'A Book of Psalmody, . . . All Set in Four Parts,' 1718. From this—the first edition—where they bear no names, come

ARUNDEL, No. 16 U.P.P., and ST ALBANS, No. 122 in P. and P.

S.S., No. 179 U.P.II., "Behold, the Lord is my salvation," is in the same work. It is also found in Israel Holdroyd's 'Spiritual Man's Companion,' fifth edition, with large additions, 1753. See Greene, Maurice, Mus. Doc.

Children's Worship.

A collection of hymns published in 1878, with tunes in 1879; edited by the Rev. Henry Allon, D.D. From the above,

LEBBÆUS, No. 372 F.C.H. It was published in 'Church Hymns with Tunes,' edited by Sir Arthur S. Sullivan, in 1874, with a slightly different reading of the second line.

Chope, Rev. Richard Robert, born September 21, 1830; educated at Exeter College, Oxford, where he graduated in 1855; took holy orders in 1856; Vicar of St Augustine's, Queen's Gate, London, since 1865.

HERBERT, No. 277 in S.H., is from his 'Congregational Hymn and Tune Book,' 1862, which is one of the most important of modern hymnals, Dr Dykes having contributed to it many of his finest hymn tunes.

Clark,[1] **Jeremiah,** born in London in 1670 or earlier, entered the Chapel Royal as a chorister under Dr Blow. After leaving the choir he became organist at Winchester College. In 1693 his master, Dr Blow, resigned in his favour the appointments of Almoner and Master of the Children of St Paul's Cathedral. About 1695 he was appointed organist of St Paul's, and in 1704 he became joint-organist of the Chapel Royal with Dr Croft. He "shot himself at the Golden Cup in St Paul's Church-Yard," December the 1st, 1707, and was buried in St Gregory's by St Paul's, December the 3d. Clark's compositions for the Church "abound in melody which time has not antiquated, and are rich in harmony and pathos." His death was lamented by Edward Ward (the London spy), who concludes what was intended to be a pathetic ode with the following lines :—

> "Let us not therefore wonder at his fall,
> Since 'twas not so unnatural
> For him who lived by Canon to expire by Ball."

---

[1] There is no record of Clark's having graduated Mus. Doc., although he is described as such in the S.H. and S.P., and several works on musical biography.

BISHOPTHORPE, No. 51 in P. and P., appears in Dr Edward Miller's 'Psalms of David,' 1790, under that name, and set to Psalm 77th. It is thought to be an adaptation.

The following tunes by Clark were first published in Henry Playford's 'The Divine Companion; or, David's Harp New Tun'd,' 1708, where they are without names—

ST MAGNUS, No. 69 S.H., 51 F.C.H., 141 S.P., 184 U.P.P., 51 and 93 U.P.H., and Doxology 1, 135 P. and P., set to Psalm 107. Riley in his 'Parochial Harmony,' 1762, gives it its present name.

CONFIDENCE, No. 205 S.H., 10 in P. and P., 337 F.C.H. (there named "Brockham"), set to Psalm 121.

KING'S NORTON, No. 100 P. and P., is set to "A Hymn for Good Fryday," beginning—

"No songs of Tryumph now be sung,
Cease all your sprightly airs;
Let sorrow silence every tongue,
And joy dissolve to tears."

MELODY OF "KING'S NORTON" AS COMPOSED BY CLARK.

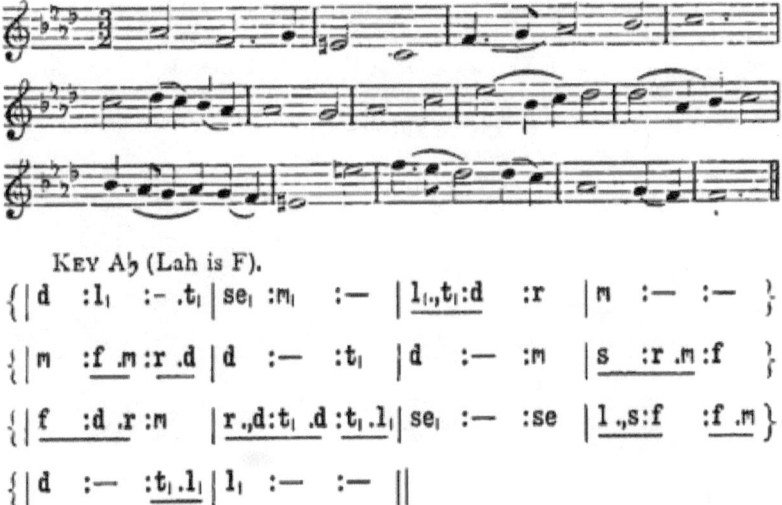

KINGSTON, No. 101 P. and P., set to "A Hymn for Christmas-day," beginning—

"What words, what voices can we bring,
Which way our accents raise,
To welcome the misterious King,
And sing a Saviour's praise."

MELODY OF "KINGSTON" AS COMPOSED BY CLARK.

KEY B FLAT.

{ :s₁ | d :— :r | t₁ :— :s₁ | d :r :— | m :— :r }

{ | m :fe :s | l :fe :— | s :— :s | s :f :m }

{ | r :m :f | m :r :d | t₁ :— :s₁ | d.r :m .f :s .m }

{ | l .s :l .s :f .m | m :— :r .d | d :— || }

The form of this tune in P. and P. is that given by William Riley in his collection of 1762, and it there bears the name of "Kingston."

HERMON, No. 89 P. and P., is set to "A Hymn for Easter-day," beginning—

"If angels sung a Saviour's birth
 On that auspicious morn,
 We well may imitate their mirth
 Now he again is born."

SECOND HALF OF "HERMON" AS COMPOSED BY CLARK. (The line between the asterisks is omitted in P. and P.)

KEY B FLAT.

{ :m | s :f | m :r | d .m :r .d | t₁ :s₁ | d :r }

{ | r :— .d | d :— | :m | l₁ :t₁ | t₁ :— .l₁ | l₁ :— || }

ST LUKE, No. 33 P. and P., is a *scandalously corrupt* version of one of Clark's tunes in Henry Playford's 'The Divine Companion, . . . 1701.' It is there set to "An Evening Hymn" of five stanzas, beginning—

CLARK.

I.

"Sleep, downey Sleep, come close mine eyes,
Tired with beholding vanities.
Welcome, sweet Sleep, that driv'st away
The toils and follies of the day.

II.

On thy soft bosom will I lie,
Forget the world and learn to die.
O Israel's watchful Shepherd, spread
Tents of angels round my bed."

MELODY OF "ST LUKE," AS COMPOSED BY CLARK.

KEY C (Lah is A).

{| 1 :l.s :f | m :— :t | d¹ :t :l | se :— :— }
{| m¹ :m¹ :m¹ | r¹ :— :d¹ | r¹ :t :— | d¹ :— :— }
{| s¹ :s¹ :f¹ | m¹ :— :m¹ | m¹ :r¹ :d¹ | t :— :t }
{| d¹ :t :l | se :— :m¹ | d¹ :— :t.l | 1 :— |— ||

S. S., No. 57 U.P.H., "My song shall be," was suggested to Dr Mason by an anthem of Clark's bearing the same title in Henry Playford's 'The Divine Companion; or, David's Harp New Tun'd,' 1701. It was first published in its present form by Dr Mason in his 'Hallelujah,' New York, 1854.

Clark, Thomas, said to have been born at Canterbury in 1775, but the writer is unable to confirm this statement; amateur composer of hymn tunes, of which he issued above twenty sets in different forms; acted as leader of psalmody at the Wesleyan church, Canterbury, and afterwards at the Unitarian church; died at Canterbury, where he had resided for many years, May 30, 1859. His tune

CREDITON, No. 71 S.H., 53 S.P., 149 U.P.P., 66 P. & P., was published in 'A Second Set of Psalm Tunes (Original), adapted to the use of Country Choirs,' about 1800. The last line has been unwarrantably tampered with

G

in the S.H., P. & P., and U.P.P. It is erroneously assigned to Jeremiah Clark in all Scotch collections.

Clarke, John, Mus. Doc., afterwards known as Clarke-Whitfeld, was born at Gloucester, December 13, 1770, and received his musical education at Oxford under Dr Philip Hayes. In 1793 he took the degree of Mus. Bac. at Oxford, Mus. Doc. at Dublin 1795, Cambridge *ad eundem* 1799, Oxford *ad eundem* 1810. He held the following offices: organist of St Lawrence's, Ludlow, from 1789 to 1794; of Armagh Cathedral, 1794 to 1797; Master of the Choristers of both Christ Church and St Patrick's Cathedrals, Dublin, 1798; organist of Trinity and St John's Colleges, Cambridge, 1799 to 1820; of Hereford Cathedral, 1820 to 1833; Professor of Music in the University of Cambridge, 1821. He died at Holmer, near Hereford, February 22, 1836, and was buried in the cloisters of Hereford Cathedral.

S.S., No. 68 U.P.H., "Behold how good and joyful," S.S., No. 66 U.P.H., "I will lift up mine eyes," appear in 'Services and Anthems' (vol. iv.), which he composed and dedicated to the Reverend the Masters and Fellows of Trinity and St John's Colleges. (No date.)

Clauder,[1] **Joseph,** Rector of the School in Altenburg early in the seventeenth century. Edited 'Psalmodia Nova,' second edition, 1630, published at Leipzig by Elias Rehefeld.

BRESLAU, No. 184 S.H., 4 P. & P., 6 F.C.H., 39 U.P.H., 71 U.P.P., is No. LXXIII. in Clauder's work, and is set to the hymn, "O Jesus Christ, mein's Lebens Licht," and the melody in the following form:—

[1] Clauder's Christian name is usually given as Israel, but that is an error. Israel Clauder was not born for upwards of thirty years after 'Psalmodia Nova' was issued.

Mendelssohn employs this tune in his oratorio "St Paul," composed for the Lower Rhine Musical Festival at Düsseldorf, 1836.

Clay, Frederic Emes, son of Mr James Clay, Liberal M.P. for Hull from 1847 till his death in 1873; born in the Rue Chaillot, Paris, August 3, 1838; in early life entered the Diplomatic Service, but forsook that pursuit in order to devote himself to musical composition; pupil of Molique, and afterwards of Hauptmann of Leipzig; in 1862 made his first public appearance as a composer at Covent Garden with the operetta "Court and Cottage," the libretto of which was written by Tom Taylor. His other works were: "Constance," 1865; "Ages Ago," 1869; "Princess Toto" and "Don Quixote," 1875; the cantata "Lalla Rookh," written for and produced at the Birmingham Musical Festival in 1877. In the last-named cantata occurs the popular song, "I'll sing thee songs of Araby." His other songs that have become popular are—"She wandered down the mountainside," "Long Ago," and "The Sands of Dee." From 1877 till 1883 Mr Clay composed no works of importance, but in May of the latter year his comic opera "The Merry Duchess" was produced, and in December of the same year his "Golden King." On the night following that of its production, Mr Clay was unhappily seized with paralysis of the tongue, the paralysis eventually spreading over his left side. He partially recovered, but was never able to resume his labours as a composer. He died at Oxford House, Great Marlow, November 24, 1889, and was buried at Brompton, November 28.

LITANY, No. 333 S.H., was composed by Clay for 'Church Hymns with Tunes,' edited by Sir Arthur S. Sullivan, 1874.

Cologne Gesangbuch.

NARENZA, No. 196 S.P., 164 U.P.P., 194 P. & P., 179 U.P.H., 129 F.C.H., 211 S.H., is ascribed by the Rev. W. H. Havergal to a Cologne Gesangbuch. None of the Cologne Gesangbücher which the writer has examined at the British Museum and elsewhere contains the original of the above.

The present form of the tune seems to have been first published in this country in Mr Havergal's 'Old Church Psalmody.'

Congregational Church Music. A Book for the Service of Song in the House of the Lord.

The above is the title of an important collection of Psalmody published in London in 1853, with a preface by the Rev. Thomas Binney. Dr W. M. Cooke had a large share in editing it. Part I.—General Psalmody—contains:

ST JOHN, No. 218 S.P., 158 F.C.H., 259 and Dox. 8 U.P.H., 166 U.P.P., 204, 269, and 392 S.H., 215 Pand. P. It had appeared in 1851 in vol. iii. of the 'Parish Choir,' with the following difference of rhythm in the first and last measures :—

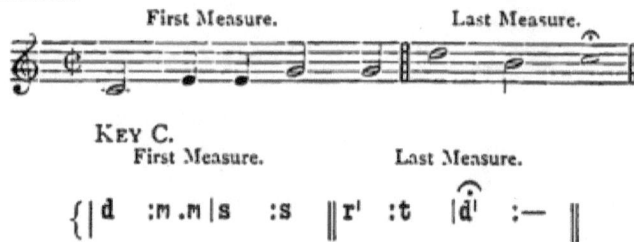

(See Havergal, Rev. W. H.)

LAVINGTON, No. 177 U.P.H., appears in a later edition, and is founded on a tune described in American collections and in R. A. Smith's 'Sacred Music,' second edition, Edinburgh (1828), as a "Venetian Melody."

Part II. of Congregational Church Music consists of Anthems and Collects.

S. S., "Unto Him that loved us," No. 29 F.C.H. and 21 U.P.H., is found there, and is anonymous.

Congregational Psalmist. An important collection of Hymn Tunes, edited by the Rev. Henry Allon, D.D., Henry John Gauntlett, Mus. Doc., and William Henry Monk, Mus. Doc. The following are the dates of the various editions :—

Part I., Tunes 1 to 104, published 1858.
Part II., Tunes 105 to 164, published 1859.
Part III., Tunes 165 to 330, published 1861.
First Appendix, Tunes 331 to 383, published 1868. (17 Tunes cancelled in this edition.)
Second Appendix, Tunes 384 to 500, published 1875.
Third Appendix, Tunes 501 to 649, published 1883.
Congregational Psalmist Hymnal, published 1885, and edited by W. H. Monk, Mus. Doc.

GHENT, No. 217 S.P. and 157 F.C.H., appears in Part III. of the above, published 1861, and is there anonymous. It is of older date, however.

Converse, Charles Crozat, born at Warren, Mass., October 7, 1834 ; studied in Germany ; was popular as a musician in the neighbourhood of New York about 1850 ; compiler of several music-books for choirs and Sunday-schools ; has been for many years a lawyer and judge, and has charge of the Burdetta Organ Co., Erie, Pennsylvania ; has written under many *noms de plume.* His tune

Paraclete, No. 370 F.C.H., is his most popular piece, and was composed at Brooklyn in 1868.

Cooke, Robert, son of Benjamin Cooke, Mus. Doc.; succeeded his father as organist of St Martin's-in-the-Fields, London, 1793; succeeded Dr Arnold as organist of Westminster Abbey, 1802. He drowned himself in consequence of a love affair, August 22, 1814, aged forty-six. Buried with his father in the west cloisters of Westminster Abbey.

Chant No. 235 in U.P.P. is his, and was composed about 1800. The same Chant is set to S.S., No. 129 U.P.H., "But now is Christ risen."

Coombs, William, known as "Coombs of Bristol," flourished about 1770; dates of birth and death unknown. The writer has been unable to trace any particulars of his life. He composed

Oxford, No. 117 in S.P., where it is wrongly assigned to James Coombs.[1] The form of the tune in the S.P. is similar to that given in the Rev. R. Harrison's 'Sacred Harmony,' vol. i. (1784), where it is named "New Oxford." Earlier copies repeat the second half with a different cadence.

Cooper, George, born in Lambeth, July 7, 1820; appointed organist of St Benet, Paul's Wharf, London, and in 1836 of St Ann and St Agnes; two years later assistant-organist of St Paul's Cathedral; on the death of his father in 1843, succeeded him at St Sepulchre's; on the death of J. B. Sale in 1856 appointed organist of the Chapel Royal; died October 2, 1876; one of the greatest organists of modern times.

St Sepulchre, No. 122 S.H. and 35 in P. and P., was composed in 1836, and published in the Rev. R. R. Chope's 'Congregational Hymn and Tune Book,' 1862. It is also known by the name of "St Agnes."

Cottman, Arthur, son of George and Susan Cottman; by profession a solicitor; amateur musician and composer; died at Ealing, June 3, 1879, aged thirty-seven years. Published about 1872 "Ten Original Tunes," one of which is

Caterham, No. 46 in S.P., which is set to the hymn, "O God, our help in ages past." It afterwards appeared, along with eight others, in the revised and enlarged edition of the 'Bristol Tune Book,' 1876.

---

[1] James Morris Coombs, born at Salisbury; chorister in that cathedral from 21st December 1776 till 1784; appointed organist of Chippenham, 1789; composed services and secular music, and edited a collection of Psalm tunes entitled 'Divine Amusement'; died March 7, 1820, aged fifty-one. It will be observed that James M. Coombs must have been in his infancy when "Oxford" was published.

Courteville, Raphael, organist and political writer, was son or grandson of Raphael Courteville, one of the Gentlemen of the Chapel Royal, and who died December 28, 1675. The organ from the Chapel Royal was presented by Queen Mary in 1691 to the Church of St James's, Westminster; and on September 7 of the same year (1691) a Raphael Courteville, who had been previously a chorister in the Chapel Royal, was appointed the first organist, at a salary of £20 per annum and £4 for a blower. The tune

St James, No. 22 U.P.H., 133 P. and P., 125 U.P.P., 137 S.P., was published in 'Select Psalms and Hymns for the Use of the Parish Church and Tabernacle of St James's, Westminster,' 1697, and is generally considered to be by Courteville. It has been in use in Scotland since 1756. In the S.P. it is wrongly referred to the elder Courteville, who died in 1675.

"It has been supposed," says Mr J. A. Fuller-Maitland in the 'National Dictionary of Biography,' "that Courteville died in 1735, and was succeeded by his son of the same name; but as the Vestry minutes of the parish, in which all appointments, &c., are carefully recorded, contain no mention of such a change of organists, while no record of the father's death can be found, we are compelled to believe that the existence of the son is a mere assumption, made in order to account for the long tenure of the post by a person or persons of the name of Courteville. This conclusion is strengthened by various entries in the Vestry minutes; in January 1752-53, and again in June 1754, letters are written to him warning him that unless he attended personally to the duties of the post he would be dismissed. Whether he endeavoured to perform the duties himself after this we do not know, but he was certainly not dismissed; and shortly afterwards an assistant, 'Mr Richardson,' was appointed. On June 12, 1771, it was reported to the Vestry that Courteville gave this assistant only one quarter of his salary for doing the whole work, and he was thereupon ordered to share the payment equally with Richardson. Seven years before this, in 1764, the assistant, with two others, was consulted as to the state of the organ and the undertaking of repairs to its structure. Neither at this time nor when the improved instrument repaired by Byfield was tried, was Courteville's advice asked in the matter, from which we may conclude that he was long past all work, although he was allowed to keep the post. This Raphael Courteville, whether he be identical with the first organist of the church or not, took a somewhat active part in politics towards the end of Sir Robert Walpole's administration. He married, on the 14th September 1735, a lady named Miss Lucy Green, with a fortune of £25,000. Courteville was the reputed author of the 'Gazetteer,' a paper written in defence of the Government; and it was probably in consequence of this production that he received the nickname of Court-evil. He died early in June 1772, and was buried on the 10th of that month, Richardson being appointed organist."

It is not incredible that a man should hold such an office for eighty years, as Charles Bridgman, who died at Hertford, August 3, 1873, was organist of All Saints' Church there for eighty-one years. He was appointed at the age of thirteen, and conducted the service twice on his ninetieth birthday. He was ninety-five at his death.

It may be noted here that in 1735 there was a Raphael Courteville, jun., as the following inscription, copied by the writer from a tablet in St James's Church, will show: "Near this place lies interred the Body of Elizabeth Courteville, late Daughter to Major Gilbert Abbot, Deceased, and wife of Raphael Courteville, Jun., of this Parish, Gent. . . . *Nat.* 1701, *Obiit* 27th May 1735, Æt. xxxiv."

Croft, William, Mus. Doc., son of Mr William Croft; born at Nether Eatington, Warwickshire; baptised December 30, 1678[1]; chorister of the Chapel Royal under Dr John Blow; first organist of St Anne's, Westminster, 1700 to 1711; appointed organist of the Chapel Royal 1707, and of Westminster Abbey in 1708; received the degree of Mus. Doc. from Oxford University in 1713; died at Bath, August 14, 1727, and buried on the 23d of that month in the north aisle of Westminster Abbey; distinguished as a composer of church music. The following tunes by Croft were first published in Henry Playford's 'The Divine Companion; or, David's Harp New Tun'd,' 1708, where they are nameless:—

EATINGTON, No. 72 in P. and P. and 126 U.P.P., set to Psalm 116.
NORTHAMPTON, No. 115 P. and P., set to Psalm 96.
CROFTS, 148TH, No. 212 P. and P., set to Psalm 136.

---

[1] The following is a copy of the entry of Croft's baptism, which the writer was the first to discover:—
"1678.
"Decemb. 30, Guilielmus, filius Guilielmi Croft, Gen. Bap."

It may be safely affirmed that Croft was born in 1678, not in 1677, although the majority of his biographers give that as the year of birth.

The form of "Northampton" in P. and P. is the same as that given by William Riley (who names it "Trinity") in his 'Parochial Harmony,' 1762. It differs considerably in rhythm from the original, which is here given:—

MELODY OF "NORTHAMPTON" AS COMPOSED BY CROFT.

KEY A.

{| m :r :d | t₁ :— :— | s :f :m | r :— :r |}

{| m :— :s | s :— :fe | s :— :r | r :—.f :m |}

{| f :— :m | m :— :r | m :— :s | d :r :m |}

{| m :— :r.d | d :— :— ||

St Matthew, No. 124 S.H., 325 U.P.H., 177 P. and P., 144 S.P., 55 U.P.P., set to Psalm 33. At the Musical Festival at York in 1823, Catalani was observed to shed tears during the singing of this tune, and was with some difficulty enabled to recover her composure and perform the song of "Angels ever bright and fair," which succeeded the psalm.

Hanover, No. 16 (First Tune) S.H., 289 F.C.H., 207 U.P.H. (called "A new tune to the 149th Psalm of the New Version, and the 104th Psalm of the Old"); St Anne, No. 309 S.H., 128 S.P., 110 F.C.H., 19 U.P.H., 219 U.P.P., 124 P. and P., set to Psalm 42, are found in the sixth and enlarged edition of the 'Supplement to the New Version of Psalms,' 1708, which is said to have been edited by Dr Croft, and they have been in use in Scotland since the middle of last century. As "Hanover" is assigned to Händel in the U.P.H., it may be here remarked that the great master did not arrive in England until 1710, two years after the tune appeared in Playford's book. Other evidence might be adduced to show that it is not his, but probably this fact will be sufficient.

Within the last few years Croft's authorship of "St Anne" has been called in question, that tune being found in the *seventh* edition of Abraham Barber's 'Book of Psalms,' 1715, where it is called "Leeds Tune," and ascribed to a Mr Denby. An earlier copy of the above work has been discovered, published probably in 1696 or 1697, but it does not contain "Leeds Tune." Whether it was added to Barber's collection before the appearance of "St Anne" in the "Supplement" of 1708 is still uncertain.

The harmony at the close of the third strain of this popular tune has been most unjustifiably altered in the Free and Church of Scotland collections. "Editors" (says the late Rev. W. H. Havergal) "fear to follow the worthy Dr Croft, as he followed his predecessors, in commencing the first note of the fourth strain on the tonal FULL chord, because of consecutive fifths. SUCH fifths no old harmonist ever declined."

"Hanover" is introduced by Sir George Alexander Macfarren in his oratorio "St John the Baptist," produced at the Bristol Musical Festival, 1873, and "St Anne" by Sir Arthur S. Sullivan in his "Te Deum Laudamus," for soprano solo, chorus, orchestra, organ, and military band, composed for the Festival held at the Crystal Palace, May 1, 1872, in celebration of the recovery of his Royal Highness the Prince of Wales.

CHANT No. 356 S.H., 222 S.P., 354 U.P.H., and 26 U.P.P. (there assigned to Purcell), is usually assigned to Dr Croft, but is considered by some to be the composition of James Hawkins, Mus. Bac., who was organist of Ely Cathedral, and died in 1729.

The same Chant is set to S.S., No. 121 U.P.H., "Who hath believed our report?"

Crotch, William, born at Norwich, July 5, 1775; from early childhood celebrated for his musical talent; in 1786 became assistant to Dr Randall at King's and Trinity Colleges, Cambridge; at fourteen years of age composed an oratorio, "The Captivity of Judah," which was performed at Trinity Hall, Cambridge, in 1789; appointed organist of Christ Church, Oxford, and in 1797 succeeded Dr Philip Hayes as Professor of Music there; graduated Mus. Bac., Oxford, 1794, and Mus. Doc. 1799; died suddenly at Taunton, December 29, 1847. In 1836 he edited 'Psalm Tunes, Selected for the Use of Cathedrals and Parish Churches.'

EXETER, No. 77 P. and P., is in the above collection named "St Martin's," but is anonymous.

His CHANTS, No. 234 S.P., 250 S.P. and 209 U.P.P., 262 S.P., 118 U.P.P., appear in 'Cathedral Chants,' edited by Bennett and Marshall, 1829.

No. 356 S.H. (Chant II.) appears in 'A Collection of Single and Double Chants,' which he edited in 1842, and is there styled "From an Ancient Harmony."

CHANT in A to S.S., No. 113 U.P.H., "Doth not wisdom cry?" and CHANT in G to S.S., No. 112 U.P.H., "Trust in the Lord." The last is the same as 118 in U.P.P. Chant in A appears in his collection issued in 1842.

Crown of Jesus Music. See Hemy, Henri Frederick.

Crüger, Johann, born at Gross-Brensen, near Guben, in Prussia, April 9, 1598; educated chiefly at the Jesuit College, Olmütz, at the School of Poetry at Regensburg, and at the University of Wittenberg; appointed Cantor of St Nicholas Church, Berlin, in 1622, a post he retained till his death, February 23, 1662. Composer of much excellent church music. Crüger edited in 1644 an important collection of hymns and tunes known as

'Praxis Pietatis Melica,' second edition, 1647. No copy of either of these editions is known to exist. In the third edition, 1648, is found

NUN DANKET, No. 141 S.H., 321 F.C.H., 148 U.P.H., there named "WITTENBERG," is the chorale "Nun danket alle Gott." Mendelssohn employs it in his "Hymn of Praise" (Lobgesang).

BERLIN, No. 325 S.H., 177 F.C.H., 101 (Second Tune) U.P.H., named CYPRUS in the last two collections, is the chorale "Heil'ger Geist du Tröster mein" in 'Praxis Pietatis Melica,' 1656.

SWABIA, No. 133 and 282 S.H., 208 S.P., 232 U.P.P., 139 F.C.H., 161 and 103 U.P.H., is adapted from the chorale, "Nun begeh'n wir das Fest," in an edition of 'Praxis Pietatis Melica' published at Berlin in 1698. As the *Hymn* appears in an edition published in 1661, it is probable the tune is also there.

NURNBERG, No. 200 F.C.H. and 215 S.H., "Wie soll ich dich empfangen," appears in 'Geistliche Lieder,' by Luther and others, which Crüger edited in 1653.

In an edition published in 1657 appears the tune from which is taken
GRÄFENBERG, No. 83 P. and P., 18 S.H., 73 S.P., 108 U.P.H. and 68 U.P.P., "Nun danket All' und bringet Ehr."

Cuisset, Frank, born in London, February 23, 1812; pupil of Sir Henry R. Bishop, Brinley Richards, and Sir George Thomas Smart; organist successively of Holy Trinity Church, Coventry—Bishop Ryden's, Birmingham—Selly Oak Church, Birmingham—Busbridge Church, Godalming, Surrey, where he now is; composer of glees, songs, part-songs, hymn tunes, and church services; author of 'The Vocalist's Indispensable Practice, a Series of Exercises for promoting the Strength and Flexibility of the Voice,' London, 1875. His tune

HARNAL, No. 75 S.P., 98 U.P.P., was first published in 'Congregational Church Music,' London, 1853.

Cummings, William Hayman, born at Sidbury, Devon, August 22, 1831 [1]; chorister in St Paul's Cathedral, London, and the Temple Church; organist of Waltham Abbey; tenor singer in the Temple Church and Westminster Abbey; professor of singing at the Royal College for the Blind, Norwood, London; composer of a cantata "The Fairy Ring," anthems, songs, part-songs, &c.; founded the Purcell Society. Mr Cummings is a noted antiquary, and has cleared up many doubtful points in musical history.

[1] Not 1835 as commonly stated.

CHANTS No. III., set to Hymn No. 333 in F.C.H., are his. The first, in C major, was published in Masters's 'Chant Book'; and the second, in A minor, was first published in the F.C.H., although in use some time previously.

BETHLEHEM, No. 27 S.H., 195 F.C.H., 31 U.P.H., was adapted by Mr Cummings about 1850 for the use of the choir at Waltham Abbey, and published soon after in folio form. The adaptation is a very excellent one, but it is seldom Mr Cummings's work has been acknowledged by editors of hymnals.

Dale, Rev. Reginald Francis, M.A., Mus. Bac.,[1] F.R.A.S., son of Thomas Dale, D.D., Dean of Rochester; born at Sydenham, Kent, September 12, 1845; educated at Queen's College, Oxford, where he graduated Bachelor of Arts, and Bachelor in Music, in 1866; took holy orders in 1870; assistant-master in Westminster School, 1870 to 1886; Rector of Bletchingdon, Oxford, since 1885. His tune

ST CATHERINE, No. 205 F.C.H., is one of 'Twenty-two Original Hymn Tunes by Two Oxford Graduates' (1867).

Darmstädter Gesangbuch, 1698. This collection contains 361 hymns and 123 tunes. Its title is 'Geistreiches Gesangbuch, vormals in Halle gedruckt, nun aber allhier mit Noten der unbekannten Melodien und 123 Liedern vermehrt, zur Ermunterung gläubiger Seelen, mit einer Vorrede Eberhard Philipp Zuehlens, jüngern Stadt - predigers und Definitoris daselbst: Darmstadt, bei Sebastian Griebel,' 1698; or, 'Spiritual Hymn-book, formerly printed at Halle, 1695-97, but now enlarged by 123 Hymns and the Notation of unknown tunes, for the encouragement of believing souls, with a preface by Eberhard Philipp Zuehlen, junior Minister and Definitor there: Darmstadt, Griebel,' 1698. Most of the hymns and tunes were of that period. The writers belong to the school of Spener, and their compositions have a pietistic tendency.

BAVARIA, No. 3 P. and P., is adapted from "Preis, Lob, Ehr, Ruhm, Dank, Kraft und Macht," a copy of which is here given—

---

[1] Wrongly described in F.C.H. as Mus. Doc.

St Gregory, No. 190 and 283 (Second Tunes) S.H., 32 P. and P., is from "Zeuch meinen Geist, triff meine Sinnen," also given below—

```
        KEY F.
SOPRANO. ⎧ :s  | m  :f   :s  | l  :-.t :d' | l  :s   :-.f ⎫
BASS.... ⎩ :d  | d  :r   :m  | f  :-.r :m  | f  :s   :s,  ⎭

⎧ | m  :m  :s   | d  :r   :m  | f  :s   :m  | r  :—   :d   ⎫
⎩ | d  :d  :t,  | l, :t,  :d  | t, :s,  :d  | t, :s,  :l,  ⎭

⎧ | r  :r  :s   | m  :f   :s  | l  :-.t :d' | l  :s   :-.f ⎫
⎩ | s, :s, :s,  | d  :—   :d, | f, :-.r,:d, | f, :s,  :s₂  ⎭

⎧ | m  :—  :s   | d  :r   :m  | f  :s   :m  | r  :r  :-.d | d  :—  ⎫
⎩ | d, :—  :t,  | l, :s,  :d  | f, :—   :d  | f, :s, :s₂  | d, :—  ⎭
```

The copies given above are from 'Freylinghausen's Gesangbuch,' as the writer has failed to meet with a copy of the Darmstadt work. It is not in any of the Darmstadt libraries.

ALL SAINTS, No. 11 (Second Tune) S.H., "Zeuch mich, Zeuch mich den Armen," appears in a more florid form than that given by Störl, 1711.

Darwall, Rev. John (not Darwell, as in U.P.H. and U.P.P.), born at Haughton, Staffordshire, where he was baptised, January 13, 1731; received his education at Manchester School and at Brasenose College, Oxford, where he graduated in 1756; took holy orders, and in 1769 became Vicar of Walsall, Staffordshire, where he died, December 18, 1789. He composed 150 tunes, one for each of the Psalms, of which the tune

DARWALL'S, No. 204 U.P.P., 65 U.P.H., 129 S.H., 216 S.P., 154 F.C.H., 213 P. and P., was the 148th. It appears in Aaron Williams's 'Psalmodist,' 1770.

Day, or **Daye, John,** printer, said to have been born in St Peter's parish, Dunwich, Suffolk, in 1522[1]; settled in London as printer before the middle of the sixteenth century; one of the earliest of English music-printers; produced about 230 works, many of them being of importance; died at Walden in Essex, July 23, 1584, aged sixty-two; buried at Bradley Parva in Suffolk, August the 2d.

Published in 1562 'The Whole Booke of Psalmes, collected into Englysh metre by T. Starnhold, I. Hopkins, and others; conferred with the Ebrue, with apt Notes to synge thē withal, Faithfully

[1] There are no records to verify this date.

perused and alowed according to the ordre appointed in the Quenes maiesties Iniunctions. Imprinted at Lōdon by Iohn Day, dwelling ouer Aldersgate. . . . An. 1562.' This contains German, Genevan, *new* and *native* tunes, the melodies only being given. In this are found

OLD 61ST, No. 41 U.P.P.

OLD 68TH, No. 173 P. and P., 185 U.P.P.

OLD 81st, No. 186 U.P.P., 124 S.H., 174 P. and P.

OLD 137TH, No. 175 P. and P., 37 and 254 U.P.H., 215 U.P.P., 81 F.C.H., 114 S.P.

ROCHESTER, No. 94, 98, 190 S.H., 29 P. and P.

DAY, No. 54 S.P., 47 F.C.H.; 12 S.H., 128 P. and P., where it is named "St Flavian"; No. 66 U.P.P., where it is named "Prescot," are abridged from the following melody in Day's book, where it is set to Psalm 132d :—

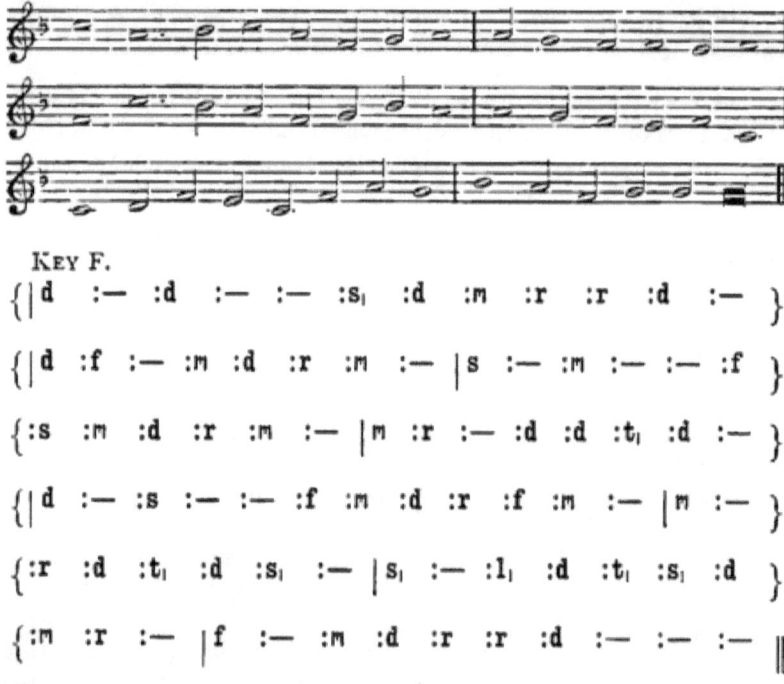

KEY F.

{| d :— :d :— :— :s, :d :m :r :r :d :— }

{| d :f :— :m :d :r :m :— | s :— :m :— :— :f }

{ :s :m :d :r :m :— | m :r :— :d :d :t, :d :— }

{| d :— :s :— :— :f :m :d :r :f :m :— | m :— }

{ :r :d :t, :d :s, :— | s, :— :l, :d :t, :s, :d }

{ :m :r :— | f :— :m :d :r :r :d :— :— :— ||

It is worthy of notice that the melody of the first strain of the Old 81st is identical with the first strain of "Tallis," No. 168 S.P., 67 F.C.H., 70 and 123 U.P.P., 308 U.P.H., 101 and 189 S.H., and the passage forms the opening of Handel's "What though I trace," from which is taken "Solomon," No. 160 S.P. and 150 P. and P.

In the following year (1563) Day published the first English Psalter in parts, adapted to the metrical version of Sternhold and his coadjutors. The tunes were harmonised by Richard Brimle, William Parsons, T. Causton, J. Hake, Richard Edwardes, Nicholas Southerton, M. Shepherd, and Thomas Tallis. It was reprinted in 1565 without material alteration. In the 1563 edition are found

OLD 44TH, No. 182 U.P.P., 97 and 200 U.P.H., 172 P. and P., 59 F.C.H. and 113 S.P.

PRESTON, No. 225 P. and P.

ST MICHAEL, No. 201 P. and P., 58 and 239 S.H., is abridged from the tune set to Psalm 101 in the Genevan Psalter, 1543.

OLD 134TH, No. 162 U.P.H. and 202 U.P.P., 125 F.C.H., 197 S.P., is the same as St Michael. See Genevan Psalters.

Dearle, Edward, Mus. Doc., born at Cambridge, March 2, 1806; chorister at King's, Trinity, and St John's Colleges, Cambridge; organist of St Paul's, Deptford, 1827, and later first organist of Blackheath Park Chapel, both of which appointments he held for some time; organist of St Peter and St Paul Parish Church, Wisbeach, 1832 to 1833; of St Mary Parish Church, Warwick, 1833 to 1835; of St Mary Magdalen Parish Church, and Master of the Song School, Newark-on-Trent, 1835 to 1864; graduated Mus. Bac., Cambridge, 1836; Mus. Doc., 1842—his exercises for these degrees being settings of the Psalms, "Sing unto God" and "I was glad"; since 1864 resident at Camberwell, London.

PENITENTIA, No. 168 (Second Tune) S.H., was first published in 'Church Hymns with Tunes,' edited by Sir A. S. Sullivan, 1874; and KELHAM, No. 3 U.P.P., in Dr Maurice's 'Choral Harmony.'

Decius, Nicolaus, born at Hof in Voigtland, was first a monk and then Prior of Steterburg, or Stettersburg, in Wolfenbüttel, about 1519. Having adopted the principles of the Reformation, he left Steterburg in 1522, and became a schoolmaster at Brunswick. In the following year, 1523, he went to Stettin, where he subsequently became Lutheran Pastor of St Nicholas's Church. He died at Stettin, March 21, 1541.

STETTIN, No. 155 S.H. and 24 U.P.H., is admitted by the best authorities to be an adaptation by him from an old melody of the Latin Church. It is assigned to Hans Kugelmann in the U.P.H., probably because it is found in his 'Concentus Nova,' published at Augsburg in 1540.

Denham, Henrie, published a Psalter in 1588. This is said to contain

DENHAM or SOUTHWELL, No. 207 S.P. and 185 P. and P., set to Psalm 70. It is in 'Barton's Psalms,' 1644, where it is named "Southwell Tune, proper for sad ditties, as the 13th Psalm." In 'Ravenscroft's Psalter,' 1621, it is described as a "Northern Tune," and is arranged by Martin Peirson, Mus. Bac.

Dibdin, Henry Edward, youngest son of Charles Dibdin the younger; born at Sadler's Wells, London, September 8, 1813; pupil of his elder sister Mary Anne, afterwards Mrs Tonna, who was an excellent harpist and musician; studied the harp under her and Bochsa; performed also on the viola and organ; his first public appearance was at Covent Garden Theatre, on August 3, 1832, when he played the harp at Paganini's last concert; settled in Edinburgh in 1833; honorary organist of Trinity Chapel, Edinburgh; skilled as an artist and illuminator; died May 6, 1866.

Edited, in conjunction with J. T. Surenne, 'A Collection of Church Music, consisting of Chants, Psalm and Hymn Tunes, principally Original, . . . Arranged for Four Voices, with an Accompaniment for the Organ or Pianoforte,' 1843—a supplement appearing in 1844. In 1865 he compiled 'The Praise Book.' The work by which he will be best remembered is 'The Standard Psalm Tune Book,' 1852, a large and important collection of old church tunes, but which is notoriously untrustworthy as regards the source and authorship of the tunes. From it are taken

UXBRIDGE, No. 159, and WOBURN, No. 166, P. and P. They are probably tunes of last century.

SOLDAU, No. 229 U.P.P., 169 U.P.H., 103 S.H., 38 P. and P., is an adaptation by him from the Chorale "Nun Bitten Wir," published in 'Luther's Psalter,' 1524.

Doane, William Howard, Mus. Doc., born at Preston, New London County, Connecticut, February 3, 1832; is the principal of the firm of A. J. Fay & Co., manufacturers of wood-working machinery in Cincinnati, Ohio; conductor of Norwich (Conn.) Harmonic Society; from 1862 to the present time has published about thirty collections of music for church and Sunday-school; degree of Mus. Doc., conferred on him by Denison University, Ohio, 1875. His tunes

EVANGEL, No. 174 S.H. and 356 F.C.H.; FAITH, No. 216 F.C.H., 419 S.H. (there named "Arms of Jesus"); and RESCUE, No. 146 S.H., were published in 'Songs of Devotion for Christian Associations,' which he edited, in 1870.

Dobson, John, sometime of Manchester; latterly resident at Richmond, Surrey; well known as a collector of Psalmody, of which he accumulated over three thousand volumes; died at Richmond, May 1, 1888, aged seventy-four; buried at Ardwick Cemetery, Manchester. Edited 'Tunes New and Old,' for use in the Methodist Church. The following are the dates of the various editions:—1st and 2d, 1864; 3d and 4th, 1865; 5th, 1866; 6th, 1867; 7th, 1869; 8th, 1871; 9th, 1873; 10th and 11th, 1876; 12th and 13th, 1877.

LEBANON, No. 93 S.P., was composed by Mr Dobson for the hymn, "All hail the power of Jesus' name," and first published in the 10th edition. The harmony is by Dr Bridge.

Dolomite Chant.
CHANT, No. 213 S.P.

Dougall, Neil, son of Neil Dougall and Jean Moir, was born at Greenock, December 9, 1776. His father (a wright by trade) was impressed into the service of his country, and died in the island of Ceylon, when Neil, the subject of the present notice, was about four years of age. He (Neil) afterwards removed to Cartsdyke with his mother, living in a small property which was now inherited by him. He was kept regularly at school till he was fifteen years of age. Fond of boating and the sea, like most boys brought up in a seaport town, he determined to be a sailor, and in 1791 was bound an apprentice on board the ship Britannia. Neil made three voyages to New York, and became a favourite with captain and owners. In 1793 war broke out with France, and the ship was laid up at Greenock. Captain William Mathie, a son of one of Neil's employers, purchased a little ship called the Clarence Yacht. He fitted her up with ten guns, and procured a letter of marque authorising him to make reprisals on the high seas. Neil was offered a transference to this vessel, which he readily accepted. He sailed for nearly a year between Shetland and the Mediterranean, finding himself still in Captain Mathie's ship at Greenock in June 1794, on the 14th day of which month news reached the seaport of Lord Howe's great victory over the French fleet. All armed vessels in port were instructed to fire a salute. Captain

Mathie was very loyal, and entered heartily into the rejoicings. He, his mate, and three apprentices, the eldest of whom was Neil, were all that were on board. Neil was ready with match in hand to fire one of the guns, when the captain hailed an old man-of-war's-man, who was looking on, and asked him to jump on board and lend them a hand. He did so; and, taking the match from Neil, fired the gun. Neil, ready for duty, sprang on the gun-carriage, and proceeded to sponge the gun; but a stupid fellow neglected to stop the touch-hole at the same moment, the result being that a spark was left within the gun. Never thinking of danger, Neil proceeded to reload the gun with a cartridge consisting of three pounds of gunpowder, and was just in the act of ramming home, when it went off, carrying away his right hand, and the outer portion of his arm up to the elbow, tearing the flesh off his right cheek, and completely depriving him of his eyesight. He fell into the water, but was immediately picked up and conveyed to his mother's house at Cartsdyke, where the two doctors who attended him found it necessary to amputate his right arm above the elbow. At first some slight hopes were entertained of a partial recovery of his left eye, but these were speedily blasted by the opinion of an eminent oculist, who came purposely to examine him. This was a sad calamity to a person of Neil's active temperament, but the kindness of a wide circle of friends, who read and conversed with him, soon reconciled him to his fate. In 1798 he was urged by friends to attend a singing-class taught by Mr Robert Duncan, precentor of the East Parish Church, Greenock. He objected, thinking people would laugh at one of his age joining a singing-class; but a friend offering to accompany him, he consented. So rapid was his progress in the study of music under Mr Duncan, that in the autumn of 1799 his friends urged him to open a singing-class, which he held annually till 1844, when he was compelled by infirmity, and especially the failure of his voice, to give up teaching altogether. In 1800 he gave his first public concert, and continued to give a concert annually until the year 1860. As early as 1810 he contributed the tune "Naples" to R. A. Smith's 'Devotional Music.' His compositions consist of about one hundred psalm and hymn tunes, an anthem from the 136th Psalm, and about a dozen songs and other pieces. He published a small volume of poems in 1854. Dougall died at Greenock, October 1, 1862. His tune

KILMARNOCK, No. 98 in P. and P., 87 S.P., and 96 U.P.P., was composed about 1823, and was widely circulated in MS. before it received a place in Brown's Robertson's 'Selection of the Best Psalm and Hymn Tunes,' published about 1834.

Its origin may be briefly told. Dougall's attention having been drawn to the peculiarity of the tune "Morven" (built on what is commonly termed the Caledonian scale—viz., without the fourth or seventh in the melody), resolved to compose one on the same principle, "Kilmarnock" being the result. It shared the fate of his other tunes—a place among his scraps. "One day R. A. Smith and John Taylor, who was then precentor in the Middle Parish Church at Greenock, paid him a visit. After conversation, Smith said, 'Anything new doing, Mr Dougall? no scraps to divert us?' Mr Dougall went to a drawer and brought the first few scraps of paper he could lay his hand on. Smith took up one, and hastily humming it over, said—'A *very* pretty melody; and what do you call it?' 'It's not christened yet,' was the answer; 'but do you observe anything peculiar about it?' 'I do,' said Smith; 'it is on the Caledonian scale, the same as "Morven."' 'Yes; the same as your tune.' 'No, no; not my tune,' said Smith. 'Will you oblige me with a copy of your nameless tune?' 'With pleasure,' said the composer, 'and we'll christen't "Kilmarnock"'; and thus ended the conference."

Drese, Adam, born in Thuringia, December 1620; studied music at Warsaw under Marco Scacchi; music director at Weimar from 1655; afterwards held similar appointments to the Duke of Brunswick, and at Arnstadt, where he died, February 15, 1701. His tune

DARMSTADT, No. 301 F.C.H., 236 S.H. (there named "Haarlem"), 217 U.P.H. (there named "Zinzendorf"), was composed for use in his family devotions, and was sung in his house as early as 1690. It first appears in print in the Halle 'Gesangbuch,' 1697; and it subsequently occurs in the Darmstadt 'Gesangbuch,' 1698, and in Freylinghausen's 'Gesangbuch,' 1704. It is associated with the hymn, "Seelenbräutigam, Jesu Gotteslamm."

The following occurs in the notice of Drese's death in the Arnstadt Church Records, and proves that the dates of Drese's birth and death are incorrectly given in the S.H.: "On the 15th February 1701, at 10 o'clock in the evening, Herr Adam Drese fell asleep in God. . . . Age, 80 years 2 months."

[Den 15 Febr. 1701, Abends um zehn Uhr ist in Gott selig entschlafen Herr Adam Drese. . . . Alter 80 Jahre 2 Monate.]

Dretzell, Cornelius Heinrich, born at Nürnberg in 1705; successively organist of the churches of St Egide, St Laurent, and St Sébald, all in his native town. He played the organ in the last-named church till he died in 1773.

BOZRAH, No. 56 U.P.H., is adapted from the Chorale "Meinen Jesum will ich danken," in his 'Choralbuch,' which he issued in 1731, and will be found on page 24.

Dublin Hymn-book. A Collection of Hymns and Sacred Poems.—Dublin: Printed by S. Powell, in Crane Lane, 1749. At the end, among "Tunes adapted in the foregoing Hymns," is

IRISH, No. 96 P. and P., 131 U.P.P., 84 S.P., in the key of G, noted in minims, and without name. It has invariably been assigned to Isaac Smith, because it appears in his collection issued about 1770, but it is *not* marked with the asterisk prefixed by him to the tunes of his own composition. In the U.P.P. it is assigned to Benjamin Milgrove, on what authority it is difficult to know.

The tune is named "Irish" by Ashworth in his collection published about 1765.

It is named "Irish" in Robert Gilmour's 'Psalm Singer's Assistant,' Glasgow, no date; and in the second edition, Paisley, 1793; also in Henry Boyd's Collection, Glasgow, 1793. This seems to be its first appearance in a Scotch Psalmody.

Dupuis, Thomas Sanders, born in London, November 5, 1730, son of John Dupuis, of a Huguenot refugee family settled in London; chorister in the Chapel Royal; organist and composer to the Chapel Royal, 1779; graduated Mus. Bac. and Mus. Doc., Oxford, 1790; died in London, July 17, 1796.

CHANT, No. 78 in U.P.P., also 235 S.P.; CHANT, No. 355 S.H. (A minor), 353 S.H., CHANT I., are from 'Sixteen Double and Single Chants, as performed at the Chapel Royal, &c.,' published before 1790.

CHANT, No. 254 S.P., is from 'A Second Set of Chants Composed for the Use of his Majesty's Chapel.'

CHANT, No. 333 F.C.H., is probably adapted from some of his works.

Dykes, Rev. John Bacchus, born at Kingston-upon-Hull, March 10, 1823; received his first musical tuition from Skelton, organist of St John's, where his grandfather was incumbent; obtained a scholarship at St Catherine's Hall, Cambridge, and during his stay there pursued his musical studies under Professor Walmisley, and became conductor of the University Musical Society; graduated as B.A. in 1847, and having taken holy orders in the same year, obtained the curacy of Malton, Yorkshire; in 1849 appointed minor canon and precentor of Durham Cathedral; in 1850 proceeded to the degree of M.A., and in 1861 had conferred on him by the University of Durham the degree of Doctor of Music; in 1862 was presented by the Dean and Chapter to the vicarage of St Oswald, Durham, on which he resigned the precentorship; died at St Leonards-on-Sea, January 22, 1876. It is admitted on all hands that as a writer of hymn tunes Dr Dykes stands unequalled. He was an able organist, and it was not uncommon for him during the illness of his organist to take that gentleman's place at the organ, read the lessons, &c., and preach the sermon. His tunes

DIES IRÆ, No. 89 S.H.;
HOLLINGSIDE, No. 192 S.H., 186 F.C.H., 133 U.P.H.;
HORBURY, No. 241 S.H. (First Tune);
MELITA, No. 21 S.H., 41 F.C.H., 327 U.P.H.;
NICÆA, No. 1 S.H., 1 U.P.H., 295 F.C.H.;
ST CROSS, No. 38 S.H., 26 F.C.H.;
ST CUTHBERT, No. 96 S.H., 274 F.C.H., 98 U.P.H.;
were first published in 'Hymns Ancient and Modern,' 1861.

GERONTIUS, No. 49 S.H.;
PAX DEI, No. 293 S.H.;
VOX DILECTI, No. 197 S.H., 81 F.C.H.;
in the Appendix to 'Hymns Ancient and Modern,' 1868.

ALFORD, No. 219 F.C.H.;
ALMSGIVING, No. 127 S.H., 18 U.P.H., 281 F.C.H.;
COME UNTO ME, No. 208 F.C.H.;
COMMENDATIO, No. 45 S.H.;
REQUIESCAT, No. 257 S.H.;
STABAT MATER, No. 41 S.H.;
VENI CITO, No. 88 S.H.;
in the Revised and Enlarged Edition of 'Hymns Ancient and Modern,' 1875.

ELVET, No. 97 U.P.P.;
ST AELRED, No. 225 S.H., 271 F.C.H.;
ST ANATOLIUS, No. 294 S.H. (Second Tune);
ST BEES, No. 161 S.H. (First Tune), 164 F.C.H.;
ST GODRIC, No. 392 S.H., 151 F.C.H., 320 U.P.H.;
ST SYLVESTER, No. 310 S.H.;
were first published in 'The Congregational Hymn and Tune Book,' edited by the Rev. R. R. Chope, B.A., 1862.

The last line of "St Aelred" originally ended in the minor and in common time, thus—

KEY E♭ (Lah is C).

SOPRANO.	d	:r	d	:—
ALTO.....	l₁	:l₁	l₁	:—
TENOR....	f	:f	m	:—
BASS.......	f₁	:r₁	l₁	:—

It was altered to its present form for the Appendix to 'Hymns Ancient and Modern,' 1868.

FERRIER, No. 367 S.H. and 348 F.C.H., appears without a name in 'Accompanying Tunes to the Hymns for Infant Children,' which was edited by Dr Dykes in 1862. It bears its present name in the Rev. R. Brown-Borthwick's 'Supplemental Tune Book.'

FAITH, No. 90 U.P.P. and 65 S.P., is one of six tunes composed by Dr Dykes for 'Psalms and Hymns for Divine Worship,' London (Nisbet & Co.), 1867.

ST OSWALD, No. 143 and 407 S.H., 228 F.C.H., was first published in 'A Manual of Psalm and Hymn Tunes,' edited by the Hon. and Rev. John Grey, 1857.

ST AGNES DURHAM, No. 170 S.H. (Part I.), 75 U.P.H., 69 F.C.H., 125 S.P., was first published in 'A Hymnal for Use in the English Church, with Accompanying Tunes,' 1866, which was also edited by the Hon. and Rev. John Grey.

ROCK OF AGES, No. 149 (Second Tune), 178 (Part II.) S.H., was composed for a Children's Hymnal published at New York in 1874, to the hymn from which it takes its name. It was first published in this country in the S.H.

LUX BENIGNA, No. 246 S.H., 310 F.C.H., appears in the Appendix to 'Hymns Ancient and Modern,' 1868, under that name, but it does not seem to have been *first* published there. In 'The Parish Tune Book,' compiled by George F. Chambers, F.R.A.S., Harmonies revised by R. Redhead, London, 1868, it is named "St Oswald."

SLINGSBY, No. 117 F.C.H., was composed for the Rev. R. Brown-Borthwick's 'Supplemental Tune Book.'

SANCTUARY, No. 119 S.H., seems to have gained acceptance through 'Hymns Ancient and Modern,' although published elsewhere before appearing in that work.

Ebdon, Thomas, son of Thomas Ebdon, cordwainer (shoemaker); born at Durham, 1738; baptised July 30, St Oswald's Parish. It is thought that he received his early musical education as a chorister at Durham Cathedral, as the name and date, "T. Ebdon, 1755," is still (1891) to be seen carved on the north side of the oak screen which divides the choir from one of the aisles. In 1763 he succeeded James Heseltine as organist and choirmaster of Durham Cathedral, an office he held till his death, September 23, 1811. Buried in St Oswald's churchyard.

S.S., No. 14 F.C.H. (Sanctus III.), Doxology 17 U.P.H. (Sanctus II.), "Holy, holy, holy," is from his Service in C published in 'Sacred Music composed for the Use of the Choir of Durham,' by Thomas Ebdon, organist of that Cathedral, London (1790).

Elliott, James William, born at Warwick, February 13, 1833; chorister at Leamington Parish Church 1846 to 1848; pupil of Sir George Macfarren and others; organist of Leamington Episcopal Chapel (now Christ Church), 1847 to 1852; organist of Parish Church, Banbury, 1860 to 1862; St Mary, Boltons, Brompton, 1862 to 1864; All Saints', St John's Wood, 1864 to 1874; since then of St Mark's Church, Hamilton Terrace. Mr Elliott has compiled several works of great utility for the harmonium, and has composed a number of good songs and glees. Among the former may be mentioned "Hybrias the Cretan," one of the best bass songs of modern production. The first correct version of his tune

DAY OF REST, No. 315 (First Tune) and 341 (Second Tune) S.H., was published in the Revised and Enlarged Edition of 'Hymns Ancient and Modern,' 1875.

Elvey, Sir George Job, Mus. Doc., born at Canterbury, March 27, 1816, and educated at the Cathedral School there; graduated Mus. Bac., Oxford, 1838; Mus. Doc., 1840; organist at St George's Chapel, Windsor, from 1835 to 1882; knighted 1871; composer of much excellent church music. His tunes

URSWICKE, No. 10 (Second Tune) S.H., and WELLESLEY, No. 273, were composed for the 'Children's Hymn Book' (1881).

DIADEMATA, No. 70 S.H., was first published in the 'Appendix to Hymns Ancient and Modern,' 1868; ADORATION, No. 67 S.H., in the 'New Mitre Hymnal,' 1874; LITTLE CHILDREN, No. 388 S.H., in 'Christmas Carols,' edited by Dr Stainer, 1871.

ST GEORGE'S, WINDSOR, No. 5 and 300 S.H., 192 F.C.H., and 52 U.P.H., was composed for 'A Selection of Psalm and Hymn Tunes,' edited and arranged by E. H. Thorne, and adapted to 'Psalms and Hymns,' compiled by the Rev. T. B. Morrell and the Rev. W. W. How, 1858.

ST CRISPIN, No. 148 S.H., was composed for an enlarged edition of the same work published in 1862.

ELVEY, No. 64 S.H. and 303 F.C.H., was composed in 1858 for Dr Maurice's 'Choral Harmony,' with Supplement, where it is named "Windsor Castle."

PILGRIMAGE, No. 246 F.C.H., was first published in the 'Appendix to Hymns Ancient and Modern,' 1868.

S.S., No. 84 U.P.H., "Arise, shine, for thy light is come," was composed for the 'Musical Times,' and first appeared there November 1, 1861.

Este, Thomas, was a printer in London between the years 1588 and 1624. In 1592 he published 'The Whole Booke of Psalmes, with their wonted Tunes, as they are Song in Churches, composed into Foure Parts.' It contains the old church and nine new tunes, harmonised by the following composers: George Kirbye, William Cobbold, Richard Allison, Edward Blancks, Michael Cavendish, John Douland, John Farmer, Giles Farnaby, Edmund Hooper, and Edward Johnston. Este's Psalter contains fifty-seven distinct tunes, exclusive of those of the 'Spiritual Songs and Hymns.' This was the first Psalter in which the tunes are named—"Cheshire Tune," "Kentish Tune," and "Glassenburie Tune," being thus distinguished—

WINCHESTER, No. 23 and 203 S.H., 165 P. and P., 178 S.P., 178 U.P.P., 291 and Dox. 2 U.P.H. (named "*Old* Winchester" in U.P. Collections), set to Psalm 84th. See Tye, Christopher.

CHESHIRE, No. 60 P. and P., 47 S.P., 52 U.P.P., 180 U.P.H. (there named "Chester"), set to Psalm 146; DUNDEE, No. 1 U.P.P., 69 P. and P., 57 S.P., set to Psalm 116, appear in the above work. "Dundee," like "Winchester," is an adaptation from Dr Tye. See that name.

CANTERBURY or PASTON, No. 207 S.H., 58 P. and P., 104 U.P.P., is there set to Psalm 4, without a name, and in the following form :—

EVANGELISCHE—EWING.   121

KEY F.
{| d :m | — :r | m :d | r :m | f :— ‖ f :m }
{| — :r | d :l, | r :— ‖ r :— | r :m | r :d }
{| d :t, | d :— ‖ m :— | r :d | d :t, | d :— ‖

The form of melody in S.H. and P. and P. is that given by Playford. See that name.

Evangelische Gezangen. A Collection of Psalms and Tunes published at Amsterdam at the beginning of the present century. First edition, 1803; second edition, 1804; third edition, 1805. The earliest edition the writer has seen is one issued in 1806, which contains on page 25

HOLLAND, No. 90 P. and P., with the following ending :—

KEY F.
{ :s | f :m | f :s | d :— | — ‖

Ewing, Alexander, son of Alexander Ewing, M.D.; born in the parish of Old Machar, Aberdeen, January 3, 1830; educated for the law at Marischal College, Aberdeen, but entered the army in 1855, and now holds the rank of staff-paymaster, with the honorary rank of lieutenant-colonel; received a medal for services in China during the campaign of 1860; married in 1867 Juliana Horatia, second daughter of the Rev. Alfred Gatty, D.D., vicar of Ecclesfield, and sub-dean of York Cathedral, well known by her writings for the young, and who died at Bath, May 1885. Lieut.-Colonel Ewing is a most accomplished amateur musician.

EWING, No. 275 S.H., 251 U.P.H., 212 F.C.H., was composed in 1853, and published in the same year on single slips. The following line will indicate the original rhythm :—

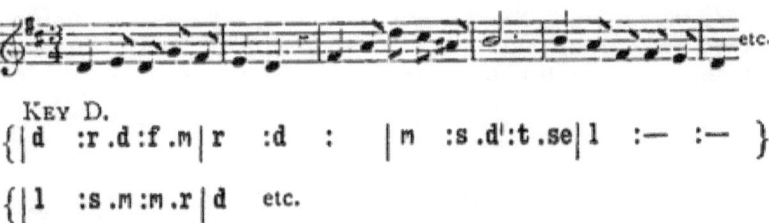

KEY D.
{| d :r.d:f.m| r :d : | m :s.d':t.se| l :— :— }
{| l :s.m:m.r| d   etc.

It was composed for a portion—but a different portion—of Dr Neale's translation of the Latin hymn of which the words to which it has generally been sung form a part, the portion beginning "For thee, O dear dear country." The tune seems to have been first published in common time in 'Hymns Ancient and Modern,' 1861, and this was done without reference to the composer, who was then in a distant quarter of the globe, but in other respects no alterations were made on the tune. "In my opinion," says the composer, "the alteration of the rhythm has very much vulgarised my little tune. It now seems to me a good deal like a polka. I hate to hear it."

The tune was often erroneously assigned to the late Bishop Ewing of Argyll (a relation of Lieut.-Colonel Ewing), until Mr Carnie, of Aberdeen, pointed out the real composer.

Farrant, Richard, a composer of sacred music, was born about 1530. He was one of the Gentlemen of the Chapel Royal, but resigned on becoming Master of the Children of St George's Chapel, Windsor, of which he is said to have been also a lay vicar and organist. On November 5, 1569, he was reappointed a Gentleman of the Chapel Royal, and remained such until his death, November 30, 1580. The tune

FARRANT, No. 67 S.P., 99 and 231 S.H., 35 U.P.P., 89 F.C.H., 43, 82, 157, 272 U.P.H., and 78 P. and P., is an adaptation by Dr Edward Hodges from S.S. No. 87 U.P.H., "Lord, for Thy tender mercies' sake," usually assigned to Farrant, but attributed by earlier writers to John Hilton, organist of St Margaret's Church, Westminster, who died about the middle of the seventeenth century. It is printed with the name of Farrant as its composer in Page's 'Harmonia Sacra,' 1800.

CHANT, No. 224 in S.P., and 77 U.P.P., is taken from the same anthem.

Feilden, Rev. Oswald Mosley, M.A., youngest son of the Rev. Robert Mosley Feilden, rector of Bebbington, Cheshire; born at Canterbury, September 16, 1837; educated at Eton and Christ Church, Oxford; graduated in 1859; ordained at St Asaph, 1861; curate of Whittington, Salop, to the present Bishop of Bedford, and by him appointed to the perpetual curacy of Welsh Frankton, Salop, 1865. His tune

ST JOHN BAPTIST, No. 208 S.H., was published in E. H. Thorne's 'A Selection of Psalm and Hymn Tunes for Morrell and How's Psalms and Hymns,' enlarged edition, 1862. The harmony of the tune is Mr Thorne's.

Felton, Rev. William, B.A., Oxford, 1733; M.A. 1736; vicar-choral in Hereford Cathedral 1741; afterwards minor canon; vicar of Norton Canon, 1751; died December 6, 1769, aged fifty-four; an excellent musician and a noted performer on the harpsichord and organ.

FABIAN, No. 278 U.P.H. and 269 F.C.H., is founded on his "Burial Chant," which appears in Harrison's 'Sacred Harmony,' vol. ii. (1791).

Filitz, Friedrich, Ph. Doc., was born at Arnstadt, in Thuringia, March 16, 1804. He studied philosophy, in which he received the degree of doctor; resided at Berlin from 1843 to 1847, removing in the latter year to Munich, where he died, December 8, 1876.[1] The following tunes are from his 'Vierstimmiges Choralbuch,' Berlin (1847), where they are marked as new:—

CAPETOWN, No. 289 S.H., 280 F.C.H. "Morgenglanz der Ewigkeit" (No. 139).

CASWALL, No. 411 S.H., 107 S.P. (there named "Neander"), 256 F.C.H. (there named "Filitz"), 347 U.P.H. (there named "Basil"). "Wem in Leidenstagen" (No. 203).

CONSTANCE, No. 49 U.P.H. (Second Tune). "Der Tag vertreibt die finstre Nacht" (No. 32).

KIRKMAY, No. 102 P. and P. "Ich singe dir mit Herz und Mund" (No. 93).

MANNHEIM, No. 229 and 348 S.H., 214 U.P.H., 247 F.C.H., is an altered copy of the chorale, "Auf! auf! weil der Tag erschienen" (No. 12). It was first published in its present form in 'Congregational Church Music,' London (1853).

ORIGINAL FORM OF "MANNHEIM" AS IN FILITZ'S 'CHORALBUCH.'

[1] Not 1860, as given by some, as the following extract from the Royal "Polizei-Direction" at Munich will show: "Dr Friedrich Filitz, man of letters, belonging to Arnstadt, died here at the age of seventy-two on 8th December 1876."

Key F.

{| d :m | s   :s | l   :s | f   :— | m   :— || s   :s }
{| l :s | ta :l | s   :— | f   :— || m :f | s   :d }
{| m :r | d   :— || d :d | r   :d | ta, :ta, | l, :— ||
{| d :d | r   :d | r   :f | f   :m | f   :— || l   :s }
{| f :m | f   :m | r   :— | d   :— || r :r | m   :d }
{| f :m | r   :— | d   :— ||

Finch, Edward, fifth son of Heneage, first Earl of Nottingham; born 1664; proceeded M.A. in 1679, and became Fellow of Christ's College, Cambridge; represented the University of Cambridge in the Parliament of 1689-90; ordained deacon at York in 1700; rector of Wigan; appointed prebendary of York, April 26, 1704; of Canterbury, February 8, 1710; died at York, February 14, 1737-38. Author of 'A Grammar for Thorough-Bass, with Examples,' the MS. of which is in the Euing Library, Glasgow.

CHANT, No. 333 in F.C.H., is assigned to him.

Fischer, Michael Gotthardt, born June 3, 1773, in the village of Alach, near Erfurt; pupil of Kittel; in 1802 appointed concert-master and organist of the Barfüsser Church, Erfurt; in 1809 succeeded Kittel as organist in the Prediger Church there. At the same time he became music teacher at the seminary; died January 12, 1829. Famous for his skill as an organist. Published at Gotha 'Choral Melodies for the Evangelical Church'; Division I., 1820; Division II., 1821. On pages 153 and 154 of the first division will be found

MARIENBERG, No. 308 F.C.H., assigned to one Scheibner, who contributes several tunes to the work, and set to the hymn "Gesund mit frohem Muthe." The reading of the last line in the F.C.H. is abbreviated from the original, which is here given—

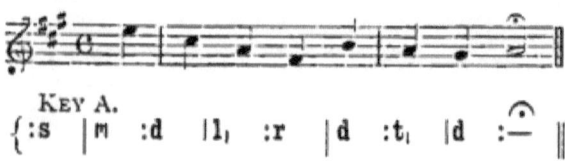

Key A.
{ :s | m :d | l, :r | d :t, | d :— ||

Fischer, William Gustavus, son of John Henry Fischer, a baker of Ludwigsburg, Würtemberg, Germany; born at Baltimore, Maryland, U.S. of America, October 14, 1835; studied under different masters; when a boy he led the singing in a Lutheran church; in 1859 elected teacher of music at Girard College, an office he resigned about ten years after; now a music-seller in Philadelphia; composer of many popular hymn tunes, one of which,

VALLEY OF BLESSING, No. 428 in S.H., was composed in 1868, and published on single slips.

Fish, J., a Lancashire composer of hymn tunes towards the end of last century.

BLACKBURN, No. 10 U.P.P., is generally considered in Lancashire to be his composition. It appears in Harrison's 'Sacred Harmony,' vol. i. (1784), and is anonymous. Some writers have ascribed it to Henry Purcell, but it may be safely said he had no connection with the tune. It is in Henry Boyd's 'Psalmody,' published at Glasgow in 1793, which seems to be its first appearance in a Scotch collection.

Flintoft, Rev. Luke, graduated as B.A. at Queen's College, Cambridge, in 1700; priest-vicar at Lincoln Cathedral from 1704 till 1714; vicar in Worcester Cathedral about 1714; gentleman of the Chapel Royal, 1715; reader in the chapel at Whitehall, 1719; minor canon of Westminster Abbey; died November 3, 1727, and was buried in the cloisters of Westminster Abbey.

CHANT, No. 236 S.P., 29 U.P.P., is in Vandernan's Collection, 1770, and was published probably a year or two earlier. It is an adaptation by Flintoft from the tune given below, which is found without a name in Playford's 'Psalms and Hymns in Solemn Music, in Foure Parts,' 1671—

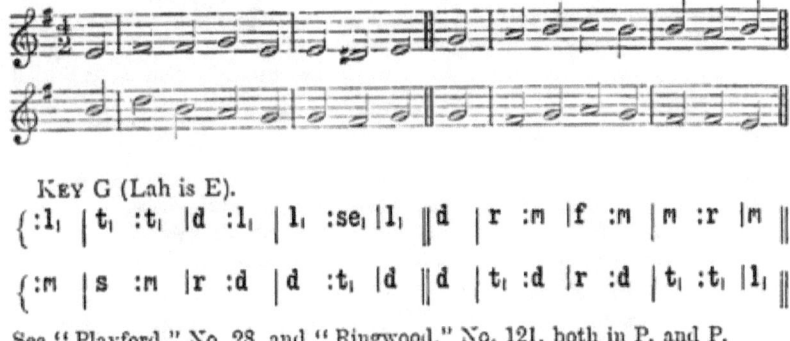

KEY G (Lah is E).

{ :l₁ | t₁ :t₁ | d :l₁ | l₁ :se₁ | l₁ ‖ d | r :m | f :m | m :r | m ‖

{ :m | s :m | r :d | d :t₁ | d ‖ d | t₁ :d | r :d | t₁ :t₁ | l₁ ‖

See "Playford," No. 28, and "Ringwood," No. 121, both in P. and P.

Foster, James, a self-taught musician, born at Bristol, September 12, 1807; by trade a builder; for some time honorary organist of the Bristol Tabernacle; assisted in the compilation and editing of Waite's " Hallelujah," in 1842; composer of many hymns and tunes; died at Bristol, June 7, 1885. His tune

CLAREMONT, No. 48 in S.P., was composed for the hymn, "There is a land of pure delight," and first published in 'The Bristol Tune Book,' 1863.

Frank, Michael, born at Schleusingen, March 16, 1609; educated at the Gymnasium in his native town; apprenticed to a baker in Coburg; married in 1628, from which time till 1640 he was a master baker in Schleusingen; after various misfortunes in time of war he returned to Coburg; died September 24, 1677. Frank devoted much time to poetry and music, and in 1657 published 'Geistliches Harpffenspiel,' a collection of thirty-six sacred songs, with tunes of his own composition, one of which is

MEININGEN, No. 193 P. and P., "Kein Stündlein geht dahin." Wrongly assigned in P. and P. and other collections to Melchior Frank.

Frech, Johann Georg, son of Johann Michael Frech, a watchmaker and organ-builder, was born at Kaltenthal, near Stuttgart, January 17, 1790. He became assistant-master of the school at Degerloch, near Stuttgart, when only sixteen years old. He afterwards studied music under J. H. Knecht and others, and in 1811 settled at Esslingen as assistant in a school, and a year later became teacher, and afterwards music director in the seminary, and organist of the church in that town. He died at Esslingen August 23, 1864. His compositions consist of psalms, motetts, songs, organ pieces, an oratorio—" Abraham "—and an opera—" Montezuma." His tune

ASPURG, No. 201 S.H. and 47 P. and P., 179 U.P.P., 88 in S.P., 52 F.C.H. (named in the two last collections "Kornthal"), is the choral "Die Ernt' ist da, es winkt der Halm" in 'Vierstimmige Choralmelodien zum Gebrauch in Kirchen und Schulen,' Stuttgart, 1844, which he edited in conjunction with Dr Conrad Kocher and Dr Friedrich Silcher.

French Melody.

AMBERG, No. 221 and 277 S.H. The original of the above appears in ' Pierre Attaignant's Thirty-four Chansons Musical,' Paris, 1529, in a piece by Claudin de Sermisy. It is an adaptation of an old French song, "Ill me suffist de tous mes maux." It is employed by Bach in his 'Grosse Passions Musik,' and set to " Was mein Gott will das gescheh allzeit."

COBLENTZ, No. 102 U.P.H., 97 S.H., 236 F.C.H., there named " Old 42d " because found in the Genevan Psalter set to that Psalm. It is adapted from the melody of a hunting song, which was a favourite of Henry II. of France when Dauphin, about 1542. This is probably the reason why Dr Layriz and others assign it to him.

REDHEAD, No. 25 S.H. (Second Tune), is adapted by Redhead from a melody that was in use in France as early as the twelfth century.

Freylinghausen, Rev. Johann Anastasius, son of the Burgomaster of Gandersheim, in Wolfenbüttel, born December 2 or 11, 1670; educated at the University of Jena, and at Halle; succeeded Franke, his father-in-law, as minister of St Ulric's Church at Halle and director of the Orphan Houses in 1727; died February 12, 1739. Edited an important collection of hymns and tunes in 1704 for use of the Orphan Houses at Halle, entitled 'Geistreiches Gesangbuch.'

BERLIN, No. 169 F.C.H. (First Tune), 35 U.P.H. (there named "Carinthia"), is the chorale "Gott sei Dank in aller Welt," on page 5 of an edition issued in 1705.

LÜBECK, No. 200 and 234 S.H. (First Tune), is another form of the same chorale.

HALLE, No. 325 S.H. (Second Tune), "Heil'ger Geist du Tröster mein," is in his 'Neues Geistreiches Gesangbuch,' 1714, and will be found on page 163.

Fripp, Edward Bowles, son of Mr Samuel Fripp; born at Kingsdown, Bristol, January 29, 1787; a self-taught musician; amateur organist and composer; honorary organist of St James's Church, Bristol, for many years; also at Westbury, Gloucestershire, and Hutton, near Weston-super-mare; died at Teignmouth, September 1, 1870; composer of a Te Deum, Anthems, Chants, and Hymn Tunes, the bulk of which are still in MS.; edited 'A Selection of Psalms and Hymns, adapted in Portions for Every Sunday and Festival of the Church of England,' fourth edition, 1851; and 'Church Psalmody; A Collection of Tunes, Harmonised for Four Voices, with an Organ Accompaniment; Expressly adapted for a Selection of Psalms and Hymns.' From this collection is taken

CHARMOUTH, No. 36 F.C.H. It is understood to be an adaptation from a movement in one of Vincent Novello's collections of sacred music.

Gadsby, Henry Robert, born at Hackney, London, December 15, 1842; chorister in St Paul's Cathedral, London, 1849 to 1858; principally self-taught in music; organist of St Peter's, Brockley, London, till 1884; Professor at Guildhall School of Music, London; succeeded Dr Hullah as Professor of Harmony at Queen's College, London, 1884; Fellow of the College of Organists.

S.S., No. 24 in F.C.H., "Suffer the little children," was composed by him, and published in 'The Psalmist: A Collection of Tunes, Chants, and Anthems for Public Worship, and for Domestic and Family Use.' Issued under the editorial superintendence of Ebenezer Prout, B.A. 'Chants and Anthems'—London: Haddon & Co., 1882.

Gall, Rev. James, born in Edinburgh, September 27, 1808; educated at the High School and University of Edinburgh; printer and publisher, of the firm of James Gall & Son—now Gall & Inglis; devoted the early part of his life till 1858 to the extension and improvement of Sabbath-schools along with his father, who did much in revolutionising the old methods, sixty years ago; inventor of a new process of printing music at the letter-press, which enabled him to publish music at a quarter of the usual price, in any size or style; founder of the Carrubber's Close Mission at Edinburgh 1861, in which year he published a Children's Hymn Book, which had an enormous sale; since 1872 he has been doing the work of an evangelist, "a work to which he had long before consecrated his life."

O COME LET US SING, No. 377 S.H., which is now associated with his hymn, was originally the tune to a hymn beginning "The voice of free grace."

Galloway, Rev. Alexander, born at Tillicoultry, February 18, 1847; educated at Edinburgh University, where he graduated M.A. in 1869, and B.D. in 1872; assistant minister at Bowden, Roxburghshire; Lasswade, Mid-Lothian; and St Mary's, Partick, Glasgow; elected minister of Milton Parish, Fife, 1876; of Minto Parish, Roxburghshire, 1878, where he still is; amateur musician, and one of the compilers of the 'Scottish Hymnal,' 1885.

AVE MARIS STELLA, No. 408 S.H. (Second Tune), seems to be an adaptation from the chorale, "Nimm von deinen Kindern, Herr," in Kocher's 'Zionsharfe,' 1855.

Ganther. To a composer of this name

HILARY, No. 232 F.C.H. and 253 U.P.H., is assigned in Kocher's 'Zionsharfe,' 1855. It is there set to "O du Liebe meiner Liebe."

Gastorius, Severus, was choirmaster at Jena in the seventeenth century; composer of songs and chorales.

BADEN, No. 216 S.H. and 173 U.P.H., "Was Gott thut das ist wohlgethan," is said to have been composed by Gastorius in 1653, after his recovery from a severe illness. It is also assigned by some to Pachelbel. See that name.

Gauntlett, Henry John, Mus. Doc., born at Wellington, Shropshire, July 9, 1805;[1] pupil of Henry Field and Samuel Wesley; organist of the Parish Church, Olney, Bucks (where his father was vicar), 1814, and also choirmaster 1819 to 1825; organist and choirmaster of St Olave's, Southwark, 1827 to 1847; degree of Mus. Doc. conferred on him by Archbishop of Canterbury, and appointed organist to the King of Hanover, 1842; choirmaster (honorary) St John, Milton-next-Gravesend, 1844 to 1851; organist of Union Church, Islington, 1852 to 1861; All-Saints, Kensington Park, 1861 to 1863; St Bartholomew the Less, Smithfield, 1872; died suddenly at Kensington, February 21, 1876; a distinguished organist and composer of Psalmody. Dr Gauntlett contributed tunes to so many hymnals that there is difficulty in tracing them to their original sources, hence it has been deemed advisable to do no more here than name his compositions in alphabetical order. They are as follows :—

ALEXANDRIA, Nos. 100 and 217 S.H., 178 P. and P.
ASCENSION, No. 57 U.P.H.
BEAMINSTER, No. 263 U.P.H.
BRAYLESFORD, No. 215 U.P.H.
BREDON, No. 104 U.P.H. and 43 U.P.P.
CAERLEON, No. 72 U.P.H.
CAIUS COLLEGE, No. 112 U.P.H.
CERTA CLARUM CERTAMEN, No. 166 U.P.H.
CROYLAND, No. 81 U.P.H.
CRY OF FAITH, No. 40 S.H.
DENBIGH, No. 40 U.P.H.
DEVONPORT, No. 269 U.P.H.
DURA, No. 100 U.P.H.
EVERMORE, No. 316 S.H. (Second Tune).
GAUNTLETT, No. 202 U.P.H.
HOUGHTON, No. 16 S.H., 8 U.P.H., 288 F.C.H.
IMMANUEL, No. 29 U.P.H. (Second Tune).
IRBY, No. 385 F.C.H., 384 S.H.
KINDLY LIGHT, No. 216 U.P.H.
LUX ALMA, No. 12 S.P., 200 U.P.P., 74 U.P.H.
MIDDLETON, No. 128 U.P.H.
NEWLAND, Nos. 44 and 157 S.H.

[1] The date 1806 given in Grove's 'Dictionary of Music and Musicians,' and many other works, is incorrect, as the following extract from the 'Birth Records of Wellington, Shropshire,' will show : "Henry John, son of the Rev. Henry Gauntlett, Curate of this Parish, and Arabella his wife; born July 9th, baptised July 28th, 1805."

Rest, No. 237 U.P.H.
Riseholme, No. 123 U.P.H.
St Albinus, No. 59 S.H., 58 U.P.H.
St Alphege, No. 153 U.P.H., 210 F.C.H., 273 and 338 S.H.
St Colm, No. 48 U.P.H.
St Fulbert, No. 126 S.H., 133 S.P., 130 P. and P., 50 U.P.H., 86 U.P.P.
St Olaf or Olave, No. 102, 206, 339 S.H., 245 U.P.H. (there also named "St George"), 112 U.P.P., 202 S.P., 130 F.C.H., 202 P. and P.
St Jerome, No. 129 U.P.H.
St Malo, No. 156 U.P.H.
St Methodius, No. 121 U.P.H.
Sonning, No. 238 U.P.H.
Southwold, No. 190 U.P.H., 99 U.P.P., 162 S.P., 220 S.H., 152 P. and P.
Toplady, No. 227 U.P.H., 89 U.P.P.
Triumph, No. 61 and Doxology 7 U.P.H., 249 F.C.H., 61 and 111 S.H.
Gloria in Excelsis, No. 353 U.P.H.
University College, No. 165 U.P.H., 232 S.H., 161 F.C.H.
Westover, No. 261 U.P.H.

S.S., No. 80 U.P.H., "Thou wilt keep him in perfect peace," is the opening movement of an anthem bearing that title, which seems to have been first published by Novello in 1863.

S.S., No. 130, "Holy, holy,"
" No. 131, "We give Thee thanks,"
" No. 132, "Hallelujah,"—all in U.P.H., were composed for a Chant Book edited by the Rev. Dr Henry Allon in 1860.

Gawthorn, Nathaniel, "at the Black Peruke in Rood Lane, Fenchurch Street," London, was clerk, or conductor of Psalmody at "the Friday Lecture in Eastcheap," early in the eighteenth century. Edited in 1730 'Harmonia Perfecta: A Compleat Collection of Psalm Tunes in Four Parts. . . . Taken from the Most Eminent Masters, chiefly from Mr Ravenscroft.' In the above appears

Barnet, No. 49 P. and P., and
Newark, No. 113 P. and P., where they are anonymous.

Thomas Moore published the first-named in his 'Psalm Singer's Pocket Companion,' Glasgow, 1756. It is there named "Wakefield."

Genevan Psalter. The skeleton of the history of the French Genevan Psalter is this:—

The Words.—Clement Marot made at different times versions of several psalms, to the number of thirty, which were collected into a volume in 1542. Before this, however, they had circulated largely in MS., and were published with an incorrect text in a psalter printed at Antwerp in 1541.

Two years before this, in 1539, when Calvin was at Strasburg, he compiled a small collection of psalms with tunes, and there are found 12 of Marot's versions which Calvin had got somewhere, but with the spurious text. This Strasburg book was the basis of the true Genevan Psalter, which Calvin prepared on his return to Geneva in 1542. In this the whole thirty psalms of Marot are included. It should be borne in mind that up to this time Calvin and Marot had no personal intercourse or acquaintance whatever with each other. But when Marot fled from Paris and arrived at Geneva soon after Calvin, the latter got him to continue the translations. Marot then wrote 19 more, which, with the Song of Simeon, make up what is known as the "Fifty Psalms of Marot." Marot left Geneva a year afterwards, and died in 1544. So the Genevan Psalter stood till 1551, when Calvin asked his friend Beza, who had then settled at Geneva, to continue the work. Beza then added thirty-four new versions, making eighty-three in all. About 1554 he added six more; another about 1555; and the remaining sixty in 1562.

The Tunes.—The tunes of the Strasburg book of 1539 were mostly German, either borrowed from local sources, or some perhaps written for the occasion. Those in the Genevan book of 1542 were taken partly from the Strasburg book and partly new. Then came the edition of 1543 with Marot's new psalms, and of course new tunes. To Beza's new psalms of 1551 and the complete edition of 1562 new tunes were also added. It should be remembered that from 1542 to 1562 alterations were made in each edition, either by modification of the existing tune, or by substitution of a new one. After 1562 no change was ever made. It will thus be seen that the Genevan Psalter was a growth of twenty years, and that the 150 psalms in it are of different dates—viz.,

30............1542.	34............1551.	1............1555.
19............1543.	6............1554.	60............1562.

The tunes as they appear in the final edition of 1562 are likewise of various dates, but not necessarily those of the psalms to which they belong. For instance, one psalm of 1542 might retain its original tune to the end. Another psalm of same date might have been set to three or four tunes in succession, till set finally in 1562. In other cases the final form of a tune was not quite the same as its first.

Composers of the Tunes.—In those days "composing" meant

"compounding." A composer troubled himself little about originality. If his purpose was answered by piecing stock musical phrases together in a new arrangement, he did so; and very many of the older tunes were so constructed. The tune we call "Old Hundredth" is highly effective, but perhaps the least original in the whole Genevan Psalter.

To assign *any* tune in the Genevan book (1542-1562) to Guillaume Franc is utterly wrong. Franc was engaged as master of the children in St Peter's Church at Geneva in 1542, but there is not a trace of evidence that he had anything to do with the editing of the Psalter. He left Geneva soon afterwards, and settled at Lausanne, where he *did* edit a psalter which was indeed printed at Geneva, but was confounded with the Genevan book by writers who did not know the facts.

The Genevan Psalter contained melodies only. After it was completed in 1562, Goudimel harmonised the tunes for private use (as singing in parts was never permitted in the "Reformed Church" till the present century). Goudimel had nothing to do with the compiling or musical editing of that work, and in fact was not even a Protestant till about 1555. On the other hand, there is positive evidence in existence that the editor from 1545 to 1557 was Louis Bourgeois; and there is every reason to believe he edited the book from the beginning in 1542.

The number of distinct tunes in the Psalter of 1562 is 125 (two of which are those to the Decalogue and Song of Simeon), so that 27 psalms are sung to tunes of other psalms.

The following tunes are from the Genevan Psalters, the dates of their first appearance and the psalms to which they are set being given:—

CALVIN, No. 47 U.P.H. and 222 U.P.P., is the same as Commandments.

CARMEL, No. 6 P. and P. 1551. Set to Psalm 35.

COMMANDMENTS, No. 8 P. and P., 6, 20, 284, 311 S.H., 33 F.C.H., 3 S.P. 1549. Set to the Ten Commandments.

LAUSANNE, No. 281 U.P.H. 1543. Set to Psalm 118.

OLD HUNDREDTH, No. 26 P. and P., 135 S.H., 224 U.P.P., Doxology 3 U.P.H., 15 and 16 S.P., 20 F.C.H. 1551. Set to Psalm 134.

OLD 117TH, No. 43 F.C.H. 1551. Set to Psalm 127; also set afterwards (1562) to Psalm 117.

OLD 124TH, No. 203 U.P.P., 217 P. and P., 214 S.P. 1551. Set to Psalm 124.

GENEVAN PSALTER. 133

OLD 134TH, or ST MICHAEL, No. 125 F.C.H., 162 U.P.H., 202 U.P.P., 197 S.P., 58 and 239 S.H., 201 P. and P. 1543. Is abridged from the following tune, which is set to Psalm 101 :—

KEY B♭.

{ | s₁ :d :— :m :— :r :r :m :s :f :m :r :— }

{ :d :— :d :— :t₁ :l₁ :s₁ :s₁ :d :d :r :m :f }

{ :m :— :m :— :s :f :m :— :r :— :d :t₁ :d :— }

{ :r :— :m :— :f :— :m :— :r :— :d :— :— :— ‖

The following is the original form of Old Hundredth :—

KEY F.

{ | d :— :d :t₁ :l₁ :s₁ :d :— :r :— :m :— : : }

{ :m :— :m :m :r :d :f :— :m :— :r :— : : }

{ :d :— :r :m :r :d :l₁ :— :t₁ :— :d :— : : }

{ :s :— :m :— :d :— :r :f :m :— :r :— :d :— :— :— ‖

It was early introduced into England, being found in John Day's Psalter, 1562. It was known as "The Hundredth," until the old version of the Psalms was superseded by that of Tate and Brady. The name "Hundredth" is peculiar to England, as in the Genevan Psalter the tune was adapted to Psalm 134. It was sometimes named "Savoy" from its use by a Huguenot congregation established in the Savoy, London, in the reign of Elizabeth. The ordinary version of the tune, as in the S.H., U.P.H., and F.C.H., is found as early as 1592.

OLD 124TH has for centuries been a popular tune in Scotland, and has remained fixed to the psalm to which it was first set. The following, by Calderwood the historian, relates how it was sung in 1582 on the return of John Durie after a temporary banishment: "John Durie cometh to Leith at night, the 3d September. Upon Tuesday the 4th of September, as he is coming to Edinburgh, there met him at the Gallowgreen 200, but ere he came to the Netherbow their number increased to 400; but they were no sooner entered but they increased to 600 or 700, and within short space the whole street was replenished even to Saint Geiles Kirk: the number was esteemed to 2000. At the Netherbow they took up the 124 Psalme, 'Now Israel may say,' &c., and sung in such a pleasant tune in four parts, known to the most part of the people, that coming up the street all bareheaded till they entered in the Kirk, with such a great sound and majestic, that it moved both themselves and all the huge multitude of the beholders, looking out at the shots and over stairs, with admiration and astonishment; the Duke of Lennox himself beheld, and reave his beard for anger; he was more affrayed of this sight than anie thing that ever he had seene before in Scotland. When they came to the Kirk, Mr James Lowsone made a short exhortation in the Reader's place, to move the multitude to thankfulness. Thereafter a psalm being sung, they departed with great joy."

German.

AUGSBURG, No. 27 U.P.H. Adapted by the Rev. W. H. Havergal.

BACH, No. 138 F.C.H.

BADEN, No. 74 U.P.P., 121 F.C.H., 187 S.P. Adapted by Dr Lowell Mason, and published in his 'Carmina Sacra,' 1841.

BOHEMIA, No. 185 U.P.H., 10 S.H.

BOHEMIA, No. 256 F.C.H. Melody of the sixteenth century.

BRANDENBURG, No. 364 U.P.H. Marked "German" in an American collection issued about 1823.

BRÜNN, No. 182 P. and P. and 171 S.H. See "Baden," which is the same tune.

COLOGNE, No. 15 and 51 U.P.P.

CULM, No. 12 P. and P. Adapted from a secular melody of the sixteenth century.

DETTINGEN, No. 66 U.P.H. Melody of the sixteenth century.

DIJON, No. 347 F.C.H., 341 U.P.H., 416 S.H.

ERLANGEN, No. 323 S.H. Adapted by Walter Hately from a melody of the fifteenth century.

GERMANIA, No. 253 S.H. "Herzlich thut mich erfreuen." 1545.

INFANT'S PRAYER, No. 364 F.C.H.

ISRAEL, No. 206 F.C.H. A melody of the sixteenth century which is found in many forms. Upon this is based "Moravia," which see.

KILSYTH, No. 318 S.H., 99 P. and P. Adapted from the chorale "Allein zu Dir Herr Jesu Christ," which was published (according to the Chorale Book for England) on a broadside at Nürnberg in 1541, and afterwards in 'Geistliche Lieder,' Second Part, Leipzig, 1545.

KREUZNACH, No. 335 S.H. This was originally a secular melody set to the harvest song, "Entlaubt ist uns der Wald," and according to Prætorius is in Georg Forster's 'Auszug guter alter und neuer teutscher Liedlein,' Part I., No. 61 (1539). In the 'Bohemian Brethren's Hymn Book,' 1544, it is set to the hymn, "Lob Gott getrost mit Singen"; and in Luther's 'Geistliche Lieder,' 1545, it is set to Kolross's hymn, "Ich dank Dir lieber Herre."

LUTZEN, No. 15 and 35 U.P.H.

MARGARETHA, No. 376 S.H., is marked "German" in Westlake's 'Hymns and Sacred Songs for the Year' (1863). It is found also in 'A Collection of Catholic Hymns,' First Series, 1853. There the melody is slightly different, and no source is given.

MELANCHTHON, No. 170 F.C.H. Melody of the thirteenth century.

MONKLAND, No. 160 F.C.H., 13 S.H. Same as "Lutzen" in U.P.H., excepting a variation in the last strain.

MORAVIA, No. 151, 264, 421 S.H., 17 U.P.H., 112 P. and P., 67 U.P.P., 103 S.P. The tune from which "Moravia" is adapted is found in many forms, set to the hymn "Aus meines Herzens Grunde," by Johannes Mathesius, minister of Joachimthal. The melody as a matter of course was ascribed to his precentor, Nicolaus Hermann, but it is not found in his works. Though it is commonly held that its earliest source is the 'Hymn Book of Bartholomäus Gesius,' 1601, Dr Faisst has found it as early as 1598 in the Eisleben Hymn Book, and in Wolder's 'Katechismus-Gesangbüchlein,' Hamburg, 1595, with some variation. In the S.P. and S.H. it is referred to the 'Greifswald Hymn Book' of 1592. A copy of this work is in the Greifswald University Library, and another, dated 1593, in the Library of St Nicholas Church there; both contain the hymn, "Aus meines," &c., but no tune is set in either work to that hymn. These books were specially examined for the writer.

NÜRNBERG, Doxology No. 11 U.P.H. This tune is not in the 'Nürnberg Gesangbuch,' as stated in the U.P.H. In an edition published in 1690 the hymn "Alles ist an Gottes Segen," with which this tune is associated, appears, but directions are given to sing it to the tune "Jesu, heil den alten Schaden," which is totally different from Nürnberg.

The readings of this melody vary considerably. The nearest approach to the form given in the U.P.H. the writer has seen is in J. S. Bach's 'Vierstimmige Choralgesänge,' vol. ii., 1769, where the melody stands No. 132 and in the following form:—

ALLES IST AN GOTTES SEGEN.

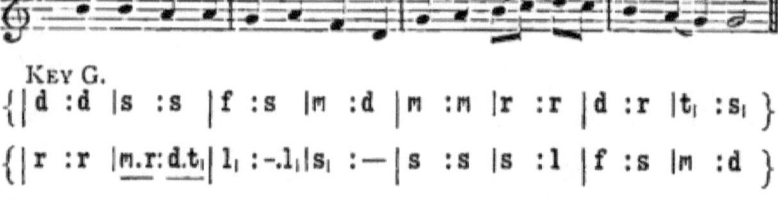

Key G.

{| d :d |s :s |f :s |m :d |m :m |r :r |d :r |t₁ :s₁ }

{| r :r |m.r:d.t₁| l₁ :-.l₁|s₁ :— |s :s |s :l |f :s |m :d }

{| m :m |r :r |d :r |t₁ :s₁ |d :r |m.f:s.f|m :r.d|d :— ||

OBERLIN, No. 300 F.C.H. According to Winterfeld, Luther in 1526 introduced the "Agnus Dei" in German, and as no other setting is known, this tune must have been in use at that date. It appears in the 'Magdeburg Gesangbuch,' 1540.

OLD SAXONY, No. 230 U.P.P., 68 U.P.H., 24 F.C.H., 17 S.P., is adapted from a chorale of the sixteenth century, "Christ, der du bist der helle Tag," and is found in many different forms.

PENTECOST, No. 106 U.P.H., 120 F.C.H. See "Germania," which is the same tune.

SAXONY, No. 81 and 254 S.H., 37 P. and P. See "Old Saxony," which is the same tune.

SPRINGTIME, No. 375 F.C.H. This is the famous German drinking-song "Crambambuli," which became popular in this country by association with W. M. Hutching's hymn, "When mothers of Salem their children brought to Jesus."

STOBEL, No. 107 S.H., 135 U.P.H. Mr Havergal, in his 'Old Church Psalmody,' refers this to John Daniel Müller's 'Choralbuch,' 1754, but that work contains no such tune. Nor is it to be found in Johann Michael Müller's 'Choralbücher,' published at Frankfort-on-Maine between 1735 and 1741.

STRASBURG, No. 53 U.P.H. See "Melanchthon," which is the same tune.

TRUST, No. 250 F.C.H. This tune was taken from a German collection, and inserted by Mr Parlane of Paisley in the 'Sabbath-School Union Hymnal' (1877).

Gerum, August, son of M. Gerum, a schoolmaster and choir-director in the neighbourhood of Weingarten; born at Spaichingen, April 21, 1818; in 1838 appointed teacher at Ravensburg, a profession he gave up in 1860 in order to devote himself entirely to music; in 1844 appointed conductor of the Ravensburg Choral Society, an office he retained till 1877; in July 1860 accepted formally the management of the Roman Catholic choir; died at Ravensburg, December 29, 1885; composer of sacred and secular music, but more distinguished as a conductor. His tune

GERUM, No. 115 S.H. (Second Tune), "Pange lingua gloriosi," appears in a slightly different form in Kocher's 'Zionsharfe,' 1855.

Gesius, Bartholomäus, or **Gese,** born 1560; published at Wittenberg in 1588 Passion-music from the Gospel of St John; became in 1598 precentor at Frankfort-on-the-Oder, where he died in 1614.

ABBEY CLOSE, No. 25 U.P.P., "Ach Gott, wem soll ichs klagen," appears in an important Collection issued by Gesius in 1605.

LUCCA, No. 249 S.H., appears in the same Collection set to the words "Man spricht; wen Gott erfreut." It is adapted from a secular song, "Venus du und dein Kind, seid alle beide blind," which occurs in Regnart's 'Schönen kurzweiligen deutschen Liedern, Nürnberg,' 1574. Vulpius, in his Collection of 1609, sets it to the hymn with which it is now associated, "Auf meinen lieben Gott."

Giardini, Felice de, an eminent violinist, was born at Turin, April 12, 1716; chorister at Milan Cathedral when a boy; pupil of Paladini in singing, composition, and the harpsichord; afterwards returned to Turin and studied the violin under Somis. In 1750 he made his first appearance in London as a violinist, creating a perfect furore; left England in 1784 to spend the rest of his life in Italy, but returned in 1790, when he started a comic opera at the Haymarket, which proved a failure; afterwards went to Russia, and died at Moscow, December 17, 1796.

MOSCOW, No. 315 F.C.H and 107 S.H. (Second Tune); 287 U.P.H., there rightly named "Trinity," was composed by Giardini for the Lock Hospital Collection, 1769 (see Madan), where it is set to a "Hymn to the Trinity." The last two notes of the melody of the sixth line, and the first three of the last line, as given in the above hymnals, are a third too low. This corrupt reading of the melody, and the unison passage (third line) harmonised, is given in the majority of tune-books.

SIXTH AND SEVENTH LINES OF "TRINITY," AS COMPOSED BY GIARDINI.

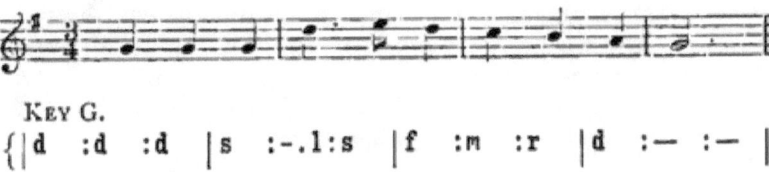

KEY G.
{ | d :d :d | s :-.l:s | f :m :r | d :— :— ||

It is found in its original form, and named "Giardini," in Henry Boyd's Collection, Glasgow, 1793. This seems to be its first appearance in a Scotch Psalmody.

PALMYRA, No. 330 U.P.H. This is a double short metre tune in the Lock Collection, 1769, where it is named "Pelham," and set to a hymn beginning

"My soul, repeat His praise
Whose mercies are so great."

The last line of each verse is repeated, as shown below, the line marked thus * being omitted in the U.P.H.

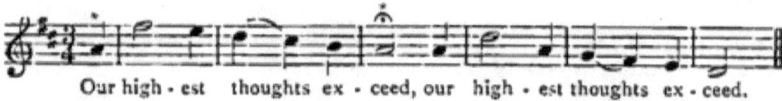

KEY D.

{ :s* | m¹ :— :r¹ | d¹ :t :l | s* :⌢ :s | d¹ :— }
  Our | high . . . est | thoughts ex . . | ceed, our | high . .

{ :s | f :m :r | d :— ||
  est | thoughts ex . . | ceed.

Gibbons, Christopher, son of Orlando Gibbons, was born 1615 (baptized August 22); chorister in Exeter Cathedral; organist of Winchester Cathedral, 1638 to 1661; of Westminster Abbey, 1660 to 1665; and of the Chapel Royal 1660 to 1676; Mus. Doc., Oxford, 1664; died, October 20, 1676.

CHANT, No. 115 in U.P.P., appears in Vandernan's Collection, 1770, with a different cadence. The present reading is found in Harrison's 'Sacred Harmony,' vol. ii. (1791), where it is wrongly assigned to Orlando Gibbons.

Gibbons, Orlando, Mus. Doc., born at Cambridge in 1583.[1] As an organist he was one of the finest of his time, and indeed one of the greatest musical geniuses of our country. At the age of twenty-one he was appointed organist of the Chapel Royal, and in 1622 admitted a Doctor of Music at the University of Oxford. In 1623 Dr Gibbons was appointed organist of Westminster Abbey, and two years later was summoned to Canterbury to attend the marriage of Charles I., for which he had composed an ode and some instrumental music, and whilst there, died after a short illness, June 5, 1625, and was buried the following day in the Cathedral at Canterbury. In 1623 he composed Tunes in two parts—Treble and Bass—for George Withers' 'Hymns and Songs of the Church.' From that Collection are taken

ANGELS' SONG, No. 16 F.C.H., 1 S.P., 130 S.H., 1 P. and P., 140 U.P.H.,

---

[1] The writer has failed to verify this date, although he has caused the Baptismal Records of the parishes then in existence to be searched.

and 162 U.P.P. (named in the U.P. Collections "Angels' Hymn"), which was set by Gibbons in three different forms, and so named from the words of one of the hymns to which it is set. The form in the F.C.H. and S.P. is almost identical with the air given below, which is set to Song XXXIV.:—

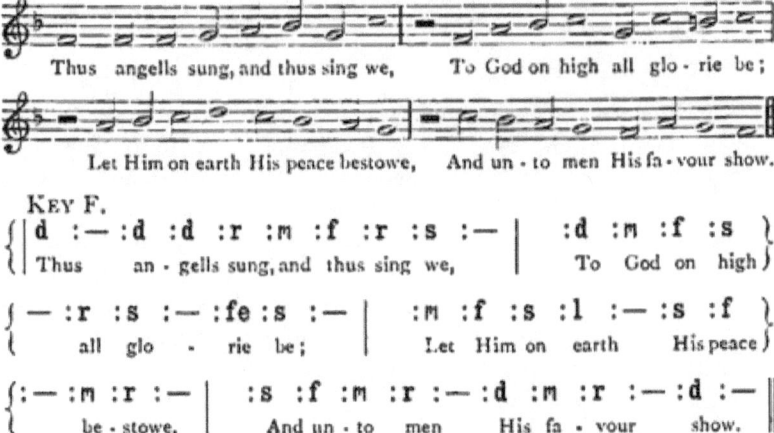

The Melody of Song XXXIV. in Withers' 'Hymnes and Songs of the Church,' 1623.

Thus angells sung, and thus sing we, To God on high all glo-rie be;
Let Him on earth His peace bestowe, And un-to men His fa-vour show.

The altered version, in 3 time, given in the Church of Scotland and U.P. Collections, has been in use since the beginning of last century. Its earliest appearance in this form in a Scotch Collection the writer has seen, is in Thomas Moore's 'Delightful Pocket Companion,' Glasgow (1762), where it is arranged for Treble and Bass.

DEPTFORD, No. 286 F.C.H., is set to Song XXII.
GIBBONS, No. 163 F.C.H., 159 U.P.H., 161 S.H., is set to Song XIII.
ST MATTHIAS, No. 137 P. & P., 145 S.P., 211 U.P.H., 105 U.P.P., is set to Song LXVII., which is for St Matthias' Day.
S.S., No. 14 F.C.H. (Sanctus II.) is his composition. Dr Boyce's 'Cathedral Music,' vol. iii., 1773, contains the earliest *printed* copy the writer has seen of it.

Gibson, Mrs Patrick—*née* Isabella Mary Scott; daughter of William Scott, teacher of elocution; born at Edinburgh about 1786; in June 1818, married to Patrick Gibson, R.S.A., and writer on art; kept a boarding-school for young ladies in Inverleith Row, Edinburgh, and in 1828 opened a similar establishment in Dollar; a distinguished vocalist and harp player; occupied a high position in the musical and literary world, and was the associate of Lord Brougham, Sir Walter Scott (to whom she was distantly related), and other celebrities of her time; contributed a song to R. A.

Smith's 'Scottish Minstrel,' "Lochnagar," words by Byron (Away, ye gay landscapes), which is still popular, also two original psalm tunes to vol. vi. of James Steven's 'Church Music,' edited by John Turnbull, Glasgow, 1833; died at Edinburgh, November 28, 1838.

COMFORT, No. 93 U.P.P., is one of four tunes contributed by Mrs Gibson to 'Sacred Harmony,' Part I., for the use of St George's Church, Edinburgh, 1820, a collection edited by Dr Andrew Thomson. It is slightly different from the original form.

Gilbert, Walter Bond, son of Samuel Thomas Gilbert; born at Exeter, Devonshire, April 21, 1829; pupil of Alfred Angel, Dr S. S. Wesley, and Sir Henry R. Bishop; appointed organist of Topsham Parish Church, Devonshire, 1847; Bideford, 1849; of Tunbridge, 1854; Maidstone, 1859; Lee, Kent, 1866; Boston, Lincolnshire, 1868; since 1869, organist of Trinity Chapel, New York; graduated Mus. Bac., Oxford, 1854; degree of Mus. Doc. conferred on him by the University of Trinity College, Toronto, Canada, 1886, and by Oxford University, 1888; Fellow of the College of Organists, 1864; composer of an oratorio, "St John," and much excellent church music. Author of 'Memorials of All Saints Church, Maidstone,' 1864; 'Antiquities of Maidstone,' 1865. His tunes

MAIDSTONE, No. 128 S.H., 349 U.P.H., 193 F.C.H.; and THANKSGIVING, No. 441 S.H., and 54 U.P.H., were first published in the 'Parish Tune Book,' compiled by Mr G. F. Chambers, 1862.

Gilmour, Robert, music-teacher at Paisley about the close of last century, and of whom no further information can be had, although it has been diligently sought for, edited 'The Psalm Singer's Assistant; Being a Collection of the most approved Psalm and Hymn Tunes. Mostly in Four Parts. Selected from the best Authors, and adapted to the different metres of the Psalms of David, and the Assembly's Translations; with a compendious Introduction, for the use of Learners, and a Collection of Hymns suited to the Tunes.' Glasgow, no date. Second edition, with Improvements, Paisley, 1793.

MONTROSE, No. 191 and 221 U.P.P., is in both editions, where it bears its present name, and is the earliest copy the writer has seen. It was commonly known as the "Burghers' Rant." The supposition that the melody of "Montrose" was originally the bass of a tune named "Dunkeld" is erroneous. Mr Carnie of Aberdeen informed the writer that exactly the opposite is the case, and that the composing of "Dunkeld" by using

"Montrose" melody as a bass was the freak of a Glasgow musical amateur. Neither is there any truth in the statement that "Montrose" is the bass of the tune set to the 84th Psalm in the 'Scottish Psalter.' In James Thomson's 'Collection of the Best Church Tunes,' third edition, Edinburgh, 1793, it is named "Montrose or Mather," and in several collections of later date it bears the latter name.

Giornovichj, Giovanni Marie, an eminent violinist; born at Palermo in 1745; pupil of Lolli; made his *début* in Paris in 1770, and for some years was all the rage in that city; visited Austria, Poland, Russia, and Sweden, and in 1791 arrived in London, where he gave his first concert in May of that year; died at St Petersburg, it is said during a game at billiards, in 1804. His insolence and conceit (says Sir George Grove) seem to have been unbounded, and to have brought him into disastrous collision with Viotti, a far greater artist than himself, and with J. B. Cramer—who went the length of calling him out, a challenge which Giornovichj would not accept—and even led him to some gross misconduct in the presence of the King and the Duke of York. He visited Scotland in 1797.

St Asaph, No. 250 S.H., 176 P. & P., 157 U.P.P., 127 S.P., 73 F.C.H., is probably an adaptation from one of his instrumental pieces. Although many of these have been examined by the writer at the British Museum, he is unable definitely to state its source. R. A. Smith's Collection, 1825, contains the earliest copy the writer has seen of the tune, and it is there assigned to Giornovichj, and set to Paraphrase 66, with which it has always been associated. In the 'Sacred Harp' by Lowell and T. B. Mason, Cincinnati, 1836, it is found in a slightly different form, and named "Fulton," no composer's name being given.

Gläser, Carl Gotthelf, born at Weissenfels, May 4, 1784; studied under his father, and afterwards at the St Thomas School, Leipzig, under Johann Adam Hiller and August Eberhard Müller, who taught him the pianoforte, and Campagnoli, who taught him the violin. In 1801 he went to Leipzig University to study law, but gave up jurisprudence to become a music-teacher at Barmen. There he took up a music-shop, which he carried on till his death on April 16, 1829. Composer of motets, school songs, and instrumental music.

Denfield, No. 56 S.P., 362 F.C.H., and 357 S.H., is by him, and appears in many books of German school songs. It is found as a hymn tune in 'The Seraph' by Dr Lowell Mason, June 1839.

Gluck, Christoph Willibald, Ritter von, German composer; born at Weidenwang, near Neumarkt, Upper Palatinate,

July 2, 1714; distinguished as an operatic composer; died at Vienna, November 15, 1787.

BOSWELL, No. 95 U.P.P., was adapted from one of Gluck's works, and bears its present name in 'Cantica Laudis,' by Lowell Mason and G. J. Webb, 1850.

Goodenough, Rev. Robert Philip, son of the Right Rev. Samuel Goodenough, Bishop of Carlisle, born at Ealing, Middlesex, 19th October 1775; baptised November 16th; studied at Westminster School and Christ Church, Oxford; graduated B.A., Oxford, 1796; M.A., 1799; Prebendary of Southwell, 1806; Carlisle, 1811; Ripon and York; Vicar of Carlton-in-Lyndrick, Nottinghamshire, 1806, and later Rector of Beelsby, Lincolnshire; died April 20, 1826. His

CHANT, set to Hymn 352 in S.H., appears in 'A Collection of Chants as used at Christ Church Cathedral,' Oxford, edited by William Cross, Mus. Bac.

Goss, Sir John, born at Fareham, Hants, December 27, 1800; son of Joseph Goss, organist of that place; chorister in Chapel Royal under John Stafford Smith, 1811, afterwards a pupil of Thomas Attwood; organist of St Luke's, Chelsea, 1824; organist of St Paul's Cathedral in 1838 in succession to Thomas Attwood; resigned in 1872 and received the honour of knighthood; composer to the Chapel Royal 1856 to 1872; Mus. Doc., Cambridge, 1876; died at Brixton, London, May 10, 1880. Composer of much excellent church music.

WATERSTOCK, No. 156 F.C.H., 202 S.H., appears in his 'Parochial Psalmody: A Collection of Ancient and Modern Tunes,' 1826.

BEVAN, No. 4 U.P.H., 121 and 251 (First Tune) S.H., was composed in 1853 for, and published in, 'Choral Harmony,' by the Rev. Peter Maurice, 1854.

PETERBOROUGH, No. 13 U.P.H., 226 U.P.P., 44 P. and P. (there named "Worcester"), was composed in 1864, and published in the Rev. William Mercer's 'Church Psalter and Hymn Book' the same year.

CLAREWOOD, No. 344 F.C.H. and 345 U.P.H., is from 'Congregational Church Music,' enlarged edition, 1871.

FAREHAM, No. 342 S.H., and CARMEL, No. 277 U.P.H., are from 'The Hymnary,' edited by Joseph Barnby, 1872.

GOSS, No. 241 S.H. (Second Tune), is from the Rev. William Mercer's 'Church Psalter and Hymn Book,' 1864. It is there named "Bede," and is an adaptation. (See Handel.)

EPHESUS, No. 101 U.P.H., is arranged by him, and appears in 'Choral Harmony,' 1858.

Humility, No. 383 S.H., was composed for 'Christmas Carols,' edited by Dr Stainer (1872).

Chants No. 81 U.P.P. and 356 S.H. are his.

He contributed the following Scripture Sentences at various dates to 'Congregational Church Music':—

S.S. No. 30 U.P.H., " My voice shalt Thou hear," was written for second supplement to 'Congregational Church Music,' 1864.

S.S. No. 98 U.P.H., "Christ is risen . . . blessing and honour"—

S.S. No. 64 U.P.H., "Wherewithal shall a young man?"—

S.S. No. 25 U.P.H., " Will God in very deed?"—appear in 'Congregational Church Music,' enlarged edition, 1871.

S.S. No. 49 U.P.H., " Praise waiteth for Thee," appears in 'A New Handbook of Anthems,' 1882.

S.S. No. 72 U.P.H., " Enter not into judgment," was first published in 'The Office of Praise,' 1870.

S.S. No. 95 U.P.H., " Behold I bring you good tidings." Published in 'Musical Times,' December 1857.

S.S. No. 120 U.P.H., " Behold my servant, whom I uphold."

S.S. No. 93 U.P.H., " Blessed be the Lord God of Israel."

S.S. No. 104 U.P.H., " I heard a voice," was published in 1870. It is an amplification of the last movement of the Burial Service composed by Goss.

S.S. No. 56 U.P.H., " O be joyful in the Lord," was published in November 1865, and first performed by the Charity Children in St Paul's Cathedral on Thursday, June 7, 1866. It was originally written in unison, a harmonised version being afterwards issued.

S.S. No. 39 U.P.H., " O taste and see," was composed for the Special Sunday Evening Choir of St Paul's Cathedral, and first performed on Sunday evening, February 15, 1863.

Gotha Cantionals. A Collection of Sacred Songs and Chorales by various authors for use in the Schools and Churches of Gotha, by Johann Michael Schallo. Part I., 1646, Feast Day Songs; second edition, 1651. Part II., 1647, Christian Church and School Songs, arranged according to the order of the Holy Catechism; second edition, 1655. Part III., 1648, Funeral Hymns; second edition, 1657. From the edition of 1651 is taken

Altenburg, No. 4 F.C.H., 21 P. and P. (there named "Luneburg"), "Herr Jesu Christ dich zu uns wend."

An edition issued in 1715, commonly called the 'New Gotha Cantional,' was edited by Christian Friedrich Witt (in 1700 Court bandmaster at Friedenstein in Gotha, where he died in 1716), and contains 359 tunes for 762 hymns. On pages 302, 303 of the above work will be found—

Sigismund, No. 46 U.P.H., 225 F.C.H., 11 and 380 S.H. (First Tune, there named "Stuttgart"), set to the hymn "Sollt es gleich bisweilen scheinen." It is also in Dretzell's 'Choralbuch,' 1731. Wrongly referred in S.H. to Störl's 'Choralbuch,' 1711.

Gould-Baring, Rev. Sabine. See Baring-Gould.

Gounod, Charles François, born in Paris, June 17, 1818; entered the Conservatoire in 1836, studying under Halévy and others, gaining the "Grand Prix de Rome" in 1839; well known by his opera of "Faust," and his oratorios "The Redemption" and "Mors et Vita." His tunes

Redemption, No. 26 S.H. (Second Tune), and Gounod, No. 243 F.C.H., are from 'The Hymnary,' edited by Joseph Barnby, 1872.

S.S. No. 81 U.P.H., "O that thou hadst hearkened," is adapted from his anthem, "Come unto Me."

S.S. No. 88 U.P.H., "Come unto Me," is from the opening and closing movements of "All ye who weep," both of which were published in 1869.

S.S. No. 90 U.P.H., "Blessed is He who cometh," is from the Benedictus in his "Messe Solennelle," composed by Gounod after he had left Rome and returned to Paris, and when he thought of becoming a priest, about 1845-50. Some movements of the Mass were performed, under Hullah, at St Martin's Hall, London, January 15, 1851. The whole work was performed in its entirety at the Birmingham Festival, 1867.

Grant, David, born at Aberdeen, September 19, 1833; educated at a public school; studied music under Herr Granz at Aberdeen; for twenty-five years carried on business as a tobacco merchant, retiring in 1878; since then resident in London; amateur composer of several excellent church tunes, one of which,

Raleigh, No. 20 in S.P., was composed in 1867, and published on single slips in 1868. "Keeping" (says Mr William Carnie in a letter to the writer) "the composer's trade in view, and in honour of the introducer of the 'weed' to this country, I gave the tune its present name."

Greatorex, Thomas, son of Anthony Greatorex, music-teacher, born at North Wingfield, near Chesterfield, Derby, October 5, 1758; pupil of Dr Cooke; organist of Carlisle Cathedral, 1780, till about 1784; travelled in Holland and Italy, 1785 to 1788; appointed conductor of the Concerts of Ancient Music, 1793; organist of Westminster Abbey, 1819, till he died, July 17, 1831; conductor of the Birmingham, York, and Derby Musical Festivals for many years. One of the greatest organists and conductors of his time. Buried in Westminster Abbey. In 1823, Greatorex published 'Parochial Psalmody; Being a Collection of the most approved Tunes, arranged expressly for this Psalm-Book,' and 'A Selection of Tunes,' &c., London, 1829. In both of the above Collections appears the tune

TOTTENHAM, No. 170 S.P. and 155 U.P.P., but there is not the slightest reference as to who composed it. It is usually assigned to Greatorex, and though there seems no proof that he wrote it, it is likely he did so.

BEVERLEY, No. 7 and 269 (Second Tune) S.H., appears in its present form in 'Parochial Psalmody,' where it is named "Hundred and Forty-Eight." There is no evidence to favour the assumption that it was composed by the Rev. John Darwall. It is found thus in Arnold and Callcott's Psalms, 1791:—

"PROPER 136TH" IN ARNOLD AND CALLCOTT'S PSALMS, 1791, P. 159.

Greek Air.

SALAMIS, No. 384 F.C.H., 338 U.P.H., 396 S.H.

Green, John and **James,** probably father and son; edited 'A Collection of Choice Psalm-Tunes in Three and Four Parts; with New and Easie Psalm-Tunes, Hymns, Anthems, and Spiritual Songs.' . . . Third edition, 1715.

ST NEOT, No. 140 P. and P., 148 S.P., 12 U.P.P., is an altered copy of "Worksop Tune" in the above work:—

THE FIRST AND THIRD LINES OF "WORKSOP TUNE."

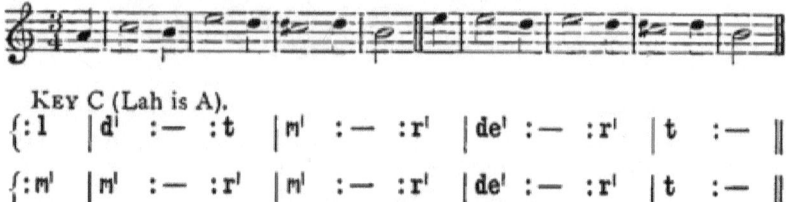

Key C (Lah is A).

{ :l | d¹ :— :t | m¹ :— :r¹ | de¹ :— :r¹ | t :— ||

{ :m¹ | m¹ :— :r¹ | m¹ :— :r¹ | de¹ :— :r¹ | t :— ||

Green, James, mentioned above, was organist at Hull,[1] and edited 'A Book of Psalmody; containing Chanting-Tunes, . . . with eighteen Anthems, and Variety of Psalm-Tunes in Four Parts,' fifth edition, 1724. From this the tune

CROWLE, No. 13 U.P.P., where it is set to Psalm 66.

WIRKSWORTH, No. 218 P. and P., and 23 U.P.P., is also there, the rhythm in the last-named Collection being identical with that given by Green. An earlier copy, with a different reading of the second half of the tune, is found in Chetham's Collection, 1718, a copy of which is here given:—

SECOND HALF OF "WIRKSWORTH" AS FOUND IN CHETHAM.

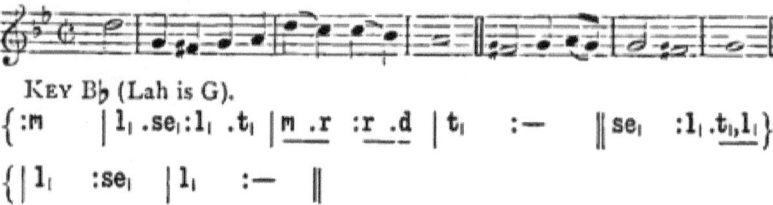

Key B♭ (Lah is G).

{ :m | l₁ .se₁:l₁ .t₁ | m .r :r .d | t₁ :— || se₁ :l₁.t₁.l₁ }

{ | l₁ :se₁ | l₁ :— ||

Greene, Maurice, Mus. Doc., born in London about 1696; chorister of St Paul's Cathedral under Charles King; on the breaking of his voice he became an articled pupil of Richard Brind, then organist of the Cathedral; in 1715 or 1716 appointed organist of St Dunstan's in the West, Fleet Street, and in 1717 of St Andrew's, Holborn; succeeded Brind (deceased) as organist of St Paul's in 1718; organist and composer to the Chapel Royal, 1727; elected Professor of Music in the University of Cambridge with the degree Doctor of Music, 1730; died December 1st[2] (not September, as commonly stated), 1755; buried in St Olave's Church, Old Jewry, December 10; reinterred in the Crypt of St Paul's Cathedral, May 18, 1888.

[1] Numerous inquiries at Hull have failed to enable the writer to add anything to Green's biography.

[2] December 1st on coffin-plate, and in 'Scots Magazine'; 3d December in Vicar Choral book.

CROWLE, ST NICHOLAS, and WIRKSWORTH have all been assigned to Dr Greene, but upon insufficient grounds. It is questionable if the Doctor ever wrote a psalm or hymn tune.

S.S. No. 179 U.P.H., "Behold, the Lord is my salvation," is assigned to Greene, in 'The Young Gentlemen and Ladies' Musical Companion,' vol. i., 1772; but this work is full of errors as to authorship. Dr Greene's name may have become associated with this anthem from the fact that it appears in James Green's 'A Book of Psalmody,' 1738. It is not in 'Forty Select Anthems in Score,' issued by Dr Greene in 1743. It is in James Thomson's Collection, Edinburgh, 1778. See Chetham, Rev. John.

Gregorian.

BETHANY, No. 61 F.C.H. In the 'Psalmist,' edited by Vincent Novello, this tune is marked "Gregorian Melody, adapted for the work by S. Wesley, 1836."

CHANT, No. 237 S.P.
CHANT, No. 234 U.P.P.
CHANTS to S.S. 124 U.P.H., "Blessed are the poor in spirit."
CHANTS to S.S. 110 U.P.H., "Man that is born of a woman."
CHANT to S.S. 109 U.P.H., "Behold, happy is the man."

Gregory, George Herbert, born at Clewer, near Windsor, December 6, 1853; pupil of Samuel Reay, Mus. Bac., organist of Newark-on-Trent; elected a Fellow of the College of Organists, London, 1873; graduated Mus. Bac., Oxford, 1874; organist of Holy Trinity Episcopal Church, Melrose, from 1872 to 1875; Parish Church, Tamworth, Staffordshire, 1875 to 1876; since January 1876 organist of Boston Parish Church, Lincolnshire; composer of Services, an Anthem for Whitsuntide, and other music, for the use of the Church of England. His tunes

CUI HABET DABITUR, No. 406, and SUAVITAS, No. 438 in S.H., were first published in the 'Church of Scotland Children's Hymnal,' 1876, the former, along with another named LUZ, being specially composed for that work.

Grell, August Edward, born at Berlin, November 6, 1800; pupil of Zelter, J. C. Kaufman, and others; at sixteen years of age became organist of St Nicholas' Church in Berlin; director of the Sing-Akademie for upwards of twenty years; appointed a professor of composition at the Berlin Royal Academy, 1858; composer of many psalms, a 16-part mass—which is his most important work, —hymns, an oratorio, "Die Israeliten in der Wüste," a Te Deum, several motets, &c.; died at Steglitz, near Berlin, August 10, 1886.

S.S. No. 96 U.P.H., "Behold the Lamb of God."
S.S. No. 53 U.P.H., "Bow down thine ear."

S.S. No. 73 U.P.H., "The Lord is gracious."
S.S. No. 5 U.P.H., "The righteous shall be glad."
The first of these is an adaptation.

The last three appear in their present form for the first time in Dr Lowell Mason's 'Hallelujah,' 1854.

Grigg. The tune

TIVERTON, No. 84 F.C.H., 169 S.P., 148 U.P.P., 113 and 267 S.H., and 157 P. and P., is one of three assigned to a composer of the above name in 'A Selection of Psalm and Hymn Tunes, from the best Authors,' 1806, edited by the Rev. John Rippon, D.D. The melody has been sadly tinkered in the Church of Scotland Collections.

Grigg, Rev. Joseph, born in humble life in the early part of the eighteenth century; at first a mechanic; assistant pastor of the Presbyterian Church, Silver Street, London; retired from the ministry in 1747, and died at Walthamstow, Essex, October 29, 1768; author of many hymns. The writer can find no authority for assigning the tune "Tiverton" to the Rev. Joseph Grigg.

Grosvenor, Simeon, born at Dudley, January 11, 1816; pupil of Moscheles and Thomas Adams; appointed organist of St Thomas's Parish Church, Dudley, 1836, and held that office till October 1854; graduated Mus. Bac., Oxford, November 3, 1852; an accomplished performer on the organ and violin; died at Dudley, 7th or 8th July 1866, and interred in Vicar Street Burial-ground on the 13th. Edited 'Hymns, Anthems, Chants, &c., as used in the Services at St Thomas's Church, Dudley.' The work bears no date, but was published before he graduated. His tune

ST MINVER, No. 146 S.P., appears without a name in the above collection, set to the words "Jerusalem, my happy home." It is better known by the name "Jerusalem."

Hamburger Musikalisches Handbuch. The exact title of this work is 'Musikalisches Handbuch der geistlichen Melodien,' Hamburg, 1690.

CRASSELIUS, No. 11 P. and P., 36 S.H., 225 U.P.P., and 192 U.P.H., where it is also named "Winchester," is adapted from the chorale "Dir, Dir, Jehovah, will ich singen," in the above work. The melody stands thus in 'Freylinghausen,' 1741 (No. 721):—

HAMBURGER MUSIKALISCHES HANDBUCH. 149

In 'A Collection of Tunes, Set to Music, as they are commonly Sung at the Foundery,' 1742, which was prepared under the direction of the Rev. John Wesley, the following reading is given, and the tune is named "Swift German Tune":—

In 'The Psalm Singer's Compleat Tutor and Divine Companion,' by Thomas Moore, Manchester, second edition, 1750, the tune is named "Winchester," and the melody is in the following form:—

Key C.

```
{ :s   | d¹  :—  :s   | l   :—  :l   | s   :—  :f   | m.,r:d    }
{ :m   | f   :—  :m   | r   :—  :s   | l   :s  :fe  | s   :—    }
{ :s   | d¹  :—  :r¹  | m¹ :-.r¹:d¹  | f¹  :—  :m¹  | r¹  :—    }
{ :m¹.,r¹| d¹ :t  :l  | s   :—  :d¹.,r¹| m¹ :—  :r¹  | d¹  :—  ‖
```

Moore also published the tune in the same form and under the same name, in his 'Delightful Pocket Companion,' Glasgow (1762). This seems to fix the date of its introduction into Scotland.

EFFINGHAM, No. 61 S.P. and 56 F.C.H., is another form of the same chorale.

There seem no good grounds for assigning this tune to Bartholomäus Crasselius, as is done by some editors.

Hanby, Rev. Benjamin Russell, American divine and amateur composer. Born, 1833; died, 1867. His tune

LOWLINESS, No. 380 F.C.H., and 391 S.H., there named "Who is He?" appears in 'The Dove: A Collection of Music for Day and Sunday Schools,' which he edited in conjunction with G. F. Root, Chicago, 1866. The hymn to which it is set is also his.

Händel, Georg Friedrich, son of Georg Händel, surgeon, was born at Halle, in Saxony, February 23, 1685; studied under Zachau, cathedral organist at Halle; settled in London in 1712, where he died, April 13, 1759; buried in Westminster Abbey. The tunes bearing his name are mostly adaptations from his oratorios, by which he is universally known.

SAMSON, No. 24 S.P. and 14 F.C.H., is adapted from the chorus, "Then round about the starry throne," in the oratorio of that name, composed in 1742.

SOLOMON, No. 160 S.P. and 150 P. and P., is from the solo, "What though I trace," in the oratorio of that name, composed in 1748. The first strain is identical with a tune by Tallis in Archbishop Parker's 'Psalter.' (See Tallis.)

THEODORA, No. 173 (Second Tune) S.H., is from the solo, "Angels ever bright and fair," in the oratorio of that name, composed in 1749, and performed in 1750.

SAUL, No. 237 U.P.H., is from the "Dead March," in the oratorio of that name, composed in 1738.

MAMRE, No. 244 S.H., is from the solo, "Shall I on Mamre's fertile plains," in the oratorio of "Joshua," composed in 1747.

DAVID, No. 338 F.C.H., is adapted from the aria, "Rendi'l sereno al ciglio," in his opera "Sosarme," performed in 1732.

SAXONY, No. 186 S.P., appears as a psalm tune in 'The Psalms of David, for the Use of Parish Churches,' edited by Drs Arnold and Callcott, 1791, and is adapted from the song, "Non vi piacque ingiusti Dei," in his opera "Siroe," performed in 1728. It is in 'Sacred Harmony,' by the Rev. Dr Andrew Thomson, Edinburgh, 1820, and was for many years a favourite tune in Scottish churches.

GOPSAL, No. 251 (Second Tune) S.H., 150 F.C.H.; CANNONS, No. 182 U.P.H. and 7 P. and P., are two of three tunes composed by Händel to hymns by the Rev. Charles Wesley, and discovered in the Fitzwilliam Library, Cambridge, by Samuel Wesley, who published them with the original words and the following account of their origin:—

"The late comedian, Rich, was also proprietor of Covent Garden Theatre, during the period when Händel conducted his oratorios at that house. He married a person who became a serious character after having formerly been a very contrary one, and who requested Händel to set to music the three hymns which I transcribed in the Fitzwilliam Library, from the autography, and published them in consequence."

"Gopsal" was composed for a hymn on the Resurrection, "Rejoice, the Lord is King," and "Cannons" for "Sinners, obey the Gospel word."

The rhythm of the tune "Chandos" or "Cannons," as given in the U.P.H. and P. and P., is considerably different from the original, a copy of which is here given:—

MELODY OF TUNE "CANNONS" AS COMPOSED BY HÄNDEL.

The third tune, KEDRON, will be found in the 'Scottish Hymnal' of 1872, set to the words for which it was composed, "O Love Divine, how sweet thou art!" It has been omitted in the new S.H., and a not very suitable one set in its stead.

GOSS, No. 241 S.H. (Second Tune), is an adaptation by Sir John Goss from the duet, "Cease thy anguish," in the oratorio "Athalia," composed by Händel in 1733. A peculiar metre tune adapted from the same source appears in the 'Sacred Harp,' Glasgow (1840).

CHANT, No. 238 S.P. and 171 U.P.P., is an adaptation from the duet, "Joys in gentle trains appearing," also in "Athalia."

The same Chant is set to S.S., No. 119 U.P.H., "Comfort ye, comfort ye, my people."

Harington, Henry, M.D., son of Henry Harington and Mary Backwell; born at Kelston,[1] Somersetshire, September 29,[2] 1727; entered Queen's College, Oxford, December 16, 1745, and matriculated at the University on the following day; graduated B.A. July 8, 1749 (not 1748, as stated by some), and proceeded M.A. June 4, 1752; Bachelor and Doctor of Medicine, July 2, 1762; established himself as a physician at Wells in 1753; settled at Bath in 1771; and was elected mayor in 1793; founded the Harmonic Society there; devoted his leisure time to the composition of glees, catches, songs, &c.; died January 15, 1816; buried at Kelston, January 23 (not in Bath Abbey, as commonly stated). Two sons by his wife, Miss Musgrave, were Sir Edward Harington and Henry Harington, D.D.

HARINGTON, No. 244 U.P.H., 109 U.P.P., 87 P. and P., 76 S.P., was published about 1780, under the title of "Retirement," for three voices, in the following form, and to the words given below:—

"RETIREMENT."

[1] His birth at Kelston is an accepted tradition, which cannot be verified by the baptismal records of that parish, as they contain no entry of the event. As his parents inherited the estate of Kelston in the year 1726, it is very probable that he *was* born there.

[2] The 20th is usually given, but the above date is from his monument in Bath Abbey. The writer has to acknowledge the kindness of the Rev. F. R. Poynton, Vicar of Kelston, who examined not only the records of his own parish, but also those of the parishes of Bath, in search of the entry of Dr Harington's birth.

I.

"Beneath the silent rural cell
    Of innocence and peace,
With sage retirement let me dwell,
    And taste each home-felt bliss.

II.

O let me pierce the secret shade,
    Chear'd by the warbling woods;
Or woo the venerable maid,
    Lull'd by the gliding floods.

III.

Then learn when noon of life be past,
    To calmly meet my end,
And feel my setting sun at last
    The grave unfear'd descend."

It appears as a hymn tune in the third set of Magdalen Hymns published before 1787.

John Wilson's 'A Selection of Psalm Tunes, Sanctuses, Doxologies, &c., for the Use of St Mary's Church, Edinburgh,' 1825, exhibits probably its first appearance in a Scottish collection.

Harrison, John,[1] born at Canterbury; pupil of Goodban of that city, and "Russian" Field; settled in Deal in 1835; for eighteen years organist of St Andrew's Church, Deal; represented the South Ward of Deal in the Town Council for nearly five years; seized with a fatal illness while accompanying a soloist at a concert in aid of St Andrew's Infant School, Deal, and died February 21, 1871, aged sixty-three. Edited in 1838 'Sacred Music; A Selection of Psalm Tunes from the Works of J. S. Bach, Händel, &c. &c.'; also a 'Kyrie Eleison,' and 'Chants Arranged for Four Voices or a Single Voice, with a Separate Accompaniment for the Organ or Pianoforte.' From this is taken his tune

GUILTON, No. 34 in S.H. (First Tune).

Harrison, Rev. Ralph, a member of a family noted in the history of Nonconformity; descended from the Rev. Cuthbert Harrison, who was ejected from Lurgan,[2] in Ireland, in 1662; born September 10, 1748, at Chinley, Derbyshire, where his father, the Rev. William Harrison, was for upwards of twenty-seven years minister of a rural chapel; educated at the Warrington Academy; appointed assistant minister of the Unitarian Chapel, High Street, Shrewsbury, 1769; minister of Cross Street Unitarian Chapel, Manchester, from 1771 till he died, November 4, 1810; classical tutor in Manchester Academy; distinguished as a teacher of ancient languages; musical amateur and composer; published an English Grammar, and other works. Edited 'Sacred Harmony; A Collection of Psalm Tunes, Ancient and Modern, set in Four Parts.' Volume I., published February 1784,[3] contains his tunes

CAMBRIDGE, No. 189 S.P.

WARRINGTON, No. 3 F.C.H., 27 S.P., 198 U.P.P., 114 and 130 S.H., 41 P. and P., absurdly set in B Flat in the S.H. and P. and P. Original key, D.

---

[1] Harrison's Christian name is wrongly given as JAMES in the S.H.

[2] There is a tradition that it was from Singleton in Lancashire that he was ejected, but those who have written the history of that district treat the tradition as unfounded.

[3] Not 1786, as in the S.H., nor 1760, as in the S.P.

RIDLEY, No. 198 P. and P., appears there under its present name, in the form given below, and is anonymous—

ORIGINAL FORM OF "RIDLEY," AS IN HARRISON, VOL. I.

KEY F.

{ :d | s :— :d | r :d :t₁ | d :— ‖ m | r :— :s }
{ | l :s :fe | s :— ‖ r | f :— :m | l :— :s }
{ | d :f :m | r :— ‖ s | f :— :m | l⁽ᵈ⁾:m :r | d :— ‖

Volume II., published May 1791,[1] contains—

PETERBOROUGH, No. 119 S.P., 151 S.H., 118 P. and P., where it is anonymous. Known in Scotland for many years by the name of "The Precentor's Apology,"—"his apology for music when he is lazy, or afraid, or when an indiscreet minister has prescribed too long a psalm."

CHANT, No. 268 S.P., is there as a L.M. named "Sterling."

Hart, Philip, born about the middle of the seventeenth century; bass singer at York Minster till 1670; gentleman of the Chapel Royal, 1670 to 1718; lay vicar Westminster Abbey, 1670 to 1718; organist of St Andrew's, Undershaft; St Michael's, Cornhill; St Dionis, Blackheath, 1724; died in London at a great age, about 1749. His 'Melodies Proper to be Sung to any of ye Versions of ye Psalms of David,' were published about the year 1713. From that collection is taken

LICHFIELD, No. 105 in P. and P., where it is named "St Michael's Melody."

Hassler, Hans Leo, son of Isaac Hassler, a musician; born at Nürnberg, 1564; in 1584 pupil of Andrea Gabrieli, then organist of the Cathedral of St Mark, Venice; in 1585 became organist to Count Fugger in Augsburg, and from 1602, in Prague, to the Emperor Rudolph II.; died at Frankfort-on-the-Maine, June 8, 1612.

STUTTGART, No. 214 F.C.H., 44 U.P.H., was originally composed in 1601, to the words of a secular song, "Mein G'müth ist mir verwirret," for which

---

[1] Not 1790, as in the S.H.

the hymn "Herzlich thut mich verlangen" was afterwards substituted. Bach inserted it in his 'Grosse Passions Musik,' and adapted it to the hymn, "O Haupt voll Blut und Wunden."

BACH'S PASSION CHORALE, No. 50 S.H., is the same tune.

Hastings, Thomas, Mus. Doc., born in Lichfield, Connecticut, October 15, 1784; from 1824 to 1832 conducted a religious journal in Utica; for nearly forty years resident in New York, where he was invited by a number of the Churches to improve their psalmody, a subject he had given much attention to from his earliest years; composer of many hymns and tunes which were published in the Collections he issued; degree of Mus. Doc. conferred on him by the New York University, May 1858; died May 15, 1872. His tune

RETREAT, No. 21 S.P., 30 F.C.H., 241 U.P.H., was composed in 1840, and first appeared in 'Sacred Songs,' which he edited in 1842.

ORTON, No. 299 (Second Tune) F.C.H., appears in 'The Manhattan Collection,' first edition, 1837, and is there named "Ortonville."

INVITATION, No. 158 (First Tune) S.H., and the hymn to which it is set, were written in 1831, and published in 'Spiritual Songs for Social Worship,' 1832. The tune is there named "Return."

HASTINGS, No. 412 S.H., and the hymn to which it is set, were written in 1836. They appear in 'The Manhattan Collection,' 1837. The tune is there assigned to a composer—K. L.-F. F.—a *nom-de-plume* adopted by Dr Hastings, which has prevented him in some instances from getting the credit of the tune. "I had found (he said) that a foreigner's name went a great way, and that very ordinary tunes would be sung if Palestrina or Pucitta, &c., were over them, while a better tune by Hastings would go unnoticed."

S.S. No. 52 U.P.H., "Let the people praise Thee," was composed in 1836, and first published in 'The Manhattan Collection of Psalm and Hymn Tunes and Anthems,' 1837.

S.S. No. 50 U.P.H., "O Thou that hearest prayer," was composed in 1854, and published in 'The Selah,' 1856.

Hately, Thomas Legerwood, born at Greenlaw, Berwickshire, September 26, 1815[1]; apprenticed when a boy to Messrs Ballantyne & Co., printers, Edinburgh, with whom he remained eleven years; afterwards entered the employment of the Messrs Constable; a self-taught musician; member of R. A. Smith's choir, St George's, Edinburgh; appointed precentor of North Leith Parish Church, 1836; of St Mary's Church, Edinburgh, December 11, 1838, resigned at the Disruption, 1843. He had the distinction, it is said, of being

---

[1] Not 1816, as commonly stated.

one of the few precentors in Edinburgh who came out with the Free Church at that time. He led the singing at the first General Assembly of the Free Church at Tanfield, and in D. O. Hill's picture of that Assembly, Hately's portrait holds a prominent place. Afterwards appointed precentor to Free Church Assembly; accepted in 1850 the precentorship of the Free High Church, Edinburgh, then under the pastorate of the Rev. Dr Gordon. About the same time he devoted himself almost entirely to the teaching of psalmody and conducting classes throughout the country, and not only in this way, but also by the training of teachers, he gave the first great impulse in recent times to the cultivation of church music in Scotland; edited the 'National Psalmody,' and other works; died at Edinburgh, March 22, 1867.

GLENCAIRN, No. 71 S.P., was composed in 1850 for Psalm 42, that being a favourite Psalm of Dr Gordon's, whose birthplace was Glencairn.

LEUCHARS, No. 210 S.P., 45 U.P.P., 208 P. and P., was composed in 1855 for Psalm 143, second version.

ZUINGLE, No 181 S.P., was composed in 1840, and published as an 'Old Swiss Tune,' but was afterwards claimed by him.

CALWOOD, No. 360 S.H., and ELMHAM, No. 374 F.C.H., first appeared in Rev. Dr J. H. Wilson's 'Service of Praise,' Edinburgh, 1865. They received their names in 'Songs of Zion,' 1877. The former is an adaptation.

MAKERSTOUN, No. 292 (First Tune) S.H., and NENTHORN, No. 312 (Second Tune) F.C.H. and 241 (Third Tune) S.H., were first published in 'The Church of Scotland Hymn Tune Book,' 1865. The last was first published anonymously, but claimed as Mr Hately's composition in 1872.

DISMISSION, No. 362 U.P.H., was first published in 'Hymn Music,' 1858. The harmonies of OLD 100TH, No. 16 S.P., and MARTYRS, No. 98 S.P. are his.

Add to his compositions CHANTS No. 225 and 269 S.P.

Hately, Walter, son of the preceding, born at Edinburgh, January 29, 1843; educated at the High School, Edinburgh; studied music at Leipzig Conservatoire under Plaidy, Moscheles, Reinecke, Hauptmann, Richter, and Dreyschock, 1861 to 1864; teacher of music in Edinburgh since 1865; first public appearance as pianist at Edinburgh, January 1867; choirmaster in Free High Church in succession to his father, from 1867 to 1871; pianoforte teacher in Ladies' College; Training College of the Church of Scotland; teacher of harmony in connection with St George's Hall classes; choirmaster, Free St George's Church, since April 1885; composer of psalm and hymn tunes, anthems, songs, and pianoforte music. His tune

St Helen, No. 212 in 'Scottish Hymnal,' was composed for the 'Scottish Hymnal,' 1872. It is indelibly associated with the Hymn to which it is set.

Inchcolm, No. 283 F.C.H., and S.S., Nos. 15, "Thou wilt keep him," and 22, "Who is a God like unto Thee," were first published in that work.

Hatton, John, born at Warrington; afterwards resided in Duke Street, St Helens, in the township of Windle; died 1793. His tune

Duke Street, No. 13 P. and P., 6 S.P., 197 U.P.P., 284 U.P.H., bears its present name in William Dixon's 'Euphonia,' published about 1800.

In the original there is no A (♩) in the last measure of the third line. The correct form is given in the U.P. Collections. This tune found a place in the Scottish Psalmodies at an early period of its existence, as it appears in Henry Boyd's Collection, published at Glasgow in 1793, under the name of 'Addison's 19th Psalm.' This is the earliest copy the writer has seen.

Havergal, Rev. William Henry, born at High Wycombe, Buckinghamshire, January 18, 1793, baptised February 15; educated at St Edmund's Hall, Oxford, where he graduated in 1815; took Holy Orders, February 24, 1816; M.A., June 25, 1819; rector of Astley, Worcestershire, 1829 to 1842; honorary canon, Worcester Cathedral, 1845; rector of St Nicholas, Worcester, 1845 to 1860, when he resigned; rector of Shareshill from 1860 to 1868; died at Leamington, April 19, 1870; published a reprint of 'Ravenscroft's Psalter' in 1844, and three years later the 'Old Church Psalmody,' which reached the fifth edition in 1864; 'A History of the Old Hundredth Psalm Tune, with Specimens,' in 1854, and in 1859 'A Hundred Psalm and Hymn Tunes' of his own composition; composer of much excellent church music. The following tunes are his, the dates of their composition being given in brackets:—

Baca (1852), No. 260 F.C.H.
Bethabara (1860), No. 131 U.P.H.
Capernaum (1860), No. 281 U.P.H. (Second Tune).
Chesalon (1854), No. 183 U.P.P.
Eden (1845), No. 88 U.P.P., 60 S.P., 74 F.C.H.
Havergal (April 16, 1870), No. 278 U.P.H. (First Tune).
Havilah (1870), Doxology No. 9 U.P.H.
Idumea (1866), Doxology No. 13 U.P.H.
Midian (1861), No. 116 U.P.H.
Patmos (1869), No. 177 S.H.
Sheba (1865), No. 248 U.P.H.
Zoan (1845), No. 285 U.P.H.

HAVERGAL. 159

HAVERGAL consists of the first three strains of a triple 7 7 7 tune he composed at the request of a friend, on Easter Eve, April 16, 1870. It was the last he ever wrote. The lines omitted in U.P.H. are here given.

KEY G.

r :r	r :r	s :s	s :—	m :m	m :d	r :d	t₁ :—
s₁ :s₁	fe₁:fe₁	s₁ :d	t₁ :—	d :d	t₁ :d	l₁ :l₁	se₁:—
t₁ :r	r :r	r :m	r :—	m :d	m :m	f :m	m :—
s₁ :t₁	r :d	t₁ :d	s₁ :—	d :l₁	se₁:l₁	f₁ :l₁	m₁ :—

d :d	d :d	r :t₁	l₁ :—	l₁ :l₁	s₁ :s₁	d :r	t₁ :—
l₁ :l₁	ta₁:l₁	l₁ :se₁	l₁ :—	l₁ :f₁	s₁ :s₁	l₁ :l₁	s₁ :—
m :f	s :f	f :m.r	d :—	d :d	m :r	m :f	r :—
l₁ :f₁	m₁ :f₁	r₁ :m₁	l₁ :—	f₁ :l₁	d :t₁	l₁ :f₁	s₁ :—

m :d	f :m	r :d	s :—	f :m	r :d	d :-.d	d :—
s₁ :s₁	f₁ :s₁	f₁ :fe₁	s₁ :—	l₁ :d	t₁ :d	l₁ :-.l₁	s₁ :—
d :d	t₁ :d	l₁ :d	t₁ :—	r :s	s :m	f :-.f	m :—
d₁ :m₁	r₁ :m₁	f₁ :l₁	s₁ :—	r₁ :m₁.f₁	s₁ :l₁	f₁ :-.f₁	d₁ :—

EVAN, No. 76 (Second Tune) F.C.H., 64 S.P., 36 U.P.P., 105 U.P.H., 76 P. and P., 24 (Second Tune) S.H., and 218, is one of the most popular tunes in use at the present time in the Churches of Scotland. Its history is interesting, and may be told in a few words.

In 1846 Mr Havergal composed music for Burns's Prayer, beginning "O Thou dread pow'r, who reign'st above," lines which the poet left lying on a table in the room where he had slept when on a visit to Dr Laurie's family at the Manse of Loudon. The music is purposely framed in the Scotch style, and was inscribed to Mrs Laurie of Monkton Manse, the profits from the sale of the song being given to the Monkton industrial schools. A copy of the melody is here given :—

Dr Lowell Mason of New York having received a copy of this song, was much struck with its beauty. He arranged the 1st, 2d, 7th, and 8th strains as a psalm tune, altered the measure to three-two time, and published it in the 'New Carmina Sacra,' copyrighted July 18, 1850. It is there named "Eva," and the letter H. only given as composer. In 'Cantica Laudis,' copyrighted August 10, 1850, it is named "Evan," and the measure altered to that of the song. In 'The Shawm,' issued in 1853, Dr Mason gave Mr Havergal credit for the melody of this tune. In the United States it is generally used in three-two time, thus—

Key A♭.

{ :s₁ | s₁ .d :m | :r | d .l₁ :s₁ ‖ etc.

Writing in March 1870, Mr Havergal says: "As the American arrangement was a sad estrangement, I have reconstructed the tune after a more correct form. Why it was called 'Evan' I know not. Still I do not approve the tune."

"EVAN," AS ARRANGED AND HARMONISED BY MR HAVERGAL,
MARCH 19, 1870.

Key A♭.

s₁	:—	s₁	:d	m	:r	d	:l₁	s₁	:— ‖ s₁	:—
m₁	:—	r₁	:s₁	s₁	:f₁	s₁	:f₁	m₁	:— ‖ s₁	:—
Je	.	sus,	the	ve	- ry	thought	of	Thee,		With	
d	:—	t₁	:d	d	:l₁	d	:d	d	:— ‖ m	:—
d	:—	s₁	:m₁	d₁	:r₁	m₁	:f₁	d₁	:— ‖ d	:—

L

```
{ |s₁ :d  |m  :d  |r  :—  ||f  :—  |m  :r  |d  :r  )
  |s₁ :m₁ |m₁ :m₁ |s₁ :—  ||l₁ :—  |s₁ :s₁ |m₁ :l₁
     sweet-ness fills my breast;   But     sweet-er far  Thy
  |r  :d  |t₁ :d  |t₁ :—  ||d  :—  |d  :t₁ |d  :l₁
  |t₁ :l₁ |se₁:l₁ |s₁ :—  ||f₁ :—  |d  :s₁ |l₁ :f₁  }

{ |m  :d  |l₁ :—  ||s₁ :—  |s₁ :d  |m  :r  |d  :—  |—  :—  ||
  |se₁:l₁ |l₁ :—  ||m₁ :—  |s₁ :fe |s₁ :—.f₁|m₁ :—  |—  :—
     face to see,     And     in   Thy pre-sence   rest.
  |t₁ :d  |d  :—  ||d  :—  |r  :d  |d  :t₁ |d  :—  |—  :—
  |m₁ :l₁ |f₁ :—  ||d  :—  |t₁ :l₁ |s₁ :s₁ |d₁ :—  |—  :—  ||
```

Here also is given the entire melody of the song in common time, arranged by Mr Havergal about 1867 :—

I heard the voice of Je-sus say, "Come un-to Me and rest:
Lay down, thou wear-y one, lay down Thy head up-on My breast!"
I came to Je-sus as I was, Wea-ry, and worn, and sad;
I found in Him a rest-ing-place, And He has made me glad.

HAVERGAL.

Key G.

{sol-fa notation for hymn tune, lyrics:}

I heard the voice of Je-sus say, "Come un-to
Me and rest: Lay down, thou wea-ry one, lay
down Thy head up-on My breast! I came to
Je-sus as I was, Wea-ry, and worn, and sad;
found in Him a rest-ing-place, And He has made me glad.

Below will be found a copy of a letter, dated May 25, 1872, from Mrs Havergal to Mr J. O. Anderson of Edinburgh, in which she gives her opinion as to the origin of the name "Evan":—

"In visiting Scotland last year, I for the first time saw the little stream Evan, and *I* have a fancy that Dr Lowell Mason took up the nomenclature from that, as he in the very year in which he first had this piece ('O Thou dread Pow'r') and sent it out to America as a hymn tune, had visited that part of Scotland—Moffat—where the stream is. I have written to ask the question of him, though when asked by my dear husband he could not remember *why* he had given the name. My reminding him of this stream may recall it to his memory."

No answer was received to Mrs Havergal's letter, as Dr Mason died a few weeks after. Mrs Havergal's surmise, however, hardly coincides with the following facts: 1st, That Dr Mason originally named the tune 'Eva'; 2d, That it was first published by him in 1850; 3d, That he did not visit Scotland till 1852, and that in his journal no mention is made of having visited Moffat; 4th, That the existence of such an insignificant stream is hardly likely to have been known to Dr Mason.

CHANT, No. 266 S.P., composed about 1834, is known as "Worcester Chant."

CHANT in A, No. 119 U.P.P., composed about 1836. Both were published in 1836 in 'A Hundred Double Antiphonal Chants, with Remarks on Chants and Chanting.'

CHANT in A is set to S.S. No. 116 U.P.H., "O Lord, Thou art my God."

S.S. No. 70 U.P.H., "Lord, we cry unto Thee," is adapted from two Kyries composed by Mr Havergal in 1863. Mr Carnie of Aberdeen, who made the adaptation, set it to Psalm 141, and published it in the Anthem Appendix to his 'Northern Psalter.'

ST JOHN, No. 215 P. and P., 204, 269, 392 S.H. For assigning this tune to Mr Havergal in the first edition of P. and P. the writer was responsible. Finding it ascribed to him by several editors of important tune books, he communicated with Miss M. V. G. Havergal (now deceased), and was positively informed that her father composed the tune about 1840 for a church missionary anniversary at Astley, Worcestershire. Her father's MS. music books not being accessible, she furnished the writer with a copy of the tune as it appears in his *own* Appendix to 'Old Church Psalmody,' and which she asserted was taken from his MS. tune book. It appears assigned to him in 'Songs of Grace and Glory,' 1879, a work prepared by the late Frances Ridley Havergal, and is now given in a few important Collections as his composition. For the following reasons the writer questions Havergal's authorship:—

1. The object of the 'Parish Choir' (in which the tune seems to have been first published) was the revival of old music, and it is doubtful if the editor would knowingly have admitted music by a living composer. The editor was of the opinion that "St John" was an old tune, although he could not distinctly trace the authorship.

2. During the progress of 'Congregational Church Music' through the press, Mr Havergal (to whom the organ score was dedicated) gave much assistance in settling the authorship and sources of many of the tunes, but he made no claim to "St John."

3. After a careful examination of Mr Havergal's MS. volumes, the tune is not found there. See 'Congregational Church Music.'

Havergal,[1] **Frances Ridley,** youngest daughter of the preceding; born at Astley Rectory, Worcestershire, December 14,

---

[1] See Memorials of Frances Ridley Havergal (James Nisbet & Co., London for full details of her career.

1836; pupil of William Marshall, Mus. Doc., and Alberto Randegger; died at Caswell Bay, Swansea, June 3, 1879; well known by her hymns (many of which she set to music) and other writings. Her tunes

EIRENE, No. 45 (Second Tune) S.H.; HERMAS, No. 365 F.C.H., 96 U.P.H., 393 S.H.; and SARDIS CHANT, No. 49 U.P.P., were composed in 1870, and published in 'Havergal's Psalmody,' which she edited in 1871.

In the U.P.H. the refrain of "Hermas" is not given. It consists of the 1st, 2d, 7th, and 8th strains of the tune.

Haydn, Franz Joseph, eldest son of Matthias Haydn, a wheelwright, was born at Rohrau, a village in Lower Austria, March 31, 1732; universally known by his instrumental compositions, and his oratorio "The Creation," finished in 1798; died at Gumpendorf, near Vienna, May 31, 1809.

AUSTRIAN HYMN, No. 234 F.C.H., 243 U.P.H. (there named "Austria"), 191 S.H. (there named "Haydn's Hymn"), was composed for Hauschka's National Hymn, January 1797, and was first publicly performed on the Emperor's birthday, February 12, following. Haydn afterwards introduced it in his quartet for stringed instruments (Op. 76, No. 3), where it is the slow movement with variations. It appears as a hymn tune in 'Sacred Music'—intended as an Appendix to Dr Watts' 'Psalms and Hymns,' edited by Dr Miller (1800). An interesting incident in connection with this tune is related in the 'Athenæum' of June 18, 1842:—

Mendelssohn was paying his seventh visit to London in that year, staying at Denmark Hill, in the southern suburbs of the Metropolis. On a summer's Sunday evening he went to St Peter's Church, Cornhill. As he entered the church the congregation were singing Haydn's well-known tune. He was asked to play the out-going voluntary, and took as his theme the tune which had been sung, "The Emperor's Hymn," "and wrought it out for more than half an hour, exhausting every contrivance (so it seemed) of reply, rejoinder, harmonic change, and episodical embellishment." On the following Thursday, at Christ Church, Newgate Street, he was asked to take again the same theme. A grand fantasia and fugue was the result, *totally different* from that on the previous Sunday, "save in its consummate variety and skill, as it had been the work of other organists' hands and feet," and—may we not add?—brains. In the course of the movement Mendelssohn held down the top A on the swell, and treated it as an inverted pedal point of great length. His auditors thought that the long A was a cipher, and that the manual would become useless; but after harmonising the note in a variety of different ways, he held it for some time alone, when the A quietly glided through G sharp to G natural, and then to F sharp. On coming down from the organ loft and rejoining his friends, he laughingly said, "You thought it was a cipher—I *know* you did." Would that Mendelssohn had written down even *one* of his masterly improvisations!—(F. G. Edwards in the 'Nonconformist Musical Journal,' November 1890.)

DAYSTAR, No. 173 F.C.H., is from the slow movement of a Symphony in E flat. OTTERBOURNE, No. 18 S.P., from a Symphony. Both appear as hymn tunes in Gardiner's 'Sacred Melodies from Haydn, Mozart, and Beethoven,' vol. i., 1812.

CASTERTON, No. 155 F.C.H. and 92 U.P.H., is assigned to Haydn, but the writer cannot trace the source.

ELAH, No. 255 (Second Tune) F.C.H., is from the slow movement in A of a Symphony in D (No. 20 in the Litolff Edition).

Haydn, Johann Michael, younger brother of Joseph Haydn; born at Rohrau, September 14, 1737; died at Salzburg, August 10, 1806; an excellent composer of sacred music, which included masses, motets, &c.

COWPER, No. 52 S.P., 76 F.C.H., 86 P. and P. (there named "Grimma"); SALZBURG, No. 156 S.P., 98 F.C.H., 37 U.P.P., 178 U.P.H., 147 P. and P.; and GREENLAND, No. 108 (Second Tune) S.H., 209 F.C.H., are all adapted from movements in a Mass composed for the use of country choirs.

These movements will be found in the Rev. C. J. La Trobe's 'Sacred Music,' 1806.

Hayes, William, Mus. Doc., son of John Hayes; born at Hanbury, Worcestershire; baptised December 12, 1706; chorister in Gloucester Cathedral under William Hine; organist of St Mary's, Shrewsbury, from 1729 to 1731; of Worcester Cathedral, 1731 to 1734; of Magdalen College, Oxford, 1734 to 1777; Professor of Music in Oxford University, 1741; Mus. Bac., Oxford, 1735; Mus. Doc. 1749; died at Oxford, July 27, 1777; buried in the churchyard of St Peter's-in-the-East, Oxford.

HEREFORD, No. 78 S.P., is from his 'Sixteen Psalms selected from the Rev. Mr Merrick's New Version; Set to Music.' (1774.)

CHANT, No. 175 U.P.P. and 239 S.P., is his.

Nos. 334 and 355 U.P.H., 272 S.P., 262 and 386 S.H., 284 and 373 F.C.H., is a reduced copy by A. H. D. Troyte of the same chant.

Hayes, Rev. William, son of the preceding, born at Oxford; baptised at St Peter's-in-the-East Church there, November 6, 1741; chorister at Magdalen College, Oxford, 1749 to 1751; graduated B.A. April 7, 1761, at Magdalen College; M.A. January 15, 1764, at New College; Minor Canon, Worcester Cathedral, 1765; of St Paul's Cathedral, 1766; Vicar of Tillingham, Essex, from July 1783; died October 22, 1790; author of 'Rules necessary to be observed by all Cathedral Singers in the Kingdom,' and other works.

LADBROKE, No. 89 S.P., is assigned to him by Dr Crotch.

Hayne, Rev. Leighton George, Mus. Doc., son of the Rev. Richard Hayne, D.D., Rector of Mistley, Essex, was born at St David's Hill, Exeter, February 28, 1836; educated at Eton and Queen's College, Oxford; graduated Mus. Bac., 1856; Mus. Doc., 1860; took holy orders in 1861; appointed Coryphæus[1] of the University in 1863, and Public Examiner in the School of Music; succentor and organist of Eton College, 1868; rector of Mistley, and vicar of Bradfield, Essex, 1871; died at Bradfield, March 3, 1883. The following tunes are from the 'Merton Tune Book,' which he edited in conjunction with the Rev. H. W. Sargeant in 1863 :—

BUCKLAND, No. 415 S.H.
COMPLINE, No. 45 F.C.H. and 79 U.P.H.
HAYNE, No. 77 S.P., is an adaptation from Spohr. (See that name.)
MISTLEY, No. 313 F.C.H.
ST ANSELM, No. 18 F.C.H., although marked as his, is anonymous in the 'Merton Tune Book.' It is an ancient melody.
ST CECILIA, No. 222 S.H., 211 S.P., 259 F.C.H.
ST LAWRENCE, No. 312 S.H.
ST MARGARET, No. 142 S.P., 87 U.P.P., 209 U.P.H.

CHALVEY, No. 248 (First Tune) S.H., was composed for the hymn to which it is set, and first published in the Appendix to 'Hymns Ancient and Modern,' 1868.

WIX, No. 86 F.C.H., was first published in that work.

Heathcote, Rev. Gilbert, M.A., Oxford; Fellow of New College, Oxford, 1788, and of Winchester College, 1804; rector of Hursley, and vicar of Andover, Hants; Archdeacon of Winchester, 1819; died in London, October 19, 1829, in his sixty-fifth year.

CHANT in A, No. 120 U.P.P., 258 S.P., appears in 'A Selection of Single and Double Chants in Score,' edited by John Clarke-Whitfeld, Mus. Doc.

Hebrew Melody.

LEONI, No. 322 F.C.H., 23 U.P.H., 235 S.H., 210 P. and P. It is said that Thomas Olivers having written the hymn "The God of Abraham praise," applied to one Leoni,[2] a Jew, and celebrated as a vocalist in London, to furnish a tune, who gave him the one named above. Another account is,

---

[1] Conductor of the Chorus.
[2] Leoni was one of the instructors of John Braham, the eminent vocalist. He was dismissed from the Synagogue for taking part in a performance of the "Messiah." He is said to have died at Jamaica, October 1796.

that Olivers first heard the tune sung by Leoni in the Synagogue, and being greatly impressed by its effect, immediately wrote the hymn to suit it. The words and music were published together in 1772. It is very doubtful if it is of Hebrew origin, as it resembles a chorale by Christian Flor, organist at Luneburg about 1560.

It seems to have been first published in a Scotch Psalmody in 1793, as it is found in Henry Boyd's Collection, issued in that year. A part of this tune is used by Sir Michael Costa in the overture to his oratorio of "Eli," produced at Birmingham Musical Festival, 1855.

S.S., No. 1 U.P. and F.C. Hymnals, "The Lord bless thee and keep thee." The history of this may be told in a few words. A German organist believing he had discovered among the Hebrew points some that were guides to the music of the Psalms and poetical part of the Old Testament, published a 'Hebrew Psalter, with Notes.' Dr Lowell Mason got the book, and tried to adapt it to English words, finding, however, nothing he could use but the above. On its publication in 'Congregational Anthems,' a copy was forwarded to the late Rev. Dr N. M. Adler, Chief Rabbi, London, by Dr W. M. Cooke, asking if the Jews had music at all like it in use in their Synagogues. Dr Adler replied in the negative, adding, "We put no faith in the German organist's book." The harmonies are wholly by Dr Mason.

Hegler, Rev. Jacob Gottfried, born December 17, 1794, in Oehringen in Würtemberg; minister of Markgröningen near Ludwigsburg; after September 15, 1865, lived in retirement at Cannstadt, where he died November 8, 1877.

Monsell, No. 142 U.P.H., "Nicht eine (diese) Welt, die in ihr Nichts vergeht," is his, and was published in the South German 'Schulbote,' 1850, afterwards in Kocher's 'Zionsharfe' (No. 684), 1855, where there is another by him (No. 1058).

Hemy, Henri Frederick, son of Henri Hemy, a native of Saxe Gotha; born at Newcastle-on-Tyne, November 12, 1818; for many years organist of St Andrew's Roman Catholic Church, Newcastle, and a professor of music at North Shields; now holds a similar position at Ushaw College, Durham; universally known by his Pianoforte Tutor, which has had an enormous sale. Edited 'Crown of Jesus Music.' Parts I. and II. consist of Latin Hymns, Part III. consists of Chants, Latin Hymns, and Benediction Services. Issued in one volume, 1864. Part IV. of Masses: no date.

Stella, No. 353 U.P.H., 46 (Second Tune) F.C.H., 397 S.H., is an English air, and appears in Part I. (page 75). The form given in the S.H. is a corrupt abridgment.

Henderson, Rev. Andrew, a self-taught musician, born at Kirkwall, Orkney, January 4, 1825; educated at Tay Square

School, and the Academy, Dundee, also at the University of St Andrews; ordained at Coldingham, Berwickshire, June 2, 1847; inducted to Abbey Close U.P. Church, Paisley, April 17, 1855; acted as Secretary to Hymnal Committee of United Presbyterian Church, and Convener of Sub-Committee for Preparing Musical Editions of Presbyterian Hymnal, Psalter, Scripture Sentences, and Hymnal for the Young; elected F.R.S.A. 1884; degree of LL.D. conferred on him by the University of St Andrews, 1887. Edited 'Church Melodies,' 1858, 1860, and 1862. Also 'The New Scottish Psalter,' 1870. These works contain several tunes by Dr Henderson.

S.S., No. 85 U.P.H., "O the Hope of Israel," was composed for that work.

Hermann, Nicolaus, was from 1518 precentor and schoolmaster at Joachimsthal, in the north of Bohemia; retired about 1548, and devoted himself to writing hymns, which he set to music and published in 1560; died May 5, 1561.

St George, No. 131 P. and P., 134 S.P., 150 U.P.P., 115 F.C.H., and 71 (Second Tune) S.H., is an altered copy of the chorale, "Lobt Gott, ihr Christen allegleich," published in his collection in 1560. It was published in Scotland about the middle of last century, in a different form from that now in use.

Hervey, Rev. Frederick Alfred John, son of Lord Alfred Hervey; born in London, May 18, 1846; graduated B.A. Cambridge, 1868; M.A. 1872; took holy orders, 1869; rector of Upton Pyne, 1876; of Sandringham, and Domestic Chaplain to the Prince of Wales, 1878; honorary chaplain to the Queen, 1882. His tune

Castle Rising, No. 97 F.C.H., appears in 'The Hymnary,' edited by Joseph Barnby, 1872, and is there set to the same hymn as in the F.C.H. It had appeared some years before in the first edition of the Rev. R. Brown-Borthwick's 'Supplemental Hymn and Tune Book,' with a slightly different reading at the end of the 3d and beginning of 4th strains.

Hewlett, Thomas, Mus. Bac., son of Mr Thomas Hewlett, of Oxford; born at Oxford, March 16, 1845; pupil of the Rev. L. G. Hayne, Mus. Doc.; graduated as Bachelor in Music at the University of Oxford in 1859; organist of the Duke of Buccleuch's Chapel at Dalkeith from 1865 to 1871, and for eighteen months of 1868 and 1869 of St Peter's Episcopal Church, Edinburgh, the duties of the morning service being performed by a deputy; of St Mary's Roman Catholic Church, Broughton Street, Edinburgh, for some time; of Newington Parish Church, Edinburgh, from November 1873 till he died, April 10, 1874; buried in Newington Cemetery, where a monument was erected to his memory by the members of the Edinburgh Choral Union "in acknowledgment of his musical talent and his great ability as organist of that Society."

DALKEITH, No. 168 (First Tune) S.H. Composed for the 'St Alban's Tune Book.'

ANGELIC SONGS, No. 247 (Second Tune) S.H., was published on single slips in 1873, and afterwards found a place in the 'Church of Scotland Anthem Book,' 1876.

Hews, George, born in Massachusetts, United States of America, in 1806; was a manufacturer of pianofortes, and an organist in Boston; died July 6, 1873. His tune

HOLLEY, No. 426 S.H., was first published in the 'Boston Academy Collection,' edited by Dr Lowell Mason, 1835, and is there set to the hymn, "Softly now the light of day."

Hill, John, born in the parish of St Michael Coslany, Norwich, April 5, 1797; baptised April 9; led the psalmody at St Mary's Chapel there for many years; appointed in 1826 chorus-master of the Musical Festivals and Choral Society, an office he held till his death, July 28, 1846.

ABRAHAM, No. 235 S.H., is one of seventeen tunes contributed by him to 'The Norwich Tune Book,' which he edited in conjunction with his son, the late James Frederick Hill, in 1844. It is there named "Dundee."

Himmel, Friedrich Heinrich, born at Treuenbrietzen, Brandenburg, November 20, 1765; studied for the Church at Halle, but the excellence of his pianoforte-playing induced the king, Frederic William II., to have him educated as a musician; chapel-master to Frederic William II. and his successor; composer of operas, psalms, masses, &c.; died at Berlin, June 8, 1814.

S.S., No. 37 U.P.H., " Incline Thine ear," was adapted by Vincent Novello to Latin words from movement No. 3 (Hope) in " Urania," a didactic poem, in six cantos, by Christoph August Tiedge, portions of which Himmel set to music. It was adapted to "Incline Thine ear" by William Patten, and published in the 'Musical Times,' January 1, 1854.

Hine,[1] **William,** son of John and Margaret Hine, born at Brightwell, Oxfordshire, 1687; baptised June 12; chorister of

---

[1] In the Baptismal Register the name is written "Hinde."

Magdalen College, Oxford, from 1694 until 1705, when he was appointed a clerk; in the same year he was dismissed from his office and removed to London, where he studied under Jeremiah Clark; in 1712 appointed organist of Gloucester Cathedral, and shortly afterwards married Alicia, daughter of Abraham Rudhall of Gloucester, the famous bell-founder; died August 28, 1730; buried in the eastern ambulatory of the cathedral. His compositions were published after his death under the title of 'Harmonia Sacra Glocestriensis.'

CHANT, No. 334 F.C.H., is assigned to him.

Holden, John, probably a native of England, seems to have settled in Glasgow about 1757, and carried on business as a potter. He was made a Burgess and Guild-brother of the city of Glasgow by purchase, July 8, 1757, and is described on the Burgess Roll as a merchant. Holden appears to have been an able scholar, and eminent as a musical theorist. He published in parts 'An Essay towards a Rational System of Music,' the whole being issued in 1770, inscribed to the Chancellor, Lord Rector, and Professors of Glasgow College, where Fetis asserts he was a Professor, but of this there is no record. It is known, however, that he took an interest in the music of the College chapel; and on May 16, 1765, the chapel committee was empowered "to pay Mr Holden five pounds sterling a year as a present to him from the chappel fund for instructing the band;" and on January 23, 1766, the same committee was instructed to purchase thirty copies of "Mr Holden's Music-book for the use of the chappel." This was doubtless his collection of tunes, the title of which is given below. On December 17, 1767, and on July 13, 1768, it was agreed to pay the "accounts of John Holden for writing the records of the minutes of the Rector, Dean of Faculty's, and Principal's meetings, . . . the accounts being judged reasonable." From the chapel accounts of June 1, 1769, we find Holden presenting the sum of fifteen pounds fifteen shillings to the chapel committee "for buying music for the College;" and on May 18, 1770, the sum of twenty-one pounds ten shillings and ninepence as a present "for the encouragement of music in this University." An edition of Holden's Essay quoted above was published at Calcutta in 1799,[1] and one at Edinburgh in 1807.[2] Francis Holden (probably a son of John

---

[1] This was edited by a gentleman who possessed the only copy of the original to be found in that country.

[2] The editor of this edition is not known to the writer.

Holden) was one of six precentors who petitioned the Magistrates and Town Council of Glasgow for an advance in salary, September 1783.

GLASGOW, No. 70 S.P. During the last forty years this tune has been assigned to Holden, but it is doubtful if he composed it. In the index to the 'Scottish Psalmody' of 1867 Holden is named as composer, and the date 1766 given. In that year (1766) Holden published 'A Collection of Church Music; consisting of New Setts of the Common Psalm-Tunes with some other Pieces. . . . Principally designed for the Use of the University of Glasgow.' That work contains a tune "St Matthew's or Glasgow," but it is totally different from No. 70 in S.P. See Moore, Thomas.

Holdroyd, Israel, "Philo-Musicæ," edited 'The Spiritual Man's Companion; or, The Pious Christian's Recreation. Containing . . . A Set of Psalm-Tunes, in One, Two, Three, and Four Parts, as they are sung in England and Scotland, &c. The Fifth Edition, with large Additions, never before Printed.' London, 1753.

ST NICHOLAS, No. 141 P. and P., 193 U.P.P., 149 S.P., appears on page 49 under that name in the above collection and set to Psalm 119, Second Part, Old Version. The earliest copy in a Scotch collection the writer can trace is in James Thomson's work next mentioned.

LAUDER, No. 7 U.P.P., is on page 8 without a name set to Psalm 16, Old Version, and in duple time, thus—

"LAUDER," AS IN HOLDROYD AND THE SCOTCH COLLECTIONS.

KEY C (Lah is A).

{| 1 :— | m :l | se :l.t | d¹ :t | l :— || d¹ :— | t :m }
{| fe :r | m :— || d¹ :— | t :l | se :d¹ | r¹ :d¹ | t :— ||
{| m¹ :— | d¹ :l | r¹ :t | l :— ||

An edition of Holdroyd's book without date does not contain "St Nicholas" or "Lauder." The writer is of opinion that this tune, "Lauder," is not Scotch, although it is so described in the U.P.P. It is not in the collections issued by Bremner, Gray, Moore, Holden, and M'Lachlan between 1756 and 1776. The earliest copy the writer has seen in a Scotch collection is in 'The Rudiments of Music: To which is added, A Collection of the best Church Tunes, Hymns, Canons, and Anthems,' by James Thomson, Philo-

Musicæ, Edinburgh, 1778, where it is named "Funeral." It is also in Robert Gilmour's 'The Psalm-Singer's Assistant,' second edition, with improvements, Paisley, 1793; and in many other Scotch collections issued about the beginning of the present century. It was commonly associated with Psalm 79, verse 3 :—

> "Their blood about Jerusalem
> Like water they have shed;
> And there was none to bury them
> When they were slain and dead."

The Rev. George Robson, late of Lauder, who was the first to show this quaint tune to the Psalmody Committee of the U.P. Church, informed the writer that upwards of fifty years ago, when preaching a missionary sermon in a church in Fifeshire, he gave as a closing psalm the 72d, verses 17, 18, and 19, when to his astonishment the precentor struck up "Funeral." It was evident he knew little about adaptation.

Hopkins, Edward John, born at Westminster, London, June 30, 1818; chorister in the Chapel Royal under William Hawes from 1826 to 1833; pupil of T. F. Walmisley; organist of Mitcham Parish Church, Surrey, 1834 to 1838; St Peter's, Islington, 1838 to 1841; St Luke's, Berwick Street, London, 1841 to 1843; of the Temple Church, London, since 1843; Mus. Doc. Cantuar., 1882; distinguished as an organist and composer of church music.

FENITON COURT, No. 147 S.H.; HADDO, No. 317 F.C.H.; WHITEFORD, No. 312 (First Tune) F.C.H.; and Anthem Music to Hymn No. 334 F.C.H., appear in the 'Hymnal of the Presbyterian Church in Canada, with Accompanying Tunes,' 1881, the music of which was prepared under the direction of Dr Hopkins.

BENEDICTION, No. 293 (Second Tune) S.H., No. 291 F.C.H., 279 (Second Tune) U.P.H., named "Ellers" in the last two collections, was published in choral unison in the Rev. R. Brown-Borthwick's 'Supplemental Hymn and Tune Book,' third edition. The harmony was written specially by the composer for the Appendix to the 'Bradford Tune Book.'

CHILDREN'S VOICES, No. 363 F.C.H., was composed for 'Church Hymns, with Tunes,' edited by Sir Arthur S. Sullivan, 1874.

CULFORD, No. 187 (Second Tune) F.C.H., is from Dr Hopkins's 'Temple Tune Book.'

ST HUGH, No. 49 F.C.H., 136 S.P., and ST RAPHAEL, No. 242 F.C.H., are in the Rev. R. Chope's 'Congregational Hymn and Tune Book,' 1862.

SHROPSHIRE, No. 1 F.C.H., appears in the Rev. Joshua Fawcett's 'Lyra Ecclesiastica,' 1844. TEMPLE, No. 292 (Second Tune) S.H., and 331 F.C.H., appears without a name in 'The Book of Praise Hymnal, with Music,' edited by John Hullah, 1868, and set to the hymn, "God that madest earth and heaven."

Dr Hopkins contributed the following to the F.C.H., the harmonies of which work he also revised:—

ST WOLSTAN, No. 302, and S.S. No. 17, "Arise, shine," S.S. No. 9, "O praise the Lord," S.S. No. 20, "The Lord is my portion," and Anthem Music to Hymn No. 333, "We praise Thee, O God"; the last-named being specially composed for that work.

CAMDEN, No. 119 F.C.H.; CRAYFORD, No. 361 F.C.H.; JEHOVAH, No. 293 F.C.H.; SPRINGTIDE, No. 296 (Second Tune) S.H.; TEMPLE BAR, No. 141 F.C.H.; and CHANT, No. 333 F.C.H. and 259 S.P. (No. 260 S.P. being the minor form), are his compositions.

Horsley, William, born in London, November 15, 1774; pupil of Dr Callcott, and others; assistant-organist at Asylum for Female Orphans, 1798; organist, 1802; Mus. Bac.[1] Oxford, 1800; Belgrave Chapel, Grosvenor Place, 1812; Charterhouse, 1837; died in London, June 12, 1858; a distinguished glee composer, and an able organist. 'A Collection of Psalm Tunes, Ancient and Modern, together with nearly Two Hundred Characteristic Interludes, the whole Selected, Arranged, and Composed by William Horsley, Mus. Bac. Oxon., organist of the Asylum and Belgrave Chapels, 1828, contains

BELGRAVE, No. 37 S.P., 145 U.P.P., and ST MARY ABBOTS, No. 201 S.P., and eight others by Horsley.

In 1844 he published 'Twenty-Four Psalm Tunes, and Eight Chants' (never printed before). From that Collection is taken

HORSLEY, No. 91 P. and P. and 341 F.C.H., where it is nameless.

Houldsworth, John, appointed organist of Halifax Parish Church, November 5, 1819, in succession to a Mr Stopford, whose assistant he had been for some time. He was disabled by a paralytic stroke for some years, and before his death a Mr Sharpe of York was appointed organist, January 17, 1836. Houldsworth was a skilled violinist, and played first violin at the Yorkshire Musical Festivals of 1823 and 1825. Published an edition of 'Chetham's Psalmody' in 1834, which had been issued by Stopford in 1811.

CHANT, No. 169 U.P.P., and CHANT II., Hymn 353 U.P.H., is said to be his composition.

Howard, Samuel, Mus. Doc., born in London, 1710; chorister in the Chapel Royal under Dr Croft; studied under Dr Pepusch; organist of St Clement Danes, and St Bridget's, Fleet Street,

---

[1] Horsley did not graduate Mus. Doc., although he is described as such in the F.C.H.

London; Mus. Doc. Cambridge, 1769; died in London, July 13, 1782. The following tunes were contributed by Dr Howard to William Riley's 'Parochial Harmony,' 1762 :—

LANCASTER, No. 60 and 301 S.H., 103 P. and P., 90 S.P., 122 U.P.P., and is there named "St Clement Danes," and set to Psalm 1, Old Version.

ST BRIDE, No. 200 S.P., 22 U.P.P., 200 P. and P., named "St Bridget's," and set to Psalm 130, New Version.

NORFOLK, No. 12 F.C.H., 299 and Doxology 4 U.P.H., 25 P. and P., bears its present name set to Psalm 95, but is in triple time, thus :—

HOWARD'S 148TH, No. 214 P. and P., and COVENTRY, No. 65 P. and P., appear in Christopher Smart's Collection, 1765, but are nameless.

HOWARD, No. 81 S.P., 158 U.P.H., 108 U.P.P., has been assigned in Scotland during the last forty years to Dr Howard, but he certainly did not compose it. See Wilson, John.

Hudson, Robert, born 1732; pupil of Charles King; tenor singer in Marylebone and Ranelagh Gardens; assistant-organist St Mildred, Bread Street, London, 1755; vicar-choral St Paul's, 1756; gentleman of the Chapel Royal, 1758; almoner and master of the children, St Paul's, 1773 to 1793; graduated Mus. Bac. Cambridge, 1784; died at Eton, December 1815.

LLANDAFF, No. 20 P. and P., is generally thought to be by Hudson, but is also assigned by some to Mary Hudson, his daughter, organist of St Olave's, Hart Street, London, and St Gregory's, Old Fish Street, 1790 to 1801; died in London, March 28, 1801.

It appears in 'A Selection of Psalm and Hymn Tunes adapted to the Various Metres now in Use in all Churches, Chapels, and Dissenting Congregations throughout Great Britain,' . . . by O. Nodes and J. Bowcher (1803); is there named "Strettons," and is anonymous.

Hullah, John Pyke, born at Worcester, June 27, 1812; pupil of William Horsley; student at the Royal Academy of Music from September 1833 to December 1835; first appeared before the public as composer of an opera, "The Village Coquettes," the book of which was written by Charles Dickens, then scarcely known to fame; was Professor of Harmony at King's College, London, and other educational establishments; Inspector of Music in Training Colleges from 1872 to 1882; degree of LL.D. conferred on him by the University of Edinburgh, 1876; elected an honorary member of the St Cecilia Academy at Rome, 1877; died in London, February 21, 1884; author of many works on music; composer of motets, anthems, and songs, one of which is very popular—viz., "The Three Fishers." Hullah was an ardent advocate of Wilhem's method of teaching singing—the fixed Doh —and he adapted it to English use. His classes held at Exeter and St Martin's Halls between the years 1841 and 1850 were attended by thousands.

In his early enthusiasm for the elevation of the working classes, Canon Kingsley wrote 'Alton Locke,' and in this novel he put into the mouth of his tailor-hero the following glowing tribute to Hullah, whose large classes at Exeter Hall were then attracting much attention: "I had no idea that music was capable of expressing and conveying emotions so intense and ennobling. My experience was confined to street music, and to the bawling at the chapel. And as yet Mr Hullah had not risen into a power more enviable than that of kings, and given to every workman a free entrance into the magic world of harmony and melody, where he may prove his brotherhood with Mozart and Weber, Beethoven and Mendelssohn. Great unconscious demagogue! leader of the people, and labourer in the cause of divine equality! Thy reward is with the Father of the people." His tune

BENTLEY, No. 198 F.C.H. and 240 (Second Tune) S.H., was composed for 'Psalms and Hymns for Divine Worship,' 1867.

ST BRUNO, No. 303 (Second Tune) S.H., was composed for the use of the scholars of the Charterhouse (where he was for some time organist), and appears in 'The Book of Praise Hymnal, with Music,' 1868.

Humfrey, Pelham,[1] born 1647; chorister in the Chapel Royal under Captain Henry Cook, 1660 to 1664; gentleman of the Chapel Royal, 1666-67; master of the choristers, 1672; died at Windsor, July 14, 1674.

CHANT No. 233 in U.P.P. and 229 S.P., known as the "Grand Chant," used to be much sung in cathedrals on the great festivals.

Hurst, William, born at Leicester, December 3, 1849; an amateur musician; studied for several years under J. T. Stone, the well-known organist and arranger.

[1] This composer's name appears as Humphrey, Humphreys, and Humphrys. The form given above is in accordance with his signature to his will—viz., Humfrey.

LEICESTER, No. 317 (First Tune) S.H., was first published in the revised and enlarged edition of 'Hymns Ancient and Modern,' 1875. It has become associated with Sir Henry W. Baker's Communion Hymn, "I am not worthy, Holy Lord."

Hutchins, William Jonas, son of Mr Jonas Hutchins; born in London (parish of Clerkenwell), March 27, 1854; chorister in the Temple Church, London, under Dr E. J. Hopkins; organist of All-Hallows-the-Great and -Less, London, from 1872 till 1878, during which time he studied under Dr Hopkins, and acted as assistant-organist at the Temple Church; from May 1878 till August 1879 organist of Esher Parish Church, Surrey; organist of Belhaven United Presbyterian Church, Glasgow, from 1879 till 1886; organist of Bridge of Allan Parish Church, 1887; private organist to the Marquis of Breadalbane at Taymouth Castle, Perthshire, from June 1888 to March 1890; now organist of Crouch Hill Presbyterian Church, North London. Composer of anthems, songs, and organ music, the bulk of which is still in MS.

S.S. No. 19 F.C.H., "In all their affliction," was composed by Mr Hutchins for that work.

Hutton, Laura Josephine, born at Spridlington, Lincolnshire, July 1852; an amateur musician. Her tune

WARFARE, No. 427 S.H., was composed in 1878, and first appeared in the 'Children's Hymn Book,' 1881.

Hymn Music. Adapted to all the peculiar metres in 'The United Presbyterian Hymn Book,' including a 'Collection of Doxologies and Chants,' edited by a member of the Committee of the United Presbyterian Synod on Psalmody [Rev. William Thomson of Slateford], assisted by eminent professional men. Designed as a Supplement to the 'Scottish Psalmody,' 1857. From the above is taken

PILGRIM SONG, No. 232 U.P.H. It is an altered copy of the tune set to Cantique 80 in 'Recueil de Cent Cantiques Chrétiens,' composed by the Rev. C. Malan, Paris, 1827. See Malan.

Indian Air.

HAPPY LAND, No. 352 U.P.H., 367 F.C.H., 432 S.H. The following regarding the origin of the hymn will be of interest: Mr Andrew Young, author of "There is a happy land," was a native of Edinburgh. His father was a successful teacher in that city for upwards of fifty years. Mr Young was master of Niddry Street School, Edinburgh, and of the Madras College, St Andrews, where he had 600 pupils. He afterwards retired, and resided in Edinburgh, where he died, November 30, 1889, aged eighty years. As to the origin of the hymn, Mr Young gave the following account: "In 1838, a lady, among many pieces she played me, incidentally brought in the Indian air, 'Happy Land.' I was greatly impressed with the simple beauty of the air, and asked her to play it over and over again till I had it in my memory. Next day I wrote this little hymn to the air I so much admired, wedding it to my simple words as a suitable hymn for children. Mr James Gall of Edinburgh was the first to hear it sung by my pupils, and he also so much admired it that he got it arranged and published it, and from that time it has gone over the world. I never heard the words of the Indian song till 1842, when I was resident in St Andrews. The opening words are, 'I have come from a happy land where care is unknown.'"

Professor Masson relates the following touching incident in the career of the novelist Thackeray: "While walking one day in a squalid street in the east end of London, he came suddenly upon a band of gutter-children sitting on the pavement and singing. As he approached he heard the words, 'There is a happy land, far, far away.' As he looked at the ragged choristers and their squalid surroundings, and watched their pale faces lit up with an expression of delighted hope, he burst into tears."

Irons, Herbert Stephen, son of Mr John Irons, and nephew of Sir George J. Elvey, Mus. Doc., born at Canterbury, January 19, 1834; chorister at Canterbury Cathedral from 1844 to 1849; pupil and assistant of Dr Stephen Elvey at Oxford; precentor and master of the choristers, St Columba College, Ireland, 1856 to 1857; organist and master of the choristers, Southwell Minster, Notts, 1857 to 1872; assistant-organist, Chester Cathedral, 1873 to 1875; since 1876 organist of St Andrew's Church, Nottingham. His tunes

SOUTHWELL, No. 268 S.H., and ST COLUMBA, No. 287 S.H. and 270 F.C.H., were first published in 'Hymns Ancient and Modern,' 1861.

Isaac, Heinrich, was born in Germany about the middle of the fifteenth century. He was chapel-master of the Church of St Giovanni, at Florence, about 1488, and entered the service of the Emperor Maximilian I. as director of the choir about 1510. The date of his death is uncertain.

INNSBRÜCK, No. 280 U.P.H., 193 S.H., "Nun ruhen alle Wälder." This was at first a secular melody to the words, "Innsbrück ich muss dich lassen." It was afterwards set to the hymn, by Johann Hesse, "O welt ich muss dich lassen," and finally to Paul Gerhardt's hymn, "Nun ruhen alle Wälder," with which it has remained associated. Bach employs the tune in his 'Grosse Passions Musik,' and Mendelssohn in his unfinished oratorio "Christus."

J.

ST LUCY, No. 417 S.H. Appears in Sir Arthur S. Sullivan's 'Church Hymns with Tunes,' 1874.

Jackson, Thomas, born about 1715, was organist of St Mary Magdalen Parish Church, and Master of the Song School, Newark-on-Trent, in succession to John Alcock, jun., 1768; died November 11, 1781; buried in the church. In 1780 he published 'Twelve Psalm Tunes and Eighteen Double and Single Chants . . . composed for Four Voices.'

JACKSON, No. 97 P. and P., 85 S.P., 69 U.P.P., 242 U.P.H., is there set to Psalm 47. It is wrongly assigned in the three last-named collections to William Jackson of Exeter. Dr Miller styles it "Byzantium" in his collection (No. 216) issued in 1800.

CHANTS No. 242 S.P. and 82 U.P.P., 267 S.P. and 207 U.P.P., were composed by Jackson, and are in his work mentioned above. They are, like his tune, wrongly assigned to William Jackson of Exeter.

Jackson, William, known to the musical world as "Jackson of Exeter," was born at Exeter, May 28, 1730, and became a pupil of John Sylvester, then the organist of Exeter Cathedral, and afterwards of John Travers, organist of the Chapel Royal. In 1777 he succeeded Richard Langdon as organist and master of the choristers of Exeter Cathedral. He died July 12, 1803.

CHANT No. 240 S.P. was composed in 1790, and published in Marsh's Collection about 1810. The copy given below is from the original, and, as will be observed, the Chant is formed upon a tonic pedal note. Writing on chants of this construction, Mr Havergal observes: "They are not common, nor is it desirable that they should be. They are said to have originated with Mr Jackson of Exeter, whose well-known chant in B Flat is the best he ever wrote, and the chief of its kind."

BIOGRAPHICAL SKETCHES.

$$\left\{\begin{array}{llllllllll} \overset{\frown}{d} & |r & :m & |f & :- & \| \overset{\frown}{r} & |m & :l_1 & |s_1 & :t_1 & |d & :- \\ m_1 & |f_1 & :s_1 & |l_1 & :- & \| s_1 & |s_1 & :f_1 & |m_1 & :s_1.f_1 & |m_1 & :- \\ d & |t_1 & :ta_1 & |l_1 & :- & \| t_1 & |d & :d & |d & :r & |d & :- \\ d_1 & |d_1 & :d_1 & |d_1 & :- & \| d_1 & |d_1 & :f_1 & |s_1 & :s_1 & |d_1 & :- \end{array}\right.$$

CHANT No. 227 S.P. was not composed by Jackson. It seems to be made up from the Double Chant given above.

DOXOLOGY No. 18 U.P.H., and TE DEUM in F, No. 354 U.P.H., are from 'Two Anthems and a complete Church Service, by the late William Jackson of Exeter. Edited, and dedicated by permission to The Venerable the Dean and Chapter of Exeter Cathedral, by the organist, James Paddon.' Vol. ii. No date.

There seems to be some doubt as to whether or not this Service was composed by Jackson, for a correspondent writes thus to the editor of 'The Musical World' of February 23, 1856:—

"JACKSON IN F."

"SIR,—No doubt you are aware that a medley which goes by the dignified name of 'Jackson in F' has been sung in many churches and places of worship for several years. 'William Jackson of Exeter,' as he is generally called, died in 1803, and this Service (!) was certainly not known before the year 1812, about which period it began to be introduced into the Exeter parish churches, and was sung at the cathedral of that city. Jackson was succeeded as organist of St Peter's by his pupil, James Paddon, who many years afterwards published Jackson's Church Music, and with it the 'Service' in F. In 1834, Paddon was on his deathbed, and some weeks before he died declared that Jackson did not write the 'Service' in F. As it is very desirable to place the saddle on the right animal, perhaps this information will be useful to some of your readers. I may add that my information can be well authenticated. Hoping your numerous readers will carefully digest the matter,—I am, &c., OBOE."

There does not seem to have been any published answer to this letter. Mr T. P. Hamlin of Exeter, who was a pupil of Paddon's, informs the writer that he has seen the original copy of the Te Deum in F in Jackson's own handwriting.

Jackson,[1] **William,** known to the musical world as "Jackson of Masham," born January 9, 1815; a self-taught musician; composer of oratorios, cantatas, glees, anthems, &c.; organist of Masham Church about 1832; settled in Bradford, 1852; organist

---

[1] Jackson, William, son of the above, was appointed organist of Morningside Parish Church, Edinburgh, May 5, 1875; died at Ripon (holding that office) September 10, 1877, aged twenty-four years.

of St John's Church, Bradford, and afterwards of Horton Lane Chapel; died April 15, 1866.

S.S. No. 86 U.P.H., "Come, and let us return," is his composition, and was written for and first published in 'Parochial Anthems by the Cathedral Composers of 1863,' edited by Dr Thomas Lloyd Fowle, M.A. Preface dated Winchester, 1863.

Jamieson, Augustus Grant, son of Mr Robert Jamieson, solicitor; born at Edinburgh, December 20, 1844; studied under J. C. Kieser and J. T. Surenne there; also at the University under Professor Donaldson, and at Stuttgart under Herr Winternitz; was appointed organist of Brighton Street Church, a post he held for eight years; afterwards organist of St George's Episcopal Church for five years; appointed organist and choirmaster of St Paul's Episcopal Church by Sir Herbert Oakeley in 1872; music-master at George Watson's Ladies' College from its opening in 1872, also at the Ministers' Daughters' College, and other institutions; conductor of the Orpheus Orchestral Society for two years; captain of No. 7 Company of the Queen's City of Edinburgh Rifle Volunteer Brigade; died at Edinburgh, January 21, 1888, and buried in the Grange Cemetery, January 25; succeeded at St Paul's by his son, Herbert Linton Eddie Jamieson, who, however, retired from the office early in 1891.

BRIERLEY, No. 64 (Second Tune) S.H., and ST SULPICE, No. 306 S.H., were composed by him for the hymns to which they are set, and were first published in the 'Book of Psalms and Scottish Hymnal,' 1872.

Mr Jamieson contributed to various hymnals, and published several compositions for the pianoforte.

His brother, Rev. William Cruickshank Eddie Jamieson, B.A., minister of St Matthew's Parish Church, Glasgow, and latterly of the Tron Church, Edinburgh, was distinguished as a preacher of the Gospel. He died in 1881. Several hymn tunes of his composition are still in MS.

Jones, John, born 1728; appointed organist of the Temple Church, November 24, 1749; of the Charterhouse, July 2, 1753; of St Paul's Cathedral, December 25, 1755; held all three posts till his death; was one of the directors of the Händel Commemoration, 1784; died February 17, 1796. His

CHANT in D (Single), No. 354 S.H., appears in Vanderuan's Collection, 1770. Chant in D (Double), No. 249 S.P., 176 U.P.P., was published by Jones in his 'Sixty Chants, Single and Double,' 1785. It was performed April 23, 1789, when George III. went in state to St Paul's to return thanks for his restoration to health and reason. For many years it was constantly used at the annual meetings of the charity children in the cathedral; and at the anniversary of 1791 was heard by Haydn, who was so pleased with it that he noted it down, suggesting a slight alteration in the last strain, and afterwards said, "This simple and natural air gave me the greatest pleasure I ever received from the performance of music."

Jones, Rev. William, born at Lowick, Northamptonshire, July 30, 1726; educated at the Charterhouse, and at University College, Oxford, where he graduated 1749; took holy orders, and in 1764 became vicar of Bethersden, Kent, and afterwards rector of Pluckley, a post which he afterwards exchanged for the rectory of Paston, Northamptonshire; in 1798 became rector of Hollingbourne, Kent; appointed perpetual curate of Nayland, Suffolk, about 1776; died February 6, 1800; author of 'A Treatise on Music,' and other works.

NEWINGTON, No. 114 F.C.H., 90 S.H., 114 P. and P., 142 U.P.P., 109 S.P. (original name "St Stephen's Tune"), was published (Key B flat) at the end of 'Ten Church Pieces for the Organ, with Four Anthems, ... composed for the use of the Church of Nayland in Suffolk,' by William Jones, M.A., March 25, 1789. It is there set to Psalm 23. It is found in John Knott's collection published at Aberdeen, 1814, this being probably its first appearance in a Scottish Psalmody. It there bears its original title. The name "Newington" seems to have been first given to it in R. A. Smith's 'Sacred Music,' second edition, Edinburgh, 1828. In John Wilson's Collection, Edinburgh, 1825, it is named "Naylor," doubtless a misprint for "Nayland."

Josephi (or Joseph), Georg, a musician in the Chapel of the Prince-Bishop of Breslau, in the middle of the seventeenth century. He wrote a large number of melodies for the hymns of Johann Scheffler (Angelus Silesius), which are published in Scheffler's 'Heilige Seelen-Lust oder Geistliche Hirtenlieder,' Breslau, 1657, in three books. They contained 123 tunes, of which 107 are by Josephi. A fourth book was soon afterwards added, with 32 tunes, of which 30 are by Josephi. The work appeared in a complete form in 1668, with a fifth part containing 48 tunes by Josephi and 2 by other composers—205 tunes in all.

ANGELUS, No. 288 S.H., 304 U.P.H., 32 F.C.H., appears in Kocher's 'Zionsharfe,' 1854-55, set to the hymn, "Du meiner Seelen gold'ne Zier." The tune set to that hymn in the 'Hirtenlieder,' Book I. (No. 22), is identical with "Angelus" as far as the middle of the second line, but the similarity ends there.

It seems more probable that it is adapted from the following tune, which is also in Book I. (No. 7), set to "Komm mein Herze, komm mein Schatz":—

JOSEPHI.

Key E♭.

{| d :— :r :m :— :m :m :— :fe :s :— :— }

{| l :— :t :d¹ :— :t :l :— :l :s :— :— }

{| m¹ :— :r¹ :d¹ :— :d¹ :f¹ :— :m¹ :r¹ :— :— }

Four-pulse Measure.
{| t .r¹:m¹.m¹ |r¹.r¹ :d¹ | s .s :l .l |t .t :d¹.d¹ | r¹.m¹:f¹.m¹ |r¹.d¹ :d¹.d¹ ||

The third line has been formed by writing the corresponding line of Josephi's tune backwards. The fourth line is constructed out of material afforded by the concluding portion of the original, which forms a sort of *coda*, and is in common time.

CULBACH, No. 234 (Second Tune) S.H., 268 U.P.H., "Ach wenn kommt die Zeit heran," is No. 2 in Book I. It is marked "After a well-known melody." Wrongly assigned in the S.H. to Dretzell, who was not born till 1705, nearly fifty years after it appeared in the above.

In J. G. Storl's 'Choralbuch,' 1711, the tune is found in the following form :—

Key D.

{| :d |d .r :m .f |s :s |f :s |m :— || :s }

{|d¹ :d¹ |t .l :t |l :l |s :— || :s |s :l .t|d¹ :s }

{|l :s .f|m :— || :s |s :s |l .s :f .m|r :r |d :— ||

SCHEFFLER, No. 168 F.C.H., is an altered copy of the tune which is set to "Bis gegrüst mein Gnaden-Thron," No. 21, Book I. It appears in its present form in Kocher's 'Zionsharfe,' 1855-56.

FRANKFORT, No. 373 (First Tune) S.H. This tune is wrongly assigned to Josephi. His name may have become associated with it from the fact that in North Germany it is usually set to a pastoral by Scheffler, "Liebe, die du mich zum Bilde." See Bach, J. C.

Kent, James, was born at Winchester, March 13, 1700. He was a chorister at Winchester Cathedral under Vaughan Richardson from 1711 to 1714, and afterwards at the Chapel Royal under Dr Croft, where he remained till 1718. He next became organist of Finedon Parish Church, resigning in 1731; organist of Trinity College, Cambridge, from 1731 till 1737; Winchester Cathedral and College from 1737, resigned 1774; died May[1] 6, 1776.

S.S. No. 28 U.P.H., "Blessed be Thou;"
S.S. No. 2 U.P.H., "Thine, O Lord, is the greatness"—the adaptation by William Shore;
S.S. No. 29 U.P.H., "Both riches and honour,"—
are the first three movements in his anthem, "Blessed be Thou."

S.S. No. 82 U.P.H., "Sing, O heavens," is adapted from an anthem of that name. The above were published in 'Twelve Anthems Composed by James Kent, Organist of the Cathedral and College at Winchester.' Printed for the Author, 1773.

Kettle, Charles Edward, born at Bury St Edmunds, Suffolk, March 28, 1833; organist successively at St Margaret's, Plumstead; St Nicholas (old Parish Church), Plumstead; Holy Trinity Church, Woolwich; Hove Parish Church; Queen Square Congregational Church, Brighton; organist and composer of many excellent church tunes.

FARNINGHAM, No. 66 S.P., was composed in 1875, and first published in the 'Bristol Tune Book' in 1876. To this collection he contributed 26 tunes.

King, Alfred, son of Mr William King; born at Shelly, Essex, April 24, 1837; educated for the Church, but turned his attention

---

[1] In the Appendix to Sir George Grove's 'Dictionary of Music and Musicians,' 1889, it is stated that Kent "died in October, not May, if his monument at Winchester may be trusted." The following extracts from the Winchester Cathedral Register should settle the point:—

"James Kent (organist) was buried May 10, 1776.

"Elizabeth Kent, Relict of James Kent (late organist of this church), was buried June 4, 1776."

to music; appointed organist at Cuddesdon Theological College, 1856; organist and choirmaster at Eastnor, Ledbury, 1857 till 1864; at St Michael's and All Angels, Brighton, 1865 till 1877; from 1877 to 1887 organist of the Parish Church, Brighton; Fellow of the College of Organists, 1868; graduated Mus. Bac., Exeter College, Oxford, 1872; Mus. Doc., October 1888; since 1878 organist to the Brighton Corporation; conductor of Kuhe's Festival Chorus, and Lecturer on Harmony at the School of Science and Art. Composer of anthems, part songs, &c.

EASTNOR, No. 188 (First Tune) S.H. and 186 P. and P., was composed in 1862, and first published in the 'Bristol Tune Book,' 1863.

Knapp, William, born at Wareham in 1698 or 1699—the exact date cannot be given, as the records of the parish were destroyed by fire in 1762; said to have been organist of one of the churches of Wareham, but this wants confirming; became parish clerk of St James's Church, Poole, and held the office for thirty-nine years; died at Poole in 1768, and buried September 26, "somewhere near the old town wall."

WAREHAM, No. 307 and 314 U.P.H., 294 F.C.H., 159 U.P.P., and 40 P. and P., appears in 'A Sett of New Psalm Tunes and Anthems, in Four Parts; on Various Occasions, . . . by William Knapp,' 1738. It is set (in Key C) to Psalm 36, "for ye holy sacrament."

The tune is also found in Knapp's 'New Church Melody,' second edition, 1754, in common time, and named "Blandford," the melody slightly altered.

Knecht, Justin Heinrich, born September 30, 1752, at Biberach, in Suabia; studied music under Krämer, organist of the Roman Catholic Church at Biberach, and afterwards from 1768 to 1771 under Schmidt, director of the music at the Collegiate Church at Esslingen; appointed in 1771 director of the music at Biberach, and, with the exception of the years 1807 and 1808, when he was music director at Stuttgart, remained there till his death, December 1, 1817; one of the greatest organists of his time.

ALTENBURG, No. 28 U.P.H., "Gott der Wahrheit und der Liebe," composed in 1797;

HOSANNA, No. 139 S.H., "Preis sey dir, Weltbeherrscher dir," composed in 1795;

KNECHT, No. 207 F.C.H., 237 and 338 (Second Tune) S.H., "Der niedern Menschheit Hülle," composed in 1793;

RAVENNA (or VIENNA), No. 165 (First Tune) F.C.H., 228 U.P.H., 173 (First Tune) S.H., 223, 349 (First Tune), "Ohne Rast und unverweilt," composed in 1797;

WALDECK, No. 147 U.P.P., 160 P. and P., "Du, Gott, bist über Alles Herr," composed in 1792,—were all published in Knecht's 'Choralmelodien,' 1799.

The fourth and fifth lines of "Hosanna" were added by Mr Walter Hately to suit the hymn "Hosanna to the living Lord!" and published in 'The Church of Scotland Psalm and Hymn Tune Book,' 1868. By omitting these lines the melody will stand as composed by Knecht.

Kocher, Conrad, Ph.D., was born at Ditzingen, in Würtemberg, December 16, 1786; from 1827 to 1865 organist of the Stiftskirche at Stuttgart, where he died, March 12, 1872. He published many compositions, including an oratorio, "Der Tod Abels."

DIX, No. 180 F.C.H., 36 U.P.H., 31 and 280 S.H., is adapted from his chorale "Treuer Heiland! wir sind hier," which was published in his 'Stimmen aus dem Reiche Gottes,' 1838. The form now in use seems to have been first published in 'Hymns Ancient and Modern,' 1861, where it is set to "As with gladness men of old," by W. Chatterton Dix, hence probably its name.

ORIGINAL FORM OF TUNE "DIX," IN KOCHER'S 'ZIONSHARFE.'

FREIBURG, No. 110 U.P.H., "Den die Engel droben," and
MINTO, No. 85 (First Tune) S.H., "Willkommen, Held im Streite," appear in his 'Zionsharfe,' 1854-55, and are marked as his.

The following are also from his 'Zionsharfe,' but are anonymous:—
ALTONA, No. 43 (Second Tune) S.H., "Ins feld geh zale alles gras." It is described by Dr Layriz as a song of the people, Paderborn, 1850.

BORLAN, No. 65 (First Tune) S.H., 231 (Second Tune) F.C.H., "Endlich kommt Er das Verlangen." The form of this tune is correctly given in the F.C.H. It has been altered to common time in the S.H. Why it should have been so tampered with is hard to understand, as it had gained acceptance in its original form in the Church of Scotland.

ELLACOMBE, No. 400 S.H., 350 F.C.H., 344 U.P.H., "Der du im heil'gen Sakrament." See St Gall Gesangbuch.

LINDEN, No. 48 (Second Tune) S.H., 40 F.C.H., 19 P. and P., "Gross ist der Herr."

NATIVITY, No. 34 U.P.H., 167 U.P.P., "Gott ist mein Hort."

ST MARK, No. 282 F.C.H., "O Mutter mit dem Himmelsfinde."

ST NINIANS, No. 3 U.P.H., "Kommst du, Jesu, Licht der Heiden?"

AVE MARIS STELLA, No. 408 (Second Tune) S.H. See Galloway, Rev. Alexander.

Krieger, Adam Philipp, born 1634, or, according to some, 1628, was chamber-musician at Dresden to the Elector of Saxony; died in 1666.

ULM, No. 158 P. and P., 11 U.P.P., there named "Silesia," "Nun sich der Tag geendet hat," appears in his 'Neuen Arien,' published posthumously in 1667.

Lahee, Henry, born at Chelsea, April 11, 1826; organist of Holy Trinity Church, Brompton, 1847 to 1874; composer of the cantatas, "The Building of the Ship" and "The Blessing of the Children"; also many prize glees and madrigals.

NATIVITY, No. 106 S.P., was first published without a name in 'The Metrical Psalter,' which he edited in 1855, and is there set to a Hymn for Christmas Day. It bears its present name in 'One Hundred Hymn Tunes,' which he published after the first-named collection.

Lamb, Rev. James, son of Mr James Lamb; born in Dovecotland, Perth, November 17, 1835; educated in the Perth schools, and at Edinburgh University, where he studied music under Professor Donaldson; ordained minister of Old Kilpatrick United Presbyterian Church, February 5, 1867, where he still is; member of the Psalmody Committee of the U.P. Church since 1868 (with the exception of one year); clerk to the Committee during the preparation of the U.P. Hymnal and Psalter.

S.S. No. 34 U.P.H., "Show me Thy ways," was first published in that work.

Four hymn tunes composed by Mr Lamb will be found in U.P. Hymnal for the Young (1882).

Lambeth, Henry Albert, a distinguished organist and conductor; born at Hardway, near Portsmouth, January 15, 1822; studied the pianoforte under Mr J. Trekell at Portsmouth; appointed organist at St James's Church, Ryde, Isle of Wight, in his sixteenth year; of St Mary's Parish Church, Portsmouth, in 1841; of St Thomas's Parish Church, Portsmouth, in October 1842; conductor of the Portsmouth Choral Society, 1843; of the Fareham Choral Society in 1844; studied the organ under Thomas Adams, Dr S. S. Wesley, and George Cooper; instrumentation under Sir W. Sterndale Bennett; singing and music generally under Henry Smart; and theory and composition under Sir George Smart; in 1853 appointed organist to the Corporation of Glasgow on the recommendation of Henry Smart,[1] a position he still holds; appointed organist of St Mary's Episcopal Church, Glasgow, December 16, 1853, and played his first service on the 25th of that month; of Glasgow Choral Union, August or September 1857,[2] retiring in 1880; from 1866 till 1889 organist of Park Church, Glasgow; founder and conductor of Lambeth's Select Choir, which had the honour of being commanded to perform before her Majesty the Queen at Balmoral, September 29, 1877, and on May 27, 1879. Mr Lambeth's compositions consist of organ and pianoforte music, songs, and many beautiful arrangements of Scotch airs as part-songs. His more important works are settings of Psalms 137 ("By the waters of Babylon") and 86 ("Bow down Thine ear"), composed for the Glasgow Choral Union, by whom the first-named was performed on March 13, 1861, and the last-named on November 7, 1873.

In 1876 he edited an important collection of church music, entitled 'The Scottish Book of Praise; being Selections from the Psalms in Prose and Verse, and other parts of Scripture, with a Collection of Hymns, Paraphrases, and Anthems. The whole Printed with Music, designed to assist in Congregational Singing.'

CHANT No. 48 in U.P.P. is from the above Collection, where it is set to Psalm 48.

Lampe, Johann Friedrich, was a native of Saxony, but in what part of that country he was born seems unknown. It is asserted by some that his place of birth was Helmstadt, but the

---

[1] Of this appointment Smart said: "I have done many good things for the art in my day, but the best thing I ever did was to send Mr Lambeth to Glasgow."

[2] Not 1858.

baptismal records of St Stephen's, St Marienburg, and St Ludger churches having been searched at the writer's instigation, no entry of his baptism can be found.[1] It is known, however, that he settled at Helmstadt to study music, and this may have given rise to the statement that he was born there. About 1725 he arrived in London, and became a bassoon-player in Handel's opera band; and tradition relates that he was one of the best performers of his time. He aspired, however, to something higher than being a mere member of the band, for in 1732 he composed the music to Henry Carey's "Amelia." His most successful effort was the music he composed for the same writer's burlesque opera, "The Dragon of Wantley," which met with unbounded success, and made him famous. Lampe's other theatrical works need not be mentioned here. He was author of 'A Plain and Compendious Method of Teaching Thorough Bass' (1737), and 'The Art of Musick,' 1740. In 1748 or 1749 Lampe went to Dublin, performing at concerts with his wife, Isabella Young,[2] a noted vocalist and actress, and daughter of Charles Young, organist of All-Hallows, Barking. About the close of the year 1750 he arrived in Edinburgh, and conducted many theatrical performances at the Canongate Theatre,[3] in all of which his wife took a part. About the 15th of July 1751, Lampe was seized with an illness which terminated fatally on the 25th[4] of that month, and was buried in the Canongate Churchyard (East Wall), where a monument—now in a dilapidated state—was erected to his memory, bearing the following inscription :—

"Here lye the mortal remains of Johann Frederic Lampe, whose harmonious compositions shall outlive monumental registers, and, with melodious notes through future ages perpetuate his fame, till time shall sink into eternity. His taste for moral harmony appeared through all his conduct. On the 25th of July 1751, in the forty-eighth year of his age, he was summoned to join that heavenly

[1] The search was from 1688 to 1710 inclusive, and the name Lampe was not once met with.

[2] Charles James Frederick Lampe, organist of All-Hallows, Barking, from 1758 to 1769, was son of the above marriage. "Kent" is wrongly assigned by some editors to him.

[3] For an account of the works performed by Lampe and his company while in Edinburgh, see a letter by the writer in the 'North British Advertiser and Ladies' Journal,' October 27, 1888.

[4] Not the 23d, as stated by some writers. Sir John Hawkins, writing in 1776, erred in stating that Lampe died in London.

concert with the blessed choir above, where his virtuous soul now enjoys that harmony which was his chief delight upon earth.

"In vita felicitate dignos mors reddit felices."

Lampe was an intimate associate of the Wesleys, and the Rev. Charles Wesley wrote a hymn on his death, which was afterwards set to music by Dr Arnold. The first stanza runs thus:—

> "'Tis done! the sov'reign will's obey'd,
> The soul by angel guards convey'd
> Has took its seat on high.
> The brother of my choice is gone
> To music sweeter than his own,
> To concerts in the sky."

KENT, No. 77 (Second Tune) and 179 (First Tune) S.H., 18 P. and P., is the composition of Lampe. It appeared in 'Hymns on the Great Festivals and other Occasions,' London, printed for M. Cooper, 1746. This collection, which consists of melodies only, with a figured bass, set to twenty-four hymns by the Rev. Charles Wesley, is without the name of either the author or the composer; but on the title-page of the second edition, issued in 1753 after Lampe's death, it is stated that the work may be obtained "at Mrs Lampe's lodging"; and in a letter of Wesley's dated December 11, 1746, the following passage occurs: "Tell Mrs Dewal not to mind that envious gentleman who slandered Lampe. His tunes are universally admired here among the musical men, and have brought me into high favour among them." It was originally set to the hymn, "Sinners, obey the Gospel word," and, like the others, had no name. Dr Miller, in his 'Psalms of David for the Use of Parish Churches,' 1790, names it "Kent"; and in Harrison's 'Sacred Harmony,' vol. ii. (1791), it is named "Invitation." For upwards of a century it has been wrongly assigned to Dr Maurice Greene, and also to a "George Greene, son of Dr Greene," but the Doctor had no son.

It must not be supposed that the introduction of this tune into Scotland is of recent date, for it is found in Thomas Moore's 'Psalm Singer's Pocket Companion,' Glasgow, 1756, and is there named "Psalm 145." Also in Cornforth Gilson's Collection, Edinburgh, 1759, where it is named "New Church Tune."

Langdon, Richard, born about 1729; appointed organist of Exeter Cathedral in room of John Silvester, deceased, June 23, 1753; resigned October 4, 1777, when William Jackson succeeded him; appointed organist of Ely Cathedral, November 26, 1777, but does not seem to have entered upon the duties; appointed organist of Bristol Cathedral in room of Samuel Mineard, December 3, 1777; elected one of the lay clerks of the Cathedral, November 30, 1778; resigned before June 25, 1781; appointed organist of

Armagh Cathedral, August 14, 1782, in succession to Dr Langrische Doyle; resigned in 1794, when he was succeeded by Dr John Clarke (afterwards Clarke-Whitfeld); graduated Mus. Bac. at Exeter College, Oxford, July 13, 1761; died at Exeter, September 8, 1803, aged seventy-four.[1]

CHANT in F, No. 241 S.P. and 79 U.P.P., is in his 'Divine Harmony; being a Collection in Score of Psalms and Anthems,' 1774. It is there anonymous, but has been generally ascribed to Langdon.

Langran, James, son of Mr Joseph Langran; born in London, November 10, 1835; pupil of J. Baptiste Calkin, Dr Gordon Saunders, and Dr J. F. Bridge; organist of Holy Trinity Church, Tottenham, from 1859 to 1870; and from 1870 to the present time organist of the Parish Church; graduated Mus. Bac., Oxford University, 1884; musical editor of the 'New Mitre Hymnal,' 1875.

DEERHURST, No. 235 F.C.H. and 112 S.H.; also

ST AGNES, No. 287 F.C.H., 279 (First Tune) U.P.H., 320 S.H., were published in 'Psalms and Hymns adapted to the Services of the Church of England,' &c., by John Foster,[2] 1863. A varied form of "Deerhurst" appears in 'Tunes and Chants used in St Anne's Church, Birkenhead,' 1864.

"St Agnes" was composed for the hymn "Abide with me," and published on single slips in 1861 or 1862. It is named "Evensong" in Foster's collection quoted above, and also in its successor 'The New Metre Hymnal,' 1875.

Latin.

EPHRATAH, No. 30 U.P.H., 226 F.C.H., melody of the fourteenth century.

---

[1] Langdon's biographers err in stating that he was the son of the Rev. Tobias Langdon, priest-vicar and sub-chanter of Exeter Cathedral, as the latter died September 4, 1712. He (Tobias) had a son named Richard, who was baptised in Exeter Cathedral, July 18, 1686, and probably he was father of the Chant writer. The statement made above, that Langdon was seventy-four years of age at death, is from his memorial tablet at Exeter.

[2] The following is offered regarding the career of this editor, vocalist, and composer, which has not appeared elsewhere: Foster, John, born at Staines, Middlesex, August 1827; elected a chorister at St George's Chapel, Windsor, 1836; in 1844 articled pupil of Dr, afterwards Sir G. J. Elvey, there; organist St Andrew, Wells Street, London, 1847; elected Gentleman of her Majesty's Chapel Royal, and lay vicar, Westminster Abbey, 1856. When at St George's, Windsor, his reputation as a soprano singer was widespread, and he is still an excellent alto vocalist, and one of the finest exponents of old English glees we have. Contributed to the 'Westminster Chant Book,' edited by James Turle.

IMMORTALITY, No. 37 S.H., an ancient tune used for the Latin Christmas hymn, "In natali domini." It appears in the 'Hymn Book of the Bohemian Brethren,' 1544.

INTERCESSION, No. 344 (First Tune) S.H., 17 P. and P., appears in 'Easy Music for Church Choirs,' 1853.

NICOMEDIA, No. 344 (Second Tune) S.H., 24 P. and P., 298 U.P.H.

ORIEL, No. 118 and 323 U.P.H., 26 and 115 (First Tunes), and 328 S.H., "A Tantum Ergo."

ST AMBROSE, No. 22 S.P. Another form of "Veni Creator," which see.

VENI CREATOR, No. 91 S.H., 39 F.C.H., 99, 115, 321 U.P.H. Melody of the fourth century, or a little later.

VENI IMMANUEL, No. 29 (First Tune) U.P.H., "Veni, veni, Immanuel! Captivum solve Israel." Said to be a melody of the thirteenth century, from a French Missal in the National Library at Lisbon.

La Trobe, Rev. Peter, son of the Rev. C. I. La Trobe;[1] born in London, February 15, 1795; educated at Fulneck, Yorkshire, for the service of the Moravian Church; in 1836 succeeded his father as Secretary of the Unity of the Moravian Brethren in England; died suddenly at Bertheldorf, near Herrnhut, September 24, 1863.

FAIRFIELD, No. 206 P. and P. and 123 F.C.H., was composed in 1852, and contributed by him to 'Choral Harmony,' edited by the Rev. Dr Peter Maurice, 1854.

Laudi Spirituali. A name given to certain collections of hymns, psalms, &c., compiled for the use of the "Laudisti," a religious confraternity instituted at Florence in the year 1310, and afterwards held in great estimation by St Charles Borromeo and St Philip Neri. A highly interesting MS. volume once belonging to a company of "Laudisti," enrolled in the year 1336 at the Chiesa d'Ogni Santi, at Florence, is now preserved in the Magliabecchi Library; and in this is found—

---

[1] La Trobe, Rev. Christian Ignatius, son of the Rev. Benjamin La Trobe; born at Fulneck, Yorkshire, February 12, 1758; educated at Niesky and at Barby in Prussia; returned to London in 1794, and appointed Secretary to the Society for the Furtherance of the Gospel; and in 1795 succeeded to the office of Secretary to the Unity of the Moravian Brethren in England; died at Fairfield, Lancashire, May 6, 1836. His 'Selection of Sacred Music,' in six volumes, published between the years 1806 and 1825, is a valuable work. Edited also the first English edition of the 'Brethren's Tune Book,' which had been compiled in 1784 by Bishop Christian Gregor; composer of hymn tunes, anthems, &c.

LAUDI SPIRITUALI. 193

ALLA TRINITÀ BEATA, No. 252 F.C.H., 8 (Second Tune) S.H. The reading of the melody in these hymnals is different from the original, a copy of which is here given, taken from Dr Burney's 'History of Music,' vol. ii. p. 328. Burney, it should be added, took his copy from that preserved in the library already named.

ALLA TRINITÀ BEATA.

Key F.

{| d :— | d :r | m :— | r :d | f :— | m :r |}
   Al .   la   Tri .   ni .   tà   be .
{| d₁ :— | m₁ :s₁ | d :— | m :— | r :— | s₁ :— |}

{| m :— | m :— | r :— | m :f | m :— | m :r :d |}
   a .   ta   da   noi   sem . pre
{| d :— | d₁ :— | s₁ :— | — :— | d :— | l₁ :— |}

{| r :f | m :r | d :— | d :— | s :— | s :l |}
   a .   do .   ra   ta   Tri .   ni .
{| f₁ :— | s₁ :— | d₁ :— | d₁ :— | de :— | l₁ :— |}

N

f	:—	|—	:—	|s	:f	|m	:r	|m	:—	|m	:—
tā		a		glo	.	rio	.	o	.	sa	
r	:—	|r	:m	|t₁	:—	|s₁	:—	|d	:—	|d	:t₁

|r	:d	|f	:r	|d	:—	|f	:m	|r	:d	|f	:r
u	.	i	.	tā		me	.	ra	.	vig	.
|l₁	:—	|f₁	:s₁	|m₁	:—	|l₁	:s₁	|f₁	:m₁	|r₁	:s₁

|d	:—	|d	:—	|s	:—	|f	:l	|f	:—	|s	:l
lio	.	sa.		Tu		sei		man	.	na	
|d₁	:—	|d₁	:—		:		:de	|r	:d	|ta₁	:l₁

|ta:l	:s	|f	:m	|f	:—	|s	:—	|d	:—	|r	:m
sa	.	por	.	o	.	sa		e		tutt'	.
|s¹	:—		:d	|l₁	:r	|t₁	:s₁	|l₁	:s₁	|f₁	:m₁

|f	:—	|m	:d	|r	:f	|m	:r	|d	:—	|d	:—
or		de		si	.	de		ro	.	sa.	
|r₁	:—	|m₁	:—	|f₁	:—	|s₁	:—	|d₁	:—	|—	:—

Lawes, Henry, son of William Lawes; born at Dinton, Wiltshire; baptised January 1, 1595-1596; pupil of Giovanni Coperario; sworn in as epistler of the Chapel Royal, and on November 3, following, one of the gentlemen, and some time after clerk of the cheque; composed in 1634 music for Milton's masque of "Comus," produced at Ludlow Castle on Michaelmas night in that year; in 1637 published 'A Paraphrase upon the Psalms of David, by G(eorge) S(andys), Set to New Tunes, for Private Devotion. And a thorow Base, for Voice or Instrument;' and in 1648, 'Choice Psalmes put into Musick for Three Voices. . . . Composed by Henry and William Lawes, Brothers and Servants to his Majestie. With divers Eligies Set in Musick by several friends upon the death of William Lawes.'[1] On the Restoration in 1660, Lawes was reinstated in his Court appointments. He is said to have been the first English musician who regularly employed bars in his music; and he had the good fortune to be celebrated in a sonnet by Milton, which begins thus—

> "Harry, whose tuneful and well-measured song
> First taught our English music how to span
> Words with just note and accent."

Lawes died in London, October 21, 1662, and was buried in the cloisters of Westminster Abbey.

[1] Killed during the siege of Chester, 1645.

CHANT No. 256 in S.P. is an adaptation by Joseph Corfe. The same chant is set to S.S. No. 118 U.P.H., "The wilderness and the solitary place."

Leipzig Melody.

PENUEL, No. 205 U.P.H., "Ich lasz dich nicht, du muszt mein Jesus bleiben," is so described in vol. i. of Johann Gottfried Schicht's 'Allgemeines Choralbuch,' 1819.

Lemon, John, son of William and Ann Lemon; a distinguished musical amateur, born at Truro, 1754; baptised November 29; successively lieutenant and major, Horse Guards, and lieutenant-colonel in the army; M.P. for West Looe, 1784, but in the same year accepted the Chiltern Hundreds; M.P. for Saltash, 1786 to 1790, and for Truro in five successive Parliaments from 1796 till his decease; colonel of the Cornish Miners; Lord Commissioner of the Admiralty, 1804; died at Polvellen, near Looe, April 5, 1814.

CHANT No. 116 U.P.P. is his, and was published in John Marsh's Collection. The same Chant is set to S.S. No. 122 U.P.H., "Ho, every one that thirsteth."

Leslie, Henry Temple (Mus. Doc. ?), born about 1825; an ardent advocate of the temperance cause, and musical authority among the Good Templars; sometime organist at Victoria Church, Leicester; afterwards at St Mary-Le-Port, Bristol; edited several collections of hymn tunes and temperance pieces; died at Sandown, Isle of Wight (not at Reading, as stated by some writers), May 5, 1876. His tune

TRUST, No. 171 S.P., appears without a name in 'Clifton Conference Hymns,' which he edited in 1872. It first received its present name in Mr Carnie's 'Northern Psalter.'

Lindeman. To a composer of this name, "Romsdal," No. 204 U.P.H., is assigned. It is perhaps the composition of Ole Andres Lindeman, Norwegian organist and composer; born 1768; organist of the Frauekirke in Trondheim; died 1855. If so, it is not in his 'Choralbuch,' issued in 1838.

Lockhart, Charles, born in London about 1745; blind from infancy; first organist of the Lock Chapel, 1772; also organist of St Katherine, Cree; St Mary's, Lambeth; Orange Street Chapel; and Lock Chapel again from 1790 to 1797; died in London, February 9, 1815 (not 1816, as in the S.P. and F.C.H.)

CARLISLE, No. 190 S.P., 184 P. and P., and 126 F.C.H., appears in a reprint of the Lock Collection, 1792. Set to the hymn "Come, Holy Spirit, come" (No. 102 in S.H., 121 F.C.H., 104 U.P.H.), and is there named "Invocation."

Lockwood, Radcliffe Boorman, a musical amateur, was born in Binghamton, New York, U.S.A., May 6, 1829, and educated principally in private schools. He is a graduate of Columbia College Law School, New York. Mr Lockwood has during his lifetime been much interested in Sunday-school work, and for many years had charge of the music at the Five Points House of Industry, New York, where he taught thousands of the little waifs who entered that institution to sing. He composed several tunes to Sunday-school hymns, one of which is

GOOD SHEPHERD, No. 414 S.H. and 377 F.C.H. It was composed in 1858 or 1859, and published by Horace Watters in 'The Sabbath-School Bell,' New York, 1859, where it is given "As sung by the children at the Five Points House of Industry." The words were written by the late Mrs Mary Woolsey Howland, wife of the Rev. Robert Howland, D.D., late Rector of the "Church of the Heavenly Rest," New York.

Löhr, George Augustus, born at Norwich, 1821; educated at Magdalen College, Oxford, as a chorister; in 1836 became an articled pupil of Dr Buck, then organist of Norwich Cathedral; in November 1845 appointed organist of St Margaret's Church, Leicester, and afterwards choirmaster, which positions he still holds.

ST FRANCES, No. 79, 213, and 219 (Second Tune) S.H., 129 P. and P., 132 S.P., 62 F.C.H., 83 U.P.P., 186 and 282 U.P.H., was composed in 1855 to a hymn translated from the Latin by the Rev. Dr J. H. Newman, beginning "Now that the daylight dies away." It was first published in 'Bemrose and Adlington's Chorale Book,' 1861, and afterwards in 'The Bristol Tune Book,' 1863.

Lomas, George, born at Birch Hull, Bolton, November 30, 1834; studied music under Dr Steggall, the late Sir W. Sterndale Bennett, and more recently under Dr J. F. Bridge, of Westminster Abbey; for seven years voluntary organist at Didsbury Parish Church, and for eighteen years voluntary organist at Emmanuel Church, Barlow Moor; altered circumstances induced him to take up music as a profession, and he graduated as Mus. Bac., at New College, Oxford, in October 1876; continued as organist at Emmanuel Church until his death, October 18, 1884, having held that post for nearly twenty-seven years.

SUBMISSION, No. 214 S.H., is one of a number of tunes composed for 'The Bristol Tune Book,' 1876.

Lowry, Rev. Robert, D.D., born in Philadelphia, Pennsylvania, United States of America, March 12, 1826; educated at

Lewisburgh University, Pennsylvania, where he graduated in 1854; entered the Baptist ministry; became, in 1869, Professor of Rhetoric at Lewisburgh; resigned his appointment in 1875, and settled at Plainfield, New Jersey, where, in 1876, he became pastor of the second Baptist Church; received the degree of Doctor of Divinity from his University in 1875. His tune

BEAUTIFUL RIVER, No. 440 S.H., and the words to which it is set, were written in July 1864, and published in 1865 in a small collection of hymns and tunes entitled 'Happy Voices.'

Luther, Martin, D.D., the great leader of the Reformation in Germany, was the son of a miner. He was born at Eisleben, in Saxony, November 10, 1483, and educated at the University of Erfurt; professor of philosophy and divinity in the University of Wittenberg; died at Eisleben, February 18, 1546. Music was Luther's favourite art. He cultivated it assiduously all his life, and taught it to his children. He excelled very much as a flute and lute player, and was fully alive to the value of music, both in the service of the Church and as an aid to private devotion. He did not hesitate to say that "music is the art of the prophets; it is the only other art which, like theology, can calm the agitations of the soul and put the devil to flight." Luther composed several hymn tunes, and adapted others from older and well-known melodies. He also wrote about forty hymns, some of which were originally printed on single slips with the tunes.

EIN' FESTE BURG, No. 182 S.H., 325 F.C.H., 144 U.P.H., named in the last two collections "Worms," is Luther's best known composition, and appears in 'Geistliche Lieder,' printed by Joseph Klug, Wittenberg, 1529, and the 'Augsburger Gesangbuch,' 1530. It is said to have been composed by Luther on his way to the Diet of Worms, April 1521; but this is considered unlikely, as it is not in the collection of 1524. Meyerbeer makes use of it in his opera "The Huguenots," and Mendelssohn in his "Reformation Symphony."

ERFURT, No. 199 U.P.P., 290 U.P.H., "Von Himmel hoch da komm' ich her," is attributed to Luther. It appears in Lotther's 'Magdeburg Gesangbuch,' 1540.

LUTHER'S 130TH, No. 125 U.P.H., "Aus tiefer Noth schrei ich zu dir," a hymn based by Luther upon Psalm 130, De Profundis. This tune is associated with that hymn, and appears in 'Geistliche Gesangbuchlein,' Wittenberg, 1524; it is probably by Luther.

LUTHER'S HYMN, No. 155 S.H., 318 F.C.H., 71 U.P.H., appears in a collection published by Joseph Klug in 1535, set to the words "Nun freut euch, liebe Christen g'mein." It was afterwards adapted to the hymn "Es ist gewisslich." It is doubtful if Luther composed this tune; a tradition exists that he wrote it on hearing it sung by a traveller. It has been associated in this country with the hymn, "Great God, what do I see and hear?" and was at one time much used at musical festivals and sacred concerts. John Braham,[1] the great tenor vocalist, used to sing it. Harper accompanying him on the trumpet with effective fanfares between the lines. The reading given in the above hymnals is found in Jacobi's 'Psalmodia Germanica,' 1722, and differs considerably from the original. The following is the reading given by Von Tucher.

SOLDAU, No. 103 S.H., 25 S.P., 229 U.P.P., 13 F.C.H., 38 P. and P., 169, 188, and 193 U.P.H. Thought to be an old German melody which Luther adapted to his arrangement of "Nun bitten wir den heiligen Geist," a hymn of the thirteenth century. The form now in use is an abridgment by Henry Edward Dibdin, who published it in his 'Standard Psalm Tune Book,' and has for many years been associated with Paraphrase 15. Nothing is more affecting than to hear this tune with its solemn plagal cadences sung by a large congregation.

THE TUNE ON WHICH "SOLDAU" WAS FRAMED.

---

[1] It was sung by Braham at the Edinburgh Musical Festivals of 1815 and 1819.

Key G.

{| d :— | r :r | d :— | l₁ :— | s₁ :— | l₁ :— | d :— | d :— |}

{| : | m :— | s :— | l :— | s :— | m :— | d :— | l₁ :— |}

{| d :— | d :— | : | m :-.m | m :r | m :— | d :d | r :r |}

{| m :— | d :— | r :r | m :— | d :— | l₁ :— | d :d | r :— |}

{| d :— | l₁ :— | s₁ :— | — :— | l₁ :-.t₁ | d :— | d :— | — :— ||

Spires, No. 231 U.P.P., 28 S.P., 42 P. and P., named in the last two collections "Wittenberg," "Erhalt uns Herr bei Deinem Wort," a children's hymn against the two arch-enemies of Christ, the Pope and the Turk, hence often called the "Pope and Turk tune." It appears in 'Geistliche Lieder,' printed by Joseph Klug at Wittenberg, 1543. According to Winterfeld it is Luther's composition.

Lyra Davidica.

A collection of hymns with tunes, published in 1708, under the title, 'Lyra Davidica, or a Collection of Divine Songs and Hymns, partly new composed, partly translated from the High German and Latin Hymns, and set to easy and pleasant Tunes,' London, 1708.

Easter Hymn, No. 54 (First Tune) S.H., 169 (Second Tune) F.C.H., is in the above work, harmonised in two parts (treble and bass), and set to the hymn "Jesus Christ is risen to-day." It is erroneously assigned in many collections to Dr Worgan, who was not born in 1708.

It is found in Cornforth Gilson's Collection, published at Edinburgh in 1759. This is probably one of its earliest appearances in a Scottish collection. C. Lee Williams has introduced the first line of this tune in his church cantata, "The Last Night at Bethany," composed for the Gloucester Musical Festival, 1889.

Macbeth, Allan, son of the late Norman Macbeth, A.R.S.A.; born at Greenock, March 13, 1856; educated in Germany, 1869 to 1871; studied music under Mr Robert Davidson, and Herr Otto Schweitzer, Edinburgh, 1871; organist and choirmaster in Albany Street Congregational Chapel there; studied at Leipzig Conservatoire under Richter, Reinecke, Jadassohn, 1875 to 1876; succeeded H. A. Lambeth as conductor of Glasgow Choral Union, 1880; resigned 1887; appointed organist and choirmaster Woodside Established Church, Glasgow, 1882; St George's-in-the-Fields (first organist), 1884; Principal of the Glasgow Athenæum School of

Music, founded in 1890. Mr Macbeth's compositions include songs, part-songs, anthems, and a cantata, "Silver Bells." His most important work is a cantata, "The Land of Glory" (words by Edward Oxenford), which gained the first prize offered by the Glasgow Society of Musicians, 1889. It was first performed at Glasgow, March 10, 1890. His "Intermezzo" for strings is exceedingly popular.

S.S., No. 2, "O that Thou wouldest bless me indeed," and No. 16, "He shall feed His flock," both in F.C.H., were composed for and first published in that work.

Macfarren, Sir George Alexander, Mus. Doc., born in London, March 2, 1813; pupil of Charles Lucas and others; appointed Principal of the Royal Academy of Music, 1875; Professor of Music in the University of Cambridge, and Mus. Doc., 1875; Mus. Doc. Oxford, 1879; received knighthood 1883; one of the greatest theorists of modern times; blind for many years; died in London, October 31, 1887.

Chant in A, No. 355 S.H., is his composition, and not Dr Dupuis's. It appears in 'Chants as used in Westminster Abbey,' edited by James Turle.

S.S., Nos. 11 and 23 U.P.H., "Arise, O Lord," and "Salvation to our God," were composed for that work.

S.S., No. 33 U.P.H., "The Lord is my shepherd," was composed for and published in 'Parochial Anthems,' by the Cathedral Composers of 1863, edited by Dr Thomas Lloyd Fowle, M.A.; preface dated Winchester, 1863.

The following are his compositions :—

    S.S., No. 42 U.P.H., "Have mercy upon me."
       " No. 99   " "I know whom I have believed."
       " No. 115 " "O Lord, I will praise Thee."
       " No. 35   " "One thing have I desired."
       " No. 60   " "Remember me, O Lord."
       " No. 40   " "The Lord redeemeth."

All but the third, "O Lord, I will praise Thee," are found in 'Introits, or Short Anthems, for the Holy Days and Seasons of the English Church,' 1866.

Macfarren, Walter Cecil, brother of the preceding; born in London, August 28, 1826; chorister in Westminster Abbey under James Turle, 1836 to 1841; studied at the Royal Academy of Music under W. H. Holmes, Cipriani Potter and his brother; since 1846, a professor at that institution, and from 1873 to 1880, conductor of its concerts. Composer and pianist of much ability.

AGATHA, No. 174 U.P.H., was composed for the hymn to which it is set, and first published in the 'Anglican Hymn Tune Book,' edited by E. G. Monk, Mus. Doc.

Madan, Rev. Martin, son of Colonel Madan of the Guards, and brother of Spencer Madan, D.D., Prebendary of Peterborough; was born in 1726; founded the Lock Hospital, London, of which he became chaplain; died May 1790; published in 1760 'Psalms and Hymns extracted from various authors,' and an appendix in 1763; author of 'Thelphthora' and other works.

HUDDERSFIELD, No. 93 P. and P., 130 U.P.P., 82 S.P., is one of 33 tunes contributed by Madan to 'A Collection of Psalm and Hymn Tunes, never Published before,' 1769, where it bears its present name. This, known as the "Lock Collection," was edited by Madan. A second edition was published in 1792.

SECOND HALF OF "HUDDERSFIELD" AS COMPOSED BY MADAN.

Main, Hubert Platt (descended from the Scotch Mains), born at Ridgefield, Connecticut, August 17, 1839; studied harmony in 1856 under Dr Thomas Hastings; composer of many anthems and pieces for Sunday-schools; connected with the firm of Biglow & Main, Music Sellers and Publishers, New York, since its formation in February 1868; an excellent authority on hymns and their writers.

BETTER WORLD, No. 433 S.H., is an adaptation by him, and was first published in its present form in 'Bright Jewels,' by Lowry, Sherwin, and Allen, in 1869.

Mainzer, Joseph, Ph. Doc., was born at Trèves, October 21, 1801. He received his education in the Maîtrise of Trèves Cathedral, and learnt to play several musical instruments. With a view to becoming an engineer, he spent some time in the coal-mines near Saarbrück, but he at length entered the ecclesiastical profession, and was ordained priest in 1826, afterwards becoming an Abbé. His political tendencies forced him to leave Germany. In 1841 he competed against Sir Henry R. Bishop for the musical professorship at Edinburgh, but was unsuccessful. He met with much success as a teacher and organiser of singing-classes; his 'Singing for the Million' was long popular, and ran through many editions. He died at Manchester, Nov. 10, 1851.

MAINZER, No. 13 S.P., 17 F.C.H., 59, 163, 213, 319 U.P.H., 201 U.P.P., 22 P. and P., 6 (First Tune) S.H., 94 (First Tune), 135 (Second Tune) S.H., appears in his 'Standard Psalmody of Scotland,' 1845, but is there anonymous. It was published a short time before in 'Mainzer's Choruses,' and is set to Psalm 107. It seems to be his composition.

Malan, Rev. Henri Abraham Cæsar, son of Jacques Imbert Malan, a professor in the College of Geneva; born at Geneva, July 7, 1787; divine, poet, and musician; educated at Geneva; ordained to the ministry, October 1810; pastor of the Chapelle du Témoignage, Geneva; degree of D.D. conferred on him by the University of Glasgow, October 10, 1826, "as a very faithful pastor, an excellent man, commendable in the highest degree for his piety and the holiness of his life, and especially worthy of the highest theological honours"; died at Vandœuvres, near Geneva, May 18, 1864.

NAZARETH, No. 73 (Second Tune) S.H., is an altered copy of the following tune, which appears in his 'Musique des Chants de Sion,' 1834 :—

KEY F.

{| .s₁:d .r | m :- .s | f :l | l .,s:s | .s₁:d .r | m :- .s }
{| f :t₁ | d :— || .s :l .s | f :- .f | m :m | m.,r:r }
{| .s :l .s | f :- .f | m :m | r :— ||

In later editions of Malan's work the tune is given in the same time form as appears in the S.H.

PILGRIM SONG, No. 232 U.P.H., is an altered copy of the tune set to Cantique 80 in 'Recueil de Cent Cantiques Chrétiens,' Paris, 1827, composed by Malan. See Hymn Music.

SILCHESTER, No. 206 S.P., 124 F.C.H., 165 U.P.P., appears in the form given below in 'Les Chants de Sion; ou, Les psaumes, les hymnes, et les cantiques de la Bible, mis en musique par Céasar Malan, Ministre de Christ,' Geneva, 1825, and set to Psalm 34:—

ORIGINAL OF "SILCHESTER" TUNE.

The form we now use appears in 'The National Psalmist,' by Mason and Webb, 1849.

S.S., No. 26 U.P.H., "O Lord, my God,' appears in 'Recueil de Cent Cantiques Chrétiens,' composed by Malan, and published at Paris in 1827. It will be found on page 200 and set to Cantique 100.

It was set to the words "O Lord, my God," by his son, the Rev. Solomon Cæsar Malan, who was born April 1812; vicar of Broadwinsor, Dorsetshire, for many years; author of numerous works on Eastern topography, ornithology, &c.

This anthem is erroneously assigned in some collections to Dr Maurice Greene. Assuredly it is not his composition.

Marshall, Frederick, son of James Marshall, a teacher of music; born at Northampton, and educated at Rugby School, where he succeeded his father as organist; afterwards organist of Christ Church, Leamington, for many years; appointed organist of Rochester Cathedral, but resigned without entering on the duties, and accepted the appointment of organist of the Parish

Church, Banbury, Oxfordshire; died near Olney, Bucks, July 1857, aged sixty-seven years. His tune

LEAMINGTON, No. 92 S.P., appears in the Rev. J. A. Baxter's 'Harmonia Sacra,' edited by Vincent Novello, 1840.

Martin, George William, a prominent figure in London musical circles about thirty years ago, was born March 8, 1828, and studied as a chorister in St Paul's Cathedral under William Hawes. He also sang sometimes in St James's Palace, when her Majesty the Queen—then a young girl—used to attend the Chapel Royal with her mother, the Duchess of Kent. Martin was professor of music at the Normal College for Army Schoolmasters, and from June 1845 to Michaelmas 1853 was resident music-master at St John's Training College, Battersea. He was also the first organist of Christ Church, Battersea, which was opened in 1849. His abilities as a conductor were of a high order, and the concerts of the National Choral Society and the Metropolitan Schools Choral Society, which he conducted, were spoken of by the London press in highly eulogistic terms. His compositions are excellent, and many of his glees and part-songs obtained prizes. Martin died at Bolingbroke House Hospital, Wandsworth, April 16, 1881. It is sad to relate that the closing years of this talented musician's life were passed in intemperate excess. A gentleman generously paid for his maintenance at the hospital where he died. Martin refused to give any address where he had lived, or the name of any friend except the gentleman who befriended him. He was evidently quite destitute, and no doubt had not had any settled place of abode for some time. He was not married. He had no personal effects. Only a few scraps of music and memoranda were found in his pockets. The simple facts show conclusively that he had drained the cup of misery to the dregs, and wished to die in obscurity. The assigned cause of death was a severe attack of rheumatic fever, induced by exposure and want. His body was buried in Woking Cemetery by the parish. The following anecdote relating to Martin is told: The Prince Consort having composed a part-song, had requested Sir George Smart to attend at Buckingham Palace with a few choir boys for the purpose of its performance. When the musical company reached the presence of his Royal Highness, the latter presented a copy of the part-song to young Martin and said, "Can you sing that at sight?" "Yes, sir," replied Martin, quite undismayed, and performed the task to the Prince's satisfaction. But that unlucky expression, "sir," called forth from punctilious Sir George's right hand a tremendous box on the ears outside the palace gates.

LEOMINSTER, No. 147 F.C.H., 248 S.H., 318 U.P.H., associated with Dr Bonar's hymn, "A few more years shall roll," was composed by Martin and published in his 'Journal of Part Music,' vol. ii. (1862). The harmony in the above hymnals is by Sir Arthur S. Sullivan.

S.S., No. 65 U.P.H., "Teach me, O Lord, the way," is his composition, and appears in his 'Journal of Part Music,' No. 21 (1862).

Mason, Lowell, Mus. Doc., son of Johnson Mason and Caty Hartshorn, was born at Medfield, Massachusetts, January 8, 1792. When not much more than a boy, his fondness and aptitude for music placed him in the position of leader of a church choir in his native town. From Massachusetts he removed to Savannah, where he was clerk in a bank. Here he conducted the psalmody of the large Presbyterian church, and compiled his first collection of church music. Obtaining leave of absence from the bank, he bent his steps to Philadelphia, and offered the copyright of his book to the publishers, if he might but receive a few copies for his own use. They all declined the offer; and when the young enthusiast went to Boston, he fared no better. He was about to return to Savannah, when he met a musical gentleman, who desired to examine his work. The gentleman expressed great satisfaction with it, and, with Lowell Mason's permission, showed the manuscript to the Board of Management of the Boston Handel and Haydn Society, of which he was a member. That Society published it, giving the author an interest in the work. It became immensely popular, and speedily ran through seventeen large editions. This success decided Lowell Mason's course of life. He took up his abode at Boston, became organist of Dr Lyman Beecher's church, and commenced the work of lecturing and publishing church music in earnest. In 1832 he established the Boston Academy of Music, and in 1838 obtained power to teach in all the schools of Boston. At the same time he founded periodical conventions of music-teachers, which have proved very useful, and are now established in many parts of the States. He also published a large number of manuals and collections, which sold enormously, and produced him a handsome fortune. His degree of Doctor in Music —the first of the kind conferred by an American college—was granted by the New York University in 1835. He died at Orange, New Jersey, August 11, 1872. Of his compositions—

AVENTINE, No. 32 S.P., is arranged from a Gregorian Chant, and was published in 'The Boston Händel and Haydn Society's Collection,' third edition, 1824, where it is named "Hamburg."

BARROW, No. 35 S.P., appears in 'The People's Tune Book,' 1860.

BETHANY, No. 201 U.P.H. Composed in 1856, and first published in 'The Sabbath Hymn and Tune Book,' 1858.

BOSTON, No. 11 F.C.H., 276 U.P.H. Another form of "Aventine."

BOYLSTON, No. 75 U.P.P., 188 S.P., 140 (Second Tune) and 342 F.C.H. First published in 'The Choir,' 1832.

BRIGHTON, No. 41 S.P. From 'Congregational Church Music,' London, 1853.

CECIL, No. 10 U.P.H. Composed in 1854, and published in 'The Hallelujah,' New York, the same year.

DILIGENCE, No. 431 S.H. and 387 F.C.H. First published in 'The Song Garden,' 1864.

ELLIOTT, No. 148 (Second Tune) S.H. Published in 'The Sabbath Tune Book,' New York, 1859. It was originally in triple time.

ERNAN, No. 9 S.P. First published in 'New Carmina Sacra,' and 'Cantica Laudis,' 1850.

EVAN, No. 24 (Second Tune) S.H., 76 P. and P., 36 U.P.P., 105 U.P.H., 64 S.P., 76 (Second Tune) F.C.H. Adapted by Dr Mason. See Havergal, Rev. W. H.

FELIX, No. 79 P. and P., 24 S.H., 101 F.C.H., 68 S.P., 151 U.P.H., and 54 U.P.P. Adapted by Dr Mason. See Mendelssohn.

GRAFTON, No. 84 P. and P., was composed in 1830. It appears in the 'Sacred Harp,' which he compiled with Timothy Battle Mason in 1836, where it is anonymous. He claims it as his composition in 'The Hallelujah,' 1854. It was published (probably for the first time in Scotland) in the 'Bon-Accord Harmonist; Being a Selection of Psalm and Hymn Tunes, in a Variety of Measures,' Aberdeen, 1845.

HEBER, No. 204 F.C.H., 108 (First Tune) S.H., was composed in 1824 for the words to which it is set, and published in 'The Händel and Haydn Society's Collection,' ninth edition, 1829.

ILFRACOMBE, No. 11 S.P., 335 F.C.H., 158 U.P.P. Adapted by Dr Mason from his tune "Brighton," and published anonymously in the first Supplement to 'Congregational Church Music,' 1859.

MILTON, No. 102 S.P., appears in Dr Mason's 'Hallelujah,' 1854, under the name of "Kinlock," and is there anonymous.

MISSIONARY, No. 134 and 294 (Second Tune) U.P.H. See "Heber," which is the same tune.

MOUNT VERNON, No. 359 (First Tune) S.H., 357 F.C.H. Composed to words by the Rev. S. F. Smith on the death of Miss M. J. C., July 13, 1833, aged sixteen, and sung at her funeral.

NAIN, No. 268 F.C.H. Composed in 1831, and published in 'Spiritual Songs for Social Worship,' January 1833.

NAOMI, No. 110 U.P.P., 105 S.P. Adapted by Dr Mason. See Nageli.

OLIVET, No. 314 F.C.H., 227 (Second Tune) S.H. Composed in 1832 for the hymn to which it is set—viz., "My faith looks up to Thee." It is related that Dr Mason having applied to Dr Ray Palmer for some words to set to music, he drew the above hymn from his pocket. It had been written a few weeks before. Both words and music were published for the first time in Hastings and Mason's 'Spiritual Songs,' vol. i., 1832.

ST AUGUSTINE, No. 199 in P. and P., is an altered copy of his tune "Lathrop," which appears in his 'New Carmina Sacra,' 1850. It had become popularly associated in the Church of Scotland and elsewhere with James Montgomery's hymn, "O where shall rest be found," the last four lines of verse 2, and the first four of verse 3, being sung to a minor part added by the late Sir John Goss, for the Rev. W. Mercer's 'Church Psalter and Hymn-Book.' It has now been separated from the hymn in 'Scottish Hymnal,' and another tune set to it that has no special claim as being suitable to the words.

OLMÜTZ, No. 116 S.P. Arranged by Dr Mason from the 8th Gregorian Tone, and first published as a metrical tune, 1834.

S.S. No. 7 U.P.H., "Holiness becometh Thine house,"
,, No. 13 F.C.H., "I love them that love Me,"
,, No. 9 U.P.H., "Not unto us,"
,, No. 20 U.P.P., "Now unto Him,"
,, No. 10 U.P.H. and 10 F.C.H., "Pray for the peace of Jerusalem,"
,, No. 18 U.P.H., "The grace of our Lord Jesus Christ,"

were all published for the first time in his 'Hallelujah,' 1854. Although no composers' names are given, they are understood to be Mason's compositions.

S.S. No. 6 U.P.H., "Blessed is the people,"
,, No. 3 U.P.H., "Our soul waiteth for the Lord,"
,, No. 69 U.P.H. and 11 F.C.H., "Search me, O God,"

are his compositions. The last-named appears in the 'People's Tune Book,' 1860.

S.S. No. 13 U.P.H., "The Lord is in His holy temple," is an adaptation by him; and the harmonies of S.S. No. 1 U.P.H. and 1 F.C.H., "The Lord bless thee and keep thee," are wholly his.

Mason, Timothy Battle, born at Medfield, Massachusetts, November 17, 1801; pupil of his brother Dr Lowell Mason; in 1834 removed to Cincinnati, Ohio, having accepted the Professorship of the Eclectic Academy of Music in that city; became director of the music in the second Presbyterian Church, Dr Lyman Beecher's, there; conductor and founder of the Cincinnati Händel and Haydn Society; from 1854 to 1856 director of the music in Vine Street Congregational Church, Cincinnati; removed to Milwaukee, Wisconsin, in 1856, where he was chorister of the second

Presbyterian Church; returned to Cincinnati, where he died February 10, 1861.

MASON, No. 10 F.C.H., appears in the 'Sacred Harp,' which he edited with Dr Lowell Mason in 1841, and is there named "Montgomery." It is wrongly assigned to Dr Mason in the Free Church and other Hymnals.

Mather,[1] **William,** was born in 1756. He was organist of St Paul's and St James's, Sheffield, where he died in 1808. His tune

SHEFFIELD, No. 134 U.P.P., 159 S.P., 149 P. and P., appears in 'Sacred Music, containing Two Hundred and Fifty of the most Favourite Tunes. . . . The music selected and adapted for Two, Three, and Four Voices, and intended as an Appendix to Dr Watts's Psalms and Hymns,' composed by Edward Miller, Mus. Doc., about 1802; it is there named "Attercliffe," and given as new and copyright.

Matthews, Rev. Timothy Richard, born at Colmworth Rectory near Bedford, November 4, 1826; educated at Bedford Grammar School; graduated B.A. at Gonville and Caius College, Cambridge, 1853; whilst private tutor in the family of the Rev. Lord Wriothesley Russell, Canon of Windsor, in 1847, he studied the organ under Sir George J. Elvey; rector of North Coates, near Grimsby, Lincolnshire, since 1869; edited the 'North Coates Supplemental Tune Book' in 1878. Of his tunes

CHENIES, Nos. 274 (First Tune), 308 (Second Tune), 363 S.H., was published on a single leaf in 1855.

LUDBOROUGH, No. 336 S.H. and 27 F.C.H., was first published in 'Church Hymns with Tunes,' 1874.

WINTHORPE, No. 296 S.H., was composed about 1862, and so named by Bishop Tozer after one of his two Lincolnshire parishes.

MARGARET, No. 385 S.H., was first published in 'Children's Hymns with Tunes,' published by the S.P.C.K.

Maurice, Rev. Peter, D.D., second son of Mr Hugh Maurice; born at Greenwich, Kent, June 29, 1803; educated at the Grammar

---

[1] The following is offered regarding his son, who was for many years a prominent figure in Edinburgh musical circles: John Mather, born at Sheffield 1781 (?); settled in Edinburgh about 1810; presided at the organ and pianoforte at Edinburgh Musical Festival, 1815; conductor of the Edinburgh Institution for the Encouragement of Sacred Music from 1815 till about 1818; pianist at the Glasgow Musical Festival in 1821; chorus-singer (tenor) at the York Musical Festivals of 1823 and 1825; chorus-master of the Edinburgh Musical Festival, 1843; died January 21, 1850.

School, Bangor; B.A., Jesus College, Oxford, 1826; M.A., New College, Oxford, 1829; B.D., 1837; D.D., 1840; deacon and priest by the Bishop of Bangor, 1827; chaplain of All Souls' College, Oxford, 1837; of New College, Oxford, 1858; about 1827 curate near Llanrwst; from 1829 to 1854 curate of Kennington, near Oxford; from 1854 vicar of Yarnton, near Oxford, till he died, March 30, 1878. Composer of hymn tunes, &c., and an Evening Service in E; author of 'What shall we do with Music?—a letter to the Earl of Derby,' London, 1856; also several works against Popery.

SPRINGFIELD, No. 32 (First Tune) S.H., is there wrongly assigned to him. It appears in his 'Choral Harmony, a Collection of Tunes in Short Score for Four Voices,' 1854, but is anonymous. It bears a strong resemblance to a tune named "St Clement," by the Rev. Richard Cecil, published in his daughter's collection in 1814.

McDonald, Alexander, was joint music-master with Archibald McDonald—presumably his father—at George Heriot's Hospital, Edinburgh, from 1807 to 1810; appointed precentor of Old Greyfriars' Church, Edinburgh, in succession to John Neil,[1] February 1, 1804, but dismissed from the office, October 29, 1817, for not attending to his duties. He is probably the same who edited 'The Notation of Music Simplified,' Glasgow, October 1826.

HERIOT'S TUNE, No. 88 P. and P., appears in 'A Collection of Vocal Music, containing Church Tunes, Anthems, and Songs, for the use of the several Hospitals of this City,' edited by McDonald in 1807. It is there named "George Heriot's Old Tune." As McDonald's work was based on a collection issued by one Lawrie at Edinburgh in 1780, it is probable "Heriot's Tune" appeared there.

Mendelssohn Bartholdy, Jakob Ludwig Felix, Ph.D.—a degree conferred on him by the University of Leipzig in 1836—was born at Hamburg, February 3, 1809. He was one of the

---

[1] At a meeting of the Edinburgh Town Council, held on March 2, 1803, complaint was made by the session of Old Greyfriars' Church that this "uptaker o' the Psalm" "had last Sunday fallen asleep in the desk during the time of the forenoon service, and was with great difficulty wakened, and could not sing the Psalm till the minister was obliged to give out the Psalm a second time." After consideration, "the Council unanimously dismiss the said John Neil from his office of precentor in the Old Greyfriars' Church of the city, and declare the office of precentor therein vacant."

greatest composers of the present century, and is universally known by his oratorios "St Paul" and "Elijah," his exquisite settings of some of the Psalms, and also his instrumental music. He died at Leipzig, November 4, 1847.

BETHLEHEM, No. 27 S.H., 195 F.C.H., and 31 U.P.H., is an adaptation by W. H. Cummings, the eminent vocalist, from the 'Festgesang,' a work produced at Leipzig, June 23, 1840, to celebrate the fourth centenary of the art of printing. See Cummings, W. H.

BUNYAN, No. 68 F.C.H., 43 S.P., and 72 S.H., is adapted from his Sonata for Pianoforte and Violoncello in D (Op. 58).

CONTEMPLATION, No. 292 U.P.H., 110 S.H., adapted from his setting of the 13th Psalm to English words by "C. B. Broadley, Esquire," for whom the work was composed in 1840.

EPIPHANY, No. 383 F.C.H., is adapted from his 'Lieder Ohne Worte' (Op. 30, No. 3).

FELIX, No. 54 U.P.P., 151 U.P.H., 101 F.C.H., 68 S.P., 24 (First Tune) S.H., 79 P. and P., although assigned to Mendelssohn, is practically the composition of Dr Lowell Mason, who published it in his 'Hallelujah,' 1854, under the name of "Baltic." The phrase on which this tune is founded is here given, and is from the chorus, "He stirreth up the Jews," in the unfinished oratorio "Christus" (Opus 97, Posthumous Works, No. 26), first performed at the Birmingham Musical Festival, September 8, 1852.

INTERCESSION, No. 330 F.C.H., 273 U.P.H. The last two lines of this tune are taken from "Look down on us," an air with chorus in "Elijah."

LEIPZIG, No. 192 P. and P., was composed for C. D. Hackett's 'National Psalmist,' London. Preface dated 1840.

In 1841, when Mr Henry E. Dibdin of Edinburgh was compiling his 'Standard Psalm Tune Book,' he requested Mendelssohn to compose a long-metre tune for that work, which elicited from the great master the following interesting reply, but unfortunately no psalm tune:—

"LEIPZIG, 9th July 1841.

"DEAR SIR,—I thank you very much for your kind and flattering letter of the 19th of last month, and enclose the page of your album, on which I have written a little prelude[1] for the organ, which I composed this morning on purpose. I was sorry I could not write exactly what you desired me to do, but I do not know what a 'long-measure psalm tune' means, and there is nobody in this place at present to whom I could apply for an explanation. Excuse me, therefore, if you receive something else than what you wished, and believe me, very truly yours,

"FELIX MENDELSSOHN BARTHOLDY.

"HENRY E. DIBDIN, Esq."

For a copy of the above letter, the writer is indebted to John Montgomerie Bell, Esq., W.S.

Merrylees, James, son of Mr John Merrylees; a distinguished musical amateur; born at Paisley, April 10, 1824, and when a boy played a flute in the local orchestral society. He studied the Tonic Sol-Fa system under the late W. D. Read, out of whose classes sprang the Paisley Tonic Sol-Fa Institute, of which Mr Merrylees was honorary conductor from its commencement until 1861, when he removed to Glasgow, and held the post of honorary choirmaster in St George's Road Reformed Presbyterian (now Free) Church till 1871. In 1867 he began the study of harmony and composition under the late John Curwen by attending his Euing Lectures in Anderson's College, Glasgow, and afterwards under Mr Colin Brown. In 1871 he gained the Euing Silver Medal for the best Hymn Tune, and in 1872 the Euing Gold Medal for the best Anthem. Mr Merrylees wrote *modal* accompaniments to Scottish songs for Mr Colin Brown's Collection, 'The Thistle,' and more recently he arranged for four voices, with pianoforte accompaniments, 'The Killin Collection of Gaelic Melodies' for Mr Charles Stewart. His compositions consist of hymn tunes, anthems, and other pieces.

ATLANTIC, No. 42 F.C.H. and 22 S.H., was composed in 1878 for the hymn to which it is set, and first appeared in a monthly periodical named 'The Dayspring' (October number, 1878). It was afterwards inserted in the Free Church Hymnal, 1882, under its present name.

FORMOSA, No. 175 F.C.H., was composed expressly for the hymn to which it is set, and first published in the 'Sunday School Union Hymnal,' which he assisted in editing in 1876.

The harmony of "Bangor," No. 34 S.P., is his.

S.S. No. 3 in F.C.H., "For the eyes of the Lord," was composed for that work.

Milgrove, Benjamin, born about 1731; precentor of the

[1] Published in facsimile by Messrs Paterson & Sons, Edinburgh.

212 BIOGRAPHICAL SKETCHES.

Countess of Huntingdon's Chapel, Bath, but how long cannot be ascertained; died 1810. Published about 1769 'Sixteen Hymns as they are sung at the Right Honourable the Countess of Huntingdon's Chapel in Bath. Set to Music.' From that collection

HARTS, No. 159 F.C.H., 15 and 53 S.H. The original had a chorus, "Praise the Lord, Hallelujah," which has long been obsolete. It is found in Henry Boyd's Collection, Glasgow, 1793, in its original form.

Miller, Edward, Mus. Doc., born at Norwich; studied under Dr Burney; elected organist of Doncaster upon the recommendation of Dr Nares, July 24, 1756, and held that post for fifty-one years; graduated Mus. Doc., at Cambridge, 1786; author of 'The Elements of Thorough Bass,' also in 1804 a 'History of Doncaster'; died September 12 or 13, 1807, aged seventy-two years. "A warm-hearted, simple-hearted, right-hearted man, an enthusiast in his profession, yet not undervaluing, much less despising, other pursuits." In 1790 he published 'The Psalms of David, for the use of Parish Churches.'

COMMUNION, No. 4 S.P., 35 F.C.H., 228 U.P.P., 9 P. and P., 47 and 319 S.H., is there named "Rockingham," and superscribed "Part of the melody taken from a hymn tune." The following seems to be the original, and is found in Seeley's 'Devotional Harmony,' 1806, under the name of "Great Shelford," and appears to be the earliest copy known:—

KEY E♭.

{ :d	m :f	:r	d :—	:d	s :ta	:l	s :— }
{ :s	d¹ :d¹	:t	l :l	:s	f :f	:m	ᵐr :— }
{ :r	s :s	:l	t :—	:d¹	r¹ :f	:m	r :— }
{ :d	f :f	:m	r :r	:d	d :—.r :t₁	d :— ‖

Another form (a copy of which is given below) is found in the Sequel to Weyman's 'Melodia Sacra,' vol. ii. p. 164. It is there named "Ceylon," and set to the hymn "Brightest and best":—

```
KEY E♭.
{| m    :m    :f .r | d    :—   :m.f | s    :s    :l    | l    :s    :    ||
 | d¹   :d¹   :t.d¹| t    :l        | s    :f    :m    | m    :r    :    ||
 | s    :—   :l„l | t    :—   :s.s | d¹   :m    :fe   | l    :s    :    ||
 | f    :f    :m   | m    :r    :d  | d.r :m    :r    | d    :—   :    ||
```

The earliest copy the writer can find of "Communion" in a Scottish Psalmody is in John Wilson's Collection, Edinburgh, 1825, and in R. A. Smith's published the same year. The name "Communion" is peculiar to Scotland, and was doubtless given to it from its association with Paraphrase 35, "'Twas on that night when doom'd to know," to which it is always sung at Communion time. The following reading of the second line is found in Smith's and Wilson's Collections; it was for a time prevalent in Scotland, but is now stamped out:—

```
KEY E♭.
{: s    | d¹   :—   :ta  | l    :—   :s   | s    :f    :m    | m    :r    ||
```

Monk,[1] **Edwin George,** born at Frome, Somerset, December 13, 1819; graduated Mus. Bac. Oxford 1848, Mus. Doc. 1856;

[1] The following facts are offered regarding the career of H. T. Monk, whose untimely end was the occasion of much regret: Monk, Henry Theophilus, youngest brother of Dr E. G. Monk, born at Frome, Somerset, March 6, 1831; studied music first under his brother, afterwards under Mr Lavington, organist of Wells Cathedral, Miss Reinagle of Oxford, and Professor Sir

organist and precentor of St Columba College, Rathfarnham, near Dublin, 1844 till 1846; of St Peter's College, Radley, 1848; succeeded Dr John Camidge as organist of York Cathedral, 1859; resigned 1883.

CHANT No. 1, set to hymn 354 in S.H., was first published in 'The Anglican Chant Book,' which he edited.

Monk, William Henry, son of Mr William and Anna Coleman Monk, was born in London, parish of St George's, Hanover Square, March 16, 1823;[1] pupil of Thomas Adams, J. A. Hamilton, and G. A. Griesbach; organist and choirmaster of Eaton Chapel, Pimlico, 1841 to 1843; St George's Chapel, Albemarle Street, 1843 to 1845; Portman Chapel, Marylebone, 1845 to 1847; choirmaster at King's College, London, 1847; organist in 1849, and Professor of Vocal Music in 1874 on the resignation of Dr Hullah; appointed organist at St Matthias' Church, Stoke Newington, in 1852; degree of Mus. Doc. conferred on him by the University of Durham, 1882; died after a short illness, March 18, 1889. Musical editor of 'Hymns Ancient and Modern,' and other important collections of church music; composer of many excellent hymn tunes that have become very popular.

EVENTIDE, No. 285 F.C.H., 245 (First Tune) S.H., 234 U.P.H.,
MISERERE, No. 166 (First Tune) S.H.,
NUTFIELD, No. 292 (Third Tune) S.H.,
ST BERNARD, No. 179 (Second Tune) S.H.,
ST ETHELWALD, No. 181 S.H.,
ST MATTHIAS, No. 350 S.H., 46 (First Tune) F.C.H.,
ST PHILIP, No. 95 and 169 (Second Tune) S.H.,
were first published in 'Hymns Ancient and Modern,' 1861.

VIGILATE, No. 277 F.C.H., 183 S.H., in the Appendix to the above, 1886.
ABER, No. 44 (First Tune) S.H., 135 F.C.H.,
ADVENT, No. 87 S.H.,
LITANY, No. 327 S.H.,
in the revised and enlarged edition, 1875.

G. A. Macfarren; successively organist of St Andrew's House and Church, Wells, Somerset; then as assistant to his brother at St Peter's College, Radley, Berks; next organist and choirmaster at St Philip's Church, Sheffield; and lastly, music-master and organist at Forest Schools, Walthamstow; drowned whilst bathing in North Wales, July 23, 1857. He contributed to the 'Anglican Chant Book.'

[1] These facts were communicated to the writer by Dr Monk shortly before his death.

Dr Monk, says one of his pupils, "would sometimes get out of bed to write down a tune." "Aber" was composed in this manner. "Advent" was composed in a railway train.

DISMISSION, No. 317 (Second Tune) S.H.,
MORNING, No. 345 S.H., 181 F.C.H.,
PENITENCE, No. 158 (Second Tune) S.H., 299 F.C.H.,
RESURRECTION, No. 153 F.C.H.,

are four of six original tunes he contributed to the 'Scottish Hymnal,' 1872, the harmonies of which work he also revised.

EASTER HYMN, No. 54 (Second Tune) S.H., gained the prize of five guineas on March 14, 1854, offered by "The Cheadle Association for Promoting Church Music," for the best setting of the hymn "Jesus Christ is risen to-day."

WORDSWORTH, No. 341 (First Tune) S.H., appears without a name, set to the hymn "O day of rest and gladness," in 'The Holy Year; or, Hymns for Sundays, Holidays, and other occasions throughout the Year, by Christopher Wordsworth, D.D., Archdeacon of Westminster, with appropriate tunes,' edited by William Henry Monk, London, 1865.

GETHSEMANE, No. 179 F.C.H. and 41 U.P.H., is an adaptation by him. See Tye, Dr Christopher.

Also the harmonies of :—
CHILDREN OF JERUSALEM, No. 371 S.H.
NINETY AND NINE, No. 378 F.C.H.
STEPHANOS, No. 163 S.H., 267 F.C.H., and 120 U.P.H.
ST TIMOTHY, No. 109 F.C.H.

"Eventide," says Dr Monk, was written for the hymn to which it is set, immediately before 'Hymns Ancient and Modern' was published, no other having been found suitable. As he sat writing it, one of his assistants was within two yards of him playing a Thalberg Fantasia.

S.S. No. 78 U.P.H., "Hallelujah! for unto us a child is born," appeared in the 'Musical Times,' December 1859.

Moore, Thomas, "Teacher of Psalmody," resided in the Pool-Fold, Manchester, in 1750. On June 18, 1755, appointed by the Magistrates and Town Council of Glasgow precentor of the "New Church in Bell's Yard" (Blackfriars), and teacher of psalmody in the Town's Hospital. On October 1, 1756, the Council "ordain the Dean of Guild and brethern to admit and receive Mr Thomas Moore, precentor in the New Church and teacher of church music, burgess and 'gild' (sic) brother of the burgh, and to remit his fines and hold them as paid." Moore taught (by order of the Magistrates) free music classes in the session-house of the Tron Kirk, and kept a bookseller's shop "opposite to the Post Office in Princes Street," and afterwards in Stockwell Street. He resigned his offices as precentor and teacher of psalmody, August 1787. From the terms of an advertisement in the 'Glasgow Courier' of November 17, 1792, he seems to have died there in that year.

Moore published the following collections of psalmody: 'The Psalm Singer's Compleat Tutor and Divine Companion,' 2 vols., second edition, 1750; 'The Psalm Singer's Pocket Companion,' Glasgow, 1756; 'The Psalm Singer's Delightful Pocket Companion,' Glasgow (1762). Another work he issued was 'The Vocal Concert,' Glasgow, 1761.

GLASGOW, No. 81 P. and P. and 70 S.P., appears in the 'Psalm Singer's Pocket Companion,' 1756. It there bears its present name, and is set in three parts. See Holden, John.

In Moore's work just quoted appear the following tunes, probably for the first time in a Scotch Psalmody: "Burford," there named "Norwich," "Crowle," "Kent" (see Lampe), "Walsal," "Wirksworth," "St Neot's." In it are also found "St Mary," "St Matthew," and "Hanover," but they appeared in Robert Bremner's Collection, published at Edinburgh the same year, and "St Matthew" was in use at Aberdeen in 1755. "Hanover" is named by Bremner and Moore 149th Psalm tune. In Moore's 'Delightful Pocket Companion,' Glasgow (1762), is found "Angels' Hymn" in triple time (see Gibbons, Orlando), "Babylon Streams" (see Campion, Thomas), "Winchester" (Crasselius), in triple time, similar to "Effingham" in S.P., "Stroudwater," and "St Thomas."

Morley, Henry L., for some time organist of St Paul's Church, Herne Hill, London; resigned December 1883.

NEWCASTLE, No. 297 F.C.H., was composed on September 16, 1876, and published in 'The London Tune Book,' 1877, edited by Edwin Moss.

Morley, William, graduated Mus. Bac., Oxford, in 1713; Gentleman of the Chapel Royal, 1715; died October 29, 1721.

CHANT 243 S.P. and 31 U.P.P. was composed by him, and is found in Dr Boyce's 'Cathedral Music.'

Mornington, Garret Wellesley, first Earl of, born July 19, 1735; graduated B.A., Dublin University, 1754; M.A., 1757; Mus. Doc., 1764; first musical professor Dublin University, 1764—resigned 1774; died at Kensington, May 22, 1781; father of the Duke of Wellington and of the Marquis of Wellesley; composer of many excellent glees and madrigals.

CHANTS No. 257 S.P. and 172 U.P.P., 244 S.P. and 173 U.P.P., are his. Both were performed at the public funeral of the Duke of Wellington at St Paul's Cathedral, November 18, 1852.

Moss, Edwin, born in London, January 4, 1838; educated for the scholastic profession; commenced duties as head-master of a school at Cardiff, January 4, 1858, where he remained four years; subsequently filled a similar position at Wantage, Berkshire; relinquished school work for the musical profession, and returned to London; in June 1866 appointed precentor of Poultry Chapel, a post he held for nine years; since January 1877 tenor vocalist at the Foundling Chapel.

Ulpha, No. 248 F.C.H., and

Giessen, No. 44 F.C.H., 74 and 164 S.H., are from 'The London Tune Book,' which he edited in 1877. The last is also found in 'The Comprehensive Tune Book,' Second Series, edited by Dr Gauntlett, 1851, being there named "Hoxton."

Mozart, Johann Chrysostomus Wolfgang Amadeus, was born at Salzburg, January 27, 1756, and died at Vienna, December 5, 1791. He was one of the most marvellous musicians ever born, and as a child he was the admiration of everybody for his playing and composing. This great master has left works in every branch of his art—for the Church, the stage, and the concert-room—and it is difficult to say wherein his versatile genius excelled. He was, said Joseph Haydn, "the most extraordinary, original, and comprehensive musical genius ever known in this or any age or nation."

Mozart, No. 167 (Second Tune) F.C.H., is from the opening movement in his Mass No. 12.

Belmont, No. 38 S.P., 83 F.C.H., 126 (First Tune) S.H. See Anonymous.

S.S. No. 101 U.P.H., "Blessing and honour, glory and power," is adapted from "Pleni sunt cœli," in his Mass No. 7.

Muenscher, Rev. Joseph, D.D., Professor of Biblical Literature in the Theological Seminary of the Protestant Episcopal Church, Gambier, Ohio; born at Providence, Rhode Island, December 21, 1798; died at Mount Vernon, Ohio, February 16, 1874.

Compiled in 1838-39 'The Church Choir': Part I., 295 pages of metrical tunes; Part II., 136 pages, comprising 12 anthems, 27 chants, 10 Gloria patrias, 3 sentences, and a few sanctuses.

In Muenscher's work is found the original of S.S., No. 44 U.P.H., "I acknowledge my transgressions."

Müller, Johann Daniel, edited a 'Choralbuch,' which was published at Frankfort-on-Maine in 1754.

FRANCONIA, No. 127 F.C.H., 193 S.P., 25 and 198 U.P.H., 113 U.P.P., 100 (First Tune), 156 (First Tune), and 252 S.H., 189 P. and P., was adapted by the Rev. W. H. Havergal from the chorale "Was ist das mich betrübt," on page 185 of Müller's work, a copy of which is given below. Although assigned in the S.H., P. and P., and several other collections, to Johann Georg Ebeling, it is questionable if he composed it. 'Geistliche Melodien,' which he edited in 1666-67, does not contain it, although the date given in S.H. would seem to imply as much. Further, a tune by Ebeling appears in several hymnals under the name "Franconia," but it is entirely different from the one in question. It seems probable that the two tunes have been confounded.

Nageli, Johann Georg, a composer of many popular songs, was born at Zürich in 1768; founded there in 1792 a music school; published 'The Teaching of Song on the Principles of Pestalozzi,' and other works; died at Zürich, December 26, 1836. The following tunes are adaptations by Dr Lowell Mason from MS. music he purchased from Nageli:—

DENNIS, No. 191 S.P. and 144 F.C.H., published in 'The Psaltery,' 1845, by Mason and Webb.

NAOMI, No. 110 U.P.P., arranged by Dr Mason in 1836, and published in 'Occasional Psalm and Hymn Tunes,' a monthly periodical.

ZÜRICH, No. 209 S.P., 148 F.C.H., 111 U.P.P., there named "Scott" (its original name), is also an adaptation by Mason, and appears in his 'Hallelujah,' 1854.

Nares,[1] **James**, Mus. Doc., son of Mr George Nares; born at Stanwell, Middlesex, in 1715; baptised April 19; was a chorister in the Chapel Royal, successively under Dr Croft and Bernard Gates, and afterwards a pupil of Dr Pepusch; appointed organist of York Cathedral, 1734; organist and composer to the Chapel Royal, 1756; master of the children in room of Gates his old master, 1757 to 1780; graduated Mus. Doc., at Cambridge, 1756; died February 10, 1783, and was buried in St Margaret's, Westminster; composer of church services, anthems, glees, catches, &c.

AYNHOE, No. 180 P. and P., although commonly assigned to Dr Nares, does not appear in Smart's or Riley's collections, to which he contributed. It is an altered form of a tune named "Haynor," assigned by Dibdin to "Christopher Clark, from Vocal Harmony, 1745," which is also found, without name of composer, in Abraham Milner's 'Psalm Singer's Companion,' 1751.

CHANT No. 114 in U.P.P., was published in vol. iii. of 'Cathedral Music,' edited by Dr Arnold in 1790.

ICONIUM, No. 83 S.P., 65 U.P.P., 94 P. and P., is assigned to Nares. It is not found in any old collections, or those to which Nares contributed. Perhaps its first appearance in Scotland is in 'The Sacred Harmony of St Andrew's Church, Edinburgh,' by Adam Ramage, 1843, where it is assigned to Nares.

ST CHAD, No. 17 U.P.P., is one of three tunes contributed by Nares to William Riley's 'Parochial Harmony; consisting of a Collection of Psalm

---

[1] The following is a copy of the entry of Nares's baptism in the parish registers of Stanwell, 1715, which has not been given elsewhere:—
"Aprel ye 19 James ye son of Mr George Nars was baptized."

Tunes in three and four Parts. . . . 1762'; it there bears its present name, set to Psalm 1, Old Version, and in four parts.

Naue, Johann Friedrich, born at Halle, November 17, 1787; pupil of Türk, whom he succeeded as organist and University Music Director in Halle; educated at the Orphanages at Halle, and afterwards at Berlin; in 1835 received the degree of Doctor from the Philosophical Faculty in Jena; died May 19, 1858. In 1829 he edited a 'Choralbuch' from which is taken

LEBANON, No. 14 U.P.H., "Nicht so traurig, nich so sehr." It is No. 152 in that collection.

Neander, Joachim, born at Bremen in 1640 (or, according to some, 1650); in 1674 appointed head-master of the Grammar School at Düsseldorf, and in 1679 second preacher at St Martin's Church, in Bremen; died May 31, 1680. The following are from his 'Bundeslieder,' 1680 :—

ARNSBERG, No. 270 U.P.H., 327 F.C.H., "Wunderbarer König, Herrscher von uns allen."

MELANCHTHON, No. 119 U.P.H., "Meine hoffnung stehet feste."

NEANDER, No. 239 F.C.H., 62 U.P.H., 68 S.H., where it is named "Magdeburg," "Unser Herrscher, unser König."

Neumarck, Georg, son of Michael Neumarck; born March 16, 1621, at Langensalza, from whence his family subsequently removed to Mühlhausen; studied jurisprudence at the University of Königsberg; and after some years of poverty and privation became, in 1651, Librarian of the Archives at Weimar, where he died, July 8, 1681. His tune

NEUMARK, No. 209 S.H., "Wer nur den lieben Gott lässt walten," published in 1657, in triple time, became (says the editor of 'The Chorale Book for England') so popular, that within one hundred years after its appearance no less than four hundred hymns had been written to be sung to it.

Newport, Walter, son of an architect; born at Manchester, December 24, 1839; educated at Clapham Grammar School, near London, where he was a chorister; organist successively of Trinity Church, Lambeth—of St George's Chapel, Albemarle Street, London—and of Hurstpierpoint Church, near Brighton; afterwards organist and choirmaster of Holywood Church, near Belfast, about 1878. His tune

LITANY, No. 136 U.P.H., was composed in 1873.

Nicolai, Philipp, son of Theodor (or Theodorich) Nicolai, Lutheran pastor at Mengeringhausen, in Waldeck; born at Mengeringhausen, August 10, 1556; pastor of St Catherine's Church, Hamburg, where he died, October 26, 1608.

NICOLAI, No. 329 F.C.H., 86 S.H., 67 U.P.H., "Wachet auf! ruft uns die Stimme." A tune founded on the 5th Gregorian tone. Mendelssohn employs it in his oratorio "St Paul" as the subject of the overture, and also as a chorale. Bach wrote a cantata on the same chorale.

MORNING STAR, No. 328 F.C.H. A secular origin has been assigned to this tune, but apparently without good ground, for it is evidently formed from an old church melody (See "Dortmund," No. 116 S.H.) found in Wolff's 'Kirchengesang,' Frankfort, 1569, where it is set to "Jauchzet dem Herren alle Lande" (Psalm 100). Also in a book printed at Strasburg about the same date, or a little earlier, and in 'Gesangbüchlein,' Bonn, 1577, set to "Hilf mir, Gott, durch den Namen" (Psalm 54). Nicolai seems to have merely recast and expanded the tune to suit his hymn (published in 1599), "Wie schön leuchtet uns der Morgenstern."

Mendelssohn employs it in his unfinished oratorio, "Christus," and Graun in his 'Der Tod Jesu.'

Norris, Thomas, Mus. Bac., son of John Norris; born at Mere, Wiltshire; baptised in Mere Church, August 15, 1741; chorister in Salisbury Cathedral; organist of Christ Church, and of St John's College, Oxford, 1765; lay clerk of Magdalen College, Oxford, 1771; Mus. Bac., Oxford, 1765; died at Himley Hall, Staffordshire, the seat of Lord Dudley and Ward, September 3, 1790; one of the most distinguished tenor vocalists of his time. His

CHANT, No. 174 U.P.P. and 245 S.P., is in John Marsh's Collection.

Novello, Vincent, born in London, September 6, 1781; chorister in the Sardinian Chapel, Duke Street, under Samuel Webbe; deputy organist to Webbe and John Danby; organist of Portuguese Chapel, 1797 to 1822; founded the firm of J. Alfred Novello, now Novello, Ewer, & Co., 1811; organist of Roman Catholic Chapel in Moorfields, 1840 to 1843; retired to Nice; died there, August 9, 1861; composer and editor of much sacred music.

S.S. No. 41 U.P.H., "Like as the hart," is an adaptation by R. R. Ross (see that name) from "In Manus tuas" in Novello's 'Evening Services,' Book 10.

S.S. No. 54 U.P.H., "The Lord loveth the gates of Zion" is assigned to him.

Nürnberg Hymn Book, 1677.

HEINLEN, No. 166 (Second Tune) F.C.H., and 33 S.H., appears on page 653 of the above work, set to the hymn, "Ans der Tiefe rufe ich zu Dir." It is one of three tunes by a composer whose initials are M. H.

HERR JESU, No. 258 S.H., appears in a slightly different time form on page 1162 of the above work, set to "Herr Jesu Christ, meins Lebens Licht." No indication is given as to the composer.

The first-named is wrongly assigned in many hymnals to Paul Heinlen, who contributed six tunes to the 'Nürnberg Hymn Book,' all of which have his initials, P. H., prefixed.

Oakeley, Sir Herbert Stanley, son of Sir Herbert Oakeley, Bart.; born at Ealing, Middlesex, July 22, 1830; pupil of Dr Stephen Elvey at Oxford, afterwards of Moscheles, Schneider, and others abroad; B.A. Oxford 1853, M.A. 1856; Professor of Music in Edinburgh University, in succession to John Donaldson, 1865 to 1891; Mus. Doc. Canterbury 1871, Oxford 1879; LL.D. Aberdeen 1881, and Composer of Music to the Queen in Scotland; knighted 1876; elected a member of Philharmonic Academy of Bologna, 1888.

ABENDS, No. 303 U.P.H., 23 (First Tune) F.C.H., 291 (First Tune) S.H., composed in 1871, seems to have been first published in 'The Church Hymnal,' edited by Sir R. P. Stewart, Dublin, 1874.

EDINA, No. 66 (First Tune) S.H., composed in 1862. First published in the Appendix to 'Hymns Ancient and Modern,' 1868.

S.S. "Come unto me," No. 14, and "Now unto the King," No. 19, both in U.P.H., were composed for that work.

Oliver.

To a composer of the above name

CHADWICK, No. 225 U.P.H., is assigned by Dibdin in his 'Standard Psalm Tune Book,' 1852.

Ouseley, Rev. Sir Frederick Arthur Gore, Bart., Mus. Doc., son of Sir William Gore Ouseley, the eminent oriental scholar, who was successively Ambassador and Minister Plenipotentiary to Persia and St Petersburg; born in London, August 12, 1825; named Frederick after the Duke of York, and Arthur after the Duke of Wellington, his godfathers; educated privately, and in 1843 entered Christ Church, Oxford, as a gentleman commoner; on the death of his father in 1844 (1842?) he succeeded to the baronetcy; graduated B.A. 1846, M.A. 1849, in which year he was ordained Deacon by the Bishop of London, and became curate of St Barnabas Church, Pimlico; graduated Mus. Bac. 1850, and Mus. Doc. in 1854, the oratorio "St Polycarp" being the exercise for the latter degree; erected at Tenbury on a portion of his property a church and college dedicated to St Michael and All Angels; appointed Professor of Music in the University of Oxford, and precentor of Hereford Cathedral, 1855; died suddenly at Hereford, April 6, 1889; composer of much excellent church music, and an organist of great ability.

ALL THINGS BRIGHT, No. 410 S.H., was composed for the hymn to which it is set, and published (melody only) in 'The Child's Book of Song and Praise' (Cassell & Co.) It was harmonised by the composer for 'The Children's Hymn Book,' edited by Mrs Carey Brock, 1881.

EASTHAM, No. 276 (First Tune) S.H., was composed for, and published in, 'The Year of Praise; being Hymns with Tunes for the Sundays and Holidays of the Year,' edited by Henry Alford, D.D.: London, 1867.

GETHSEMANE, Nos. 37 and 42 S.H., was composed for, and published in, 'The Sarum Hymnal, with Proper Tunes'; the music edited by Theodore Edward Aylward (1869).

ST GABRIEL, No. 286 (First Tune) S.H., composed for, and published in, the Appendix to 'Hymns Ancient and Modern,' 1868.

Pachelbel, Johann, born at Nürnberg, September 1, 1653; studied at Altdorf in 1669, and subsequently at Regensburg; in 1672 went to Vienna, and spent three years there in the office of assistant to the celebrated Johann Caspar Kerl till 1675, when he was called as organist to the Augustine Church in Erfurt; in 1690 called to Stuttgart by Duke Friedrich Carl of Würtemberg as Court organist; on November 8, 1692, he received the post of organist in the chief church at Gotha, where he remained till 1695, when he succeeded to the office of principal organist of his native town; died at Nürnberg, March 3, 1706.

BADEN, No. 216 S.H. and 173 U.P.H., "Was Gott thut das ist wohlgethan," is thought to have been composed by Pachelbel about 1678. It was first printed in the Appendix to the 'Nürnberg Gesangbuch,' 1690, and will be found there on pages 1205, 1206.

The first line stands as given below, thus showing that the fifth note of the first line in the U.P.H. is a third too high:—

Key B♭.

{ :s₁ | d :r | m :f | s :-.f | m :l | s :f | m .r }
{ :m | r :— | d : ||

Palestrina, Giovanni Pierluigi da, born about 1524 at Palestrina, a town in the States of the Church, from which he derived his name; died at Rome, February 2, 1594; one of the greatest composers of church music that ever lived.

PALESTRINA, No. 278 (Second Tune) F.C.H., 118 S.P., 126 U.P.H.;

RESIGNATION, No. 123 S.P., 106 F.C.H.;

VICTORY, No. 57 (First Tune) S.H.,—are different forms of the same tune, adapted from his "Lamentatio in Cœna Domini."

Palmer, Horatio Richmond, born at Sherburne, New York State, April 26, 1834; a teacher of music, leader of conventions, composer, &c.; from 1867 to 1886 has published twenty-nine distinct musical works, of which, perhaps, his 'Theory of Music,' issued in 1876, is the best known. The degree of Mus. Doc. conferred on him by the University of Chicago, June 1879; by Alfred University of New York in June 1880. His tune

FORTITUDE, No. 386 F.C.H., and the words to which it is set, were written in 1867, and first published in his 'Sabbath School Songs,' 1868.

Parr (not *Park*, as in U.P.P.), **Rev. Henry,** son of Mr Thomas Parr; born at Lythwood Hall, Shropshire, August 16, 1815; educated at Magdalen College, Oxford, and St Bees, Cumberland; took holy orders, 1845; vicar of Taunton, Somersetshire, 1849 to 1858; curate of Tunbridge, 1859 to 1861; perpetual curate of Ash Church, Gloucestershire, 1861 to 1862; curate-in-charge of Yoxford, Suffolk, 1867; vicar, 1872; one of the greatest living authorities on the sources of our psalm and hymn tunes. His 'Church of England Psalmody' has passed through numerous editions.

CHANT, No. 33 in U.P.P., was composed by him in 1836, and appears in 'Church of England Psalmody.'

Peace, Albert Lister, son of Mr Lister Peace; born at Huddersfield, January 26, 1844; a self-taught musician; appointed organist of Holmfirth Parish Church, Yorkshire, 1853; of Dewsbury Parish Church, 1858; St Thomas's Church, Huddersfield, 1859; Brunswick Street Chapel, Huddersfield, 1861; Providence Place

Chapel, Cleckheaton, 1863; Trinity Congregational Church, Glasgow, 1865; the University, 1870; organist and choirmaster St John's Episcopal Church, 1873; Maxwell Parish Church, 1875; Hillhead Parish Church, 1876; St Andrew's Halls, 1877, and in 1879 of the Glasgow Cathedral, a position he still holds; graduated Mus. Bac., at the University of Oxford, 1870; Mus. Doc. 1875, for which examinations he composed respectively a setting of the 138th Psalm, and a cantata—"St John the Baptist" —for solo voices and double choir (published 1887); elected a Fellow of the College of Organists (*honoris causa*), session 1886-87. His published works for the Church include the Morning and Evening Service, together with the office for the Holy Communion in D, including Te Deum, Jubilate, Kyrie, Creed, Sanctus, Gloria, Magnificat, and Nunc Dimittis; Morning and Evening Service in D (No. 2), including Te Deum, Benedictus, Magnificat, and Nunc Dimittis; anthems, "Awake up, my Glory," "Come, let us go up to the mountain of the Lord." As an organist Dr Peace is one of the most distinguished living. He has "opened" the majority of organs in Scotland, and has done much to make the instrument popular. Musical editor of the 'Scottish Hymnal,' 1885, 'Psalms and Paraphrases with Tunes,' 1886, 'The Psalter with Chants,' 1888, and the 'Scottish Anthem Book,' 1891.

ANGELS, No. 378,
ASPIRATION, No. 418,
BEATITUDE, No. 270 (Second Tune),
CHILDHOOD'S YEARS, No. 420 (First Tune),
CRUX CRUDELIS, No. 390 (First Tune),
EDOM, No. 399 and 61 (First Tune),
FIGHT OF FAITH, No. 180,
GREEN HILL, No. 389,
IN EXCELSIS GLORIA, No. 387,
INFANTS' PRAYER, No. 362 (Second Tune),
LITANY, No. 382,
LUX BEATA, No. 246 (Second Tune),
LYRA, No. 243 (Second Tune),
PROCLAMATION, No. 429,
ST MARGARET, No. 176,
ST MARTIN'S, No. 305,
SILOAM, No. 430,
were all composed for, and first published in, the S.H.

CHANT set to Hymn No. 356 S.H. is also his.

SUBMISSION, No. 214 (Second Tune) S.H., was composed for the revised reprint issued in 1889.

CONWAY, No. 207,
NEW 136TH, No. 216,
NEW 137TH, No. 168,
ST MUNGO, No. 139,
were composed for, and published in, 'Psalms and Paraphrases,' 1886.

Peregrine Tone.

CHANT, No. 27 U.P.P.

Pitts, William, son of Mr William Pitts, organ-builder and amateur musician; born at Tansor, near Oundle, Northamptonshire, April 17, 1829; pupil of his father; organist at the Oratory, Brompton, from its establishment in England.

PRINCETHORPE, No. 66 (Second Tune) S.H., 253 F.C.H., was composed for a collection of hymns and tunes used at the Oratory, and is there set to "A Daily Hymn for Mary."

Playford, John, born 1623, was a music publisher and clerk of the Temple Church, London; died 1693. In 1671 he issued 'Psalms and Hymns in Solemn Musick of Foure Parts.' In it are found the present readings of

CANTERBURY or PASTON, No. 207 S.H. and 58 P. and P. That given in U.P.P. differs at the close of the third strain from Este's and Playford's.

GLOUCESTER, No. 153 U.P.P., 11 and 219 U.P.H., 82 P. and P., and 72 S.P.; and

LONDON NEW, No. 94 S.P., 107 P. and P., 19 S.H., 274 U.P.H., 216 U.P.P.

PLAYFORD, No. 28 P. and P., is there set to Psalm 121, but is nameless.

RINGWOOD, No. 121 P. and P., is another form of the previous tune.

In 'The Whole Book of Psalms, . . . Composed in Three Parts,' and published by Playford in 1677, appear the present readings of

ST MARY, No. 153 (Second Tune) S.H., 136 P. and P., 122 U.P.H., 2 U.P.P., 143 S.P., 91 F.C.H.; and

ST DAVID, No. 108 (Second Tune) F.C.H., 126 P. and P., 16 U.P.H., 124 U.P.P., 130 S.P.

In the S.P. and F.C.H., and indeed in nine out of every ten collections issued, "St Mary" is referred to Playford, 1671; but, as will be seen from the example below, the tune bearing that name is totally different from the one published by Playford in 1677. Truly, "long standing errors are hard to kill."

TUNE "ST MARY" IN PLAYFORD, 1671.

Key G.

{| d :— | r :m | r :d | d :t, | d :— || d :— |}

{| m :s | s :fe | s :— || s :— | m :d | f :m |}

{| r :d | t, :— || m :— | r :m | f :r | d :— ||}

"St David" is also wrongly referred in P. and P. and U.P. Collections to Playford, 1671.

For the earliest known source of "St Mary," see Prys.

Pleyel, Ignaz Josef, born in Ruppersthal, near Vienna, June 1, 1757; pupil of Joseph Haydn; for several years chapel-master at Strasburg Cathedral; established in Paris a music-selling and publishing business, and afterwards founded (1807) the pianoforte manufacturing firm now known as Pleyel, Wolff & Co.; died near Paris, November 14, 1831: composer of much instrumental music.

PLEYEL, No. 167 (First Tune) F.C.H., appears as a L.M. tune in 'Arnold and Callcott's Psalms,' 1791, set to Addison's hymn, "The spacious firmament on high."

PLEYEL, No. 73 U.P.H. (different from above), is an adaptation, and appears in a slightly different form in William Gardiner's 'Sacred Melodies, from Haydn, Mozart, and Beethoven, Adapted to the best English Poets,' vol. ii. (1815).

Poole, Clement William, son of a solicitor; born at Ealing, Middlesex, June 7, 1828; educated at the Islington Proprietary School under the late Bishop of London (Jackson); pupil of the late Joseph Thomas Cooper; amateur musician, and composer of several excellent hymn tunes; officiated from time to time as organist and choirmaster (honorary) at the Parish Church, Kingston-on-Thames; Trinity Church, Ramsgate; and Christ Church, Ealing.

WESTENHANGER, No. 142 F.C.H., was composed about 1858 for the hymn "I was a wandering sheep," and published in the 'Congregational Psalmist,' 1861.

Praetorius, Jacob, organist at Hamburg in the beginning of the seventeenth century.

NICOLAI, No. 86 S.H., 329 F.C.H., 67 U.P.H., "Wachet auf! ruft uns die Stimme," is assigned to him by Kühnau and Umbreit. (See Nicolai, Philipp.)

Praetorius, Michael (or **Schulz**), born at Kreuzberg, Thuringia, February 15, 1571; chapel-master and organist to the Duke of Brunswick, and secretary to his consort Elizabeth; died at Wolfenbüttel, February 15, 1621; composed much music for the Church, and was a learned writer on the art.

PRAETORIUS, No. 121 S.P., 77 F.C.H., 151 U.P.P., 394 S.H., 119 P. and P., 246 U.P.H., "In Bethlehem ein Kindelein," from his 'Musæ Sioniæ,' 1609.

Prout, Ebenezer, born at Oundle, Northamptonshire, March 1, 1835; B.A., London University, 1854; successively organist of St Thomas's Square Chapel, Hackney; the Congregational Church, Kentish Town; the New Tabernacle, Old Kent Road; and St Mary, Newington Butts; Union Chapel, Islington, 1861 to 1873; eminent as a composer, conductor, and critic.

S.S. No. 15 U.P.H., "Glory to God,"
„ No. 76 „ "Remember now thy Creator,"
„ No. 89 „ "Suffer the little children,"
„ No. 107 „ "The Spirit and the Bride say, Come,"
were all composed for the U.P.H.

S.S., No. 45 U.P.H., "Create in me a clean heart," was composed about 1864, and first published in J. Locke Gray's 'Congregational Psalter.'

S.S., No. 36 U.P.H., "Sing unto the Lord," was composed for the Rev. Dr Henry Allon's 'Anthem Book' in 1872.

Prys, Ven. Edmund, Archdeacon of Merioneth early in the seventeenth century. He edited 'Llyfr y Psalmau wedi eu cyfiethu, ai cyfansodi ar fesur cerdd yn gymraeg,' 1621. The tune to Psalm 2 in Prys's work is the original of

ST MARY, No. 136 P. and P., 2 U.P.P., 122 U.P.H., 143 S.P., 91 F.C.H., 153 S.H. The second strain originally ended thus—

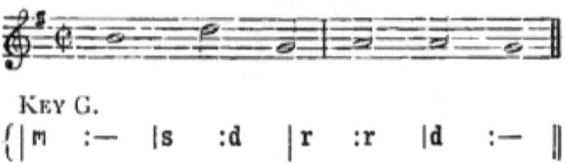

KEY G.
{ | m :— | s :d | r :r | d :— ||

The form of the tune now in use was first published by Playford. (See that name.)

Purcell, Henry, son of Henry Purcell, a Gentleman of the Chapel Royal in the reign of King Charles II.; born in St Ann's

Lane, Old Pye Street, Westminster, 1658; chorister of the Chapel Royal successively under Captain Cook and Pelham Humfrey, 1664 to 1674; pupil of Dr John Blow, whom he succeeded as organist of Westminster Abbey in 1680; organist of the Chapel Royal, 1682; Composer in Ordinary to the King, 1683; died at Dean's Yard, Westminster, November 21, 1695, aged thirty-seven; buried in Westminster Abbey, November 26; one of the greatest of English composers. The following couplet was written by Henry Hall, at one time organist of Hereford Cathedral :—

"Sometimes a hero in an age appears,
But scarce a Purcell in a thousand years."

BURFORD, No. 44 S.P., 14 U.P.P., 54 P. and P., is probably the composition of Purcell. It appears without a name in 'A Book of Psalmody, containing Variety of Tunes. . . . All set in Four Parts,' 1718, and edited by the Rev. John Chetham, to whom it has also been assigned.

Mr W. H. Cummings, probably the greatest living authority on Purcell's music, favoured the writer with the following opinion: "That 'Burford' was composed by Henry Purcell I have no doubt, and I have seen it in contemporary (?) MS. with his name."

COLCHESTER, No. 146 U.P.P., 62 P. and P., 50 S.P. (See Tans'ur, William, and Harrison, Rev. Ralph.)

STROUDWATER, No. 166 S.P., 55 (First Tune) U.P.H., 190 U.P.P., 155 P. and P. (See Wilkins, Matthew.)

ST THOMAS, No. 154 S.P., 222 U.P.H., 62 U.P.P., 145 P. and P. (See Ashworth, Charles.)

WALSALL, No. 173 S.P., 9 U.P.P. (See Wilkins, Matthew.)

These tunes have all been assigned to Purcell in the Scottish Psalmodies published during the last fifty years, but there seems to be no evidence whatever that he composed one of them. It would be better if compilers of tune books would name the earliest, or one of the earliest, collections in which these tunes are found, instead of ascribing them to Purcell, whose connection with them is so questionable.

Purcell, Thomas, uncle of the preceding, was a Gentleman of the Chapel Royal about 1660; Master (jointly with Pelham Humfrey) of the King's Band, 1672; died July 31, 1682; buried in the cloisters of Westminster Abbey.

CHANTS, No. 230 S.P., 334 F.C.H. (Chant II.), also 353 U.P.H., 46 U.P.P., 334 F.C.H. (in G minor), are both assigned to Thomas Purcell by Dr Boyce in his 'Cathedral Music.' The last was performed at the public funeral of Viscount Nelson, at St Paul's, January 9, 1806. It is known as "Funeral Chant."

Purday, Charles Henry, son of a bookseller, born at Folkestone, Kent, January 11, 1799; at one time a vocalist of some repute; sang at the coronation of Queen Victoria; engaged in music publishing for the greater part of his life; was an ardent advocate for the revision of the law in matters of copyright in musical publications; for several years director of the psalmody in the Scotch Church, Crown Court, London; composer of many hymn tunes; died April 23, 1885.

NOTTING HILL, No. 110 S.P., appears in 'Crown Court Psalmody; One Hundred Psalm Tunes and Chants, Selected and Arranged for the Congregation of the National Scotch Church, Crown Court, Covent Garden,' which he edited in 1854.

SANDON, No. 310 (Second Tune) F.C.H., appears in 'The Church and Home Metrical Psalter and Hymnal,' edited by the Rev. W. Windle, M.A. (1862). In an edition of the same work edited by Purday in 1860, the tune appears on page 161, but is anonymous.

ST ULRICH, No. 199 F.C.H., appears without a name in 'Songs of Peace and Joy.' The words selected from "The Ministry of Song" and "Under the Surface," written by Frances Ridley Havergal, the music by Charles H. Purday. 1879. It is named "St Ulrich" in 'Church Praise' (Nisbet), 1883.

Randall, John, Mus. Doc.; chorister in the Chapel Royal under Bernard Gates from about 1730 to 1735; organist of Trinity and St John's Colleges, Cambridge; of King's College, about 1745; also of the University Church, and of Pembroke Hall; Mus. Bac., Cambridge, 1744; Mus. Doc. 1756; appointed Professor of Music in Cambridge University in succession to Dr Greene, 1755; died March 18, 1799, aged eighty-three.

His tune, "Cambridge New," No. 57 P. and P. (absurdly set on Key G), appears in 'A Collection of Psalm and Hymn Tunes, some of which are new . . .' Cambridge, 1794. It was published before that time in 'A Collection of Psalm Tunes for Publick Worship,' edited by the Rev. Stephen Addington. Sixth edition, 1786. Henry Boyd's Collection, Glasgow, 1793, contains the tune, and this is its first appearance, so far as the writer knows, in a Scotch Psalmody.

UNIVERSITY, No. 172 S.P. and 132 U.P.P., appears in his collection quoted under "Cambridge New," but is not marked as his. John Pratt, who had been a pupil and deputy of Dr Randall, assigns it to him in his 'Psalmodia Cantabrigiensis; A Selection of Ancient and Modern Psalm Tunes, . . . for the Use of the University Church.' Published about 1805. No collection of any importance assigns the tune to Edward Harwood.

CHANT, No. 246 S.P., is his composition.

Randegger, Alberto, born at Trieste, April 13, 1832; pupil of Lafont and Ricci; since about 1854 resident in London; composer of sacred and secular music, but better known as a successful voice-trainer.

RANDEGGER, No. 373 S.H. (Second Tune), was published in his 'Sacred Songs for Little Singers,' words by Frances Ridley Havergal, with a pianoforte accompaniment, 1872. It was arranged in four parts for the 'Children's Hymnal' issued by the Church of Scotland in 1876.

Ravenscroft, Thomas, born 1592; educated as a chorister in St Paul's Cathedral; graduated Mus. Bac. at Cambridge, when fourteen years of age; supposed to have died about 1630.

In 1621 he published 'The Whole Booke of Psalmes . . . composed into 4 parts by sundry Authors.'

From the above collection—
BRISTOL, No. 53 P. and P., 42 S.P., 60 U.P.P., set to Psalm 64,
CHICHESTER, No. 136 U.P.P., 61 P. and P., set to Psalm 110,
GLOUCESTER, No. 82 P. and P., 72 S.P., 11 U.P.H., 153 U.P.P., set to Psalm 10,
NORWICH, No. 116 P. and P., set to Psalm 102,
OLD 22d or HURSTBOURNE, No. 170 P. and P., set to Psalm 38,
SALISBURY, No. 146 P. and P., 155 S.P., 138 U.P.P., set to Psalm 54, where they are styled English Tunes.
DURHAM, No. 59 S.P., 210 U.P.H., 181 U.P.P., 71 P. and P., set to Psalm 71,
OLD CARLISLE, No. 42 U.P.P., set to Psalm 79.—Northern Tunes.
LUDLOW, No. 24 U.P.P., set to Psalm 45,
ST DAVID, No. 130 S.P., 108 (Second Tune) F.C.H., and 126 P. and P., set to Psalm 95.—Welsh Tunes.

The readings given by Ravenscroft of "Gloucester" and "St David" are slightly different from those now in use, as will be seen from the extracts given below. See Playford, John.

MELODY OF "ST DAVID" AS IN RAVENSCROFT, 1621.

Third line of "Gloucester" as in Ravenscroft 1621.

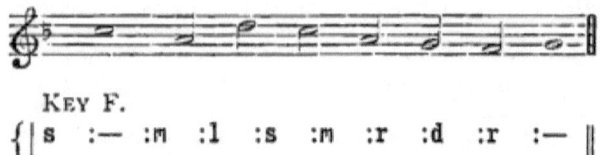

Key F.
{| s :— :m :l :s :m :r :d :r :— ||

Reading, John, son of John Reading, organist of Winchester Cathedral; born 1677; educated in the Chapel Royal under Dr John Blow in the latter part of the seventeenth century; in 1700 became organist of Dulwich College; appointed junior vicar and poor clerk of Lincoln Cathedral, November 21, 1702; master of the choristers, October 5, 1703, and instructor of the choristers in vocal music, September 28, 1704; resigned in 1707, and returned to London, where he became organist of St John, Hackney; St Dunstan's in the West; St Mary Woolchurchhaw, Lombard Street; and St Mary Woolnoth; died September 2, 1764.

Adeste Fideles, No. 33 U.P.H., 28 S.H., 306 F.C.H., there styled "Portuguese Hymn," a name it obtained from its use at the Chapel of the Portuguese Embassy, London, whence it was supposed to be a melody of Portuguese origin, is assigned to Reading by Vincent Novello, who was organist of the Portuguese Chapel from 1797. It appears in Samuel Webbe's 'Collection of Motetts or Antiphons,' 1792, but was in use before that date. Dr Gauntlett (says the Rev. Henry Parr) was investigating the history of the tune shortly before his death. He could find no authority for assigning it to Reading. "I have always heard" (he writes) "it was made by a Portuguese priest for South Street Embassy. My date has been all along about 1770—I suppose from my father, who was more learned than I."

Reay, Samuel, son of Mr George Agnew Reay; born at Hexham, Northumberland, March 17, 1822; chorister in Durham Cathedral, and while there studied under the Rev. P. Penson; studied the organ under the late James Stimpson; organist of St Andrew's, Newcastle, 1843; St Peter's, Tiverton, Devonshire, 1847; St John's, Hampstead, 1854; St Saviour's, Paddington, and St Stephen's, Paddington, successively, 1854 to 1859; organist and precentor of St Peter's College, Radley, 1859; organist and choirmaster, Parish Church, Bury, Lancashire, 1861; since 1864 organist and master of the Song School of the Parish Church, Newark-on-Trent; graduated Mus. Bac., Oxford, 1871.

Bickleigh, No. 215 S.P., was composed in 1856, and first published in Chope's 'Congregational Hymn and Tune Book,' 1862.

Redhead, Richard, born at Harrow, in the county of Middlesex, March 1, 1820; educated at Magdalen College, Oxford; pupil of the college organist, Walter Vicary, Mus. Bac.; appointed organist of Old Margaret Chapel, Margaret Street, London, in 1839; afterwards of All Saints' Church, Margaret Street, till 1864, and since then of St Mary Magdalen Church, Paddington; editor of several important collections of Psalmody, and composer of many tunes which are extensively used.

ST BEDE, No. 288 U.P.H., appears without a name in 'The People's Hymnal Tune Book' (Part I.), which he edited in 1870.

ST NICOLAS, No. 154 S.H., was published in the second series of 'Church Hymn Tunes for the Several Seasons of the Christian Year. With an Appendix and Index of Tunes to "Hymns Ancient and Modern." Edited by Richard Redhead, Organist.' No date. First series, 1853.

ST EBBE, No. 255 U.P.H., ST VICTOR, No. 337 (First Tune) S.H., and

METZLER'S REDHEAD (No. 66), No. 170 S.H. (Part II.) and 101 S.P., appear without names in 'Ancient Hymn Melodies and other Church Tunes, as used at All Saints' Church, Margaret Street. Arranged, Composed, and Harmonised by Richard Redhead, Organist.' Preface dated 1859.

ADORATION, No. 224 F.C.H.,

DUNSTAN or ST DUNSTAN, No. 166 (First Tune) F.C.H., 80 U.P.H., 255 S.H., and

PETRA, No. 178 (Second Tune) F.C.H., 132 (First Tune) U.P.H., 78 and 149 S.H., appear without names in 'Church Hymn Tunes,' edited by Richard Redhead in 1853, the full title of which is given above.

REDHEAD (No. 45), No. 25 (Second Tune) S.H., is from the same collection. It is an adaptation. See French Melody.

Reinagle, Alexander Robert, born at Brighton, August 21, 1799; son of Joseph Reinagle, at one time leader of the band at the Edinburgh Theatre, and well known in Scotland during last century for his fine performances on the violoncello; appointed organist of St Peter's-in-the-East, Oxford, 1822 or 1823; resigned 1853; died at Kidlington, near that city, April 6, 1877; buried in Kidlington churchyard. About 1830 he published 'Psalm Tunes for the Voice and Pianoforte.' His tune

ST PETER, Nos. 160 and 186 S.H., 143 P. and P., 151 S.P., 63 F.C.H., 85 U.P.P., 76, 83, 170, 283 U.P.H., is in the above collection set to Psalm 118, but bears no name.

Reynolds, John, was a Gentleman of the Chapel Royal from 1765 to 1770.

S.S., No. 32 U.P.H., ' My God, look upon me," appears in John Page's 'Harmonia Sacra,' 1800.

Rhaw, Georg, born at Eisfeld, in Franconia, in 1490 (or, according to some, in 1488); precentor of St Thomas's Church, Leipzig, about 1519; afterwards settled in Wittenberg, where he became a publisher, author, and composer; died at Wittenberg, August 7, 1548. In 1544 he published a Tune-Book for Schools, containing 123 tunes, harmonised in four and five parts, by fifteen of the most eminent composers of the time.

EISFELD, No. 7 S.P., appears in Rhaw's work, harmonised in five parts by Johannes Stahl, and set to the hymn "Nun lasst uns den Leib begraben." It is thought to be the composition of Stahl.

Richardson, John, was born at Preston, December 14, 1816. He received his education at the Fox Street Catholic School in that town. In early boyhood he showed a great taste for music, and was a member of St Wilfrid's choir. In 1829 he sang at the reopening of St Patrick's, Liverpool, when his ability as an alto singer attracted attention. In the same year he was engaged as principal alto singer at St Nicholas Catholic Chapel, Liverpool, at a salary of eight or ten pounds a-year; he was afterwards apprenticed as a house painter and decorator, but did not at the expiration of his apprenticeship follow that business. At nineteen years of age he was appointed organist at St Mary's Catholic Church, Liverpool; and two years later he returned to St Nicholas Church as organist—a post he held for over twenty years. He taught music at St Edward's College from 1844 to 1857, and had an extensive practice as a teacher: among his pupils was the now famous organist, Mr W. T. Best, who speaks of Richardson's abilities as an organist in the highest terms. Richardson was a voluminous composer; his principal compositions are several Masses, including a Requiem, also a setting of Collins's "Ode to the Passions," and a Benediction Service. In 1839 he obtained a prize from the Liverpool Beefsteak Club for his glee, "O fill the Wine Cup high!" and shortly afterwards was presented with a silver snuff-box by the Preston Catch and Glee Club. His Holiness Pope Pius IX. presented him with a magnificent ring, bearing the image of the Blessed Virgin; he also received a similar gift from Cardinal Wiseman—both in recognition of his musical abilities, either as composer or performer. In 1860 he returned to Preston broken down in health and constitution, and remained an invalid up to the time of his death, April 13, 1879.

TICHFIELD, Nos. 5 and 349 (Second Tunes) S.H., 189 F.C.H., is one of nine tunes contributed by Richardson to Formby's Collection of Catholic Hymns, 1853.

St Bernard (also known as "Resignation"), No. 129 S.P., 88 F.C.H., 84 U.P.P., 38 and 77 U.P.H., 125 P. and P., 194, 264, and 351 S.H. (Second Tunes), was also composed by him. The 'Merton Tune Book,' 1863, contains the earliest copy the writer has seen of this tune, and it is there anonymous. It is No. 255 in Frederick Westlake's 'Popular Hymn and Tune Book,' and is assigned to Richardson.

Richardson, William, educated in the Chapel Royal under Dr John Blow; appointed organist of St Nicholas Church, Deptford, 1697 (the church having been rebuilt in that year); died 1731 or 1732, the duties being performed during his illness by his brother Mr Pelham Richardson.

Greenwich, No. 85 P. and P., 140 U.P.P., 74 S.P., is from 'The Pious Recreation, containing A New Sett of Psalm-Tunes, in Three Parts,' . . . which he published in 1729. It there bears its present name, and is set to Psalm 105.

Rimbault, Edward Francis, son of Stephen Francis Rimbault, organist of St Giles's-in-the-Fields; born in London, June 13, 1816; eminent musical antiquary; pupil of his father, also of Samuel Wesley and Dr Crotch; organist of the Swiss Chapel, Soho, London, 1832; of St Peter's, Vere Street, 1866 till 1871; afterwards of St John's Wood Presbyterian Church, London; received the degree of LL.D. from the University of Göttingen in 1842; died in London, September 26, 1876.

Delhi, No. 143 U.P.H., was composed in 1857, and appears in Dr Maurice's 'Choral Harmony, with Supplement.'

Rinck or Rink, Johann Christian Heinrich, born at Elgersburg, Gotha, February 18, 1770; pupil of Forkel and others; organist at Giessen 1789, and afterwards Professor at the Music School there; organist and Professor at Darmstadt University 1806; Court organist at Darmstadt, 1813; Ph. Doc., Giessen University, 1840; died at Darmstadt, August 7, 1846; organist of great ability.

Waldeck, No. 15 F.C.H., is assigned to him in several collections, but its original source the writer is unable to trace.

Rabenlei, No. 408 (First Tune) S.H., is assigned to Rinck in several German collections, and is dated 1827.

S.S., No. 5 F.C.H., "Wait on the Lord," is an adaptation, and appears in Dr Mason's 'Hallelujah,' where it was published for the first time.

Ritter, Peter, was born at Mannheim, 1760; pupil of the Abbé Vogler, and in 1811 was appointed chapel-master to the Grand Duke of Baden; died at Mannheim, July 31, 1846.

PASCAL or HURSLEY, No. 291 (Second Tune) S.H., 132 (Second Tune) U.P.H., 23 (Second Tune) F.C.H., and 178 (First Tune) F.C.H.

The late Dr Rimbault states ('Notes and Queries' for April 11, 1868) that in a MS. collection of German chorales in his possession, the tune "Pascal" is ascribed to Ritter, and dated 1792. Dr Rimbault considered the ascription authentic. In some German collections it is assigned to the same composer.

In a Sequel to David Weyman's 'Melodia Sacra,' published after 1814, it is named "Stillorgan," and set to the words "Jesus, and shall it ever be?" This (says the Rev. Henry Parr) seems to be its first adaptation to English words.

Robinson, John, born 1682; chorister in the Chapel Royal; organist of St Lawrence, Jewry, London, 1710; of St Magnus Church, London Bridge, 1713; assistant organist of Westminster Abbey; organist, 1727, retaining his previous appointments; died April 30, 1762; one of the most remarkable organists of his time.

CHANT, No. 247 S.P., 170 U.P.P., appears in Dr Boyce's 'Cathedral Music.' It is said to have been a special favourite with George III.

Rogers, William, publisher, "at the Sun against St Dunstan's Church, in Fleet Street," London, published 'A New and Easie Method To Learn To sing by Book whereby one (who hath a good Voice and Ear) may, without other help, learn to Sing true by Notes. Design'd chiefly for, and applied to, the promoting of Psalmody; and furnished with a variety of Psalm Tunes in Parts, with Directions for that kind of Singing.' Licensed January 29, 1685-86. This contains, on page 102, the original of

LEEDS, No. 191 P. and P., where it is set to Psalm 25, and without a name. Gawthorn in 'Harmonia Perfecta,' 1730, calls it "Bella." Harrison in his 'Sacred Harmony,' vol. i. (1784), names it "Leeds," and gives the same reading as that in P. and P. The following is a copy of the melody as found in Rogers's work :—

It is in 'The Psalm Singer's Assistant,' by Robert Gilmour, Glasgow, no date, and in the second edition, Paisley, 1793. It there bears the name "Derby," and this is its first appearance, so far as the writer knows, in a Scotch Psalmody.

Romberg, Andreas Jacob, Ph.D. and Mus. Doc., was born at Vechte, in Hanover, April 27, 1767. In 1809 the University of Kiel conferred on him the degrees of Doctor in Philosophy and Music. Romberg wrote seven operas, several symphonies, &c. He is best known in this country as composer of the music to Schiller's "Lay of the Bell." Romberg died at Gotha, November 10, 1821, having settled there the year previous, as music director in succession to Spohr.

KIEL, No. 164 (Second Tune) F.C.H., is adapted from the last movement in his "Was bleibet und was schwindet" ("The Transient and the Eternal").

S.S., No. 28 F.C.H., "Now unto Him," is an adaptation from a movement in his setting of Schiller's "Die Glocke" ("The Lay of the Bell"), composed in 1808.

Root, George Frederick, son of Mr Frederick Ferdinand Root; born at Sheffield, Massachusetts, August 30, 1820; teacher of singing and organ at Boston, 1834 to 1843; music-teacher in New York, where he established a school for the training of music-teachers, 1844 to 1855; removed to Chicago (where he still resides), and founded the firm of Root & Cady, 1860 to 1880, now Root & Sons; degree of Mus. Doc. conferred on him by the University of Chicago in 1872; well known in this country by his cantatas, "The Flower Queen," "Daniel," "Pilgrim Fathers," "Bethlehem," &c.

INVITATION, No. 369 F.C.H., and
WHEN HE COMETH, No. 442 S.H., 381 F.C.H., there named "Christ's Crown," were first published in 'The Prize' (a Sunday School Collection), 1870.

ELLON, No. 335 U.P.H. First published in 'Chapel Gems,' 1868, under the title of "Because He loved me so."

LANGDON, No. 91 S.P.; and LYRA, No. 95 S.P., are the compositions of Dr Root, and appear in his 'Sabbath Bell,' 1857. "Lyra" is not in 'Carmina Sacra,' as stated in S.P. They were first published in this country by Mr William Carnie of Aberdeen.

Rosenmüller, Johann, born in Saxony; studied at Leipzig about 1647; assistant-master in St Thomas's School, Leipzig, and director of the choir there, and subsequently at Wolfenbüttel, where he died in 1686.

NASSAU, No. 323 F.C.H., 329 U.P.H., there named "Bonn," "Straf mich nicht in deinem Zorn," is said to have been composed by him in 1655. It appears in 'Hundert Geistliche Arien,' Dresden, 1694; also in 'A Collection of Hymns and Anthems for the use of the Episcopal Church of Scotland,' Aberdeen, 1790.

SCHÖNBERG, No. 186 (Second Tune) F.C.H., "Alle Menschen müssen sterben," appears in the nineteenth edition of Johann Crüger's 'Praxis Pietatis Melica,' 1678, and is generally considered to be the composition of Rosenmüller.

Ross, Roger Rowson, son of Mr Thomas Ross; born at Montrose, August 25, 1817; for many years resident at Manchester; a distinguished musical amateur; founded, in 1890, two complete scholarships at the Royal Academy of Music, London, one being to give encouragement to the study of sacred vocal music, and the other for players on wind instruments.

S.S., No. 41 U.P.H., "Like as the hart," is an adaptation by him. See Novello, Vincent.

Rousseau, Jean Jacques, son of Isaac Rousseau, a watchmaker at Geneva, where he was born June 28, 1712; author of a musical dictionary and of several pamphlets on music, but best known by his literary and philosophical works. He wrote an opera, "Le Devin du Village," which was performed for the first time October 18, 1752, at Fontainebleau, before Louis XV., King of France, and the Court. Rousseau died at Ermenonville, near Paris, July 3, 1778.

ROUSSEAU (or ROUSSEAU'S DREAM), No. 370 S.H., 358 F.C.H., 332 U.P.H., is founded on the following melody, headed "Pantomime" in scene 8 of his opera "Le Devin du Village," where it is scored for strings.

Perhaps its first appearance, under the name of "Rousseau's Dream," is as an 'Air with Variations for the Pianoforte, composed and dedicated to the Rt. Hon. the Countess of Delaware, by J. B. Cramer: London, Chappell' (1812), the melody as we now use it. It is found (with very slight changes) a quarter of a century earlier, under the title of 'Melissa. The words by Charles James, Esq., adapted to the Pianoforte, Harp, or Guitar': London, J. Dale, 1788. In Scotland it has become associated with the children's hymn, "Lord, a little band and lowly."

Rowton, Rev. Samuel James, M.A., born in London, July 3, 1844; educated at University College, Durham, where he gained the University classical scholarship in 1870; took holy orders in 1872; and has been since that date senior assistant-master, assistant-chaplain, organist, choirmaster, and Professor of Music in the Royal Medical College, Epsom; graduated Mus. Bac., Trinity College, Dublin, 1889. His tune,

EPSOM COLLEGE, No. 409 S.H., was first published in the 'Children's Hymn Book' (1881).

Russell, William, born in London, October 6, 1777; deputy-organist of St Mary's, Aldermanbury, 1789; organist of Great Queen Street Chapel, 1793; of St Ann's, Limehouse, 1798; of the Foundling Hospital, 1801, all in London; Mus. Bac., Oxford, 1808; died November 21, 1813.

CHANT, No. 353 S.H., appears in John Marsh's Collection.

No. 210 in U.P.P. is also his, and is set to S.S., No. 123 U.P.H., "Arise, shine, for thy light is come," and No. 127, "Blessed be the Lord God of Israel."

St Gall. Katholisches Gesangbuch

is the title of an important collection of chorales, published at St Gallen, Switzerland, in 1863, for use of the Church of St Gallen. The melodies were harmonised by Dr Carl Greith and R. L. de Pearsall, both of whom contributed several original pieces.

PEARSALL, No. 353 F.C.H., 63 U.P.H., 109 (Second Tune), 335 (First Tune) S.H., will be found on page 257 of the above work. The composer is unknown.

ELLACOMBE, No. 344 U.P.H., 350 F.C.H., is on pages 225 and 269. It was published elsewhere before 1863. See Kocher's 'Zionsharfe.'

Chorale books have been issued from time to time for the use of the Church at St Gallen, one dating as far back as the beginning of the seventeenth century.

'Sabbath School Union Hymnal, with accompanying Tunes.'

For Sabbath Schools and Children's Services. Compiled and Selected by a

Committee, and issued under the Authority of the Glasgow Sabbath School Union. 1876.

CHILD'S SONG, No. 349 F.C.H., was first published in its present form in the above collection, and was adapted by Mr James Merrylees from an old Border melody printed about one hundred years ago.

Sacred Melodies.

A work edited by the late Rev. C. H. Bateman and Robert Inglis in 1872, containing 200 Tunes, one of which is

JESUS SAVIOUR, No. 374 S.H. It seems to the writer that this tune is adapted from a music-hall song once very popular—viz., "Why did my Sarah sell me?" published about 1859. If so, adaptations of this kind are not to be commended.

Salvatori, S——. The writer is unable to identify this composer.

ENDSLEIGH, Nos. 212 (Second Tune) and 354 F.C.H., was adapted by James Turle, and published in 'Psalms and Hymns for Divine Worship,' 1867. (Nisbet & Co.)

Dr Paul, in his 'Handlexikon der Tonkunst,' Leipzig, 1873, mentions a Domenico Salvatori, a composer of talent, born at Modena, April 5, 1748; died October 23, 1774.

Latrobe also mentions a Salvatore who lived in the seventeenth century, and whose compositions were (1809) much used in the Pope's Chapel at Rome.

Sangster, Walter Hay, born in London 1835; chorister in the Temple Church, London, under Dr E. J. Hopkins; organist at the Chapel of the British Embassy, Berlin, from 1855 to 1856; of St Michael's, Chester Square, till 1861; All Saints, St John's Wood, 1861 to 1864; St James's Parish Church, Weybridge, 1865 to 1872; organist and master of the children of St Michael and All Angels, Paddington, 1872 to 1878; organist of St Saviour, Eastbourne, 1880; graduated as Mus. Bac., Oxford, 1870; Mus. Doc. 1877. His tune,

AD INFEROS, No. 46 S.H., was first published in the Revised and Enlarged Edition of 'Hymns Ancient and Modern,' 1875.

Scheffler, Johann, born at Breslau, in Silesia, 1624; studied medicine at the University of Breslau, and took the degree of M.D. at Padua; adopted the name of Angelus, by which he is commonly known, after Johannes ab Angelis, a Spanish mystic of the sixteenth century, usually adding to it "Silesius," from his native country; physician to the Duke of Würtemberg-Oels, and afterwards to the Emperor Ferdinand III.; joined the Church of Rome in 1653; some time afterwards took priest's orders, and died at the Jesuit Monastery of St Matthias, in Breslau, July 9, 1677. Writer of many hymns, which were published under the title of 'Heilige Seelenlust, oder geistliche Hirtenlieder' (1657)—second edition, enlarged, 1668—the tunes being provided by Georg Josephi and others. The following are in Scheffler's work:—

ANGELUS, No. 288 S.H., 304 U.P.H., 32 F.C.H.
CULBACH, No. 234 (Second Tune) S.H., 268 U.P.H.
SCHEFFLER, No. 168 F.C.H.

The first-named is wrongly assigned in the U.P.H. and F.C.H. to Scheffler, who did not compose any tunes. See Josephi, Georg.

Schein, Johann Hermann, born at Grünhayn, near Zwickau, Saxony, January 20, 1586; from 1599 to 1603 was in the choir of the chapel of the Elector of Saxony, at Dresden; studied theology and philosophy at Leipzig; became music-director at Weimar in 1613; precentor in St Thomas's School, Leipzig, in 1615; died November 19, 1630. His principal work is the 'Cantional' or 'Gesangbuch Augsburgischer Confession' (Hymn-book for the Lutheran Church), Leipzig, 1627. It contains 286 hymns and 206 tunes, of which 57 were by him. In the second edition of 1645, 22 more tunes of his composition were added.

EISENACH, No. 77 (First Tune) S.H., 14 P. and P., "Mach's mit mir, Gott, nach deiner Güt'," appears in the second edition of the 'Cantional,' issued in 1645.
GÖLDEL, No. 9 S.H., 15 P. and P., 220 S.P., "Ach Gott und Herr! wie gross und schwer"; and
ST LUKE, No. 93 F.C.H., "Herzlich vertrau du deinem Gott,"
are from the 1627 or first edition.

Schicht, Johann Gottfried, born at Reichenau, near Zittau, in 1753; appointed precentor in St Thomas's School, Leipzig, where he died in 1823. Edited 'Allgemeines Choralbuch,' 2 vols., 1819.

WALDHEIM, No. 76 (Second Tune) S.H., "Ach! es sind der Thränen auf der Welt," is No. 383 in vol. ii., and seems to be his composition.

Scholefield, Rev. Clement Cotterill, M.A., born at Edgbaston, near Birmingham, June 22, 1839; youngest son of the late Mr William Scholefield, who was for twenty years M.P. for Birmingham; educated at Pocklington Grammar School, Yorkshire; graduated at St John's College, Cambridge; ordained pastor of the Parish Church, Hove, Brighton, in 1867, where he remained for two years; afterwards pastor of St Peter's, South Kensington, for eight years; since 1880, chaplain of Eton College, Windsor; a self-taught musician and composer of psalmody.

Fides, No. 2 S.H.;

Irene, No. 266 F.C.H. and 236 U.P.H.,

were first published in Sir A. S. Sullivan's 'Church Hymns with Tunes,' 1874.

Litany (No. 2), No. 167 (Second Tune) S.H., was wrongly assigned to him in the first edition of the S.H. See Sullivan, Sir A. S.

Scholinus.   To a composer of this name,

Mamre, No. 346 U.P.H., 172 (First Tune) S.H., there named "Milton," is assigned in several German collections of school songs.

Schop, Johann, appears to have been born and to have died at Hamburg; music director in 1641, and "Rathsmusikant" in 1654; eminent as a violinist; composed tunes for many of the sacred songs of his friend Johann Rist, one of which is

Eilenburg. No. 324 S.H., "Werde munter mein Gemüthe," in 'Himmlische Lieder,' 1641-42.

Schulthes, Wilhelm, son of an officer in the German army; born at Hesse Cassel, September 9, 1816; brought up as a Lutheran, but became a Catholic through reading Frederick Faber's books—being received into the Church at the Oratory, South Kensington, London, about 1852, where shortly after he became director of the Oratory choir, a position he held till 1872; teacher of music at the Convent of the Sacred Heart, Roehampton, from 1868 to 1879; died suddenly at Bois-de-Colombes, near Paris, August 16, 1879; buried there. Composer of much sacred music for the Catholic Church.

Requiem, No. 123 S.H., was composed by him about 1868 for Hymn 34 (Consolatrix Afflictorum) in the Oratory Collection published at that time.

Schulz, Johann Abraham Peter, was born at Lüneburg in 1747; pupil of Kirnberger; from 1780 to 1787 chapel-master to Prince Henry of Prussia at Rheinsberg; from 1787 to 1794 Court chapel-master at Copenhagen, whence he returned in 1794 to Germany; died at Schwedt, June 10, 1800. Composer of oratorios, songs, &c.

Dresden, Nos. 326 and 351 F.C.H., 309 U.P.H., 297 and 364 S.H., "Wir pflügen und wir streuen," is his best-known composition.

Paran, No. 37 F.C.H., appears in Mason and Webb's 'National Psalmist,'

Boston, 1849, in a slightly different form, named "Canton," and is marked as "arranged from Schulz." It is also in 'New Carmina Sacra,' 1850, under the name of "Paran," and identical with the form given in the F.C.H. In several German collections of school songs it is assigned to Schulz.

Schumann, Robert Alexander, Ph. Doc., a title conferred on him by the University of Jena in 1840; youngest son of Friedrich August Gottlob Schumann, a bookseller; born at Zwickau, in Saxony, June 8, 1810; renowned as a composer and critic; married Clara Wieck, the eminent pianist, September 12, 1840; died at Enderich, near Bonn, July 29, 1856.

BUCER, No. 211 and 243 (First Tunes) S.H., 183 P. and P., and 140 (First Tune) F.C.H., is said to be an adaptation from one of his works. It appears in 'Cantica Laudis,' by Dr Lowell Mason and George James Webb, 1850, and is there named "White." Madame Schumann has informed the writer that she is doubtful if it is adapted from any of her husband's compositions.

Scotch Chant.

CHANT, No. 333 F.C.H., appears in 'Harmonia Sancta,' by Hamilton and Müller, 1839 (preface dated January 1838), where it is anonymous. This is probably the reason it is named "Scotch Chant."

Scottish Psalters.

In order to trace, however briefly, the history of the first Scottish Metrical Psalter, it is necessary to deal with the editions which led up to the completed work. The first of the versions which ultimately came to be used in the churches were by Thomas Sternhold, who, according to Strype, composed them originally for his own "godly solace," and without any view to their being adopted by the people. Sternhold occupied a position at Court, and it is said that King Edward VI., one day overhearing him singing his psalms, was so delighted with them that he suggested their publication. The first edition of these psalms—undated, but generally ascribed to the year 1547—was dedicated to the boy-king and contained nineteen renderings.

A second edition followed in 1549 having forty-four psalms, seven of which were by John Hopkins, a Suffolk clergyman, of whom very little is known. This latter edition proved to be the foundation of both the English and the Scottish complete Psalters. It was several times republished in England, but, so far as can be learned, without addition or change. The psalms thus versified seem to have been employed in worship to some extent, for it is evidently to this period that Burnet in his 'History of the Reformation' refers when he speaks of psalms translated into verse "which were much sung by all who loved the Reformation, and in many places used in churches." But the psalm-singing did not long continue without interruption; with the death of Edward VI. in 1553 and the succession to the throne of Mary, the persecution of the Protestants began, and most of them were forced to leave the country. Some sought shelter in Scotland, but a large number fled to Frankfort, whither we must go in following out the development of the metrical Psalter. A congregation was soon formed at Frankfort, but it was not long before dissensions arose in regard to the use of a liturgy; and towards the end of 1556 a number of the members removed to Geneva, where Calvin was then at the height of his reputation.

Here they at once proceeded to bring into use a form of service, and this was published under the following title: 'The Forme of Prayers and Ministration of the Sacrament, &c., used in the Englishe Congregation at Geneva; and approved by the famous and godly learned man John Calvyn. Imprinted at Geneva by John Crespin, MDLVI.' This substantially is the work which afterwards became known as 'The Order of Geneva' and 'The Book of Common Order.' It contained the forty-four psalms of Sternhold and Hopkins, already published in England, and seven new renderings by W. Whittingham. This collection is exceedingly interesting, because every one of the psalms, as well as forty-two of the tunes, were subsequently transferred without change to 'The Scottish Psalter,' which may thus be said to begin its history at this point. Soon after the death of Mary in 1558, the exiles returned to England, but Kethe and one or two others remained, in order "to finishe the Bible and the Psalms both in meeter and prose." In the year 1560 an edition was published at Geneva having fourteen new psalms, and in 1561 another was issued containing twenty-five more — from the pen of Kethe — the number now versified being in all eighty-seven. In 1562 the Psalter was completed and published in England. In this perfected edition the forty-four psalms of 1549 were retained, and of the forty-three added at Geneva in 1556-61 twenty were retained and twenty-three rejected. The eighty-six renderings required to finish the work, and a duplicate version of Psalm 51, were all new.

Here we may now leave the English Psalter, and come to the work with which we are more particularly concerned. The first General Assembly of the Scottish Church was held in 1560. The records of these early meetings have unfortunately perished, so that there is no means of ascertaining whether or not the matter of the Psalter engaged attention at this time. At any rate, if not in 1560, the question must have been taken up soon after, for in a paper ascribed to Calderwood the historian, we read that "In the General Assembly convened at Edinburgh in December 1562, for printing of the Psalmes the Kirk lent Robert Lekprivik twa hundredth punds [Scotch money] to help to buy irons, ink, and paper, and to fie craftsmen for printing." The exact date at which the process of printing was completed cannot be fixed, but it must have been before the meeting of Assembly in 1564, as is plain from the following entry in 'The Book of the Universal Kirk': "Sess. 2nd, holden in the 26 of December 1564. It was ordained that everie minister, exhorter, and reader sall have one of the Psalme Bookes latelie printed in Edinburgh, and use the order contained therein in prayers," &c. Only one copy of this work is known to remain—that in the library of Corpus Christi College, Oxford. Copies of an impression of the following year, identical with the other as to contents, are in the Advocates' Library, Edinburgh, and in St John's, Cambridge. The tunes number one hundred and five—forty-two more than in the English Psalter of 1562. With regard to the psalms themselves, the forty-four by Sternhold and Hopkins (1549) are retained, as well as the forty-three added by the exiles at Geneva. Of the eighty-seven added to the 1562 English Psalter, forty-two are retained, and the whole is completed by twenty-one from new sources. The printing, both in the literary and musical divisions, is executed with great accuracy and clearness. Very little is known of Lekprivik, though his place of business in Edinburgh appears to have been somewhere about the eastern nook of the old town, near the Netherbow Port. Some time after 1568 he seems to have removed to St Andrews, and several books bearing to be "Imprentit at Sanctandrois by Robert Lekprivik," are noted under the date of 1572 in Ames's 'Typographical Antiquities.'

Many editions of the Psalter were issued from this time forward, but the more important of these can only be noticed. The editions of Thomas Bassandyne deserve to be mentioned not only on their own account, but also because from the press of Bassandyne came the first Bible printed in Scotland. In 1568 this printer incurred the displeasure of the General Assembly by issuing a "Psalme Booke" containing an objectionable song "callit Welcum Fortoun." No copy of this edition is known to exist—probably the stock was destroyed, as the Assembly ordained that the sale should be stopped, and all copies called in. In 1575 Bassandyne issued another edition of the Psalter, the printing of which was remarkably good, the references to the tunes being in a peculiar script-like type which occurs in no other edition. Here the so-called "Spiritual Songs" appear for the first time; and there is also a "Gloria Patri" attached to one of the psalms (the 136th). Bassandyne is believed to have died early in 1579. He was succeeded by Arbuthnot, whom he had previously taken into partnership; and although Arbuthnot had obtained a monopoly for printing the psalms to last for seven years, no edition of the Psalter by him is known. Ross, one of Bassandyne's contemporaries, also printed one or two editions of the Psalter. An edition in black-letter, title-page wanting, belongs to the Society of Antiquaries of Scotland; and in Ross's will mention is made of, among others, "27 psalme buikes with the noittis."

We now reach an edition which ranks among the first in importance, and—so far at least as the literary contents are concerned—forms one of the leading stages in the Psalter's history. The edition to which we refer is that printed "be Henrie Charteris" at Edinburgh in 1596. Charteris was established as a printer in the capital about 1580, and an edition of the Psalter has been mentioned as coming from his press in 1594. Of this, however, no information can be obtained. The 1596 Psalter is peculiar in several respects: it contains a remarkable series of prayers in the Scottish dialect, one being appended to each psalm, and "agreeing with the meaning thereof"; it presents for the first time the full set of metrical doxologies termed "conclusions," and the contents of the psalms are considerably abridged. Unfortunately the printing of the music cannot be commended, this part of the work being disfigured by numerous inaccuracies. Andrew Hart next comes into view as the leading printer of the Psalter, his name appearing on many title-pages interesting to the Scottish musical antiquary. Hart's place of business was on the north side of the High Street, Edinburgh, opposite the Cross—the identical spot, it may be added, where the 'Edinburgh Review' was commercially hatched. He was at first a bookseller only, then he became a publisher, and at last he added a printing-office to his establishment. His most important work was perhaps an edition of the Bible, printed in 1610. This was so much esteemed for its correctness, that one or two subsequent editions bore on their titles, "conform to the edition printed by Andrew Hart." But it is with Hart's Psalters that we have here to deal. Two editions of 1611 need only be mentioned, as the printing of the music in both is very faulty and inaccurate, and neither is of much historical value. The 1615 edition is, on the other hand, one of the most handsome, and, in regard to the musical department, one of the most correctly printed of all editions up to this date. It introduces for the first time a selection (12) of four-line tunes, ranked as a separate class from the proper or fixed tunes, and bearing the general designation of "Common Tunes," with a name to each. Another of its features is the almost uniform equalisation of the length of the notes, former editions showing many vagaries in this respect. Hart died at an advanced age in 1621, and subsequent editions of the Psalter bear to have been printed by his heirs. One of these editions we have yet to consider; but in the meantime, following strictly chronological order, we shall deal with the editions printed at Aberdeen by Edward Raban.

Raban was the pioneer of the bookselling and printing trade in Aberdeen. He was an Englishman, and started first, at the sign of the "A B C," in the Cowgate Port, Edinburgh, in 1620. So far as is known, he printed only one book in the capital; and at any rate he soon removed to St Andrews, where the University appointed him their printer. In 1622 he went to Aberdeen, where he was allowed a salary of £40 (Scots) annually, as printer to the town and University. The date of his death is given in most accounts as 1649, but this is erroneous. He died in 1658, as is proved by the entry of his burial in the Aberdeen Kirk and Bridge Work Accounts: "1658, Decr. 6, Edward Rabein at wast dyk"— *i.e.*, the west wall of St Nicholas churchyard. Raban was evidently a man of taste and some literary faculty, but his work does not rise above that of his contemporaries.

Up till quite recently the earliest edition of the Psalter printed by Raban in Aberdeen, recorded by bibliographers, was that of 1629. The following extract, however, places it almost beyond doubt that Raban printed an edition with the music four years before this date: "There is now lying before me an edition of the version of the Psalms by Sternhold and Hopkins, 'together with the tunes diligently revised and amended by the most expert musicians in Aberdene,' printed at Aberdeen by Raban in 1625."—('Book of Bon Accord,' by Joseph Robertson, page 124; see also Kennedy's 'Annals of Aberdeen.') Besides this, an edition in 24mo, "printed in Aberdeen by Edward Raban for David Melvil, 1626," has been discovered, and a copy was some time ago in the hands of Mr Quaritch of London.

In 1629 we come to the edition at one time believed, as we have said, to be the earliest. So far as we are able to learn, no complete copy of this edition is known; but there is one, minus the title, which the following notice shows to be Raban's: "Here follow the Common Tunes in foure parts, in more perfect forme than ever heretofore; Together with the Tunes to the whole Psalmes, diligently revised and amended, By the most expert Musicians in Aberdene." This edition contains fifteen common tunes, all of which are harmonised in four parts, one, "Bon-Accord," being in what was then known as "Reports."

This is the first appearance of printed harmony in the history of the Psalter, as well as of the "Report" class of tune. Raban's best known and most important Psalter is, however, that of 1633. Here the music is, on the whole, well and carefully printed; and the proper tunes are evidently based upon the original edition of 1564. The twelve common tunes (all harmonised) of 1615 are continued, with three additions, and there are also two tunes in "Reports,"— "Bon-Accord" and "Montrose." A peculiarity belongs to these two latter tunes—viz., that the "Trebble" is designated the "Church part." No instance of this is found in other editions, and no other instance even in this. It is evident that in these two cases the "Trebble" is the melody; but nevertheless the tenor is termed the Church part in those as in all other cases. These Psalters of Raban's—though, as we have remarked, not rising above the typographical work of contemporary printers—are a lasting credit to the city of Aberdeen. They were the first published out of Edinburgh; and they possess features distinctive enough to give them a place of no mean importance in the history of the Psalter itself.

We have said that after Hart's death in 1621 several editions of the Psalter were published by his heirs. One of these now falls to be dealt with—the famous issue of 1635. It may be worth while transcribing the title-page of this interesting work. It runs as follows: "The Psalmes of David in Prose and Meeter, With their whole Tunes in foure or mo parts, and some Psalmes in Reports. Whereunto is added many godly Prayers, and an exact Kalendar for xxv years to come. [Woodcut of David with harp.] Printed at Edinburgh by the Heires of Andrew Hart, Anno Dom. 1635." In this very fine edition the Scottish Psalter may be said to have reached its climax. The whole of the tunes were now furnished with harmony for the first time; the number of common tunes was increased to thirty-one, besides eight in "Reports"; and a distinct individual first came into view as editor. Except in these particulars no change of any importance was made, though the upside-down arrangement of the parts of the common and "Report" tunes is a novelty in the printing which should be noted. The editor contributes an interesting preface, in which he refers mainly to the musical branch of the work. To this preface the initials "E. M." are appended, and these letters have been clearly identified with Edward Miller, who studied at the University of Edinburgh, and took the degree of M.A. in 1624. In some MS. lists, dated 1627, the name occurs of Edward Millar, in Blackfriars Wynd, Edinburgh, "who teaches bairns"; but whether the "bairns" belonged to a music or only a general school cannot be said.

Here the history of the first Scottish Psalter may be said to take end. After 1635 only two editions appear to have been published, —one in 1640, consisting simply of remaining copies of Hart's 1635 edition; and another, a quarto, of the same date, both these being issued from the press of James Bryson. By this time the agitation for a new metrical Psalter had begun, and in 1650 the present version of the Psalms was adopted by the Church. The Psalter was now printed without accompanying tunes, and no compensation was made for the loss by issuing these tunes in a separate form. What result could be expected but that the old work should vanish entirely from public view, and in a few years pass into oblivion? Ultimately, as the Rev. Dr Neil Livingston remarks in his reprint of the 1635 Psalter, our country seems to have become chiefly dependent on England for its supply of music, only some half-dozen of its old Psalter tunes being retained, and nine-tenths of its precentors, it may be affirmed, being entirely ignorant that such a work ever existed.—J. CUTHBERT HADDEN.

The edition of 1565 has the following title: 'The Forme of Prayers and Ministration of the Sacraments, &c., used in the English Church at Geneua, approved and received by the Churche of Scotland, whereunto besydes that was in the former bokes, are also added sondrie other prayers, with the whole Psalmes of Dauid in English meter. . . . Printed at Edinburgh by Robert Lekprevik. MDLXV.' In it are found :—

OLD 1ST, No. 111 S.P. Set to Psalm 1.
OLD 8TH, No. 213 U.P.P. Set to Psalm 8.
OLD 9TH, No. 40 U.P.P. Set to Psalm 9.
OLD 21ST, No. 196 U.P.P. Set to Psalm 21.
OLD 29TH, No. 214 U.P.P., 112 S.P., 171 P. and P. Set to Psalm 29.
OLD 49TH, No. 53 U.P.P. Set to Psalm 49.
OLD 78TH, No. 56 U.P.P. Set to Psalm 78.
CROMARTY, No. 137 U.P.P. Set to Psalm 46.

The 1615 edition, published by Andro Hart, printer in Edinburgh, has the following title: 'The CL Psalmes of David, in Prose and Meeter With their whole usuall Notes and Tunes.' The melodies only are given. In it are found :—

ABBEY (there called Abbay), No. 29 S.P., 87 F.C.H., 20 U.P.H., 58 U.P.P., 45 P. and P.

DUKE'S TUNE, No. 68 P. and P.

DUNFERMLINE, No. 58 S.P., 12 and 247 U.P.H., 152 U.P.P., 298 S.H. 70 P. and P.

FRENCH, No. 69 S.P., 112 F.C.H., 207 (Second Tune) S.H., 80 P. and P., 218 U.P.P.

MARTYRS, No. 98 and 99 S.P., 19 and 194 U.P.P., 110 P. and P.

OLD GLASGOW, No. 180 U.P.P.

YORK, No. 179 S.P., 105 F.C.H., 141 U.P.P., 120 S.H., 167 P. and P.

In "The Cottar's Saturday Night," Burns writes of "Martyrs"—

"Perhaps *Dundee's* wild warbling measures rise,
Or plaintive *Martyrs*, worthy of the name."

He joins it also with "Elgin" and "Dundee" as being—

"The sweetest far of Scotia's holy lays."

Of "York," Sir John Hawkins wrote: "Within memory, half the nurses of England were used to sing it by way of lullaby, and the chimes of many country churches have played it six or eight times in four-and-twenty hours from time immemorial." It is named "The Stilt" in the Scottish Psalter, and "York" by Ravenscroft. It has usually been assigned to John Milton, father of the poet, who "composed it into four parts" for Ravenscroft's Psalter; but one Simon Stubbs did so also, who might, therefore, share the authorship.

In the edition "Printed . . . by the Heires of Andrew Hart" in 1635—the title of which has already been given—are found the following tunes :—

ABERFELDY, No. 219 P. and P.

BON-ACCORD, No. 221 P. and P., 40 S.P. (where an abridged form is given).

CAITHNESS, No. 45 S.P., 121 U.P.P., 55 P. and P., 318 (Second Tune), 219 (First Tune) S.H.

CULROSS, No. 8 U.P.P., 67 P. and P.

ELGIN, No. 74 P. and P., 62 S.P., 6 U.P.P.

INVERNESS, No. 95 P. and P.

LONDON NEW (originally named Newtoun), No. 94 S.P., 107 P. and P. 19 S.H., 216 U.P.P., 274 U.P.H. See Chalmers, James, in Appendix.

MELROSE, No. 100 S.P., 59 U.P.P., 111 P. and P.

WIGTON, No. 163 P. and P.

Several of these tunes had appeared a few years previous to 1635 in the Psalter published by Raban at Aberdeen.

Sewell, John, organist and choirmaster of St Leonard's Church, Bridgnorth, and a music-seller there.

S.S. No. 63 U.P.H., "This is the Day," was composed by him about 1858, and published in Novello's 'Octavo Anthems.'

Shrubsole, William, youngest son of Mr Thomas Shrubsole, farrier; born at Canterbury; baptised in the parish of All Saints, January 13, 1760; chorister at the Cathedral there from Lady-day 1770 to Michaelmas 1777, and doubtless studied the organ under Samuel Porter, then organist at the Cathedral; settled in London as a music teacher, and among his music pupils were William Russell, organist of the Foundling Chapel, and Benjamin Jacob, of Surrey Chapel fame. Appointed organist of Spa Fields Chapel, London, in 1784, and held the office till his death on January 18, 1806; buried in Bunhill Fields, London.

MILES LANE, No. 55 F.C.H. A tune very popular in Scotland at one time, but now rarely heard; is generally considered to be the composition of Shrubsole. It was composed for the hymn "All hail the pow'r of Jesus' name," and seems to have been first published in the 'Gospel Magazine' for November 1779, where the hymn (one verse only) and tune appear without author's or composer's names. Five months later (April 1780) the complete hymn (eight stanzas) appears without music, anonymously, and for the first time, in the same periodical, an editorial footnote saying, "For the music of this hymn, see our Magazine for November 1779."

COPY OF "MILES LANE" AS IN 'GOSPEL MAGAZINE,' NOVEMBER 1779.

CHORUS.

										tr					
d¹	:—	d¹	:—	d¹	:—	t	:—	d¹	:—	—
s¹	:—	l¹	:—	s¹	:—	s¹	:—.f¹	m¹	:—	—
Crown		Him		Lord		_tr_ of		all.		
m¹	:—	f¹	:—	m¹	:—	r¹	:—	d¹	:—	—
d	:—	f	:—	s	:—	s,	:—	d	:—	—

The tune appears as "Miles's Lane" in the Appendix to the sixth edition of 'A Collection of Psalm Tunes,' compiled by the Rev. Stephen Addington, D.D., who was minister of Miles's Lane Meeting House (now demolished), London, hence probably the name of the tune. Miles Lane, close to London Bridge, still remains.

In Thomas Williams's 'Psalmodia Evangelica,' vol i., 1789, the tune is found on page 49, named "Harborough,"—the town in which Dr Addington (see above) ministered before he came to Miles's Lane—but indexed "Miles's Lane—see Harborough," and assigned to Shrubsole. In vol. ii. of the same work (1790?) there is another tune by Shrubsole named "St Peter's."

The writer of the hymn "All hail the pow'r of Jesus' name" was the Rev. Edward Perronet, who died at Canterbury, January 4, 1792. His will, dated October 4, 1789, was proved at Canterbury on the 12th of that month by Duriah Perronet, the relict, William Shrubsole, and John Halbet, the executors. Its concluding clause runs thus: "Lastly, I do here give and bequeath all and every property I am at this time or may at the time of my decease be possest of both real and personal to the afore-mentioned Mr William Shrubsole youngest son of Mr Thomas Shrubsole aforesaid and now or late of the parish of St Bride's in London and to the male heirs of his body lawfully begotten to be by them (subject to the dividends aforementioned) possest enjoyed and disposed of as they shall see meet for ever in consideration of his respect for me his services to me and that pure and disinterested affection he has ever shown me from our first acquaintance even when a proverb of reproach cast off by all my relations disinherited unjustly and left to sink or swim as afflictions and God's providence should appoint."

Perronet seems to have been a musician as well as a hymn-writer, as a tune of his composition named "St Barnabas" appears in the same collection which contains Shrubsole's "St Peter's." "An interesting incident is told in connection with 'Miles's Lane' and the late Henry Smart. It was formerly the custom for the organist to play a short interlude between every verse of the hymn. In Smart's early days there were some grumblers (the race is not yet quite extinct) who adversely criticised his manner of playing the organ in the service. Smart said nothing, but waited his opportunity. It came when 'Miles's Lane' was to be sung. He started it in the original key, C. All went well at the first verse, and a 'hearty sing' was in prospect. In the interlude between verses one and two Smart modulated, almost imperceptibly, into D flat, a semitone higher. Between verses two and three he modulated into D, when it was found the high notes on 'Crown Him' did not come quite so easily. Between verses three and four a semitone higher still, until the high notes of these and the remaining verses must have made the acquaintance of the 'Lost Chord.' Needless to say that the young organist effectually silenced his critics by this clever display of skill."—(F. G. Edwards in 'Nonconformist Musical Journal,' September 1890.)

SCARBOROUGH, No. 158 S.P., is a corrupt abridgment of "Miles Lane," and, like that tune, has been in use in Scotland since 1793, as they are both found in Henry Boyd's Collection issued in that year. Speaking of "Scarborough" in his 'Sacred Choir,' the late Rev. Dr William Anderson gave this characteristic advice to precentors: "As they would deprecate being regarded barbarians, let those precentors not intermeddle with this gorgeous tune who cannot guide a congregation in the singing of it without taking the octave at the end of the second measure. It produces the sensation as if one would vomit."

In several Scotch collections, issued about the middle of this century, the second line of "Scarborough" is printed thus—

KEY C.
{ :s | l :s .f¹ |m¹ :r¹ | d¹ :— |— ||

It may be here remarked that musical writers have confounded William Shrubsole, the organist and composer, with his contemporary, the hymn-writer of the same name.

Sicilian Melody.

MARINERS, No. 360 F.C.H., 199 S.H., there named

O SANCTISSIMA, No. 348 U.P.H., there named

SICILIAN, appears as "Sicilian Mariners' Hymn," in Dr Watts's 'Psalms and Hymns,' set to new music, 1800, a collection edited by Dr Edward Miller. It was published previous to that date on single slips.

Siegel, Michael, or **Sigillus,** of Thum, was in 1623 cantor in Hayn; little seems to be known of his career. The tune

SIGILLUS, No. 258 F.C.H., 212 S.P., and 171 U.P.H., "Sag, was hilft alle Welt," appears, assigned to him, in the third part of the 'Gotha Cantional' of 1648.

Silcher, Friedrich, born at Schnaith, a village in Würtemberg, June 27, 1789; pupil of Auberlen at Fellbach from 1803 to 1806; appointed assistant-teacher in the town of Schorndorf in 1806; removed to Stuttgart in 1811, and in 1817 to Tübingen, having been appointed to the newly instituted office of music director in the University there; in 1852 received the degree of Ph. Doc.;

died August 28, 1860; composer of much music for men's voices, which is still popular in Germany.

INFANT PRAISES, No. 364 (Second Tune) F.C.H., 340 U.P.H., 423 S.H., appears in his 'Melodies for Youth,' edited by Lindsay Sloper, 1853. It was also published in Book II. of 'Twelve Child's Songs for School and House,' Tübingen (no date), to the words "Lehr' mich beten, Gott der Herrlichkeit." The form of melody in the U.P. and F.C. Hymnals is the correct one.

LOUISBERG, No. 298 F.C.H., "Urquell aller Seligkeiten," was composed in 1823, and published in the 'Würtemberg Gesangbuch,' 1828.

RAVENSBURG, No. 122 S.P., 139 U.P.P., 120 P. and P., is adapted from the chorale "Preis ihm! er schuf und er erhält" (No. 104), in the Rev. J. L. E. Punschell's 'Evangelisches Choralbuch,' second edition, 1844, where it is assigned to Silcher. This work was issued in 1840 to suit the hymn-books of the German, Lettish, and Esthonian congregations of the Russian Baltic Provinces.

Simpson,[1] **Robert**, a weaver to trade, was born at Glasgow. He led the psalmody for some time in Dr Wardlaw's church there, but how long cannot now be ascertained. In August 1823 he was appointed precentor and session-clerk of the East Parish Church of Greenock at a salary of forty pounds a-year—positions he was well qualified to fill, as he is said to have been a man of good education, and an excellent musician and vocalist. Old residenters have related to the writer that the singing of the choir in the East Church under Simpson was a thing to be remembered. On his removal to Greenock he made music his profession, and was much and generally respected, being a quiet unobtrusive man of simple and studious habits. He was of rather delicate constitution, and died, after a short illness, July or August 1832, aged about forty years.

BALLERMA, or more correctly BELERMA, No. 38 and 57 U.P.P., 33 S.P., 48 P. and P., with which Simpson's name is now associated, was found among his papers shortly after he died. It was first published in 'A Selection of Original Sacred Music, in Four Vocal Parts. . . . Intended to form the Sixth Vol. of Steven's Collection of Sacred Music,' edited by John Turnbull, Conductor of Music, St George's Church, Glasgow (1833), where it is set to Psalm 40. It is not an original composition, but seems to be adapted from the first half of the melody given below, which was published with a harp accompaniment after 1796 by F. H. Barthélémon, the eminent violinist:—

---

[1] Probably Robert Simpson, son of William Simpson and Sarah Chapman, born at Glasgow 4th November 1790, and baptised on the 14th of that month, is the same.

256 BIOGRAPHICAL SKETCHES.

DURANDARTE AND BELERMA.
[.1 *Pathetic Scotch Ballad.*

The words to which the above melody is set consist of ten stanzas, and relate how a brave knight, Durandarte, was slain by the Moors at the siege of

Roncesvalles in Spain. They appear in 'The Monk,' a romance in three volumes, by Matthew Gregory Lewis, Esq., M.P., 1796. In an advertisement Lewis says: "The poem 'Belerma and Durandarte' is translated from some stanzas to be found in a collection of old Spanish poetry, which contains also the popular song of Gayferos and Melisindra, mentioned in 'Don Quixote.'" This may have led to the supposition that the melody is of Spanish origin.

The late Mr William Chappell, author of 'Popular Music of the Olden Time,' &c., favoured the writer with his opinion regarding this melody. He writes: "The melody is quite unlike Spanish music or any kind of sixteenth century music. I should say it is not older than the last century, and far more likely to have been composed within the present by a singer or violin-player who had a feeling for melody."

It is very probable this melody was composed by Barthélémon, for the learned G. F. Graham, writing in the middle of the present century, speaks of it as Barthélémon's composition.

An original tune by Simpson will be found in J. P. Clarke's 'Parochial Psalmody,' Glasgow. No date. Second edition (1832).

Smallwood, William, born at Kendal, December 31, 1831; pupil of Dr Camidge, Henry Phillips, and J. H. Pollard; since 1847 organist of St George's Church, Kendal; composer of anthems, songs, &c., but more widely known by his pianoforte tutor and instrumental music.

S.S. No. 12 F.C.H. is part of "The path of the just," composed by him in 1868, and first published by B. Williams in 'Select Sacred Harmony.'

Smart, Sir George Thomas, son of George Smart, music-seller in London; born May 10, 1776; chorister in the Chapel Royal under Dr Ayrton; studied the organ under Dr Dupuis, and composition under Dr Arnold. On quitting the choir of the Chapel Royal in 1791, he obtained the appointment of organist of St James's Chapel, Hampstead Road; after successfully conducting some concerts in Dublin, he was knighted in 1811 by the Lord Lieutenant; on April 1, 1822, appointed one of the organists of the Chapel Royal, in room of Charles Knyvett, deceased; in 1838 appointed one of the composers to the Chapel Royal; conducted the music at the coronations of William IV. and Queen Victoria, and at numerous provincial festivals, at one of which, Liverpool, in 1836, Mendelssohn's "St Paul" was first performed in England; died at his house in Bedford Square, London, February 23, 1867. About the end of last century, or the beginning of the present, Smart issued 'Divine Amusement, being a Selection of the most admired Psalms, Hymns, and Anthems used in St James's Chapel. . . . The whole composed and compiled by George Thomas Smart, Organist of St James's Chapel, and late one of the Children of His

Majesty's Chapel Royal. Printed by E. Lavenu, 28 New Bond Street.' In this is found

WILTSHIRE (better known in Scotland as "New St Ann"), No. 164 P. and P., 177 S.P., 129 U.P.P. A copy of the melody is here given:—

KEY B♭.

{ :s₁	m₁ :s₁	:d	d :t₁	:d	f :m	:r	ʳm :— ‖
{ :s₁	s₁ :— :s₁	s₁ :m	:d	d :t₁ ‖ r	d :— }
{ :t₁	d :— :r	m :f	:m	ʳr :— ‖ m.d	l₁ :— }
{ :r	t₁ :—.l₁:t₁.s₁	d :— ‖

It appears in the same form in Jane Clarke's 'Select Portions of Psalms and Hymns, adapted to Music, . . . as Sung at Oxford Chapel' (published before 1809).

In Peck's 'Pocket Arrangement' or 'General Collection of Psalm and Hymn Tunes,' 3 vols., 1833, it is published, "by permission," thus:—

KEY B♭.

{ :s₁	s₁ :— :d	d :t₁	:d	f :m	:r	r :m }
{ :s₁	s₁ :— :s₁	s₁ :m	:d	d :t₁	:r	d :— }
{ :t₁	d :— :r	m.d:f	:m.f	m :r	:m.d	l₁ :— }
{ :r.d	t₁ :—.l₁:t₁.s₁	d :— ‖

The alteration in the first line was probably made on account of its similarity to a melody by Haydn, the few crotchets introduced in the third line being added for effect; but the writer questions if the composer sanctioned these changes.

About 1856 the Rev. Mr (now Dr) Henderson of Paisley received permission from Sir George to insert the tune in his 'Church Melodies.' It was revised by him for that work, and he informed Dr Henderson at the same time that he did not approve of the alterations made on his tune by some editors.

Melody of "Wiltshire," as revised by the composer for 'Church Melodies':—

Again, in 1863, Smart published 'A Collection of Sacred Music, Respectfully Dedicated by express Permission to Her Most Gracious Majesty Queen Victoria.' Vol. i. contains the tune in the same form as first published in his 'Divine Amusement.' It is there set to Psalm 31.

It has been erroneously ascribed in several Scotch psalmodies to Dr Croft, apparently through some confusion with the name of "St Ann." It was doubtless named "New St Ann" in the Scotch collections, as a tune "Wiltshire," by one Stevenson, was in use when Smart's tune was introduced into Scotland, and the prefix "New" would be adopted to distinguish it from Croft's tune, "St Ann." The editors of the S.P. have taken care to state that "Wiltshire" appears in that collection in its "authentic form." It is to be regretted that they cannot say the same of several other tunes, notably Samuel Stanley's "Doversdale," which has been left, like the man who fell among thieves, stripped and wounded, even half dead.

Smart, Henry, son of Mr Henry Smart, an eminent musician, and nephew of Sir George Smart, was born in London, October 26, 1813. After receiving a commission in the Indian army, which he did not accept, he was articled to a solicitor, but finally adopted music as his profession, and studied chiefly under Mr W. H. Kearns.

From 1831 till 1836 organist of the Parish Church, Blackburn, in Lancashire; of St Philip's, Regent Street, London, 1838 to 1839; St Luke's, Old Street, 1844 to 1864; from 1865 till he died, July 6, 1879, organist of St Pancras Church, London. Smart composed many anthems, services, part-songs, trios, duets, and several cantatas, one of which—"Jacob"—was specially composed for the Glasgow Musical Festival, and performed there November 10, 1873. It is, however, as a writer of music for the organ that he will best be remembered, his compositions for that instrument being of the highest order. As an organ-player his reputation was great, especially in extemporising; he devoted much study to the mechanism of the instrument, and was chiefly consulted as to the designing of the organ in the City Hall, Glasgow (which he opened October 11, 1853); the organs in the Town Hall, Leeds; St Andrew's Halls, Glasgow; and many others. For the last fourteen years of his life, Smart was quite blind.

BETHANY, No. 56 S.H., 230 F.C.H., there named CRUCIFER;
COLUMBA, No. 103 U.P.P.;
EVERTON, No. 60 and 366 U.P.H.;
HEATHLANDS, No. 178 S.H., 183 F.C.H., 141 U.P.H.;
LANCASHIRE, No. 55 S.H., 203 F.C.H., 26 and 294 (First Tune) U.P.H.;
LONDON, No. 2 (First Tune) F.C.H.;
NORTHUMBERLAND, No. 94 F.C.H., 187 U.P.P.;
REGENT SQUARE, No. 82 (Second Tune) S.H., 237 F.C.H., 293 U.P.H.;
ST LEONARD, No. 210 S.H., 140 S.P., 99 F.C.H.,

are nine of twenty tunes he contributed to 'Psalms and Hymns for Divine Worship': (Nisbet) London, 1867. "Lancashire" was composed about 1836 for a missionary meeting among the Nonconformists at Blackburn.

ASHGROVE, No. 206 U.P.H.
BETHESDA, No. 359 U.P.H.
MOREDUN, No. 264 U.P.H., 296 F.C.H., 132 S.H.
THEODORE, No. 154 U.P.H.
ERSKINE, No. 188 U.P.P.
GILLESPIE, No. 101 U.P.P.

The first four of the above he contributed to the U.P.H. in 1877, and the last two to the U.P.P. in 1878. He revised the harmonies of both these works. The Coda to "Veni Creator," No. 99 U.P.H., is also his.

PARADISE, No. 270 (First Tune) S.H.;
PILGRIMS, No. 247 (First Tune) S.H., 233 U.P.H.;
VEXILLUM, No. 424 S.H.,

were composed for the Appendix to 'Hymns Ancient and Modern,' 1868.

EDINBURGH (first published under that name in the 'Northern Psalter'),

No. 438 (First Tune) S.H. and 73 P. and P.; and SMART, No. 238 S.H., are from 'The Hymnary,' edited by Joseph Barnby in 1872.

MISERICORDIA, No. 278 (First Tune) F.C.H., 131 (First Tune) U.P.H., was composed for the Revised and Enlarged Edition of 'Hymns Ancient and Modern,' 1875.

The following were composed for the U.P.H.:—
DOXOLOGY 6, "From all that dwell."
DOXOLOGY 16, "Hallelujah!"
S.S., No. 4, "Great is the Lord."
    ,, No. 17, "God is a Spirit."
    ,, No. 22, "Worthy is the Lamb."
    ,, No. 24, "Great and marvellous."
    ,, No. 26 in F.C.H., is the same as No. 17 U.P.H.

Smith, Isaac, was clerk to the Alie Street Meeting, London; died about 1800; said to be the first Dissenting clerk that ever received for his services £20 per annum.

ST STEPHEN, originally named "Abridge," No. 144 U.P.P., 296 U.P.H., 144 P. and P., 153 S.P., is one of twenty-five tunes by him in 'A Collection of Psalm Tunes in Three Parts' he issued about 1770. The correct reading of the last strain is given in the U.P. collections and P. and P.

Smith, John Stafford, son of Martin Smith, organist of Gloucester Cathedral; born at Gloucester, 1750; baptised March 30; pupil of his father and Dr William Boyce; Gentleman of the Chapel Royal, 1784; vicar-choral of Westminster Abbey, 1794; organist of the Chapel Royal in succession to Dr Arnold, 1802; master of the choristers, 1805 till 1817; died September 21, 1836.

CHANT, No. 251 S.P. (252 being the minor form), is from his 'Twelve Chants, composed for the Use of the Choirs of the Church of England.'

S.S., No. 23 F.C.H., "Come unto me," is his composition, and appears in 'Anthems composed for the Choir-Service of the Church of England.' No date.

Smith, Robert Archibald, son of Archibald Smith and Ann Whitcher, was born at Reading, Berks, November 16, 1780, and baptised December 27 the same year, in St Lawrence parish. His father was a silk-weaver in Paisley, but owing to a depression of trade, had left that town, and settled at Reading in 1774. About a year and a half after, he married, and Robert was the only child of the marriage who survived. At a very early period he gave indication of his genius for music. As a little boy, he was noted for his performances on the rustic whistle, which was soon supplanted by a small German flute, which, in its turn, gave place to the violin. His father, not thinking that his musical talents would prove beneficial to him further than an innocent relaxation from labour, at once placed him in his own workshop. At weaving he proved a dull scholar, and the parent had often the mortification, after explaining the mysteries of the craft, to find, on looking up to observe whether due attention had been paid to his instructions, that his pupil was intently scratching musical notes with a pin on the framework of the loom. In 1800 his father returned to Paisley with his wife and child, and took to weaving muslin. Weaving was now doubly wearisome to Smith, as he was totally unacquainted with the management of a muslin web; his spirits sank under his daily toil, and a deep melancholy made inroads on his health. The parents wisely allowed him to give up weaving, and in 1803 he began teaching music, an employment that harmonised with his feelings. About the same time he married Mary McNicol, a native of Arran.[1] In 1807 he was appointed precentor and session-clerk of the Abbey Church, Paisley, having assisted Mr Love, his predecessor, from 1803. For this appointment, Smith was indebted to Dr Boog, then senior minister of the Abbey parish, who, being himself passionately fond of music, soon discovered his merits, and became one of his earliest patrons and friends. A choir was formed, and, under his judicious management, it soon became one of the best in the West of Scotland. At this time he made the acquaintance of the Rev. Dr Young, minister of Erskine, from whom he derived much assistance in the study of harmony. At an early period after his settlement in Paisley, Smith was introduced to the poet Tannahill, and the acquaintanceship thus formed gradually ripened into a warm and steady friendship, that was never interrupted in a single instance till the poet's death. It was in commemoration of a convivial meeting with Smith and other three kindred spirits that Tannahill carelessly threw into rhyme the song entitled "The Five Friends," in which he sketched off the former in these lines—

> "There is Rab, frae the south, wi' his fiddle and his flute,
> I could list to his strains till the starns fa' out."

In 1808 Smith published his setting of Tannahill's song—"Jessie, the Flow'r o' Dunblane"—which speedily ran through several editions, and made his name known far and wide. His first collection of Psalmody, entitled 'Devotional Music, Original and Selected,' was published in 1810, and nine years after, he issued

[1] Died at Lamlash, May 20, 1848, aged seventy-one years.

'Anthems in Four Vocal Parts.' He next undertook his great work, 'The Scottish Minstrel,' which was published in six volumes at intervals from 1821 to 1824. Smith was a member of the Paisley Volunteer Band, but this he gave up, having found that the playing of a wind instrument was prejudicial to his health; as a performer on the viola, however, he distinguished himself, and played that instrument at the Glasgow Musical Festival of 1821.

He had now been settled in Paisley for twenty-three years, and had long been anxious to remove to Edinburgh, as presenting a better field for his exertions. He was on intimate terms with Dr Andrew Thomson, minister of St George's Church there, and had assisted him in the compilation of 'Sacred Harmony, Part I., for the Use of St George's Church, Edinburgh,' 1820, contributing himself five tunes, two sanctuses, and two anthems. Dr Thomson was fully aware of Smith's worth as a leader and choirmaster, and on the resignation of Richard Atkinson as precentor of St George's on March 24, 1823, Smith was asked by the kirk-session if he would accept the appointment if it could be procured for him. His answer to this was a decided "Yes." The Lord Provost, Magistrates, and Town Council had next to be consulted, and at a meeting held on April 2, 1823, the following petition was read:—

"The Kirk-session of St George's parish take this opportunity through me, their Clerk, to solicit your Lordship and the Honourable Town Council that you will have the goodness to appoint Mr R. A. Smith, at present precentor and session-clerk of the Abbey Church of Paisley, to be Mr Atkinson's successor in St George's Church.

"Our minister, Mr Thomson, and all the members of the Kirk-session, are exceedingly desirous of improving the psalmody of the congregation, and of procuring an able musician as well as a person of respectable character to fill the vacancy.

"In contemplation of the present change occurring, we applied to Mr R. A. Smith, whom we know to be an individual of most excellent private character, no less than eminently distinguished as a musician, composer, and teacher of sacred music; and Mr Smith having signified his willingness to accept the office if it could be procured for him, we now humbly presume to hope that your Lordship and the Town Council will gratify us by appointing him to be our precentor. I conclude, therefore, by hoping that your Lordship and the Town Council will have the goodness to nominate Mr Smith to our precentor's desk, which I can confidently affirm will be a gratification to the Session and congregation at large; and I believe will be doing good service to the city itself by bringing into it a person of such admitted acquirements and respectability of character. (Signed) SIR ROBERT DUNDAS."

The request of the kirk-session being granted, Smith entered on his duties about the month of August, and soon endeared himself as much to the St George's congregation as he had done to the one he had just left. A marked improvement immediately took place in the psalmody of St George's Church—an improvement due in a great measure to the uncommon taste and skill which he displayed in conducting it. Between teaching, editing collections of psalmody and other works, he spent a busy life. He also appeared at the most important concerts given in Edinburgh and other parts of the country, and he even journeyed to York to take a place in the chorus at the Musical Festival of 1825, being possessed of a good tenor voice. In addition to the works already mentioned, he published 'Sacred Music, consisting of Tunes, Sanctuses, Doxologies, Thanksgivings, &c., Sung in St George's Church, Edinburgh,' 1825—second edition, carefully revised and improved, with considerable additions (1828); 'The Sacred Harmony of the Church of Scotland, in Four Vocal Parts, adapted to the Version of the Psalms, Paraphrases, Hymns, &c., used in the Presbyterian Churches,' (1828). The contents of these collections are much the same, but the last-named contains the larger number of tunes. Another publication, named 'Sacred Harmony,' which was issued in parts, is noticed below. His other works are,—'The Irish Minstrel, a Selection from the Vocal Melodies of Ireland, Ancient and Modern,' (1825); 'An Introduction to Singing, comprising various Examples, with Scales, Exercises, and Songs,' &c. (1826); 'Select Melodies, with appropriate Words, chiefly original, collected and arranged with Symphonies and Accompaniments for the Pianoforte (1827). As to his detached pieces, they are so numerous that to point them out would be an extremely difficult task.

Smith had by nature an exceedingly sensitive organisation of mind. For many years, too, this was increased by bodily ill health, which it was found impossible to subdue, and it at length triumphed over a frame that for a long period had been gradually debilitated by its almost incessant attacks. After being confined to bed for about a fortnight, he calmly expired at Edinburgh on the 3d of January 1829. The event, being quite unexpected except by his intimate friends, caused a deep sensation in the city and in the West of Scotland, where he was so generally known. His funeral was very numerously attended, and in its progress many persons—unasked—joined, and followed the body to the tomb in St Cuthbert's churchyard.

"Smith," says Mr George Hogarth, "was a musician of sterling talent. His merits have long been recognised, but the extreme modesty of his character prevented them being so fully appreciated as they ought; and his labours were only beginning to gain for him the reputation and emolument they deserved, when he was cut off by an untimely death. His compositions partake of the character of his mind; they are tender and generally tinged with melancholy, simple and unpretending, and always graceful and unaffectedly elegant. He had not the advantage of a regular musical education, or having his taste formed upon the classic models of the art. But there was in his mind a native delicacy, and an intuitive soundness of judgment, which enabled him to shun the slightest tendency to vulgarity, and to make his productions always fulfil his object, whatever it was. His melodies are expressive, and his harmonies clear and satisfactory. He had the admirable good sense to know how far he could safely penetrate into the depths of counterpoint and modulation without losing his way; and accordingly, his music is entirely free from that scientific pedantry which forms the prevailing vice of the modern English school. Mr Smith has enriched the music of our own country with many melodies which have deservedly become national, and will probably descend in that character from generation to generation in Scotland. His sacred music is uniformly excellent, possessing in a high degree the simplicity of design and solemnity of effect which this species of music requires. . . . His own personal exertions as precentor of St George's Church, and the example which that church has given, have already wrought a wonderful change in the muscial part of our church service." In any history of Scottish song or Scottish psalmody, Smith's name must ever be mentioned with profound respect.

St Lawrence, No. 139 S.P., 64 U.P.P., 134 P. and P., is one of fourteen tunes he composed for his 'Devotional Music' (1810). It is there set to Paraphrase 24, verse 1, and in Key E flat, and was probably named after the parish in which he was baptised. Another of the fourteen is his once popular tune "Hamilton."

S.S. No. 12 U.P.H., "How beautiful upon the mountains," was composed for the same work.

Invocation, No. 183 S.P., 102 U.P.P., 222 P. and P., and
Doxology, No. 14 U.P.H., "Lord, bless us still,"
S.S. "Blessed be the Lord," No. 8. U.P.H.,
St Mirren, No. 147 S.P., 220 U.P.P., 138 P. and P., and
Selma, No. 203 P. and P., 203 S.P., 72 U.P.P.,

were first published in his 'Sacred Music, . . . sung in St George's Church, Edinburgh,' 1825. The first-named, "Invocation," is indelibly associated with Psalm 43, 3. Since its publication in 1825, editors have been content to give it in their collections as composed by Smith; not so the editor of P. and P., who has most unwarrantably tampered with it. Possibly the tune has faults, but the writer ventures to say that Smith's tunes will have a more lasting place in the psalmody of the Church than some of the modern tunes that now fill our Hymnals. In the churches where this tinkered form is used, the effect can be better imagined than described. "Selma"—generally thought to be Smith's composition—is described in 'Sacred Music' as an "Ancient Scotish Melody noted in the Island of Arran and harmonized by Mr Smith." It is there set to Psalm 67, "Lord, bless and pity us."

MORVEN, No. 104 S.P., appears in No. VI. of 'The Edinburgh Sacred Harmony, for the Use of Churches and Families, consisting of Psalm and Hymn Tunes, Doxologies, Thanksgivings, and Dismissions,' and is described as an "Ancient Scotish Melody," and set to Psalm 142. The late Mr T. L. Hately, who in early life was a member of Smith's choir at St George's, Edinburgh, was of the opinion that Smith composed the tune. Smith's work, 'The Edinburgh Sacred Harmony' (folio size), was issued in something like ten numbers, at intervals of three months, but was not completed at his death. A supplementary number contains a lengthy preface (dated December 24, 1829), written, it is understood, by the Rev. Dr Andrew Thomson.

Smith, Samuel, son of Edward Woodley Smith, lay clerk of St George's Chapel, Windsor, and brother of Alfred Montem Smith and the late George Townsend Smith; born at Eton, August 29, 1821; in 1831 admitted as one of the Children of the Chapel Royal under William Hawes; pupil of Sir George J. Elvey; organist for a short time of Hayes Church, Middlesex; afterwards at Eton and Egham, where he remained twelve years; from December 1858 to October 1861 organist at Trinity Church, Windsor; and since 1861 at the Parish Church, Windsor.

RUTH, No. 254 F.C.H., 310 U.P.H., 299 S.H., was composed by him, while organist at Egham, to a harvest hymn of Dr Monsell's, the Vicar, "Earth below is teeming." It was first published in a small collection of tunes printed for private circulation, 1865, and afterwards appeared in 'Church Hymns,' edited by Sir Arthur Sullivan, 1874, set to the words with which it has become familiar, "Summer suns are glowing."

Smith, Thomas, son of Mr Thomas Smith; born at Arnold, Notts, February 20, 1832; pupil of Henry Farmer; teacher at Bury St Edmunds; appointed organist of St John's Church, Bury, 1873; since 1880 organist at Hozzinger, near Bury, the seat of the Marquis of Bristol; some time organising choirmaster to the Church Music Society for the Archdeaconry of Sudbury; author of 'Rules of Simple Harmony,' and other works; composer of many anthems, which have had an extensive circulation.

The following S.S. in U.P.H. were composed by him, the dates of composition being given in brackets :—

No. 77, "Behold a Virgin shall conceive" (1873).
No. 97, "Christ is risen" (1873).
No. 55, "O worship the Lord" (1875).
No. 51, "Thou crownest the year" (1873).

Soaper, John, chorister in St Paul's Cathedral under William Savage ; Gentleman of the Chapel Royal, and vicar-choral of St Paul's Cathedral ; died June 5, 1794, aged fifty-one ; buried in St Paul's Cathedral. He had considerable reputation as a vocalist.

CHANT No. 80 in U.P.P. and 263 in S.P., appears in Vandernan's Collection, 1770.

Southgate, Rev. Frederic, son of Mr Francis Southgate, solicitor ; born at Gravesend in Kent, October 7, 1824 ; educated as a boy at the Rev. Christian Lenney's school at Ramsgate ; afterwards entered his father's office, intending to study for the legal profession, which he subsequently abandoned for the Church ; graduated B.A. at Emmanuel College, Cambridge, 1848 ; ordained deacon in 1849, priest in 1850, and soon afterwards became curate at Castle Headingham, Suffolk ; a few years later, became incumbent of St Mark's, Rosherville, Kent ; in 1858 presented by the Crown with the living of Northfleet ; died there January 30, 1885. Amateur musician, and composer of several hymn tunes.

ST AGATHA, No. 52 S.H., is one of sixteen tunes composed by him and published in his collection entitled 'Favourite Hymn Tunes . . . used at St Botolph's Church, Northfleet, London,' 1873. It is there set to the hymn "Lord of mercy and of might."

Southgate, Thomas Bishop, born at Hornsey, Middlesex, June 8, 1814 ; educated in the school of the Chapel Royal, where he was a chorister ; studied harmony under Thomas Attwood and Sir John Goss, and the organ under Samuel Wesley ; organist of Hornsey Church from 1834 to 1853, and of St Anne's, Highgate Rise, London, from the latter year until his death, which occurred at Highgate, November 3, 1868.

EVENSONG, No. 320 F.C.H., was published in sheet form in 1858, set to the words "God that madest earth and heaven."

Spohr, Louis, Mus. Doc., son of Karl Heinrich Spohr, a physician ; born at Brunswick, April 5, 1784 ; at an early age showed musical talent ; studied harmony at Brunswick under

Hartung, and the violin under Kunisch and Maucourt; after travelling a great deal, he settled at Cassel in 1822, and was appointed director of the Court Theatre orchestra there, an office he held till 1857, when he retired on a pension; died at Cassel, October 22, 1859. Composer of operas, oratorios, and much instrumental music.

FLENSBURG, No. 82 F.C.H., 114 U.P.H., is adapted from the Andante in F in the Quartet in A minor for stringed instruments, Op. 58, No. 2. It appears as a hymn tune in Dr Gauntlett's 'Comprehensive Tune Book,' Second Series, 1851.

SPOHR, No. 153 P. and P., 136 S.H., 163 S.P., 90 F.C.H., and No. 42 U.P.H. (where it is given in a more extended form), is adapted from an air and chorus in his oratorio "Calvary," composed in 1835, and performed at Norwich in 1839.

HAYNE, No. 77 S.P., is adapted from a quartet and chorus, "Blessed are the departed," in his best known work, 'The Last Judgment,' first produced at Cassel in 1826, and in England at Norwich in 1830.

Stade, Sigmund Gottlieb, born at Nürnberg, 1607; from 1635 organist of the church of St Lawrence there; died in 1655.

DILHERR, No. 2 (Second Tune) F.C.H., "Hör' liebe Seel' dir ruft der Herr," is one of the melodies he furnished for the 'Seelen-musik' of his pastor, J. M. Dilherr.

Stadler, Maximilian, Abbé, born at Melk, Lower Austria, 1748; educated in the Jesuit College of Vienna; composer of psalms, masses, oratorios, &c.; the friend of Haydn and Mozart; died at Vienna, 1833.

S.S., No. 61 U.P.H., "Praise ye the Lord," is adapted from a movement in his oratorio "The Restoration of Jerusalem," composed in 1816. It was first published in its present form in Dr Lowell Mason's 'Hallelujah,' 1854.

Stainer, John, Mus. Doc., the son of a schoolmaster; born in London, June 6, 1840; when seven years of age, became a chorister at St Paul's Cathedral, and remained there eight or nine years, during which period several chants and an anthem of his composition were performed at the services; graduated as Mus. Bac., at Oxford, 1859; Mus. Doc., 1865; B.A. in 1863; M.A. in 1866; organist of St Benedict and St Peter, Paul's Wharf, London, 1854; St Michael's College, Tenbury, 1856; Magdalen College, Oxford, 1859; St Paul's Cathedral in succession to Sir John Goss, 1872; resigned 1888, and received the honour of knighthood; appointed in 1880 Principal of the National School of Music, and in 1883

Inspector of Music in Training Colleges; succeeded Sir F. A. G. Ouseley as Professor of Music in Oxford University, 1889; composer of the cantatas "Daughter of Jairus" and "Mary Magdalen," and of many anthems and services for use in churches and cathedrals.

CREDO, No. 73 (First Tune) S.H.;

THE BLESSED HOME, No. 265 (First Tune) S.H., 262 F.C.H.;

SEBASTE, No. 290 S.H., 332 F.C.H.;

ST FRANCIS XAVIER, No. 194 (First Tune) S.H.,—were published for the first time in the Revised and Enlarged Edition of 'Hymns Ancient and Modern,' 1875; and

CHARITY, No. 289 (First Tune) S.H., in the Appendix to that work, 1868.

SUDELEY, No. 167 S.P., was composed for the Rev. R. Brown-Borthwick's 'Supplemental Tune Book.'

The following Sentences were composed by him:—
No. 100 U.P.H., "Blessed is the man."
No. 103 U.P.H., "Hallelujah! what are these?"
No. 91 U.P.H., "My soul doth magnify the Lord."

The first is No. 23 of 'Short Anthems or Introits, by various Composers, for Particular Seasons and for General Use,' edited by the Rev. Walter Hook, M.A. (1871). The second was composed for the Dedication Festival of All Saints' Church, Lathbury, Bucks, 1871.

Stanley, Samuel, was born in Staffordshire about 1767. When twenty years of age he was made leader of the singing at Carr's Lane Meeting House, Birmingham. The congregation was small; but after 1796 it increased, and the singing grew into notice. In 1802 the music became famous; members of other congregations would often slip out of their own places of worship as soon as the sermon was over and run to Carr's Lane Meeting House, and hear the last hymn. Stanley played the violoncello; other instruments were used; and a choir of sixteen or twenty singers led the hearty song of the congregation. The congregation removing to a new chapel built in Steelhouse Lane in 1818, the last four years of Stanley's musical work were in connection with this chapel. It seems that the music here was the admiration and envy of all hearers. Stanley died October 1822. He was an excellent violoncello-player, and was in the band of the Birmingham Theatre, and of the Festival Choral Society from 1802 till 1818, and in the newspapers of the period his name always appears along with those of the best instrumentalists of the time. Among his pupils was Chattway, one of the best double-bass players in England, who succeeded him at Steelhouse Lane. Stanley's ideas of the correct mode of rendering Händel's music were quoted and obeyed at the meetings of the Festival Choir for a generation after his death. His tunes

DOVERSDALE (originally named "Stonefield"), No. 5 S.P., 160 U.P.; and

WARWICK, No. 175 S.P. and 133 U.P.P.,—were first published in 'The Appendix to Dr Watts' Psalms and Hymns, set to New Music,' a collection edited by Dr Edward Miller, 1800.

SHIRLAND, No. 205 in S.P., appeared in Stanley's 'Twenty-four Tunes, in Four Parts.' The first-named has been sadly mutilated in the S.P.

Statham, Rev. William, B.A., Mus. Doc., born at Tarporley Rectory, Cheshire, September 29, 1832; eldest son of the late Rev. Richard Jervis Statham, B.A., who was for thirty-five years Rector of Tarporley; educated at Marlborough; about 1856 graduated B.A. at University College, Durham; ordained to the curacy of Tunstall, 1858; since 1866 vicar of Ellesmere Port; degree of Mus. Doc., conferred on him by Durham University, 1876; composer of an oratorio "The Beauty of Holiness." His tune

ST MARGARET, No. 39 S.H., was first published in the Revised and Enlarged Edition of 'Hymns Ancient and Modern,' 1875.

Steggall, Charles, Mus. Doc., son of Mr Robert William Steggall; born in London, June 3, 1826; received his musical education at the Royal Academy of Music principally under Sir W. Sterndale Bennett; appointed a professor at that institution in 1851, and graduated Mus. Bac., and Mus. Doc., at Cambridge University in 1852; organist of Christ Chapel, Maida Hill, 1847; Christ Church, Paddington, London, 1855; organist of Lincoln's Inn since 1864; since 1882 examiner at Cambridge for the degree of Mus. Doc.; composer of much sacred music, and an organist of great ability.

BONAR, No. 136 F.C.H.;

CHRISTCHURCH, No. 152 F.C.H.; and

STEGGALL'S, No. 301 U.P.H.,

are from 'Hymns for the Church of England, with Proper Tunes' (1865).

ST AMBROSE (original name), No. 164 S.P., where it is also named "Steggall," 56 P. and P., there named "Calvary," was composed in 1847; and

ST CLEMENT, No. 199 U.P.H., in 1848, and published in his 'Church Psalmody' (1849).

TABOR, No. 351 U.P.H.; and

WESTMORELAND, No. 53 (Second Tune) U.P.H.,
were first published in 'Psalms and Hymns for Divine Worship' (Nisbet & Co.), 1867.

GROSVENOR, No. 30 S.H., was composed for Dr Maurice's 'Choral Harmony,' 1853.

Stevenson, Sir John Andrew, Mus. Doc., son of John Stevenson, a native of Glasgow, who settled in Dublin as a violinist; born in Dublin about 1762; chorister in Christ Church Cathedral, Dublin, 1771 to 1775; in St Patrick's Cathedral, 1775 to 1780; stipendiary in Christ Church, 1781; vicar-choral in St Patrick's, 1783; vicar-choral in Christ Church, 1800; received the honour of knighthood, 1803; graduated Mus. Doc., Trinity College, Dublin, 1791; died at the seat of his daughter, the Countess of Headfort, Meath, September 14, 1833.

VESPER HYMN, No. 295 (Second Tune) S.H., or "Vespers," No. 244 F.C.H. This melody is believed to be of Russian origin. It was published under the name of "Hark! the vesper hymn is stealing," in 'Popular National Melodies,' by Thomas Moore, arranged by Stevenson (1818).

HOWARD, No. 81 S.P., 92 P. and P., 108 U.P.P., and 158 U.P.H. About 1845 a copy of this tune in MS. was presented to the late Mr John Dobson of Richmond as being the composition of Sir John Stevenson. It was published in Bembridge's 'Psalmody' under the name of "Stevenson" about 1854. In the organist's MS. music-book at All Saints' Church, Derby, and in 'The Sacred Harp,' by Robert Burns, Glasgow, 1840, it is assigned to him. See Wilson, John.

Stewart, Sir Robert Prescott, Mus. Doc., born in Dublin, December 16, 1825; educated in the school of Christ Church Cathedral, where he was one of the children of the choir, and became in 1844 the organist; was appointed in the same year organist of the Chapel of Trinity College, and in 1852 a vicar-choral of St Patrick's Cathedral; graduated Mus. Doc. at Dublin University, 1851, and was appointed University professor in 1861; received knighthood in 1872, from the Lord Lieutenant of Ireland, Earl Spencer; composer of anthems, services, glees, and songs, also two cantatas. His tunes in S.H.,

ST AUDOËN, No. 131; ST HELENS, No. 163 (Second Tune); VESPERS, No. 287 (Second Tune); CŒLI ENARRANT, No. 315 (Second Tune), were composed for the 'Irish Church Hymnal,' 1874.

Stiastny (or Stiasny), Johann, son of Johann Stiastny, a distinguished hautboy-player; born at Prague in 1770 (1774?); member of the orchestra of the Theatre at Prague, and subsequently a conductor at Nürnberg and at Mannheim; date of death seems unknown; distinguished as a performer on the violoncello, and composer for that instrument.

STIASTNY, No. 117 (First Tune) S.H., is adapted from one of six solos composed by Stiastny for the violoncello.

Störl, Johann Georg Christian, born at Kirchberg in 1676; chapel-master and organist of the Stift (a kind of sacred college) at Stuttgart, where he died in 1743; composed much chamber and sacred music, and in 1711 edited a 'Choralbuch,' from which is taken

LUCERNE, No. 240 F.C.H., "Ruhet wohl, ihr Todtenbeine."

ALL SAINTS, Nos. 11 and 65 (Second Tunes) S.H., "Zeuch mich, zeuch mich mit den Armen" (No. 144). See Darmstadt Gesangbuch, 1698.

Strang, Walter, born at Edinburgh, December 26, 1825; in early life removed to the west of Scotland; studied music first under his schoolmaster, and afterwards under Mr Alfred McClure of Glasgow and Dr Joseph Mainzer, the latter appointing him leader of psalmody in St Bernard's Free Church, Edinburgh, when little more than eighteen years of age; studied under Edinburgh professors for a year or two, after which he went to London, continuing his studies under the late Dr John Hullah and Signor Crivelli, and while there taught classes in King's College and in the Royal Training College, Westminster (1847-48); returned to Edinburgh on being appointed Lecturer on Music in the Training College, Moray House, a position he still holds; from 1848 to 1885 conductor of psalmody in St George's Free Church, Edinburgh, and precentor to the General Assembly of the Free Church from 1867 to 1889; among other appointments Mr Strang has held the office of singing-master in George Watson's Ladies' College since its opening.

S.S., No. 18 F.C.H., "The sun shall be no more thy light by day," was composed for that work.

Strasburg Psalters.

The Strasburg Psalters began in 1525, and were continued in various editions for more than half a century. While resident at Strasburg in 1539, Calvin issued a Psalter which had for its title, "Aulcuns Pseaulmes et mys en Chant." This formed the basis of the Psalter afterwards issued at Geneva, the tunes being mostly

German, or borrowed from local sources. From these Psalters come the following tunes :—

LINTZ, No. 196 F.C.H.

STRASSBURG, No. 41 (Second Tune) F.C.H.

OLD 113TH, DOXOLOGY 10 U.P.H., is generally considered to be the composition of Matthäus Greitter of the Strasburg Cathedral. It is considerably reduced in the U.P.H.

Strattner, Georg Christoph, born at Ungarn in 1650; organist at the Chapel of the Prince of Durlach; afterwards chapel-master at Frankfort-on-the-Main, and at Weimar, where he died in 1705. He composed tunes for Neander's 'Bundes und Himmelslieder' in 1691, one of which is

STRATTNER, No. 316 (First Tune) S.H., 171 F.C.H., " Himmel, Erde, Luft und Meer" (page 136), where it is in 6-time. It appears in common time in Freylinghausen's 'Gesangbuch,' 1705; also in the Rev. John Wesley's 'Foundery Tunes,' 1742, this being perhaps its first appearance in an English collection. It is there named "Herrnhut Tune."

Sullivan, Sir Arthur Seymour, born in London, May 13, 1842; son of Mr Thomas Sullivan, a musician, a native of Cork; was a chorister in the Chapel Royal, 1854 to 1857; elected Mendelssohn scholar at the Royal Academy of Music, 1856; studied there under Sir John Goss and Sir W. Sterndale Bennett till 1858; afterwards at Leipzig under Plaidy, Moscheles, Richter, Rietz, and Hauptmann, from 1858 to 1861; organist of St Michael's, Chester Square, till 1867, and St Peter's, Cranley Gardens, London, till 1871; received the degree of Doctor in Music from the University of Cambridge 1876, and from Oxford University 1879; knighted May 15, 1883; universally known by his vocal and instrumental compositions.

LACRYMÆ, Nos. 137, 169 (First Tune) S.H.;
LUX MUNDI, No. 75 S.H.;
ST GERTRUDE, No. 142 S.H., 255 (First Tune) F.C.H.,
were composed for 'The Hymnary,' edited by Joseph Barnby, and published September 1872. The last-named appeared in 'The Musical Times,' December 1871.

CLARENCE, No. 304 S.H., 172 F.C.H., 313 U.P.H.;
CŒNA DOMINI, No. 226 (First Tune) S.H.;
EVELYN, No. 106 S.H.;
LITANY (No. 2), No. 167 (Second Tune) S.H.;
SAMUEL, No. 413 S.H., 345 F.C.H., 342 U.P.H.;
ST FRANCIS, No. 314 S.H.,

were first published in 'Church Hymns with Tunes,' which he edited in 1874, also the harmonies of—

LEOMINSTER, No. 248 (Second Tune) S.H., 318 U.P.H., and 147 F.C.H.; and

LITANY (No. 1), No. 167 (First Tune) and 381 S.H.

SALEM, No. 66 F.C.H., 156 U.P.P., there named "Evangel."

"Clarence" is marked "arranged," because the first and second lines were taken from another work of his.

"Litany" No. 2 was wrongly assigned in the first edition of the S.H. to the Rev. C. C. Scholefield.

NOEL, No. 29 S.H., 169 P. and P., 60 F.C.H., 32 U.P.H., is an old melody arranged and partly composed by him, and published as a sacred part-song (Boosey & Co.), 1871.

MOUNT ZION, No. 176 F.C.H., is one of three tunes he composed for 'Psalms and Hymns for Divine Worship' (Nisbet & Co.), London, 1867.

ECCLESIA, No. 146 F.C.H., and

CARROW, No. 305 F.C.H., are from 'The Congregational Psalmist.'

LUX EOI, No. 329 S.H., 229 F.C.H., first published in 'Hymns for the Church of England, with Proper Tunes.'

S.S., No. 38 U.P.H., "O love the Lord," was first published in 1864.

Summers, Joseph, Mus. Doc., youngest son of Mr George Summers of Charlton, Somersetshire; born 1843, and in early life was a chorister in Wells Cathedral, where he received a musical education as an organist under Mr C. W. Lavington; studied also under Dr Gauntlett, Sir W. Sterndale Bennett, and others; graduated Mus. Bac. at Oxford in 1863, but the degree was not conferred on him till 1887; appointed organist at St Andrew's College, Bradfield, in 1861; organist of the Parish Church of Weston-super-Mare in 1864; of St Peter's Church, Notting Hill, in 1865; emigrated to Melbourne in 1865, and for fourteen years filled the offices of choirmaster and organist of St Peter's Parish Church; in 1876 appointed Government Inspector of Music for State schools; acts as Musical Examiner for the Tasmanian Council of Education; also the Education Department of Victoria, and assists Professor Ives (late of Glasgow) as Examiner at the University of Adelaide; composer of cantatas, anthems, hymn tunes, and instrumental music, the bulk of which are still in MS.; degree of Mus. Doc. conferred on him by the Archbishop of Canterbury, 1890.

REFUGE, No. 261 S.H., was composed by him, and first published in 'The Bristol Tune Book,' 1863.

Sutcliffe, Alfred Lister, son of Mr Thomas Lister Sutcliffe; born at Leckhampstead, Bucks, November 13, 1859; studied music under the Rev. L. G. Hayne, Mus. Doc.; appointed organist of Bradfield Church, 1875, and of Mistley, with Bradfield, 1878. His tune

DEDHAM, No. 58 F.C.H. and 55 S.P.; and MANNINGTREE, No. 108 (First Tune) F.C.H., were first published in these works, and are named after places near Bradfield and Mistley.

Tallis, Thomas, one of the greatest of English musicians; flourished about the middle of the sixteenth century. He was a Gentleman of the Chapel Royal in the reigns of Henry VIII., Edward VI., and Mary, and organist to Elizabeth and of Waltham Abbey till its dissolution in 1540. Tallis composed many anthems, which were published in Barnard's Selected Church Musick,' 1641. He died November 23, 1585, and was buried in the chancel of the Parish Church of Greenwich. His tune

EVENING HYMN, No. 10 S.P., 285 S.H., 22 F.C.H., 302 U.P.H., is abridged from the eighth tune composed for Archbishop Parker's 'Whole Psalter translated into Englysh Metre,' about 1560. Thomas Ravenscroft (1621) reduced it to its present form, and set it to "A Psalme before Morning Prayer." Early in the last century it became associated with Bishop Ken's Evening Hymn, "All praise to Thee, my God, this night," after which it underwent great corruptions, the melody being altered and the canon omitted.

TALLIS, 168 S.P., 67 F.C.H., 70 and 123 U.P.P., 308 U.P.H., 101 and 189 S.H., 156 P. and P., was composed for the Ordination Hymn in Archbishop Parker's 'Psalter.' Of this tune the Rev. W. H. Havergal said, "A child may sing it, while manly genius will admire it." Compare it with Händel's "Solomon," No. 160 S.P. and 150 P. and P.

CHANT, No. 226 S.P., and 76 U.P.P., is an arrangement of the first Gregorian tone—formerly called "Christ Church" tune—for the "Venite" in his Full Service. The same chant is set to the following:—

S.S. in U.P.H., No. 128, "Lord, now lettest Thou Thy servant."
"   "   No. 125, "Our Father which art in heaven."
"   "   No. 114, "Remember now thy Creator."

Tans'ur, William, a noted psalmodist of last century, was born at Dunchurch, County Warwick, in 1699 or 1700. His baptism did not take place till 1706, as the following extract from the Dunchurch Records will show: "William Tanzer, the son of Edward and Joan Tanzer of Dunchurch, was baptized November 6, 1706." Tans'ur was author of numerous works on psalmody, several of which contain the earliest known copies of a few of our most popular psalm tunes. He dates his published works in 1737 from Barnes, in Surrey; in 1754 and 1776 from Cambridge; in 1756 and 1759 from Stamford, and in 1761 from Boston, Lincolnshire. He is said to have been living at Leicester in 1770. There are traces of him also at Ware, and here he married Elizabeth Butler on May 20, 1730. She died at Ware, January 9, 1767. He seems to have been at Witham, in Lincolnshire, as well as at Market Harborough, where he buried his son David, January 8, 1743. Later in life he adopted the name and style of William Le Tans'ur, Senior, *Musico Theorico*. He also styled himself Psalmodist, Philo Music and Theology, and Professor, Corrector, and Teacher of Musick above fifty years. He had a son who had been a chorister of Trinity College, Cambridge, and who joined his father as a teacher of music, and is said to have been living in 1811. The last forty years of Tans'ur's life were spent chiefly at St Neot's as a stationer, bookseller, and teacher of music. He died there October 2 or 7, and was buried October 9, 1783, aged eighty-three years. Tans'ur's 'A Compleat Melody; or, The Harmony of Sion,' 1736 (preface dated 1734), contains

BANGOR, No. 34 S.P. and 5 U.P.P., set to Psalm 11. It is wrongly referred in some collections to Thomas Ravenscroft's Psalter, 1621. The tune named "Bangor" there is a "Welsh Tune," and is totally different from that of Tans'ur's. John Holden's Collection, Glasgow, 1766, contains the earliest copy the writer has seen in a Scotch collection.

COLCHESTER, No. 62 P.P., 146 U.P.P., 50 S.P., is also there in the following form, under its present name, and given, as composed in four parts, W. T.:—

MELODY OF "COLCHESTER TUNE" IN TANS'UR.

St Andrew, No. 126 S.P., 128 U.P.P., 123 P. and P., is not in the above Collection, as indicated in S.P. and U.P.P., but appears in 'The New Harmony of Sion,' Book II., 1764, set to Psalm 150, named "Barby Tune," and given as "composed in four parts, W. T." These initials may merely indicate that the harmonies are by Taus'ur.

Tenney, John Harrison, son of John Tenney; born in Rowley, Essex County, Massachusetts, U.S.A., November 22, 1840; a self-taught musician; compiled, alone and in conjunction with others, upwards of eighteen volumes of sacred and secular music; for the last sixteen years honorary organist and choirmaster at the Congregational Church in Seinebrook Parish, Ipswich, U.S.A.

S.S., No. 30 F.C.H., 105 U.P.H., "I heard a voice from heaven," was published for the first time in the 'New York Musical Gazette,' June 1868. It was altered to its present form by Sir John Goss, and published in 'Congregational Church Music,' Enlarged Edition, 1871.

Teschner, Melchior, was precentor at Fraustadt, in Posen, about 1613, and subsequently pastor of Oberprietschen, near Fraustadt. His biography is obscure.

Theodulph or St Theodulph, No. 35, 109 and 240 (First Tunes) S.H., 336 U.P.H., 177 U.P.P., 201 F.C.H., there named

Vienna, is the chorale, "Valet will ich dir geben, du arge falsche Welt," composed by him about 1613.

Thom, Rev. Robert Riach, born at Montrose, December 16, 1831; educated at Montrose Academy, Edinburgh Free Church Normal School, and University; also at the English Presbyterian College, London; ordained at Exeter in 1861; successively minister at Worcester and of Free St David's, Glasgow, and since December 1876 of the Free High Church, Kilmarnock; amateur musician and composer; published in 1868 'A Manual of Praise,' which contains several original compositions; author of a large number of ballads and poems published by the Religious Tract Society.

S.S., No. 4 F.C.H., "He knoweth the way that I take," was composed for that work.

Thommen, Johann, precentor in St Peter's Church at Basel last century; held the office for forty-five years; died at Basel in 1783. Edited in 1745 'Erbaulicher musicalischer Liederschatz,' containing 500 hymns and about 275 melodies.

Cassel or Lucerne, No. 185 F.C.H., 17 and 303 (First Tune) S.H., 195 and 316 U.P.H., appears on page 173 of Thommen's work, set to the hymn

"O du Liebe meiner Liebe." This is a much earlier source than is usually given. In the Rev. Christian Gregor's 'Choral-Buch,' 1784, it is the chorale "O gesegnetes Regieren," No. 167A.

BATTY or TURNAU, No. 185 and 331 S.H., 220 (First Tune) F.C.H., there named.

GENEVA, No. 223 U.P.H., there named.

INVITATION, is also in Thommen's work, and will be found on page 275, No. 209, set to "Ringe recht, wenn Gottes Gnade," and in the following form:—

KEY F.

{| d :r |m .r :d .r |m :f |s .f :m |l :s |s :f .m |}
{| r :s .f |m :— |s :s |s :r |m :f |m :— |}
{| r :— |d :r |m .f :s .f |m :r |d :— ||

Dr Layriz, in his 'Kern des Deutschen Kirchengesangs,' 1854, refers this to the 'Gnadau Choralbuch,' 1735, but no such work exists. He doubtless means the 'Herrnhut Hymn Book' of 1735, prepared for use of the United Brethren at Gnadau; but that work has no tunes. The hymn "Ringe recht" appears on page 229. In the Rev. Christian Gregor's 'Choral-Buch enthaltend alle zu dem Gesangbuche der Evangelischen Brüdergemeinen,' 1784, it is set to the words "Glück, zu Kreuz, von ganzem Herzen," on page 10. As this tune is constantly referred to Freylinghausen's 'Gesangbuch,' 1714, it may be here remarked that the hymn to which it is sometimes set —viz., "Ringe recht, wenn Gottes Gnade"—appears there on page 515 without a tune, but at the heading there is reference to the melody "O! der Alles," which is totally different. It is also given by some as from J. B. König's Collection, 1738; but although the first line of the hymn, "Ringe recht," &c., appears in the index, neither hymn nor tune is found in that work.

Thomson,[1] **Rev. Andrew Mitchell**, son of the Rev. John Thomson; born at Sanquhar, Dumfriesshire, 1778, and baptised July 11; licensed by the Presbytery of Kelso, 1802, and in the same year ordained minister of the parish of Sprouston, Roxburgh-

[1] His son John, born October 28, 1805, died at Edinburgh, May 6, 1841, was appointed Professor of Music to Edinburgh University, being the first Professor under General Reid's bequest.

shire; married Miss Jane Carmichael of Greenock, April 26, 1802; in 1808 elected minister of the East Church, Perth, and in 1810 of New Greyfriars', Edinburgh; on the erection of St George's Church, Charlotte Square, Edinburgh, he was appointed by the Town Council minister of that church, and inducted June 16, 1814; degree of M.A. conferred on him by Edinburgh University, March 14, 1811; D.D., by Marischal College and University, Aberdeen, November 1, 1823; died suddenly, while returning from a meeting of Presbytery, February 9, 1831; buried February 15, close to St Cuthbert's churchyard, in a piece of ground which now belongs to the trustees of St John's Episcopal Church.

"He was one of those characters who appear only in an age. Though full of levity and frolic when a boy, yet, after devoting himself to the ministry, he became one of the most zealous, energetic, and eloquent, both in his country and town charges, more especially when occupied in his last. To the circulation of the Holy Scriptures in purity he devoted his majestic talent with overpowering effect in the 'Apocrypha Controversy,' and pleaded with surpassing and amazing oratory for the immediate abolition of slavery in the British colonies shortly before the termination of his earthly career."

Dr Thomson was an enthusiastic musical amateur, and composed many psalm tunes. In 1820 he published 'Sacred Harmony, for the use of St George's Church, Edinburgh,' in which will be found—

REDEMPTION, No. 223 P. and P., 184 S.P.; also

ST GEORGE'S, EDINBURGH, No. 224 P. and P., 185 S.P., and 189 U.P.P. The work contains other eleven original tunes by Dr Thomson.

Thorne, Edward Henry, born at Cranbourne, Dorset, May 9, 1834; pupil of Sir George J. Elvey; organist and choirmaster Parish Church, Henley-on-Thames, 1853 to 1863; Chichester Cathedral, 1862 to 1870 (entered on the duties of the office, February 1863); St Patrick's Church, Brighton, 1870 to 1873; St Peter's, Onslow Gardens, South Kensington, 1873 to 1875; since 1875 of St Michael's, Cornhill.

ST ANDREW, No. 144 (First Tune) S.H., was first published in the Revised and Enlarged Edition of 'Hymns Ancient and Modern,' 1875.

ST LAWRENCE, NEW, No. 145 U.P.H.; and SEPULCHRE, No. 49 (First Tune) U.P.H., were composed for and first published in the enlarged edition of 'A Selection of Psalm and Hymn Tunes, edited and arranged by E. H.

Thorne, and adapted to Psalms and Hymns compiled by the Rev. T. B. Morrell and the Rev. W. W. How,' 1862.

Tochter Sion.
A German collection of hymns and tunes published last century, in which appears, according to Dr Conrad Kocher,

FREIBURG, No. 159 S.H.

Tomlinson, Richard, born at Sheffield, August 22, 1822; a self-taught musician; choirmaster for the last thirty years of the Primitive Methodist Chapel at Heeley, near Sheffield; writer of hymns, anthems, and tunes, which he published under the following title: 'Original Tunes, Anthems, and Words, for Sabbath School Anniversaries, and Services of Song. . . . Arranged for the Pianoforte and Organ.' Part I., 1879; Part II., no date.

ST HILDA, No. 366 F.C.H., was composed by him in 1870, and published by the Sheffield Sabbath School Union on single slips.

Tours, Berthold, born December 17, 1838, at Rotterdam; pupil of his father, who was organist of the St Lawrence Church and Verhulst; afterwards studied at the Conservatories of Brussels and Leipzig; since 1861 resident in London; composer of many excellent songs, anthems, hymn tunes, and services. His tune

TOURS, No. 395 S.H., was composed in 1872, and published the same year in 'The Hymnary,' edited by Joseph Barnby. Its original key is F.

Troyte, Arthur Henry Dyke, born May 3, 1811; second son of Sir Thomas Dyke Acland, Bart. of Killerton, Devonshire; educated at Harrow School and Christ Church, Oxford, where he graduated in 1832; assumed the name of Troyte instead of that of Acland in 1852; died near Dorchester, June 19, 1857.

CHANT, No. 245 (Second Tune) S.H., 271 S.P., 174 and 234 U.P.H., 50 U.P.P., 276 F.C.H., is his composition, and was first published in the 'Salisbury Hymn Book,' 1857.

CHANT, No. 334 and 355 U.P.H., 262 (Second Tune) and 386 S.H., 284 and 373 F.C.H., 272 S.P., is an adaptation by him from a chant composed by Dr William Hayes.

Turle, James, son of Mr James Turle; born at Somerton, county Somerset, March 5, 1802; chorister at Wells Cathedral from July 1810 to December 1813. He was afterwards articled as a pupil to an uncle of Sir John Goss; organist of Christ

Church, Blackfriars, Surrey, 1819 to 1829; next of St James's, Bermondsey, London, to 1831; acted as assistant to George Ebenezer Williams, organist of Westminster Abbey, and afterwards became the permanent deputy of Thomas Greatorex, Williams's successor. On the death of Greatorex, July 1831, Turle, who was then only twenty-nine, was appointed organist and master of the choristers by Dean Ireland. Turle acted as organist at some of the great English musical Festivals, notably the one held at Norwich in 1839, when Spohr's oratorio "Calvary" was produced under the direction of the composer. He was also one of the organists at the Händel Festival held in Westminster Abbey in 1834; and the Earl of Mount Edgcumbe, in his 'Musical Reminiscences' of that year, praised his playing very highly. Turle retired from active duty at the Abbey on September 26, 1875, when his Service in D was sung, but he retained a titular connection with the sacred building, and lived in his cloister-house till his death, which took place on June 28, 1882.

His works consist of Church services, anthems, organ music, &c. He compiled 'The People's Music Book' in conjunction with Professor Taylor, 1844, and the 'Westminster Chant Book,' and was editor of 'Psalms and Hymns for Public Worship; with Appropriate Tunes,' published by the Society for Promoting Christian Knowledge, London, 1862. For the latter work he composed—

CLOISTERS, No. 49 S.P.

ST JOHN'S, WESTMINSTER, No. 65 F.C.H.

ST PETER'S, WESTMINSTER, No. 245 F.C.H., 70 U.P.H.

WESTMINSTER, No. 176 S.P., 54 F.C.H., 9 and 89 U.P.H., 161 P. and P., 217 U.P.P., was composed for 'The Psalmist,' and appears in Part II., 1843, being there named "Birmingham."

TURLE, No. 265 U.P.H., from 'The Hymnary,' edited by Joseph Barnby, 1872.

CHANTS No. 28 U.P.P. and 253 S.P. are his, and appear in 'Chants as used in Westminster Abbey,' which he edited.

Turner, William, born 1651[1]; son of Charles Turner, cook of Pembroke College, Oxford; chorister of Christ Church, Oxford, under Edward Lowe, and afterwards of the Chapel Royal under Captain Henry Cooke; lay vicar and master of the choristers

---

[1] The writer is unable to verify this date, although the Baptismal Records of Pembroke College and Christ Church have been carefully searched at his instigation.

of Lincoln Cathedral, 1667; on October 11, 1669, he was sworn in as a Gentleman of the Chapel Royal, and soon afterwards became a vicar-choral of St Paul's, and a lay vicar of Westminster Abbey; graduated as Mus. Doc. at Cambridge in 1696; died at his house in Duke Street, Westminster, January 13, 1739-40, aged eighty-eight, having survived his wife, with whom he had lived nearly seventy years, only four days, she dying on January 9th, aged eighty-five. They were buried January 16th in one grave, in the west cloister of Westminster Abbey. Turner's compositions consist principally of anthems and church services.

EGHAM, No. 188 P. and P. It is questionable if this tune is by Dr Turner, as it is not found in the collections to which he contributed. In the 'Temple Tune Book,' Division I., it is assigned to him by the editor (Dr E. J. Hopkins), but nothing is said as to its source. Probably Dr Hopkins followed Dibdin, who ascribes it to Turner in his 'Standard Psalm Tune Book,' 1852.

Turpin, Edmund Hart, Mus. Doc., born at Nottingham, May 4, 1835; pupil of Charles Noble of Nottingham and others; organist of St Barnabas Catholic Church, Nottingham, from 1850 to 1864, performing by deputy from 1857, when he removed to London; organist of St George's, Bloomsbury, from 1869 to 1888; now organist of St Bride's, Fleet Street; editor of the 'Musical Standard' from 1880 to July 1886, and again from 1889 to 1890; editor of 'Academic Gazette,' and 'Organ World,' in connection with 'Musical World'; Honorary Secretary of the College of Organists since 1875; degree of Mus. Doc. conferred on him by the Archbishop of Canterbury, 1889; a distinguished living organist. His tune

ARGYLE, No. 322 S.H., was composed about 1866; and EYNSHAM, No. 340 S.H., in 1872. Both were published for the first time, December 1872, in a Collection he edited entitled 'Hymn Tunes.'

Turton, Rev. Dr Thomas, Bishop of Ely, born in Yorkshire in 1780, or, according to some, 1782; educated at Cambridge, and in 1805 proceeded B.A., being Senior Wrangler; in 1806 elected a Fellow of his College, and in the following year succeeded to the office of tutor; proceeded M.A. in 1808, and served the office of Moderator for the years 1810, 1811, 1812. In 1816 graduated as B.D., and in 1830 obtained the Deanery of Peterborough, an office he held until 1842, when he was appointed Dean of Westminster; in 1845 raised to the See of Ely, and died holding that office, January 7, 1864. Amateur musician and composer.

Ely, No. 8 S.P., 25 F.C.H., 223 U.P.P.; 6, 224, and 361 U.P.H.; 3, 34 (Second Tune), and 334 S.H., was composed in 1844, and published the same year in 'The People's Music Book,' edited by James Turle and Professor Edward Taylor. It is there named "St Catherine," and set to a version of Psalm 100, " With one consent let all the earth."

St Cyriac, No. 107 U.P.P., was composed in 1862; and

St Ethelreda, No. 131 S.P., 102 F.C.H., 100 U.P.P., 127 P. and P., 153 (First Tune) S.H., in 1860. Both appear in 'Psalms and Hymns, with appropriate Tunes,' published by the Society for Promoting Christian Knowledge, and edited by James Turle, 1862.

Tye, Christopher, graduated as Mus. Bac. at Cambridge in 1537; proceeded Mus. Doc. 1545, and in 1548 was admitted *ad eundem* at Oxford. Recent investigations by W. B. Squire, Esq., show that Tye was in orders, and held successively the rectories of Little Wilbraham, Newton, and Doddington-cum-March. He was at Wilbraham in 1564, and on September 12, 1567, John Walker was presented to the living on his resignation. On March 15, 1570, the rectory of Newton was conferred on George Bacon on Tye's resignation, and on March 15, 1572, Hugh Bellet was presented to the living of Doddington-cum-March on the death of Tye. He was a Gentleman of the Chapel Royal in 1545; musical preceptor to King Edward VI., and organist of Ely Cathedral from 1541 till 1562. In Samuel Rowley's play, " When you see me you know me, or the Famous Chronicle Historie of King Henry VIII., with the Birth and Virtuous Life of Edward, Prince of Wales,' 1605, occurs the following reference to Tye:—

> " England one God, one truth, one doctor hath
> For Musicke's art, and that is Doctor Tye,
> Admired for skill in musicke's harmony."

Anthony Wood states that Tye restored church music after it had been almost ruined by the dissolution of the monasteries. In 1553 Tye published 'The Actes of the Apostles, translated into Englishe Metre, with Notes to eche Chapter.' The first fourteen chapters only were published. From Tye's work come several of our best known tunes.

Apostle's Tune, No. 220 P. and P., is the music to chapter iv., the first verse of which runs thus:—

> " When that the people taught they had,
>   There came to them doutles;
> Priests rulers as men nye mad,
>   And eke the Saduces,

Whome it greued that they should mouve
The people and them leave
That Jesus Christ by powre aboue
Should ryse up from the deade."

DUNDEE, No. 57 S.P., 1 U.P.P., 69 P. and P. This is an adaptation from Tye's work already quoted, as will be seen by comparing it with the extract given below, which is the treble part of the music set to chapter iii. To the Rev. Henry Parr belongs the credit of observing this:—

In Damon's 'Music to the Psalms,' 1591, it is harmonised in four parts, and set to Psalm 116. It is not in Damon's earlier work of 1579. As no complete set of parts of this book is known to exist, the melody only can be quoted:—

TYE. 285

"DUNDEE" AS IN DAMON'S PSALMS, 1591.

KEY C (Lah is A).

```
{ |   :    :    :    :l   :—  :l   :t   :d¹  :—  :—  :t   }
{ :l  :l   :—  :se  :    :d¹  :m¹  :—  :r¹  :d¹  :—  :t   }
{ :d¹ :—  :    :    :d¹  :m¹  :r¹  :d¹  :t   :l   :l   }
{ :se :—  :    :    :    :    :    :l   :d¹  :t   :—  }
{ :l  :—  :se :l   :—  :    :    :    :d¹  :m¹  :r¹  :d¹  }
{ :t  :l   :l   :se  :—  :    :    :    :    :l   :d¹  }
{ :t  :—.l :l   :—  :se  :l   :—  :—  :l   :l   :—  :—  :—  ‖
```

In 'The Whole Booke of Psalmes,' by Thomas Este, 1592, it appears without a name, set to Psalm 116, the melody in the tenor as shown below, and the harmony by G. Kirbye:—

286 BIOGRAPHICAL SKETCHES.

Key F.

f	:—		s	:m	—	:r	—	:de	r	:f		m	:—		
l₁	:—		ta₁	:s₁	l₁	:—	—	:m₁	l₁	:l₁		l₁	:—		
r	:—		r	:m	f	:—	m	:—	r	:r		de	:—		
r	:—		s₁	:d	l₁	:—	—	:-.s₁	f₁	:r₁		l₁	:—		

	:d	f	:—	m	:l	s	:—	f	:—	d	:f	—	:r
	:l₁	r	:—	t₁	:l₁,d	d.ta₁:s₁		l₁	:—	l₁	:d	—	:ta₁
	:f	l	:—	s	:f	—	:m	f	:—	f	:l	—	:s
	:f₁	r₁	:—	m₁	:f₁	d	:—	f₁	:—	f₁	:f₁	—	:s₁

l	:-.s	f	:s	m	:—	r	:m	—	:f	s	:m	fe	:—
l₁	:de	r	:ta₁	l₁	:—	l₁	:l₁	—	:l₁	ta₁	:l₁	l₁	:—
f	:m	r	:r	de	:—	f	:m	—	:r	r	:de	r	:—
r₁	:l₁	ta₁	:s₁	l₁	:—	r	:de	—	:r	s₁	:l₁	r₁	:—

In Thomas Ravenscroft's 'The Whole Booke of Psalmes,' . . . 1621, it is set, as shown below, to Psalm 108, and named "Windsor or Eton," and called an "English Tune," the harmony being by Ravenscroft, and the melody in the tenor:—

TYE.

KEY F.

$$\left\{\begin{array}{l}
\text{f :— :f :m :r :— :de :— :r :f :m :— | :f} \\
\text{l}_1\text{ :— :l}_1\text{ :l}_1\text{ :l}_1\text{ :— :l}_1\text{ :— :l}_1\text{ :l}_1\text{ :l}_1\text{ :— | l}_1\text{ :d} \\
\text{r :— :r :m :f :— :m :— :r :r :de :— | f :l} \\
\text{r}_1\text{ :— :r :de :r :— :l}_1\text{ :— :f}_1\text{ :r}_1\text{ :l}_1\text{ :— | f}_1\text{ :—}
\end{array}\right\}$$

$$\left\{\begin{array}{l}
\text{:f :m :l :s :f :— | l :— :f :m :r :— :l :—} \\
\text{:— :d :d :—.ta}_1\text{:l}_1\text{ :— | l}_1\text{ :— :d :d :l}_1\text{ :— :d :—} \\
\text{:— :s :f :m :f :— | f :— :l :s :f :— :m :—} \\
\text{:f}_1\text{ :d :l}_1\text{ :d :f}_1\text{ :— | :f}_1\text{ :f}_1\text{ :d :r :— :l}_1\text{ :—}
\end{array}\right\}$$

$$\left\{\begin{array}{l}
\text{:f :s :m :— | l :s :— :f :s :m :fe :— :— :— ‖} \\
\text{:ta}_1\text{ :ta}_1\text{ :l}_1\text{ :— | d :d :— :l}_1\text{ :ta}_1\text{ :l}_1\text{ :l}_1\text{ :— :— :—} \\
\text{:r :r :de :— | f :m :— :r :r :de :r :— :— :—} \\
\text{:ta}_1\text{ :s}_1\text{ :l}_1\text{ :— | f}_1\text{ :d :— :r :s}_1\text{ :l}_1\text{ :r}_1\text{ :— :— :—}
\end{array}\right\}$$

In the 'Scottish Psalter,' published by Andro Hart in 1615, it is named "Dundie Tune," and the melody only is given, of which the following is a copy, the modern clef being used:—

KEY F (Lah is D).

$$\{ \text{l}_1\text{ :— :l}_1\text{ :t}_1\text{ :d :t}_1\text{ :l}_1\text{ :l}_1\text{ :s}_1\text{ :— : : : }\}$$
$$\{ \text{: :d :— :m :r :d :r :d :— : : : }\}$$
$$\{ \text{:d :— :m :r :d :t}_1\text{ :l}_1\text{ :l}_1\text{ :s}_1\text{ :— : : }\}$$
$$\{ \text{: : :d :— :t}_1\text{ :l}_1\text{ :l}_1\text{ :s}_1\text{ :l}_1\text{ :— :— :— ‖}\}$$

As will be observed, a slight difference occurs in the second strain, and the leading note is omitted in the first, third, and fourth strains.

In Raban's Psalter, published at Aberdeen in 1633, the accidental was restored to the penultimate note of the last strain, and throughout the tune in the 'Scottish Psalter' of 1635. (See Scottish Psalters.)

GETHSEMANE, No. 41 U.P.H., 179 F.C.H., is adapted from the tune which is set to chapter xii., beginning—

> " And in that tyme Herode the Kynge,
> He dyd his hand let slyp,
> To trouble men of good living
> And Godlye fellowship," &c.

SOUTHWARK, No. 151 P. and P., 161 S.P., 53 F.C.H., 154 U.P.P., 94 U.P.H., consists of the first four strains of the tune that is set to chapter viii., and

WINCHESTER, No. 165 P. and P., 178 S.P., 23 and 203 S.H., 291 and Doxology 2 U.P.H., is certainly adapted from the second half of the tune set to the same chapter. This fact has not been noticed elsewhere. (See Este, Thomas.)

SECOND HALF OF TUNE SET TO CHAPTER VIII.

Tyrolean Air.

EDEN, No. 435 S.H.

Ulenberg, Rev. Caspar, born 1549 at Lippstadt, in Westphalia, of Lutheran parents; educated 1567 to 1569 in Brunswick, and completed his studies at the University of Wittenberg; went over to the Catholic Church in 1572, and in the same year became teacher in the Gymnasium at Cologne; in 1575 took holy orders, and became minister of Kaiserswerth; in 1583 canon of St Swibert's; from 1593 to 1615 director of the Gymnasium in Cologne, where he died as minister of St Cunibert's, February 16, 1617. Edited, in 1582, the Psalms of David, from which is taken

EBER, No. 189 U.P.H. It is there set to Psalm 6, and will be found on pages 16 and 17. A second edition appeared in 1606, where the tune will be found set to the same Psalm, on pages 18, 19, 20, and 21.

Urhan, Chrétien, born at Montjoie, near Aix-la-Chapelle, February 16, 1790; in early life showed great aptitude for music;

the Empress Josephine having heard him perform in 1805, caused him to be instructed in composition by Lesueur at Paris; became famed for his performances on the Viola d'amour, Meyerbeer having written the solo for that instrument in the "Huguenots" specially for Urhan; solo violinist in the orchestra of the opera; organist for some years of St Paul's Church; died at Belleville, near Paris, November 2, 1845.

RUTHERFORD, No. 235 U.P.H., 213 F.C.H., 266 S.H., is an altered copy of the following tune, which is set to Cantique 52 in 'Chants Chrétiens,' Paris, 1834, and there assigned to Urhan. It appears in its present form in 'Psalms and Hymns for Divine Worship' (Nisbet & Co.), 1867, and was adapted and harmonised by Dr Rimbault. One would like to know for what reason the harmony at the close of the second-last strain of this popular tune has been altered in the S.H. from that given in the U.P. and F.C. Hymnals, which is Dr Rimbault's. The writer had occasion, some time ago, to hear it sung in a parish church by a mixed congregation, and, to say the least of it, the effect was most unpleasant:—

ORIGINAL FORM OF TUNE "RUTHERFORD."

KEY F.

{ :m .m | m :— | r :— .r | d :— | — :d | f :— .f | m :f }

{ | m :— | r :r | s :— .s | f :— .f | m :— .m | r :— .r | d :— }

{ | t₁ :— | d :— | :d .d | d :— | d :— .r | m :— | — :d .d }

{ | d :— | d :— .r | f :— | m :m .f | s :— | l :— .s | s :— }

{ | f :— | m :m a | r :— .d | d :— | ‖

Viner, William Litton, born at Bath, May 14, 1790; studied music under Charles Wesley; appointed organist of St Michael's Church, Bath, about 1820; resigned 1838, in which year he became organist of St Mary's, Penzance, Cornwall, a post he held till 1859; died at Westfield, Massachusetts, U.S.A., July 24, 1867. He composed and published songs, anthems, and hymn tunes, as well as several compositions for the organ, the pianoforte, and the harp; edited 'A Useful Selection from the most approved Psalms,' '100 Psalm and Hymn Tunes in Score,' and 'The Chanter's Companion.'

KINGSTON, No. 355 F.C.H. and 343 in U.P.H., was composed by Viner at Penzance to "Lord, dismiss us with Thy blessing." It is "inserted by permission of the Author" in Edwin Flood's 'Psalmodist' (1845), where it is named "Helston," and set as long metre.

Vulpius, Melchior, born at Wasungen, in Thuringia, 1560; about 1600 became precentor at Weimar; died there 1616, or, according to some, 1621. Published in 1604 a valuable collection of hymns with tunes, one of which is

LUSATIA, No. 359 F.C.H., 229 (Second Tune) S.H., "Weltlich' Ehr' und zeitlich Gut." From the second edition, published in 1609, come

BREMEN, No. 197 F.C.H., 85 (Second Tune), 118 (First Tune), 337 (Second Tune) S.H., 164 U.P.H., there named HEIDELBERG, "Christus, der ist mein Leben."

VULPIUS, No. 5 F.C.H, "Die helle Sonn' leucht jezt herfür."

WEIMAR, No. 191 F.C.H., 51 and 166 (Second Tune) S.H., 78 U.P.H., there named HEBRON, "Jesu, deine Passion."

Wade, James Clifft, born at Coven, Staffordshire, January 26, 1847; pupil of Drs Winn and Bradford; organist at Coven, 1860 to 1865; organ student at Birmingham, 1865 to 1866; organist Parish Church, Iver, near Uxbridge, 1867 to 1869; organist to W. S. Dugdale, Esq., Merevale, Warwickshire, 1869 to 1875; since 1880 organist and choirmaster of St Mary's Church, Maidenhead, Berks; conductor of the Orchestral Society there.

IVER, No. 273 F.C.H., was composed in 1867.

HOLY CROSS, No. 79 S.P., was adapted by him from an anonymous organ "Andante," which was said to be based on a theme by Mozart.

Wainwright, John, son of John Wainwright, "Joyner," and Mary Heginbotham, his wife; born at Stockport; baptised April 14, 1723; said to have been organist of that parish for some time, but of this there is no record; resident in Manchester in 1757; officiated as deputy or assistant organist of the Collegiate Church for several years; appointed to that post, May 12, 1767; was an able performer on the violin and organ. The celebrated Joah Bates used to say that the first notion of his own grand style of organ-playing was received "from hearing old Wainwright at the Collegiate Church;" buried at Stockport, January 28, 1768.

YORKSHIRE, No. 376 in the Scottish Hymnal of 1872, is his composition, although there, and in many other Hymnals, assigned to his son, Dr Wainwright. It was published in 1766 in his 'Collection of Psalm Tunes, Anthems, Hymns, and Chants, for One, Two, Three, and Four Voices,' and is associated with Byrom's hymn, "Christians, awake, salute the happy morn."

Wainwright, Robert, Mus. Doc., son of John Wainwright; succeeded his father at the Collegiate Church; accumulated the degrees of Bachelor and Doctor in Music at Oxford University, April 29, 1774, on which occasion a grand Te Deum of his composition was performed; appointed organist of St Peter's, Liverpool (now the Cathedral), March 1, 1775; celebrated for the great rapidity of his execution on the organ; composed oratorios, anthems, and services; died July 15, 1782, aged thirty-four years.

LIVERPOOL, No. 106 P. and P.; and MANCHESTER, No. 127 U.P.P., 96 S.P., 108 P. and P., are first found in Richard Langdon's 'Divine Harmony,' 1774, where they are without names. They receive the above titles in Harrison's 'Sacred Harmony,' vol. i., 1784; vol. ii., 1791.

ST GREGORY, No. 135 U.P.P., 135 S.P., 132 P. and P., appears under that name in 'A Collection of Original Psalm Tunes, for Three and Four Voices. . . . By Samuel Webbe, Senior and Junior.' It has been sadly tinkered in the S.P.

In 1766 Wainwright competed for the situation of organist at Halifax. Dr Edward Miller, in his 'History of Doncaster,' tells the story of the contest to the following effect: A new organ by Snetzler had been erected in the Parish Church, and was opened with an oratorio by Mr Joah Bates. There were seven candidates for the situation of organist, among whom were Robert Wainwright and F. W. Herschel, then leader of the concerts at Halifax, and an intimate friend of Dr Miller. Concerning the others we have no information. On the day of trial, August 30, they attended at the church, and the order in which they were to play was decided by lot. The second was drawn by Wainwright, and the third by Herschel. Wainwright's execution was so rapid that old Snetzler ran about exclaiming, "Te tevil, te tevil, he run over te key like one cat; he vil not give my piphes room for to shpeak!" During this performance, Miller said to Herschel, "What chance have you to follow this man?" He replied, "I don't know, but I am sure fingers will not do." In due time he ascended the gallery, and drew from the organ such a full volume of slow solemn harmony as Miller could by no means account for. After a short extempore effusion of this character, he finished with the Old Hundredth tune, which he played better than his opponent had done. "Ay, ay!" cried Snetzler, "tish is very goot, very goot inteet; I will luff tish man, for he gives my piphes room for to shpeak." Herschel being afterwards asked by Miller by what means he had produced so uncommon an effect, answered, "I told you fingers would not do," and taking two pieces of lead from his waistcoat-pocket, he said, "One of these I placed on the lowest key of the organ, the other on the octave above; thus, by accommodating the harmony, I gained the power of four hands instead of two." Herschel was thereupon appointed, but soon after entered upon other pursuits, and the musician has been long forgotten in the astronomer.

Wainwright, Richard, brother of the preceding; some time organist of the Collegiate Church, and St Ann's, Manchester; succeeded Dr Wainwright at St Peter's, Liverpool, September 1782; afterwards organist of St James's, Toxteth Park; reappointed to St Peter's, 1813; wrote many psalm tunes, and some popular glees; is said to have excelled in left-hand execution; died August 20, 1825, aged sixty-seven. His tune

WAINWRIGHT, No. 196 S.H., appears in 'A Collection of Hymns, with appropriate Symphonies and Accompaniments, as originally composed for the Children of the Liverpool Blue Coat Hospital' (about 1790). Its original name is "Newmarket," and it was first published to "My God, and is Thy table spread?" In Harrison's 'Sacred Harmony,' vol. ii., 1791, it is wrongly assigned to Dr Wainwright.

The following anecdote is related of him: Being one evening at a tavern in Liverpool, as he sat with his left arm hanging over the back of the seat, a man who owed him some grudge came in, and going stealthily behind, caught hold of the extended hand, and forced several fingers back so as to dislocate them. The offender was immediately seized by those present, but Wainwright said, "Let him go; God forgive him." The injured members were thenceforward useless; yet such was Wainwright's skill, that he continued to perform with effect. An old singer who related this to the Rev. Henry Parr, added, "Ay, so long as a Wainwright was in the town, there was never a man fit to hold a candle to him."

Walch, James, son of Mr John Walch; born at Egerton, near Bolton, June 21, 1837; pupil of his father, and lastly of Henry Smart; in 1851 appointed organist of Dukes Alley Congregational Church, Bolton; in 1857 of Walmsley Church; in 1858 of Bridge Street Wesleyan Chapel, both of which appointments he held at the same time; in 1863 of St George's Parish Church, Bolton; in 1870 appointed conductor of the Bolton Philharmonic Society; in 1874 retired from the musical profession; since 1877 honorary organist of the Parish Church, Barrow-on-Furness.

SAWLEY, No. 157 S.P., and 80 F.C.H., was composed in 1857 for a children's anniversary, and published in 1860 with other tunes for private circulation. It was wrongly assigned, in the earlier editions of the F.C.H., to the Rev. F. Pigou.

Wallis, Ebenezer John, amateur musician and composer; born in London, May 9, 1831; died at Sutton-at-Hone, Kent, October 26, 1879.

BAROSSA, No. 2 S.P., 31 F.C.H., was composed for use in Heath Street Baptist Chapel, Hampstead, and afterwards revised and published in 'Anthems, Canticles, and Hymns,' 1869.

Warren, Samuel P——,[1] son of Mr S. R. Warren, organ-builder; born in Montreal, Canada, February 18, 1841; studied at Berlin under Haupt and others, 1861 to 1864; returned to Montreal in 1864, and in 1865 became organist of All Souls Church, New York, till 1868; now organist of Grace Church there; composer of church services, anthems, and songs.

MONICA, No. 91 U.P.H., is adapted from a tune named "Dana," composed by Warren, and published in 'The Church Hymn Book, with Tunes,' New York and Chicago, 1872. The adaptation was made by the Rev. Dr Andrew Henderson, Paisley.

Watson,[2] **James,** born at Glasgow, June 10, 1816; received his education at the Grammar School there, under Dr Angus, and afterwards at the High School, under Dr Dymock; removed to London in 1832, but returned to Scotland in 1838; about 1844 became joint editor, with Dr Horatius Bonar, of the weekly newspaper the 'Border Watch' (now the 'Border Advertiser'), to advocate the spread of Free Church views; in 1845 became a partner in the well-known firm of James Nisbet & Co., publishers, London, and at Mr Nisbet's death, chief partner; member of the London School Board from 1870; died in London, September 1, 1880, and buried in Highgate Cemetery. His tune

HOLYROOD, No. 84, 157 (Second Tune), 422 S.H., 134 and 346 F.C.H., and 267 U.P.H., was composed about 1865, and published anonymously in 'Psalms and Hymns for Divine Worship,' 1867. In the editing of this collection for the English Presbyterian Church he had a large share, and published the work at his own risk.

Watts, Joseph Virgo, born at Wotton-under-Edge, Gloucestershire, June 27, 1822; pupil of Hullah, Mainzer, and George William Martin; at ten years of age appointed organist of the Independent Chapel, Kingswood, Gloucestershire; afterwards successively organist of the following parish churches in the same county: Chromhall, Lydney, and Berkeley; Midsomernorton, Somersetshire; Box Parish Church, Wilts; afterwards removed to Bath, and was organist of All Saints Chapel for six years; of Kensington Episcopal Chapel for a similar period; of Laura Chapel, and finally obtained the important position of choirmaster at Bath Abbey; teacher of music at King Edward's College for twenty years, and the Wesleyan

---

[1] This name cannot be ascertained.

[2] Those who wish a fuller account of this Christian gentleman's career will find it in 'The Weekly Review' for September 11, 1880.

College for six years; retired from the musical profession in 1885. His tune

OLIVET, No. 115 S.P., was first published in 'Original Hymn Tunes, Chants, Kyries, and Chant Services,' which he published in 1876.

Weale, William (or **Wheall**), graduated Mus. Bac., at Cambridge in 1719. He was organist at St Paul's Church, Bedford, and probably received that appointment when the organ was erected by Gerard Schmidt in 1715. Weale's biographers, without exception, give his year of death as 1745; but this is far wide of the correct date, which is here given as entered in the Burial Register of St Paul's, Bedford: "Sept. 4, 1727, Bury'd Mr William Weale, Organist." In the list of Cambridge graduates the name is also given as Weale.

BEDFORD, No. 36 S.P., 50 P. and P., 195 S.H., 143 U.P.P., 152 and 155 U.P.H., is generally considered to be Weale's composition. The Rev. W. H. Havergal states that the earliest dated publication in which he finds this tune is 'The Psalm Singer's Magazine,' 1729. This is thought to be an earlier edition of B. Smith's 'Harmonious Companion; or, The Psalm Singer's Magazine,' published in 1732, where the tune appears set in four parts. Michael Broom, a singing-master at Isleworth, Middlesex, in the early part of last century, gives the tune a place in his 'Choice Collection of Psalm Tunes,' published about 1731, and it is there assigned to "W. Wale, organist of Bedford, B. of M.," as well as by local tradition. It was played hourly by the chimes of St Paul's, Bedford, from the middle of last century till the bells were taken down recently for repair of the tower. A somewhat scarce work, entitled 'The Divine Musick Scholar's Guide, . . . issued by one Francis Timbrell, for the use of his Scholars, and all such as delight in Church Musick,' contains "Bedford" set to the 84th Psalm, in three parts, with "Wm. Wheal" as composer. This work bears no date, but the British Museum authorities suggest 1715 as the year of publication. Mr F. G. Edwards of London has two copies of this work, and the following dates in MS. are scattered about the pages—1725, 1733, 1734, and 173¾. If the dates 1715 and 1725 are to be trusted, then "Bedford" was published at a much earlier period than has been generally supposed. In Matthew Wilkin's 'Book of Psalmody' (circa 1730) "Bedford" appears in triple time, and in two parts only, the melody as shown below:—

PSALM YE 84TH, "BEDFORD TUNE," TWO VOC.

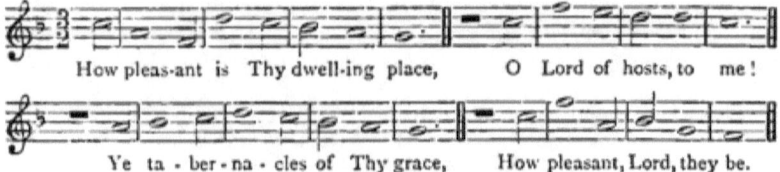

How pleas-ant is Thy dwell-ing place,   O Lord of hosts, to me!

Ye ta - ber - na - cles of Thy grace,   How pleasant, Lord, they be.

```
KEY F.
{ :s  | m :— :d  | l :— :s  | f :m :—  | r :— :— ||
{ How | pleas . ant | is    Thy | dwell-ing  | place,

{| :  :s  | d¹ :— :t | l :l :—  | s :— :— || :  :m  }
{|    O   | Lord  of | hosts, to | me!           Ye }

{| f :— :s  | l :— :s  | f :m :—  | r :— :— ||
{| ta . ber - | na - cles | of   Thy | grace,

{| :  :s  | d¹ :— :m  | f :r :—  | d :— ||
{|    How | pleas . ant, | Lord, they | be.
```

The syncopation at the close of every line of the tune, is followed in Broom's and Timbrell's work already mentioned, but in the 'Harmonious Companion' it occurs only at the second and fourth lines. In John Wesley's 'Foundery Tunes,' 1742, the syncopations are entirely absent.

Perhaps the first appearance of the tune in common time is in William Gardiner's 'Sacred Melodies' (page 19), 1812, and he makes the following lame excuse for so altering it: "This fine old tune was written by Wm. Wheal, organist of Bedford. I have changed the key to D, and written it in common time, a measure that is more stately, and better accords with that solemn grandeur in which it is disposed to move." The nearest approach to the original form in modern books may be found in the U.P. Collections.

Cornforth Gilson's Collection, published at Edinburgh in 1759, exhibits probably the first appearance of this tune in a Scotch collection. It is there named "New Grey Friers Tune."

Webb, George James, was born in Rushmore Lodge, near Salisbury, Wiltshire, June 24, 1803. His father was a farmer, but a man of educated taste and ample means, and intended his son for the ministry; the latter, however, manifesting a strong preference for the musical profession, his wishes were yielded to, and music became his chosen calling; studied under Alexander Lucas, professor of music in the School at Salisbury; appointed organist of a church at Falmouth, an office he resigned in 1830, in which year he removed to Boston, U.S.A.; organist of the Old South Church there for forty years; appointed in 1833, with Dr Lowell Mason, professor of music in the Boston Academy of Music; established in 1836 (also with Dr Mason) conventions for the instruction of music - teachers; elected president of the Boston Händel and Haydn Society in 1840; conductor for a time of the Mendelssohn Choral Society; in 1870 removed from Boston to Orange, New Jersey, and in 1876 to New York, but returned to Orange, New Jersey, in 1885, and died there, October 7, 1887. In religion

Webb was a Swedenborgian, and performed an important work for that Church in arranging its musical service. He was also organist in the new churches both in Boston and New York. He edited, with Dr Mason and others, about twenty volumes of sacred and secular music, and a work entitled 'Voice Culture' with Chester G. Allen, M.D. He will be best remembered by his tune

MORNING LIGHT, No. 403 S.H., 215 F.C.H., which he composed on the ocean in 1830, and which was first published as a secular song in 'The Odeon,' 1837, to the words "'Tis dawn, the lark is singing." It was published as a hymn tune in 'The Wesleyan Psalmist' in 1842. It is named "Goodwin" in 'Cantica Laudis,' by Mason & Webb, 1850. In America it is associated with the hymn "The morning light is breaking," hence its name.

S.S., No. 58 U.P.H., "Bless the Lord, O my soul," is adapted from his anthem, "Bless Jehovah, O my soul," composed in 1859 and published in 'Cantica Ecclesiastica.'

S.S., No. 31 U.P.H., "The Lord will be a refuge," the writer cannot trace.

Webbe, Samuel, one of the greatest of English glee composers, was born in 1740 in Minorca, where his father held a Government appointment. He was self-educated, and afterwards, under circumstances of great difficulty, became master of several foreign languages; died in London, May 25, 1816 (not 1817 as stated in S.P. and S.H.), and was buried in the churchyard of old St Pancras. In 1792 he published 'A Collection of Motetts or Antiphons,' from which is taken

MELCOMBE, No. 14 S.P., 45 U.P.H., 227 U.P.P., 93 and 279 S.H., 23 P. and P., where it is set to an "O Salutaris."

BENEVENTO, No. 164 (Third Tune) F.C.H.
WÄHRING, No. 256 S.H., "Veni Sancte Spiritus."
HOLYWOOD, Nos. 82 and 347 (First Tunes) S.H., 251 F.C.H., there named
DISMISSION, No. 317 and 357 U.P.H., there named
AUGUSTINE.

CORINTH, No. 241 F.C.H., 137 U.P.H., 8 (First Tune) S.H., and 83 (Second Tune) S.H., are Tantum ergos, and

MILAN, S.S., 7 F.C.H., and Doxology No. 15 U.P.H., a "Stabat Mater." Whether he composed the three last-named tunes or not is quite uncertain.

BELMONT is assigned to him in the U.P. collections, but there seems no evidence that he composed it. It has also been assigned to

Webbe, Samuel, jun., son of the preceding, born in London, 1770; studied under his father and Clementi; organist successively of Unitarian Church, Paradise Street, Liverpool, Spanish Ambassador's Chapel, London, St Nicholas Church and St Patrick's Roman Catholic Chapel, Liverpool; died at Hammersmith, London, November 25, 1843. Composer of sacred and secular music.

Weber, Frederic, born at Würtemberg in 1819; received his musical education at Stuttgart; from 1840 to 1841 second music-master at the Government Institution for schoolmasters at Esslingen; from 1841 to 1844 music-master at the Pestalozzian Institution for boys at Worksop, Notts; from 1845 to 1849 organist at the Hamburg Church, London; since 1849 resident organist at the German Chapel Royal, St James's Palace; author of 'Pianist's Practical Guide for Theoretical Knowledge and Manual Execution' (four editions), 'Family Singing Book' (six editions), 'School Singing Book' (two editions). His tune

ORLESTRUND, No. 379 S.H., was first published in the 'Church of England Choral Book,' which he edited in 1857.

Weldon, John, born at Chichester, January 19, 1676; pupil of Henry Purcell; organist of New College, Oxford, 1694; Gentleman of the Chapel Royal in 1701; organist of the Chapel Royal in 1708; composer to the Chapel Royal, 1715; organist of St Bride's, Fleet Street, and St Martin's-in-the-Fields, London, 1726; died May 7, 1736.

CHANT, No. 232 in S.P., and 47 in U.P.P., and 353 (Chant II.) in U.P.H., appears in Dr Boyce's 'Cathedral Music,' 3 volumes, 1760-78.

S.S., No. 75 U.P.H., "O praise God in His holiness," and
„ No. 74 „ "O praise the Lord, for it is a good thing,"
appear in Henry Playford's 'Divine Companion,' 1701.

Werner, Johann Gottlob, born at Hayn, near Leipzig, 1777; chorister at Hohenstein, Prussia; afterwards music director at Merseburg; died at Chemnitz, July 19, 1822. He edited 'Choral-Buch zu den neuen protestantischen Gesangbüchern vierstimmig. . . . Leipzig,' 1815 (1813 according to Koch), which contains the earliest copy the writer has seen of

NORMAN, No. 233 S.H., 87 U.P.H., there named "Oberlin," "Meine Hoffnung stehet feste" (No. 112).
It is also in vol. i. of J. G. Schicht's 'Allgemeines Choralbuch,' 1819, "Auf Gott setz' ich mein Vertrauen (No. 138).

RATISBON, No. 174 F.C.H., 86 and 111 U.P.H., is "Jesu, meines Lebens Leben" in Werner's book, and is partly borrowed from a chorale by Neander.

Wesley, Charles, son of the Rev. Charles Wesley, and nephew of the Rev. John Wesley the Methodist leader; born at Bristol, December 11, 1757; became a pupil of Kelway; organist of several churches in London; died, May 23, 1834.

EPWORTH, No. 75 P. and P., and 113 F.C.H., appears in 'The Psalmist' assigned to him, and arranged by his brother, Samuel Wesley, and named "Loughton." The close has been slightly modified.

It is wrongly assigned to his father in P. and P.

Wesley, Samuel, brother of the preceding, born at Bristol, February 24, 1766; from 1782 pupil for a short time of David Williams, organist of St James's, Bristol; officiated as deputy organist for one Tyler at the Abbey Church, Bath; came to London, and was candidate for the organistship of the Foundling Hospital in 1798, when, through the interest of Joah Bates, John Immyns, an amateur, was elected; organist of Camden Chapel (now St Stephen's Parish Church, Pratt Street, Camden Town), 1824; died October 11, 1837; buried in Marylebone old churchyard. From an early age Wesley excited great interest among musicians by his extraordinary genius for music; became the greatest organist of his time, and was the first Englishman to make known in this country the music of Bach; composer of much excellent church music.

BETHLEHEM, No. 156 and 282 (Second Tunes) and 206 (First Tune) S.H., 192 S.P., and 146 U.P.H., there named "Doncaster," appears in J. B. Sale's 'Psalms and Hymns for the Service of the Church,' 1837.

CHRISTCHURCH, No. 188 (Second Tune) S.H.; and
PHILIPPI, No. 92 U.P.P., 120 S.P.,
were both composed in 1835 for 'The Psalmist, a Collection of Psalm and Hymn Tunes.'

CHANTS, No. 231 U.P.H. and 117 U.P.P., 265 S.P. and 32 U.P.P., are his compositions.

CHANT to S.S., No. 108 U.P.H., "My heart rejoiceth in the Lord," is the same as No. 265 in S.P.

Wesley, Samuel Sebastian, Mus. Doc., son of the preceding, born in London, August 14, 1810; chorister at the Chapel Royal, St James; in 1827 appointed organist at St James's Church, Hampstead Road, London, and two years afterwards of St Giles, Camberwell; subsequently organist of St John's, Waterloo Road, and of Hampton-on-Thames; in 1832 organist of Hereford Cathedral, and in 1835 organist of Exeter Cathedral; in 1842 to Leeds Parish Church, to Winchester Cathedral in 1849, and to Gloucester

Cathedral in 1865—this post he held till the time of his death, April 19, 1876. One of the greatest organists and composers of church music of modern times.

ALLELUIA, No. 67 (Second Tune) S.H., was composed for the Appendix to 'Hymns Ancient and Modern,' 1868.

ARRAN, No. 222 (First Tune) S.H.;
AURELIA, Nos. 198, 272, 330 S.H.; 95, 218, 260 U.P.H.; 217 F.C.H.;
CASTLEFORD, No. 59 P. and P.;
TRINITY, No. 1 (Second Tune) S.H.;
WIMBLEDON, No. 286 (Second Tune) S.H., 90 U.P.H.;
are all found in 'Psalms and Hymns,' which he edited with the Rev. Mr Kemble in 1864.

"Aurelia" was originally set to "Jerusalem the golden." It was one of the tunes sung at St Paul's Cathedral at the National Thanksgiving Service for the recovery of the Prince of Wales, February 27, 1872.

"Castleford" was harmonised by him, and is probably a tune of last century.

ST SEBASTIAN, Nos. 150 and 326 S.H., was composed for 'A Hymnal for Use in the English Church, with Accompanying Tunes,' by the Hon. and Rev. John Grey, 1866, where it is set to "Rock of Ages, cleft for me."

HAWARDEN, No. 265 (Second Tune) S.H.; and
WETHERBY, No. 162 P. and P.,
are in his 'European Psalmist,' 1872.

HEREFORD, No. 162 (Second Tune) S.H.; and
MEMORIA, No. 321 S.H.,
are from the 'Hymnary,' edited by Joseph Barnby, 1872.

FIDUCIA, No. 183 U.P.H.; and
RADFORD, No. 346 S.H.,
were composed for 'Church Hymns with Tunes,' edited by Sir Arthur S. Sullivan, 1874.

BOWDEN, No. 181 P. and P., was harmonised by him, and published in his 'European Psalmist.' It is probably a tune of last century.

S.S. No. 27 U.P.H., "O Lord my God," was published in the 'Musical Times,' April 1, 1869.

S.S. No. 133 U.P.H., "We praise Thee, O God,"
„ No. 94 „ "Lord, now lettest Thou," and
„ No. 92 „ "My soul doth magnify the Lord,"
are from his Service in F, composed for use at Leeds Parish Church when Dr Hook was vicar. It seems to have been first published in 1855.

West, Rev. Lewis Renatus, a minister of the United Brethren's Church; son of Mr John West; born in London, May 3, 1753; entered the Moravian Boys' Boarding School at Fulneck, Yorkshire, in 1776, as one of the "masters"; settled in Bedford,

June 5, 1782, as tutor in a family, and assistant preacher, resigning December 29, 1783; settled in Dublin, January 28, 1784, as assistant minister, with special care of the young men of the Moravian Congregation; ordained deacon of the Brethren's Church by Bishop Traneker, April or May 1785; from about 1790 till 1795 minister of Gracehill, Ireland; afterwards resident at Mirfield, Yorkshire, Bath, and Bristol; became minister of the Brethren's Church at Tytherton, Wiltshire, in 1809; died there, August 4, 1826, and is buried at the Moravian burial-grounds. Amateur musician and composer, who did much to promote the study and practice of sacred music. His tune

PRAGUE, No. 199 S.P., 113 U.P.H., and Dox. 5, 163 U.P.P., 197 P. and P., was published in 'The Hymn Tunes of the Church of the Brethren, . . . arranged for Four Voices in Score, by John Lees,' 1824.

Westlake, Frederick, son of Mr John Westlake, born at Romsey, February 25, 1840; received his musical education at the Royal Academy of Music, 1855 to 1859; now a professor at that institution; well known as a pianist and teacher; composer of vocal and instrumental music.

ST URSULA, No. 57 F.C.H., appears without a name, arranged for four voices, in 'Hymns and Sacred Songs for the Year,' Part I. (1863), published by Messrs Lambert & Co. They subsequently detached the hymns from the other pieces and published them as 'The Popular Hymn and Tune Book.' Here the tune appears both in its harmonised form and also in its original form for singing in unison.

Weyman, David, appointed half vicar of St Patrick's Cathedral, Dublin, January 13, 1801; full vicar, February 19, 1819; died August 1822, and was buried in St Patrick's. Edited 'Melodia Sacra; or the Psalms of David, . . . arranged for One, Two, Three, or Four Voices,' Dublin, 1812-14. A Sequel consisting of Hymns and Anthems, published some years after, contains (in common time) the tune.

BEAUFORT, No. 359 (Second Tune) S.H. The composer is unknown. The writer finds it in a German Collection issued in 1850, and slightly different in form from that given in S.H.

Wharton, Rev. George, third son of Mr Joseph Wharton, born March 31, 1803, at Ledsham, Yorkshire; educated at Leeds Grammar School, and St John's College, Cambridge, where he graduated Second Senior Optime; B.A. 1829, afterwards M.A.; ordained deacon, 1829, by Bishop of Hereford; priest, 1830, by

Bishop of St Asaph; appointed head-master of Kinver Grammar School, 1832, and vicar of the parish, 1834; both appointments he held until his death in 1867; author of an essay upon 'The Best Means of Improving the Condition of the Agricultural Labourer,' 1844.

WARBURTON, No. 174 S.P., is one of four tunes by him, which were first published in the Rev. J. A. Baxter's 'Harmonia Sacra,' edited by Vincent Novello, 1840.

Whitaker, John, born about 1776; organist of St Clement, Eastcheap, London; in 1808 became a music-seller and publisher in St Paul's Churchyard, London; composer of the once popular songs, "Thine am I, my faithful fair," "Oh! say not woman's heart is bought," and a number of glees, one of which, "Winds gently whisper," is still popular; died in London, December 4, 1848. About 1818 he issued 'The Seraph, a Collection of Sacred Music. . . . Consisting of the most Celebrated Psalm and Hymn Tunes,' Two volumes. From vol. i. comes

HARWICH, No. 401 and 420 (Second Tune) S.H., where it is named "Morning Hymn," and set to "Awake, my soul, and with the sun."

Whitfeld, Clarke, Mus. Doc. See Clarke, John, Mus. Doc.

Wilkes, John, about 1860 organist at Monkland Church, near Leominster, Herefordshire, when the Rev. Sir Henry W. Baker was vicar; probably the same who studied at the Royal Academy of Music, London, from 1842 to 1846, and afterwards settled as a music-teacher at Aberystwith.

LYTE, No. 137 F.C.H., 228 S.H., was composed by him for 'Hymns Ancient and Modern,' 1861.

Wilkins, Matthew, son of Mr William Wilkins; baptised at Great Milton, County Oxford, August 2, 1704; by trade a butcher; author of several works on psalmody, which state that he "collected, printed, taught, and sold the same"; buried at Great Milton, August 3, 1772. About 1730 he issued 'A Book of Psalmody, containing some easy instructions for young beginners; to which is added a select number of Psalm-tunes, Hymns, and Anthems'; this work contains the earliest known copies of

STROUDWATER, No. 166 S.P., 55 (First Tune) U.P.H., 190 U.P.P., 155 P. and P.; and WALSALL, No. 173 S.P., 9 U.P.P.

The first is named "Stroudwater New Tune." "Walsall" appears in Thomas Moore's 'Psalm Singer's Pocket Companion,' Glasgow, 1756, and

"Stroudwater" in his 'Psalm Singer's Delightful Pocket Companion,' Glasgow (1762). This seems to be their first appearance in Scotch Psalmodies.

The date 1699 assigned in all Scottish Tune Books as the year in which Wilkins published the above work is, as will be seen, erroneous.

Williams, Aaron, born 1731; was a music-engraver and publisher, and clerk of the Scotch Church, London Wall; also taught psalmody; died 1776. Published a number of important collections of psalmody, one of which—'Psalmody in Miniature,' in three books, published in 1770 or before—contains

HAMPTON, No. 195 S.P., 289 U.P.H., 217 (Second Tune) S.H., 190 P. and P. Its original name was "Durham." The form given in the S.P. is the correct one.

BLOXHAM, No. 39 S.P., appears under that name in Book II. of Williams's work, reprinted posthumously, with additions, in 1778, with the following reading of the last line:—

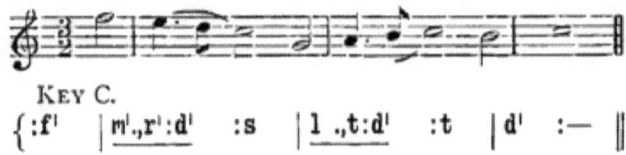

KEY C.
{ :f¹ | m¹.,r¹:d¹ :s | l .,t:d¹ :t | d¹ :— ‖

Willing, Christopher Edwin, son of Christopher Willing, alto singer and assistant Gentleman of the Chapel Royal; born in Devon, February 28, 1830; when a few weeks old, he was brought to London, where he has since resided; chorister at Westminster Abbey under James Turle, whose pupil and deputy he afterwards became; appointed organist at Blackheath Park Church when fifteen years of age; appointed organist at the Foundling Chapel, London, March 11, 1848; resigned November 12, 1879; for a few years at All Saints, Margaret Street, and St Paul's, Covent Garden; for many years organist, and sub-conductor to Sir Michael Costa, of the Sacred Harmonic Society; conductor of the Festivals of the St Alban's Choral Union since its formation some twenty years ago; for several seasons "Mæstro al Piano" at the Italian Opera, Her Majesty's Theatre, by desire of Sir Michael Costa, then the conductor.

ALSTONE, No. 425 S.H., 336 F.C.H., was composed for the Appendix to 'Hymns Ancient and Modern,' 1868, and was originally in the key of D flat.

Wilson, Hugh.

MARTYRDOM, No. 124, 160, 208 U.P.H., 109 P. and P., 97 S.P., 34 U.P.P. No Psalmody of any importance issued in this country within the last sixty years has failed to contain "Martyrdom"; as early as 1829 it was included in an Irish Psalmody, and for upwards of thirty years it has found a place in many German collections. All seem agreed as to its excellence as a congregational tune, but considerable diversity of opinion has existed among editors as to the composer. It has been described as being "partly borrowed from an old Covenanting melody," and the writer has even seen it assigned to David Rizzio and Orlando Gibbons! Had editors of tune-books taken trouble to inquire, they would have found that the composer was none other than a humble shoemaker named Hugh Wilson.

As an ardent admirer of the tune, the writer was astonished to find that little was known of its history and the career of the composer. In several works he found, "Hugh Wilson, a weaver at Kilmarnock early in the present century," a scant notice indeed. Inquiries at Kilmarnock proved, too, that this information—first published in a Scotch Psalmody—was entirely wrong; that Wilson's birthplace was a little village a few miles to the north-east—one that is rich in Covenanting legend—and his occupation that of shoemaker. Further inquiries led to the discovery of some of his descendants, and these related that he spent his last days at the village of Duntocher. From a visit to the churchyard of Old Kilpatrick his age at death was ascertained, and a search of the Baptismal Records of Fenwick discovered his year of birth and parents' names.

Briefly told, the following is the result of the writer's investigations: Hugh Wilson was born at Fenwick, Ayrshire, in 1764, and baptised December the 2d. He received his education at the village school, and afterwards learned the shoemaking trade with his father, John Wilson. In his spare moments he applied himself assiduously to the study of mathematics and kindred subjects. A favourite pastime of his was the making of sun-dials, and one constructed by him may still be seen at Fenwick. He occasionally led the psalmody in the Secession Church there, and was able to add to his income by teaching the villagers the ordinary branches of education and music. About the end of last century Wilson removed to Pollokshaws, where he made the acquaintance of Mr William Dunn, in whose mills at Duntocher he afterwards for several years held an important situation. He filled the office of a manager in the church there (now the United Presbyterian), and founded, with one James Slimmond, the first Sunday-school at Duntocher. On Saturday the 14th August 1824 Wilson died, and his remains were interred in the churchyard of Old Kilpatrick, where a plain stone marks the last resting-place of one who has left an abiding monument in the psalmody of our Church.

Wilson composed many psalm-tunes, but only two of these seem to have been published—viz., "Martyrdom" and "Caroline," and the latter is not now in use. While on his deathbed, he caused his manuscript tunes and a few poems to be destroyed—a circumstance that is to be regretted, as there may well have been other work as excellent as "Martyrdom." This tune was composed by Wilson before he left Fenwick, from which village it took its first name; and indeed, in the churches there, it was, until lately, still announced under that title. It was originally written in common time, and first published on single slips with the air and bass only, for the use of teachers in music classes, thus:—

FENWICK, C.M.

A writer in a musical magazine of 1856, referring to the introduction of "Martyrdom" into St George's Church, Edinburgh, says that "'Martyrdom' was more than once the subject of a legal and antiquarian dispute;" and this *cannot* be doubted, for Mr John Fulton, a relation of Wilson's, informs the writer positively that such was the case. He gave the following facts, which had been told him repeatedly by his father: The tune "Martyrdom" (or Fenwick as we always name it) became the private property of John Robertson, a well-known music-teacher in Glasgow (see Robertson in Appendix). It was subsequently published, without permission, under the name of "Martyrdom" in a slightly altered form, the measure being changed from common to triple time, and described by the editor as "partly borrowed from an old Covenanting melody." Mr Fulton is of the opinion that R. A. Smith was the defender in the legal dispute that ensued. This is very probable, as Smith was the first to publish the tune in triple time in his 'Sacred Music, for use in St George's Church, Edinburgh,' 1825, and he there describes it as being partly borrowed from an old Covenanting melody. "This," says Mr Fulton, "was the contention of the defenders; but it found no support in evidence, for two witnesses from Fenwick, named John and Robert Fulton, proved that Wilson composed the tune, and had taught it to his classes in Fenwick a quarter of a century before 'Martyrdom' appeared." The most conclusive evidence was given by John Fulton, who had a share in writing the bass part. The Sheriff, according to Mr Fulton, decided that the copyright of the tune "Martyrdom" or "Fenwick" was Robertson's, and that Wilson was the composer.

Further, Mr Thomas Macfarlane, a prominent musician in the West of Scotland early in this century (see Appendix), informs the writer that he remembers the legal dispute regarding the authorship of "Martyrdom," and that it was proved that a man named Wilson, a native of "Phinnick" (an old way of spelling Fenwick), was the composer. Wilson's granddaughter, now in Canada, also states that she heard her mother say repeatedly that her father was composer of the tune. It may be worthy of mention, that in 1847 a copy of the tune in Wilson's handwriting was given to a relation of his resident in Ayr. It was shown as a curiosity to all who visited the house, but about 1864 it disappeared mysteriously.

Wilson,[1] **John,** son of John Wilson; born in Edinburgh, December 25, 1800; when ten years of age apprenticed as a printer to the firm of Walker & Greig; afterwards engaged with Ballantyne, the printer of the Waverley Novels, as reader or corrector of the press; studied music under John Mather and Benjamin Gleadhill of Edinburgh; member of the choir of Duddingston Church during the pastorate of the Rev. John Thomson, the landscape-painter; appointed precentor of Roxburgh Place Relief Church, his beautiful tenor voice and admirable musical taste attracting great crowds; appointed on February 9, 1825, precentor of St Mary's Church, Edinburgh, and shortly afterwards devoted his time to music-teaching; studied singing under Finlay Dun of Edinburgh, and afterwards in London under Signor Lanza and Crivelli; studied harmony and counterpoint under Aspull; on January 29, 1830, resigned his office at St Mary's, and made his first appearance in March of that year on the Edinburgh stage as Harry Bertram, in the opera of "Guy Mannering"; appeared also

---

[1] As Wilson's year of birth has been variously given, the following from the records of the Canongate parish, Edinburgh, will set the matter at rest:—

"John Wilson, coach-driver, and Mary Edwards, his spouse, had a son, born 25th December 1800, and baptised January 4, 1801, named John. Witnesses, Hector McGowan and Robert Lawson."

at Covent Garden and Drury Lane, London, in other operas; afterwards became famous as an exponent of Scottish song; appeared before her Majesty the Queen at Taymouth Castle in 1842. After a short illness Wilson died at Quebec, July 8, 1849. David Kennedy, the Scottish vocalist, restored his tomb in Quebec, and left a sum of money for its continued preservation. Edited 'A Selection of Psalm Tunes, Sanctuses, Doxologies, &c., for the use of the Congregation of St Mary's Church, Edinburgh,' 1825. This contains the earliest copy the writer has seen of

HOWARD, No. 81 S.P., 92 P. and P., 108 U.P.P., 158 U.P.H. It there bears that name, and is anonymous. See Stevenson, Sir John A.

Wilson, M. C., wife of the Rev. Dr James Hood Wilson, minister of Barclay Free Church, Edinburgh; writer of several hymns and tunes.

NINETY-AND-NINE, No. 378 F.C.H., was composed by Mrs Wilson, and published anonymously in 'Gospel Hymns Harmonised' (1874). Her initials were added in 'Songs of Zion' (1877). The harmony in the F.C.H. is by W. H. Monk, Mus. Doc.

Wilton, Earl of, Thomas Egerton, born December 30, 1799; died March 7, 1882; composer of vocal music.

S.S. No. 62 U.P.H., "O praise the Lord, all ye heathen," is his composition, and was published in the 'Musical Times,' February 1865.

Winter, Peter von, violinist and chapel master to the King of Bavaria, was born at Mannheim; composer of an oratorio, "Der Sterbende Jesus," masses, psalms, motets, operas, &c.; died at Munich, October 17 (not August 14, as stated by some), 1825, aged seventy-one years.

WINTER, No. 138 U.P.H., is adapted from a "Stabat Mater," and appears as a hymn tune under the name of "Munich" in Lewis Benton Seeley's 'Devotional Harmony, containing Psalms and Hymns, . . . for Three and Four Voices,' 1806. It is also in vol. ii. of La Trobe's 'Sacred Music' (1809).

S.S. No. 71 U.P.H., "Hear my pray'r," is an adaptation by William Shore, from some of his works.

Wittenberger Liedersammlung or Achtliederbuch, 1524—the first collection of Reformation hymns, published at Wittenberg—contained eight hymns (four by Luther), most of which had been previously issued as fly-leaves. They were set to four melodies, the authors of which are unknown. One of these is

ERK, No. 324 F.C.H., "Nun freut euch, lieben Christen gmein."

Wolff, Johann, printer or publisher at Frankfort-on-the-Main, about 1560. Published 'Kirchen Gesäng, aus dem Wittenbergischen, und allen andern den besten Gesangbüchern. . . . Frankfurt-am-Mayn,' 1569. In the above is

DORTMUND, No. 116 and 162 (First Tune) S.H., set to "Jauchzet dem Herren alle Lande" (Ps. 100). See Nicolai, Philipp.

Wood, Thomas, was in 1762 organist of St Giles'[1]-in-the-Fields Church, London. How long he held office cannot be ascertained.

OXFORD, No. 27 P. and P., is one of four tunes contributed by Wood to William Riley's 'Parochial Harmony; consisting of a Collection of Psalm Tunes in three and four parts,' 1762. It is there named "St George's Tune," and is set to Psalm 14, New Version.

Woodbury, Isaac Baker, born at Beverley, Massachusetts, October 23, 1819; apprenticed to a blacksmith in Boston, and spent his spare time in educating himself and learning the violin; in 1839 he became a member of the Bay Street Glee Club; visited England in 1841, 1851, and 1856 or 1857; settled in New York, 1849; in 1858 started on a trip to the south for his health, and only reached Columbia, South Carolina, where he died, October 26, 1858.

MONTGOMERY, No. 252 U.P.H. and 132 F.C.H., was first published in the 'Choral Advocate,' a monthly musical periodical, 1852. The original has a coda which is not now used.

Woodd, Rev. Basil, born at Richmond, Surrey, August 5, 1760; in May 1778 entered as a commoner at Trinity College, Oxford; graduated B.A. Oxford, 1782; ordained priest at Westminster Abbey, 1784; appointed morning preacher at Bentinck Chapel, Lisson Green, in the parish of St Marylebone, 1785; presented to the living of Drayton, Beauchamp, Bucks, 1808; resigned in 1830, and was succeeded by his eldest son; died at Paddington, April 12, 1831; author of 'A New Metrical Version of the Psalms of David,' and other works. His tune

PADDINGTON, No. 195 P. and P., appears in the 'Bentinck Chapel Collection,' published about 1800. It seems to be an adaptation of Boyce's "Westminster Chant" given below:—

---

[1] Not St George's-in-the-Fields, as stated by Dibdin in his 'Standard Psalm Tune Book.'

Key D.

{| d' | s :f | m :— ‖ m | r :s | s :fe | s :— ‖

{| s | l :t | d' :— ‖ l | s :f .m | m :r | d :— ‖

Woodward, Richard, son of Richard Woodward, vicar-choral of St Patrick's and Christ Church Cathedrals, Dublin; born in Dublin about 1744; organist of Christ Church Cathedral, Dublin, 1765; vicar-choral of St Patrick's Cathedral, 1772; and master of the choristers of both cathedrals; graduated Mus. Bac., Dublin, 1768; Mus. Doc., 1771; died at Dublin, November 22, 1777.

CHANTS Nos. 228 S.P., 206 U.P.P., 264 S.P., 208 U.P.P., appear in his 'Cathedral Music; consisting of One complete Service, Seven Anthems, Several Chants, and Veni Creator Spiritus in Score. . . . Opera Terza' (after 1771). These chants are also set to

S.S., No. 117, " In that day ;"
  „ No. 111, " Where shall wisdom be found?"
  „ No. 126, " My soul doth magnify the Lord,"
all in U.P.H.

Worgan, John, born 1724; pupil of James Worgan, his brother, and afterwards of Roseingrave and Geminiani; graduated Mus. Bac., at Cambridge University, 1748; appointed organist of St Andrew's, Undershaft (with St Mary Axe), about 1749; Vauxhall Gardens, 1751 to 1774; St Botolph, Aldgate, 1758; St John's Chapel, Great James Street, Bedford Row, 1760; Mus. Doc., Cambridge, 1775; died August 24, 1790, aged sixty-six; buried in St Andrew's, Undershaft. Worgan seems to have been a remarkable performer on the organ. Händel said of him : "Mr Worgan shall sit by me, he plays my music very well at Vauxhall." Battishill considered him a finer player than even Händel himself. The Rev. Richard Cecil, an able amateur musician, at whose chapel Worgan played for some time, writes : " Admiration and feeling are very distinct from each other. Some music and oratory enchant and astonish, but they speak not to the heart. I have been overwhelmed by Händel's music; the 'Dettingen Te Deum' is perhaps the greatest composition in the world; yet I never in my life heard Händel but I could think of something else at the same time. There is a kind of music that will not allow this. Dr Worgan has so touched the organ at St John's that I have been turning backward and forward over the Prayer-book for the first lesson in Isaiah, and wondered that I could not find Isaiah there: the musician and the orator fall short of the full power of their science, if the hearer is left in possession of himself."

Worgan, No. 43 P. and P., is one of two tunes contributed by him to William Riley's 'Parochial Harmony, . . . ' 1762, and is there named "Apostles Tune," set to Psalm 112, New Version, and in four parts.

Wright, Thomas, born at Stockton-on-Tees, September 18, 1763, was the son of Robert Wright, organist of that town, and early evinced great musical ability. When eleven years old he was assistant to Garth, organist of Sedgefield, on a powerful old organ said to have been built by Father Schmidt; and after a year or two as pupil and assistant with Thomas Ebdon, organist of Durham Cathedral, young Wright was appointed to the organ at Sedgefield, an office he held from 1785 until he succeeded his father in 1797 as organist at Stockton. Wright was in extensive repute as a music-master in the counties of Durham and North Riding of Yorkshire. He published an admirable 'Primer' and 'Supplement' for his pupils; a concerto with accompaniments (in 1795), "in which was first suggested a mode of indicating the rate of each movement by a pendulum of thread measured on the keys of the piano—anticipating by many years the invention of the metronome;" the music of an (unacted) operetta called "Rusticity," written by his wife, in 1800; a simple "Anthem," on occasions of peace, in 1802, and several songs. Besides being an excellent musician, Wright excelled as an extempore player on the organ. He was expertly ingenious in mechanics, and skilled in astronomy and physical science. He resigned the organ at Stockton Church in 1818. During a professional engagement at Archdeacon Headlam's, Wright was seized with fatal illness, and died at the Rectory, Wycliffe, near Barnard Castle, November 24, 1829; buried at Norton, near Stockton. His tune

Stockton, No. 230 S.H., 154 P. and P., 165 S.P. (originally named "Elizabeth"), was among others used in the church services at Stockton. About 1820 the name was changed from "Elizabeth" to "Stockton," but it still remained in MS. It was introduced into Wakefield Parish Church, where it became popular, and in 1861 was published for the first ime in 'Hymns Ancient and Modern,' with the last strain of the melody slightly altered by Dr J. B. Dykes. The second strain has now been altered in 'The Scottish Hymnal.'

Tune "Stockton" as composed by Wright.

Key E.					Key B t.			f. Key E.
{:d	m :f	s :d¹	f :m	r	ʳs₁	l₁ :t₁	d :t₁	ᵈs ‖
{:d¹	m :l	s :d	r :f	m	s	l.t:d¹	m :r	d ‖

Würtemberg Gesangbuch. The first Würtemberg hymn book was published in 1583, and authorised to be used in the churches. A new edition, with a supplement, was published in 1664, and an enlarged edition in 1711.

Munich, No. 274 (Second Tune) S.H., 211 F.C.H., 21 and 250 U.P.H., "O Gott, du frommer Gott," was composed about the end of the seventeenth century, and inserted in the enlarged edition of the above in 1711. The composer is unknown.

Würtemberg Melody, 1760.

Nina, No. 4 S.H., is so described in Kocher's 'Zionsharfe,' 1855, where it is the chorale "Sollt' es gleich bisweilen scheinen," on p. 191, No. 416.

Wyvill, Zerubbabel, son of John and Sarah Wyvill; born at Maidenhead, Berks; baptised September 4, 1763; professor of music at Maidenhead, and organist of the Chapel of SS. Mary Magdalen and Andrew; died at Hounslow, Middlesex, May 14, 1837; buried in Trinity churchyard there. Composer of glees, anthems, and hymn tunes.

Eaton, No. 92 S.H., 38 F.C.H., and Doxology 12 U.P.H., was first published in 'Anthem, two Hymns and two Dismissions, selected and composed for the General Thanksgiving,' June 1, 1802. It is there headed "Hymn for Morning Service," but has no special name.

The following incident was related to the writer, by one who was present, regarding Robert Wyvill (who is noticed below) and his father's tune "Eaton": "When the so-called revival (?) in church music was at its height, old-fashioned musicians were often snubbed and ridiculed. Mr Robert

Wyvill was then (and had been for many years) organist of St Mary's Chapel. At a choir practice one Sunday evening, when 'Eaton' was being sung, a 'revivalist'—a chapel official—who had interfered on other occasions, told the venerable organist that he was playing the tune wrongly. I shall never forget how Mr Wyvill jumped off the stool, and said, 'What! not know how to play my father's tune!' and left the organ. The next day he resigned his post, and St Mary's Chapel lost the services of a genuine musician—one who played even a simple tune from the *heart*, and made his hearers *feel* what he was playing."

Wyvill, Robert, son of the preceding, was for many years organist of St Mary's Chapel, Maidenhead; afterwards of the Episcopal Church there; died August 1869, aged eighty years, having bequeathed a sum of money to a local charity. Edited a collection of hymn tunes and chants in 1840.

Zingarelli, Niccolò Antonio, born at Naples, April 4, 1752; eldest son of Riccardo Tota Zingarelli, a tenor singer and teacher of singing; pupil of Fenaroli and Padre Speranza; in 1794 appointed chapel-master of the Cathedral at Milan; from 1804 to 1811 chapel-master of St Peter's, Rome, and in 1816 chapel-master of the Cathedral, Naples; composer of masses, motets, Te Deums, &c., and an oratorio, "The Destruction of Jerusalem"; died near Naples, May 5, 1837.

S.S., No. 106 U.P.H., "Blessed are the dead," is adapted from a motet. The whole movement will be found in vol. i. of 'Part Music,' edited by John Hullah in 1842. It is there set to the words, "Be not far from me."

APPENDIX

CONTAINING

A LIST OF THE PRINCIPAL COLLECTIONS
OF PSALMODY

ISSUED IN SCOTLAND FROM THE YEAR 1700
TO THE PRESENT TIME.

NOTE TO APPENDIX.

The writer wishes it to be understood that the list here given by no means includes *all* the Collections of Psalmody issued in Scotland since 1700, but the principal ones only.

APPENDIX.

'**A Collection** of Hymns and Anthems for the use of the Episcopal Church of Scotland,' Edinburgh, Murray & Cochrane, 1781, contains many tunes now in use. The fourth edition was published at Aberdeen in 1790. Other editions were issued, varying slightly in their contents.

Adam, Alexander, Glasgow, printed in 1773 'The Psalms of David in Metre, newly translated, and diligently compared with the Original Text, and former Translations; more plain, smooth, and agreeable to the Text than any heretofore. Allowed by the Authority of the General Assembly of the Kirk of Scotland, and appointed to be sung in Congregations and Families. With Twenty-Three Select Psalm-Tunes particularly adapted to the Subject of the Psalms to which they are set.'

There is nothing in this Collection deserving of special mention. It consists of tunes from the Scottish Psalters and those introduced into Scotland by Thomas Moore in 1756 and 1762. It has "Coleshill" set to Psalm 103.

Anderson, Rev. William, son of the Rev. John Anderson; born at Kilsyth, Stirlingshire, January 6, 1799[1]; educated for the ministry at Glasgow University; licensed as a preacher of the Gospel by the Relief Presbytery of Glasgow, September 5, 1820; appointed minister of John Street Church, Glasgow, 1821, celebrating his jubilee as a minister of the Gospel in 1871; received the

[1] The date 1800, commonly given, is an error, as the following extract from the Kilsyth Birth Records will show: "The Rev. Mr John Anderson, minister of the Relief congregation, and Margaret Watt, had a son, born the 6th and baptised the 26th January 1799, named William."

degree of LL.D. from the University of Glasgow in 1850; died at Uddingston, near Bothwell, September 15, 1872. An enthusiastic musical amateur and composer of psalmody; author of 'Apology for the Organ as an assistance of Congregational Psalmody,' 1829, and other works. Edited

'The Sacred Choir; A Collection of Music adapted to the Psalms, Paraphrases, and Hymns in general use in Scotland; and specially to the Collection of Hymns sanctioned by the Synod of Relief' (1841). This contains two tunes by the editor, and other originals by Samuel Barr, Ludovick Nicolson, Alexander Duncan, and Rev. M. M'Gavin, musicians then resident in the West of Scotland.

Also 'A Selection of Psalm and Hymn Tunes, adapted to Various Measures,' Glasgow (1844).

Boyack, George, born at Falkirk, March 19, 1792; to trade a shoemaker; member of the Falkirk Parish Church choir; afterwards became a teacher of vocal and instrumental music; about 1825 appointed precentor of Bristo Street Chapel, Edinburgh; in 1830 appointed to Lady Yester's Church, resigning November 16, 1831, on being appointed precentor and session-clerk of the Parish Church of St Andrews; teacher of music in the Madras College, St Andrews; composer of psalm and hymn tunes that are still in MS.; died suddenly at St Andrews, February 10, 1854. During his residence at St Andrews, Mr Boyack was much respected, and was presented with his portrait by the inhabitants, "in testimony of their opinion of the able manner in which he has for many years conducted the psalmody, and of their esteem for him as a citizen." He was one of a select choir organised by Mr Peacock of Perth to lead the psalmody at Crathie Church, during one of the early visits of her Majesty the Queen and Prince Albert to Balmoral. Edited

'A Collection of Psalm Tunes for use in Bristo Street Chapel.'

James Duncan Boyack, son of the above, is well known in the West of Scotland as an able musician and conductor.

Boyd, Henry, teacher of Psalmody in Glasgow last century, and precentor in the Methodist Chapel, John Street; died November 17, 1792.

'A Select Collection of Psalm and Hymn Tunes, Adapted to a great Variety of Measures; To which is prefixed an Introduction to the Art of Singing, by the late Henry Boyd,' was published in 1793, for the benefit of his widow. It contains "187 tunes, set in three parts, among which are twelve favourite pieces, an anthem on 67th Psalm, and some original tunes."

This book is of some importance. It offers the earliest copies of the following tunes the writer has seen in a Scotch Psalmody: "Blackburn" (Fish), "Duke Street" (Hatton), "Artaxerxes" (Arne), "Trinity" (Giardini) "Harts" (Milgrove), "Carey's" (Henry Carey), "Miles Lane" (Shrubsole), "Scarborough," "New Cambridge" (Randall), "Leoni" (Hebrew Melody).

Bremner's, Robert, Collection. See page 83.

Brown, William, teacher of vocal music in Glasgow; precentor in the Wynd Church (now St George's Parish Church) there for many years, resigning in March 1807. Edited

'The Precentor; or an Easy Introduction to Church Music; with a Choice Collection of Psalm Tunes, all in three and four parts, suited to the different Metres of the Version of the Psalms used in the Church of Scotland,' sixth edition, 1799. The work contains an original tune by Brown, and thirty-nine others, the majority of which are still in use.

The earlier editions of 'The Precentor' were edited by John McLachlan. See that name.

Bruce, Thomas, schoolmaster, resided in the Cowgate, near the College Wynd, Edinburgh. Published there in 1726

'The Common Tunes; or, Scotland's Church Musick made plain, with a Description of the Antiquity, Use, Authors and Inventers of Musick,' forty-two pages being taken up with "The Gam-ut, or Scale of Musick Explain'd." The work contains about thirty tunes, harmonised in three parts and taken from the Scottish Psalters. One is named "Bruce's Tenor," which is presumably his own composition. There are also some curious verses, "for lettering the Common Tunes." It contains a dedication "To the Much Honoured Sir Thomas Bruce-Hope of Kinross and Craighall, Baronet."

A second edition (no date) was afterwards published with slight changes in the contents.

Bruce's work is one of the earliest collections issued in Scotland after the Scottish Psalter.

Campbell, John, son of Malcolm Campbell; born at Paisley; an enthusiastic musical amateur and organist; one of the first members of the Glasgow Choral Union; merchant in Glasgow for many years; died there October 1860, aged fifty-three years. Edited

'The Sacred Psaltery, in four Vocal Parts, consisting principally of Original Psalm and Hymn Tunes,' Glasgow (1854). The above contains about forty original tunes by Campbell, one of which is "Orlington," for many years the fixed tune in some parts of Scotland to Psalm 23. In the same work is his anthem, "Rejoice in the Lord," which was immensely popular with country choirs.

Carnie, William, son of William Carnie; born at Aberdeen, November 12, 1824; originally a letter engraver; became a student of literature and music; precentor of the Established Church, Banchory-Devenick, Aberdeenshire, 1845; Inspector of Poor for same parish, 1847; sub-editor of the 'Aberdeen Herald,' 1852; precentor of the West or High Church, Aberdeen, from January 1856 to December 1871; since 1861 clerk and treasurer to the Managers of Aberdeen Royal Infirmary and the Lunatic Asylum; minor poet and dramatic and musical critic.

Mr Carnie's labours (says a writer) have done everything to promote good psalmody in the North of Scotland. In 1854, at the request of the local Young Men's Christian Association, he delivered a lecture on Psalmody to an audience numbering over 2000 persons. This lecture was illustrated by the Harmonic Choir in a style which awakened great local interest in regard to the 'Service of Sacred Song.' Indeed, to this meeting may be ascribed the great desire for psalmody improvement which arose over the whole of the north-eastern districts of Scotland. Continuing his efforts to raise the standard of congregational singing, Mr Carnie's name became widely known. His 'Northern Psalter' (a work not yet surpassed) has attained immense popularity all over Scotland and amongst all Presbyterian denominations, and at the present time upwards of 60,000 copies of his psalmodic works have been published.

Chalmers, James, printer of the 'Aberdeen Journal' and other works; died at Aberdeen, 1764.

St Paul, No. 142 P. and P., 61 U.P.P., 130 U.P.H., 85 F.C.H., 150 S.P., is stated on page 84 (under Bremner) to have been in use in Aberdeen in 1755, if not earlier. Since that part of the book was passed for press, a small collection of church tunes issued by Chalmers has come into the writer's possession. The title is unfortunately wanting, but the book contains a dedication to the provost, bailies, and town council, which enables us to fix almost the exact year of publication. Through the kindness of Mr Carnie of Aberdeen, the Records of the town council of that city have been searched, and they show that the provost and bailies to whom the work is dedicated were together in office only in the years 1748 and 1749. Chalmers's book must then have been issued in one of these years. The work contains "St Paul" in two parts, air and bass, and is set to Psalm 65, verses 3 and 4. This shows the tune to be several years older than has been supposed. Chalmers's book is made up of tunes principally from the psalters of Este, Ravenscroft, and those issued by Andrew Hart and others. It contains a corrupt version of "Newtoun" or "London New," which was in use in some parts of Aberdeen in the middle of this century.

Chalmers, James, printer, son of the above; born March 31, 1742; appointed precentor of the West Church, Aberdeen, November 21, 1774, at a salary of "two hundred pounds Scots"; resigned 1797; died June 17, 1810. It may be mentioned that this is the Mr Chalmers on whose stair, in the autumn of 1787, Burns met the son of the author of "Tullochgorum," which event John Skinner celebrates in the lines—

> "O happy hour for evermair,
> That led my chil' [child] up Cha'mers' stair."

Church of Scotland Collections.

I. 'The Church of Scotland Hymn Tune Book. A Collection of Tunes for the "Hymns for Public Worship." Selected by the Committee of the General Assembly on Psalmody.' Edinburgh, T. Nelson & Sons and Paton & Ritchie, 1862. Prefatory Note signed by the Rev. Dr David Arnot, Convener of the Committee on Psalmody.

II. 'The Church of Scotland Hymn Tune Book. A Collection of Tunes for the "Hymns for Public Worship." Authorised by the Committee of the General Assembly on Psalmody Improvement.' Edinburgh, T. Nelson & Sons, 1865.

The above Collections were published under the superintendence of Mr T. L. Hately. They seem to have been issued at the publishers' risk, and recommended by the Assembly's Committee as suitable for use in the Church of Scotland.

III. 'The Church of Scotland Psalm and Hymn Tune Book. Prepared under the superintendence of the Committee of the General Assembly on Psalmody.' Edinburgh, T. Nelson & Sons. Preface dated January 1868, and signed by Mr A. T. Niven. It was issued in three divisions. The Preface says: "The present publication is the first collection of Psalm tunes published under authority or sanction of the General Assembly of the Church of Scotland since 1650." During the progress of this work through the press, Mr T. L. Hately died, and the work was brought to a conclusion by his son, Mr Walter Hately. The late Mr T. K. Longbottom also assisted in the editing of these works.

IV. 'The Book of Psalms and the Scottish Hymnal, with Accompanying Tunes. Published for use in Churches, by authority of the General Assembly. The Harmonies of the Tunes revised by W. H. Monk, Professor of Vocal Music in King's College, London,' 1872. This last was in use until 1885, when the enlarged 'Scottish Hymnal' was introduced.

V. 'The Psalter; Being the Authorised Version of the Psalms, Together with Selected Passages of Scripture, Pointed for Chanting, with accompanying Chants. The Harmonies of the Chants revised by W. H. Monk.' Edinburgh, Thomas Nelson & Sons, 1874.

VI. 'Book of Anthems; For Use in Public Worship. Published by Authority of the General Assembly of the Church of Scotland. Revised by William Henry Monk.' Edinburgh, Thomas Nelson & Sons, 1875.

VII. 'The Children's Hymnal. Harmonies revised by William Henry Monk.' Edinburgh, Thomas Nelson & Sons, 1876.

Clarke, James P., teacher of singing and pianoforte at Glasgow early in this century; some time a music-seller's assistant at Edinburgh; leader of psalmody in St George's Church, Glasgow, in 1829; married Ellen Fullarton, December 25, 1831; appointed organist of St Mary's Episcopal Chapel in succession to Thomas Macfarlane, January 28, 1834; resigned in 1835, and emigrated to Canada. Clarke had the reputation of being an excellent musician and vocalist; he taught his pupils on the Logierian system. Edited

'Parochial Psalmody; A New Collection of approved Psalm Tunes, including several composed expressly for this Work; the whole arranged for Four Voices, with an Accompaniment for the Pianoforte or Organ,' no date, second edition (1832). The work has several originals by Clarke and others, but none of them are now in use.

Daniel, John, born at Aberdeen about 1803; studied under John Ross, organist of St Paul's Church, where he acted as clerk for a time; practised as a music-teacher in Aberdeen for several years; about 1833 became precentor of St John's *quoad sacra* Church, Montrose, now St John's Free Church; settled in New York as teacher and composer about 1843 or 1844; died there June 21, 1881. Edited

'The National Psalmody of the Church of Scotland; A Collection of the most esteemed Psalm and Hymn Tunes, adapted to the various Metres of the Psalms and Paraphrases, &c., used in that Church. . . . The whole newly arranged for Four Voices, with an Accompaniment for the Organ, Pianoforte, or Seraphine. To which are prefixed a few practical observations on the Performance of Church Music, the duty of Choirs, &c.' Preface dated Montrose, November 1, 1842. This contains five tunes by Daniel, and several adaptations; also four originals by Finlay Dun.

Davie, James, born (probably at Aberdeen) about 1783; choirmaster in St Andrew's Church, Aberdeen, for many years; noted for his ability as a flute-player; founded and conducted the Aberdeen Choral Society; died at Aberdeen, November 19, 1857. Edited

Three collections of church music, the most important being 'The Music of the Church of Scotland; being a numerous Selection of Psalm and Hymn Tunes, Ancient and Modern, in Four Vocal Parts, &c.,' Aberdeen (1841).

Duncan, Alexander, teacher of music in Glasgow; appointed precentor of the Outer High Church (now St Paul's) in succession to J. R. Macfarlane, February 1829, and held the appointment till 1836, when he was dismissed from the office. Edited in 1828

'The Choir; A Collection of Psalm and Hymn Tunes, adapted to various Measures, selected and composed by Alexander Duncan, with copious Rudimental Instructions in the Art of Vocal Music.' The work contains one hundred and fifty tunes, several of which are still in use, and has a preface written by W. A., presumably the Rev. William Anderson.

Ebsworth, Joseph, born at Islington, October 10, 1788; vocalist and glee writer; librarian to the Edinburgh Harmonists' Society; compiled 'General Index to First Hundred Volumes of the Music in Library of Edinburgh Harmonists' Society. . . .' Edinburgh, 1844; appointed leader of psalmody in St Stephen's Church, Edinburgh, March 1829, "on the express condition of his giving up his connection with the theatre;" died at Edinburgh, June 23, 1868. Author of 'A Short Introduction to Vocal Music, adapted either for Private Tuition or Class Singing,' Edinburgh, no date. Edited

'A Collection of Psalm and Hymn Tunes, arranged for Four·Voices, as sung in St Stephen's Church, Edinburgh; with an Introduction to Vocal Music, intended for the use of the General Assembly's Normal Institution,' no date. The work contains forty-five tunes, the majority of which are in use at the present time.

Farquharson, James, Scottish musician and teacher in Edinburgh. Published

'A Selection of Sacred Music, suitable for Public and Private Devotion,' Edinburgh, 1824. It contains one hundred and thirty-one tunes, the majority not now being in use.

Free Church of Scotland Collections.

I. 'The Psalmody of the Free Church of Scotland. Prepared under the superintendence of George Hogarth, Esq., by T. L. Hately, Precentor to the General Assembly. Issued by Authority of the Committee on Psalmody.' Edinburgh, 1845. This Collection contains ninety tunes, and is an excellent one in many respects. The Preface says: "There are two characteristics of the present publication which will, it is trusted, render it a means of promoting this desirable end of unity in singing in the Free Church. In the first place, it discards all theatrical and jig-like, and almost all repeating tunes, which, if admissible in secular meetings, are justly deemed out of place in the house of God; and it limits itself very much to that more solid and simple class, of which the established tunes of Scotland are the type and specimen. And in the second place, its harmonies are constructed on a plain and simple principle, not requiring the foreign aid of instruments or of a trained band, but adapted to the easy use of the mass of the people themselves."

Professor Taylor of Gresham College, and James Turle, organist of Westminster Abbey, warmly praised the work. It was also published for general use under the title of 'The National Psalmody, with a Practical Guide to Psalm-Singing,' by T. L. Hately.

II. 'Scottish Psalmody; Being a Selection of Tunes with the prevailing Harmonies used throughout Scotland, with Elementary Lessons for Beginners, and a Table of Appropriate Tunes for all the Psalms. Issued by the Education Committee of the Free Church of Scotland' (1854). Contains sixty-seven tunes, No. 1 being "Arnold's," and No. 67, "Old 148th."

Another edition (1855) contains fifty-six additional tunes, No. 68 being "Abbey," and No. 123 "St John."

An enlarged edition (1858) contains twenty-eight additional tunes, No. 124 being "Bishopthorpe," and No. 151 "Goldel."

A supplement to the above (1866) contains thirty-two additional tunes, No. 152 being "Antwerp," and 183 "Zurich."

This work was used in the Presbyterian Churches of Scotland for a considerable time, and it is questionable if the singing in our churches was ever heartier than during the time it was employed. At all events, one had the assurance on entering a strange church that no discord or confusion would take place through the use of different tune-books.

III. A revised edition of the above was published in 1873, the harmonies by Mr Colin Brown.

To this was added the same year 'A Collection of Hymn Tunes, the harmonies by Mr D. Cunninghame, assisted by Mr John Ireland.' These were afterwards combined in a cut-leaved book entitled 'The Book of Psalms in Metre; And the New Selection of Paraphrases and Hymns Authorised for Use in Public Worship by the General Assembly of the Free Church of Scotland, with Accompanying Tunes,' 1873.

Here we find many German tunes, published in this country for the first time, and an interesting feature of the work are the notes on some of the less known Continental composers, which have been of service to the writer in the compilation of this work.

Geikie, James Stewart, son of Archibald Geikie and Helen Bayne; born at Edinburgh, January 12, 1811, and baptised February 2; choirmaster of St Augustine Congregational Church there from about 1843 till 1880; conductor of several choral societies; musical critic for the 'Scotsman' many years; died at Ormiston, East Lothian, August 14, 1883. Composer of psalm and hymn tunes, anthems, and songs, one of which, "My Heather Hills," was for a time very popular. Two of Mr Geikie's sons are eminently distinguished as geologists. Edited

A 'Supplement to R. A. Smith's Sacred Harmony, adapted to the Psalms and Hymns used in the Churches and Chapels of Scotland,' no date; and 'Songs of the Sanctuary; a Collection of Psalms, Scripture Hymns, &c., arranged for Chanting,' 1863.

Gilmour's, Robert, Collection. See page 140.

Gilson, Cornforth, born in England; chorister in Durham Cathedral, but how long the records do not show; appointed by the Edinburgh Town Council in 1756 master of music in the city churches, in which year a praiseworthy movement was begun to improve psalmody in Edinburgh; elected music-master at Heriot's Hospital, January 14, 1757; resigned the office of master of church music, April 1764, having resolved to settle in London; reappointed August 21, 1771, but how long he held the office is uncertain. He was resident in Edinburgh in 1774, if not later. Some facts regarding Gilson's efforts to improve the psalmody in the Edinburgh churches will be found in an article by the writer published in the 'Scotsman' of May 31, 1890. Edited

'Lessons on the Practice of Singing, with an Addition of the Church Tunes, in Four Parts, and a Collection of Hymns, Canons, Airs, and Catches, for the improvement of Beginners,' Edinburgh, 1759. The majority of the tunes in this work are taken from the Psalters issued by Este, Ravenscroft, and Andrew Hart.

Girvin, John, probably a native of Edinburgh; schoolmaster in the Gorbals, Glasgow, in 1760; in 1761 taught English and church music in the Bakers' Hall, Gibson's Wynd, Glasgow; precentor in the Tron Church, Glasgow, from 1761 to November 1762; taught church music "in the Edinburgh method" in conjunction with one John Sigismond Peters, "late chorister in the Cathedral, Carlile" (sic). Girvin seems to have settled at Port-Glasgow as schoolmaster in 1762, succeeding one John McEwen, who removed to Greenock. Edited

'A New Collection of Church Tunes,' Glasgow, 1761. No copy of this work seems to be known. From an advertisement in the 'Glasgow Journal,' it is stated to contain thirty-eight tunes in all, thirty in four parts and eight in three parts.

'The Vocal Musician. Part I. Wherein the grounds of music are distinctly handled,' Edinburgh, 1763. This work is dedicated to George Murdoch, Esq., late Provost, and the ministers of the City of Glasgow, . . . with no other view than to express in public a sense of their favours and regard on several occasions shown to their most humble and most obedient servant, John Girvin. The preface is dated Port-Glasgow, September 1763.

In 1761 Girvin issued, in conjunction with one Collet, 'Proposals for printing by subscription, Vocal Music, Moral and Divine, in three books.'

Gray, W., signed the preface to

'A Collection of Psalm Tunes, in Four Parts. Neatly engraved on copper. To which is prefixed a short Introduction, for explaining in an easy manner the chief difficulties that commonly hinder the progress of those that are learning to read and sing Music.' Edinburgh, 1758. The above contains eighteen tunes, principally taken from the Scottish Psalters.

Hamilton, David, Scottish organ-builder, music-seller, and writer; born at Edinburgh, April 2, 1803; organist in St John's Episcopal Church, Edinburgh; died at Edinburgh, December 1863. Inventor of the *pneumatic lever* action for organs, and writer of musical articles in Chambers's 'Encyclopædia.' Edited with J. M. Müller

'Harmonia Sancta; A Collection of Chants, Psalm Tunes, Sanctuses, Responses, &c., adapted to the Service of the Episcopal Church of Scotland, from the Works of the most eminent Ancient and Modern Composers; including a number of Original Chorales of the German Protestant Church, never before published in this country; also a few contributions composed expressly for this work; to which is prefixed an Explanation of the System of Chanting according to the most approved Method.' Preface dated January 1838. A supplement was added about 1858, edited by David and Adam Hamilton.

Hamilton, William, music publisher, Glasgow; born about 1812; died at Kirn, April 25, 1887. Edited

'Select Psalmody, arranged for Four Voices, with an accompaniment for the Pianoforte or Organ.' No date. This was again issued in 1853 under the title of 'Hamilton's Diamond Psalmody.' It contains many tunes still in use, and a large number of originals by musicians then resident in the west of Scotland.

Henderson's, Rev. Andrew, Collections. See page 168.

Holden's, John, Collection. See page 171.

Hume, Alexander, son of William Hume and Elizabeth Robertson; born at St John's Hill, Edinburgh, February 7,[1] 1811; engaged in business and teaching in Edinburgh and Glasgow; died at Glasgow, February 4, 1859. Composer of church music, glees, duets, songs, &c.; minor poet. Edited

'British Psalmody; A Collection of Four Hundred and Thirty-Seven Psalm and Hymn Tunes.' . . . Edinburgh (1844). This contains many tunes by Hume, none of which have obtained popularity. In the compilation of this work Hume was assisted by Thomas Clark and Benjamin F. Flint, both of Canterbury. The above was also published in two volumes as 'The Psalm Tune Book' and 'The Hymn Tune Book.' Hume also edited 'Anthems and Sacred Songs, containing Fifty-four Pieces selected from

---

[1] Not the 17th, as stated by all his biographers.

the most Popular Composers, together with several Original Compositions.' His name will not readily be forgotten as a composer, for his setting of "Afton Water" by Burns has become indelibly associated with these words.

Hume, William, son of the preceding; born at Edinburgh, September 25, 1830; now teacher of music at Glasgow; musical critic of the 'Bailie,' Glasgow, for several years; correspondent of London musical journals; composer of the cantatas "Bartimeus," "The Call to Battle," and Psalm 67, for treble voices; also many excellent glees and arrangements of popular airs. Edited

'Psalm and Hymn Tunes,' with supplement of Anthems; 'Union Sacred Tune Book,' and other works.

Hunter, Thomas Munro, a native of Alloa; born 1820; studied under Finlay Dun in Edinburgh, also under Romer in London; appointed precentor of Morningside Church, Edinburgh, about 1837, and in 1843 to a similar position in Greenside Church, resigning in 1845 on being chosen leader of psalmody in Rose Street U.P. Church (afterwards Palmerston Place U.P. Church), an office he held till his retirement in 1883. For a long period he held a prominent position as a teacher of singing in Edinburgh, and in this capacity he acted in very many of the schools and institutions of the city, including George Watson's Hospital (from 1848); Heriot's Hospital outdoor schools (from 1847); Donaldson's Hospital (from 1857); Heriot's Hospital (from 1860). When the Merchant Company's schools were opened, he acted as singing-master in George Watson's College, and in James Gillespie's school. He was also a Fellow of the Educational Institute of Scotland. Hunter rendered good service in connection with the Society for the Revival of Sacred Music in Scotland. This Society, which was instituted as early as 1842 under Dr Mainzer, seems to have been in abeyance for some time, but was revived under the presidency of Lord Murray, and Hunter held the appointment of musical director as late as 1862. He was a man of untiring industry, and his stalwart figure was a familiar one in Edinburgh for nearly half a century. Although he had retired from active duty, his death on July 16, 1886, was unexpected, being the result of a carriage accident. He compiled in 1858, for use of the Rose Street congregation,

'A Supplement to R. A. Smith's Sacred Harmony, consisting of Doxologies, Anthems, Tunes, &c.' It contained upwards of sixty numbers, including several of his own composition. This Supplement was afterwards extended at different times by additional supplements of anthems, hymn tunes, &c., until it reached over two hundred numbers. In 1868 he prepared for the use of Queen Street (now Eyre Place) U.P. Church a Psalmody containing about one hundred tunes. These collections were printed and lithographed for private use, and with the exception of the one dated 1858, were not published.

Hunter was author of 'The Elements of Vocal Music,' also many collections of songs for junior and senior classes, which had an extensive circulation.

Hutcheson, Charles, born 1792; amateur musician and composer; merchant in Glasgow; died 1856. Published

'Christian Vespers,' Glasgow, 1832, containing hymn tunes harmonised in three and four parts, and an introductory essay on church music. His once popular tune "Stracathro," associated with the hymn "O for a closer walk with God," appears in the above collection, but from some unexplained cause has not found a place in the works now in use.

Hymn Music. See page 177.

Jamieson, Robert Dickson, born at Glasgow, September 6, 1834; appointed leader of Psalmody in Free St Stephen's Church, Glasgow, 1854, a position he resigned in 1890; minor poet; secretary of the West of Scotland Branch of the Tonic Sol-fa College. Edited in 1871,

'Twenty (original) Psalm and Hymn Tunes,' one of which, "Arden," will be found in the 'The Scottish Hymnal,' 1872. Also 'The Children's Tribute of Praise,' 1879, a work of more than ordinary merit, for Sunday-schools.

Johnson, James, a native of Ettrick; music-seller and engraver in Edinburgh; flourished at the end of last and beginning of the present century; said to have been the first who attempted to strike music upon pewter plates; died at Edinburgh, February 26, 1811. Edited

'The Complete Repository of Psalm and Hymn Tunes, adapted to all the various Metres used in the principal Churches, Chapels, and Dissenting Congregations in Scotland.' Part First contains about 116 tunes and several anthems; Part Second about 131 tunes. It was published about the beginning of the present century. He will best be remembered by his 'Scots Musical Museum,' a work to which the poet Burns contributed some of his finest songs. It was issued in six volumes, the melodies being arranged by Stephen Clarke, a native of Durham, who came to Edinburgh in 1764 to compete for the vacant office of Master of Church Music, and though unsuccessful, settled in the capital, and became organist of the Episcopal Chapel in the Cowgate. Clarke died in 1797, before Johnson's work was finished, but William Clarke, his son, was intrusted with its completion.

Kenward, William Daniel, born in the Cliff, Lewes, Sussex,

March 21, 1797; educated at the Grammar School there; on the advice of Thomas Greatorex he became a pupil of the Ashleys; chorister in York and Durham Cathedrals successively; chorister at the York Musical Festival, 1823; appointed precentor of the West Church, Aberdeen, in succession to John Knott, 1824; resigned 1828, on being appointed to a similar position in the High Church, Edinburgh; singing-master at Heriot's Hospital from 1837, and conductor of the Edinburgh Harmonists' Society from 1829 till he died, May 1, 1860. Edited four books of psalmody, entitled—

'Sacred Harmony,' 1839;
'Sacred Harmony,' *circa* 1848;
'The Psalmody of Scotland,' 1855, and 'The Scottish Psalm and Tune Book,' 1855.
These works contain a number of tunes by Kenward, none of which have gained a place in the collections now in use, although one of them, "Lewes," was for a time popular, and is worthy of a place in any Hymnal.

Knott, John, probably born at Seven Oaks, Kent, where his father was a Baptist minister; said also to have been a chorister in Durham Cathedral; appointed precentor in the West Church, Aberdeen, and public teacher of vocal music in that city in 1811; resigned 1824, on being elected precentor of the New North Church, Edinburgh; music-master at Heriot's Hospital from 1827 till he died in 1837. "An excellent tenor vocalist and a gentlemanly man." Edited

'Sacred Harmony; Being a Collection of Psalm and Hymn Tunes and Select Pieces of Sacred Music.' Dedicated to Charles Forbes, Esq., M.P., Aberdeen, 1814. Second edition, 1815. There are about one hundred tunes in the work, harmonised in three parts. Also, 'A Selection of Tunes, in Four Parts, adapted to the Psalms and Paraphrases of the Church of Scotland,' Edinburgh. No date: *circa* 1828. Contains about one hundred tunes, many of which are still in use.

Lithgow, William Hume, son of Andrew Lithgow and Catharine Hume; born at Leith, February 15, 1806; pupil of an Edinburgh professor, and also of several Italian masters in London, where he studied for nearly five years; appointed conductor of psalmody in St Enoch's Parish Church, Glasgow, and music-master at the High School, May 1842,[1] holding both offices till he died,

---

[1] He had performed the duties at St Enoch's gratuitously for some years previous to his appointment, by way of assistance to his predecessor, John McDougall, who held the office for the long period of forty years.

August 22, 1874; a prominent figure in Glasgow musical circles about thirty years ago. Edited

'Parochial Sacred Music,' no date, which contains many original tunes by Lithgow; also

'A Selection of Sacred Music; with Accompaniments for the Organ or Pianoforte,' no date. The sixth edition contains upwards of twenty tunes by Lithgow and several arrangements.

Livingston, Rev. Neil, D.D., was Free Church minister of Stair, Ayrshire, from 1844 till 1886, when he retired to reside in Ayr. He was one of the small committee of the Church which brought out the 'Scottish Psalmody' (see Free Church Collections). This committee adopted various means to promote in congregational worship the singing of simple and tasteful tunes in parts. They issued a monthly periodical, which was continued for a year, and gave public lectures to congregations. In this work Dr Livingston took a large share.

The Reprint of 'The Scottish Metrical Psalter of A.D. 1635,' with copious Dissertations and Notes, published in 1864 through the munificence of the late William Euing of Glasgow, remains as a monument of Dr Livingston's industry and research. It may be considered as the ground on which the University of Glasgow conferred on him the degree of D.D.

McDonald's, Alexander, Collection. See page 209.

Macfarlane, John Reid, son of Duncan Macfarlane, a member of the Ayrshire Militia Band; born 1800; appointed precentor of Outer High Church (now St Paul's), Glasgow, March 1824; resigned December 1828; settled in London as composer and teacher for some years; died at Middlesex Hospital, June 10, 1841. Revised the harmonies of

'Harmonia Sacra; A Selection of Sacred Music, Ancient and Modern, in Four Parts,' Glasgow, about 1835. Two of Macfarlane's tunes enjoyed for a time considerable popularity—viz., "Merksworth" and "Laigh Common," but they belong to a class of tunes now obsolete.

Macfarlane, Thomas, brother of the preceding; born at Horsham, Sussex, 1808; baptised November 11; pupil of the late Andrew Thomson of Glasgow, afterwards of J. B. Cramer, Henry Herz, Bergotti, and Garcia; in January 1827 appointed organist of the Old Episcopal Chapel, Glasgow; afterwards of St Mary's Episcopal Church (then in Renfield Street), resigned January 28, 1834; next of St Jude's, Glasgow; precentor of Park Church from 1859 to 1866; harmoniumist in Camden Road Presbyterian Church, London, from 1871 till 1882; conductor of Camden Road Choral Society for a few years; retired from all professional duties in 1882; editor of several collections of psalmody; composer of songs, pianoforte music, anthems, and psalm and hymn tunes. Mr Macfarlane was from an early period conductor of the Glasgow Amateur Musical Society, and on April 2, 1844, conducted[1] the first performance of Händel's "Messiah" ever given at Glasgow, Sims Reeves singing the tenor solos. Edited

'Congregational Psalmody of St Jude's Church, Glasgow,' no date.

'Selection of Sacred Music, containing a Selection of Psalm and Hymn Tunes, Chants, Te Deums, &c.,' no date.

'Park Church Psalmody,' Glasgow, 1860.

'The Chorale and Supplementary Psalmody; A Selection of Ancient German and other Chorales,' no date.

Machray, Alexander, son of Mr John Machray, dyer in Aberdeen; born at Aberdeen, June 7, 1837; studied singing and pianoforte-playing under Richard Latter (now one of the teachers in the Guildhall School of Music, London), and harmony under the late W. R. Broomfield; leader of psalmody in the East Church, Aberdeen, from about 1855 to December 1876; secretary, at various dates, of the following musical societies—The Harmonic Choir, Aberdeen Choral Union, and the Aberdeen Musical Association; member of the firm of Messrs Cochran & Macpherson, advocates, in Aberdeen; president of the Society of Accountants in Aberdeen, 1889. Edited

'The Scottish Psalmist: a Manual of Standard and Choice Psalm and Hymn Tunes for Christian Worship,' Aberdeen, 1876. The work, which was originally intended for the special service of the congregation of the East Church, Aberdeen, contains upwards of four hundred tunes and several chants, the harmonies being revised by the late W. R. Broomfield.

McLachlan, John, teacher of music at Glasgow last century; appointed precentor of the North West Church there, February 1774; died 1791. Edited

'The Precentor; or, An Easy Introduction to Church Music, with a Choice Collection of Psalm Tunes, all in three and four parts,' Glasgow, 1776. Second edition, 1779. (See Brown, William.) In the compilation of this work McLachlan was assisted by one Finlay, doubtless the Rev. Dr Robert Finlay, who was minister of the North West Church when McLachlan was precentor. The majority of the tunes in 'The Precentor' are still in use.

[1] In some works this honour is wrongly bestowed on J. R. Macfarlane.

Maclean, William, Scottish poet and amateur musician; born at Glasgow, March 22, 1805. Educated at Glasgow University; manufacturer and merchant in Glasgow; justice of the peace for the counties of Renfrew and Lanark. Published

'Maclean's Sacred Music, arranged for Four Voices, with Organ and Pianoforte Accompaniment,' two parts, 1854-55. His tune "Golgotha,' in the above, was for a time popular. Composer of a large volume of 'Sacred Melodies' in manuscript, now deposited in the Mitchell Library, Glasgow.

Mainzer's, Joseph, Collection. See page 201.

Maitland, William, a shoemaker to trade; appointed precentor in the East Church, Aberdeen, in 1821, and held office till 1827; emigrated to Canada and became minister of a Congregational church there; died December 1873. Edited in 1823,

'The Aberdeen Psalmody; Being a Collection of Tunes, in four parts, adapted to the Psalms and Paraphrases of the Church of Scotland. Intended chiefly for the use of the East Church Congregation. Carefully selected and arranged from the best Authors, and respectfully Dedicated to the Rev. Dr Ross and the Rev. Robert Doig.' The work contains 89 tunes (two of which are the compositions of Maitland), and was for many years extensively used in Aberdeen.

Miller, William Mackie, a distinguished teacher of the Tonic Sol-fa method; born at Glasgow, 1831; educated at Wilson's Bluecoat School, which he entered about 1838; received his first musical instruction from William Logan, the well-known Glasgow missionary; appointed leader of psalmody in East Campbell Street Free Church, Glasgow, 1856; teacher of the music-classes in Greendyke Hall, Glasgow, 1860; from 1866 leader of psalmody in Free St Matthew's Church, Glasgow, resigning in 1875 on being appointed Musical Inspector for the Church of Scotland; lecturer on music in the Free Church Normal College, Glasgow, since 1873; appointed music-master to the Glasgow School Board, 1874, and had the honour of arranging the schemes of instruction in music at present carried on in all the schools of the Board; founded the Glasgow Tonic Sol-fa Choral Society, which existed for about twenty-five years, and performed for the first time in Scotland several of Händel's oratorios, and Dr A. C. Mackenzie's "Rose of Sharon." Since the introduction of the Tonic Sol-fa system into Scotland, Mr Miller has held a foremost place as a teacher of the method, and has done much to spread a knowledge of music among the people.

His collections of school songs are very numerous, and are extensively used. Edited

'The Presbyterian Psalter,' Glasgow, 1872.

Mitchison, William, was a well-known figure in Glasgow musical circles in the middle of this century. About 1833 he became manager of Mrs Brown's music warehouse, and in 1839 began business on his own account in Buchanan Street as an English and foreign music-seller. About 1854 he gave up business and went to New York. Edited

'The Psalmist's Companion; A Collection of Devotional Harmony for the use of Presbyterian Churches, selected from the Works of Steven, Robertson, R. A. Smith,' &c., Glasgow. No date. About 1843. An improved and enlarged edition of Robertson's 'Selection of Sacred Music,' 1830. This was published as 'Mitchison's Selection of Sacred Music,' 1834. These works are now of little value. Mitchison was author of 'A Few Remarks on the Pianoforte,' giving details of the mechanical construction of that instrument. Glasgow, 1845.

Moore's, Thomas, Collections. See page 215.

Neukomm, Chevalier Sigismund, composer and pianist; born at Salzburg, July 10, 1778; studied under Michael and Joseph Haydn; chapel-master to Emperor of Russia at St Petersburg, 1806; Chevalier of Legion of Honour, 1815; chapel-master to Dom Pedro of Brazil, Rio Janeiro, 1816 to 1821; appeared in London 1829, and spent much of his time in England and Paris; died at Paris, April 3, 1858. Composer of oratorios, masses, psalms, &c. He set to music, at the request of the Association for the Revival of Sacred Music in Scotland,

'Twenty Psalms selected from the Authorised English Version.' In this work, which is handsomely got up, the *whole* of each prose psalm is set to music, and the voices are divided into two choruses of four parts each, which respond to each other. The year of publication was 1853.

Nicol, James, Aberdeen, printed in 1714

'Twelve Tunes for the Church of Scotland.' This collection the writer has not seen, but it was doubtless formed by a selection of tunes from the Scottish Psalters.

Nicolson, Ludovick, a weaver to trade; born at Paisley about 1770; amateur musician and composer of psalmody; an intimate associate of Robert Tannahill and R. A. Smith; died at Paisley,

August 3, 1852, and buried in the West Relief churchyard. Published in 1852

'A Collection of Psalm and Hymn Tunes in four parts, adapted to various Metres, and may be used in the principal Churches, Chapels, and Dissenting Congregations in Scotland.'

His tune "Paisley" was for many years much used, and is quite worthy of a place in any collection. It was composed, on returning home from the funeral of his wife, to Paraphrase liii., verse 8 :—

"A few short years of evil past,
We reach the happy shore,
Where death-divided friends at last
Shall meet, to part no more."

"Low Church," also popular for a time, he composed for R. A. Smith's 'Devotional Music,' Paisley (1810).

Palmer, James, born at Southwold, Suffolk, December 7, 1796 ; teacher of music at Edinburgh ; precentor in Broughton Place U.P. Church there from 1830 to 1851 ; died at Edinburgh, July 23, 1863. Edited

'Sacred Harmony, Original and Selected ; in four vocal parts, suited to the Psalms, Paraphrases, and Hymns, used in all the Congregations of Scotland,' Edinburgh, no date. This contains twenty tunes by Palmer, and 'A Companion to Sacred Harmony' three others.

'Christian Harmony ; A Collection of Sacred Music. Adapted to the various Metres in general use.' Published in parts: no date. Part I. has a number of originals by Palmer, and one by H. E. Dibdin.

Palmer seems also to have edited a work entitled 'The Sacred Minstrel.'

Ramage, Adam, born at Edinburgh, October 10, 1788 ; a pewterer to trade ; afterwards a music-teacher ; appointed precentor of St Andrew's Parish Church, Edinburgh, in succession to Alexander Maclagan, February 13, 1838 ; singing-master at Heriot's Hospital outdoor schools, Edinburgh, 1846 ; died April 5, 1863. Edited

'The Sacred Harmony of St Andrew's Church, Edinburgh, in four vocal parts, with Accompaniment for the Organ or Pianoforte,' 1843. The above was designed as a supplement to R. A. Smith's Collections. It contains forty-six tunes, two of which are originals by Ramage. There are several by John Thomson, Professor of Music at Edinburgh University (died 1841).

Robertson, John, teacher of vocal and instrumental music at Glasgow early in the present century; died there March 11, 1827, aged fifty years. Edited in 1814

'A Selection of the best Psalm and Hymn Tunes, some of which are original, in four parts ; adapted to the various Metres used in the Established

Churches, Chapels, and Dissenting Congregations in Scotland.' This contains many tunes still in use.

Also, 'The Seraph; A Selection of Psalm and Hymn Tunes, many of them original, for four voices:' no date. (Published September 1827.) This has thirteen original tunes, which were "the private property of Robertson," notably Hugh Wilson's "Martyrdom," bearing the name "Fenwick" as well, and another by Wilson, although anonymous—viz., "Caroline," associated with the hymn "Our life contains a thousand springs."

Later editions of this were issued by John Robertson, Jun. In 1834 it was enlarged and improved, and published as 'Brown's Robertson's Selection of Sacred Music.'

Ross, John, born at Newcastle-on-Tyne, October 12, 1763; pupil of Hawdon, organist of St Nicholas Church there; appointed organist of St Paul's Church, Aberdeen, in 1783 or 1784, and held the office for fifty-three years; organist to the Aberdeen Musical Society; died at Craigie Park, Aberdeen, July 28, 1837. A musician of more than local celebrity. Contributed several airs to R. A. Smith's 'Scottish Minstrel.' Edited

'Sacred Music, consisting of Chants, Psalms, and Hymns, for three voices, with a part for the Organ or Pianoforte,' London (1828). The tunes are principally originals by Ross, but are not now in use.

'**Sacred Harmony**; A Collection of Popular Psalm and Hymn Tunes, for the use of St Thomas's English Episcopal Chapel; the whole carefully revised and arranged for four voices after the old standard harmonies, with an Accompaniment for the Organ and Pianoforte by an eminent Professor.' Edinburgh (1861). Contains eighty-eight tunes, the majority of which are still in use.

Shaw, William Maxwell, probably a native of Aberdeen; pupil of Urbani; precentor for a time of the High Church, Inverness; afterwards resident in Dingwall; appointed by the magistrates of Aberdeen, December 1797, precentor of the West Church, and teacher of vocal music in that city; resigned in 1805, and removed to Boston, U.S., where he died in July of that year.

"His manner of singing the psalms was characterised by a fine simplicity, blended with sparing ornament; and his taste was so much admired that the congregation accompanied him very softly, that they might be able to hear his beautifully round and manly voice, which appeared to fill the church without any exertion or disagreeable loudness."

Shaw was a frequent performer at the high-class concerts given in Edinburgh at the close of last century. Edited

'A Collection of Church Tunes, compiled and composed for the improvement of those who may not have the opportunity of teachers to instruct them, with the simple graces the author uses in singing. Dedicated to the Honourable the Lord Provost, Bailies, and remanent Members of the Town Council of Aberdeen.' It contains thirty-one tunes, six of which are originals by Shaw. There is also one by John Ross of Aberdeen, and one by Stephen Clarke of Edinburgh.

Sievewright, John, a well-known teacher of psalmody in the north of Scotland, was settled in Old Meldrum, Aberdeenshire, at the beginning of the present century, and probably earlier. He succeeded John Barbour as precentor in the Parish Church there, and held the office till 1835, when he retired, the kirk-session granting him an allowance of £3 yearly. Sievewright possessed a good knowledge of music, and had a fair compass of voice; but he was afflicted with an impediment in his speech, which was not in his favour. During the years he held office as precentor, he never attempted to train a choir, but always had a few good singers to assist him in leading the congregation, and had them placed in front of him in the first seat of the gallery, and some still live who remember him calling out to them the names of the tunes to be sung for the day. Sievewright died at Old Meldrum about 1846. Two of his sons, John and James—the former a teacher and the latter a doctor—emigrated to Upper Canada. Sievewright's sole occupation seems to have been the teaching of psalmody. He had an old white pony on which he used to ride about through the counties of Aberdeen, Banff, and Kincardine, to meet his classes. His connection with the latter county began, it seems, in 1794, as may be gleaned from the following verse, which formed part of a "skit" written about the beginning of the present century:—

> "In t' year o' 1794,
> When Hielant John the hills came o'er,
> He taught them a' to gape and glower,
> And sing the tunes in Fordoun."

The second verse refers to an incident which took place one Sunday when the precentor was absent, and one after another of Sievewright's pupils mounted the *lettern* to fill his place, but not one of them could sing correctly a single psalm-tune:—

> "Up startit then the bricht Dunbar,
> Instead o' better he did waur,
> An' a' the singin' he did maur,
> An' lost the lines in Fordoun."

It seems probable that Sievewright was resident in Fordoun at one time, as on the title-page of the work mentioned below he styles himself "Teacher of Music, Fordoun." One who knew him states that he was "a canty weel-faured man, who wore a black coat somewhat browned with age." He published

'A Collection of Church Tunes and Anthems in three parts; with a few Duets, Catches, Glees, &c., selected from the best authors. A New Edition, Enlarged;' no date. The work contains about sixty tunes, and is now very scarce.

Smith's, R. A., Collections. See page 261.

Smith, William, son of the Rev. Dr Alexander Smith, minister of the Chapel of Garioch; born at Garioch, December 6, 1803; educated at the Grammar School, Aberdeen, for many years; a merchant in that city; amateur musician and composer of psalmody; died at Newtyle, near Dundee, August 31, 1878. Edited

'The People's Tune Book,' Aberdeen, 1844. "Whatever" (says Mr William Carnie of Aberdeen) "southern or western critics may claim or say —whatever finical fault-finders amongst ourselves may pretend—there is unchallengeable proof that 'The People's Tune Book' contained the best lesson our modern psalmodists and precentors ever got as to what is noble, pure, and beautiful in Scottish congregational music."

Smyth, William Hugh, born in the parish of Ballyeaston, Co. Antrim, 20th March 1836; first studied under the organist of St Nicholas Church, Carrickfergus, and later under several masters in Glasgow; gained the first prize at the Society of Arts examinations in harmony and counterpoint in 1861, and in 1862 was appointed organist of St John's Episcopal Church, Glasgow; in 1864 appointed to Sandyford Parish Church, Glasgow, which appointment he held till 1877, when other more important avocations obliged him to relinquish the duties of organist. Edited in conjunction with Dr E. J. Hopkins (see that name)

'The Choral Psalter, Containing The Authorised Version Of The Psalms, And Other Portions of Scripture, Pointed for Chanting, With A Selection of Chants,' 1869.

Besides containing the standard chants by composers of the seventeenth and eighteenth centuries, this work contains original compositions by Sir George J. Elvey, Dr Stephen Elvey, Henry Smart, Sir H. S. Oakeley, Mus. Doc., and A. L. Peace, Mus. Doc. It is said to be the first appearance of the Bible translation of the Psalms in a complete form pointed for chanting.

Steven, James, "music-seller in the New Town," Glasgow, early in the present century, and leader of psalmody at the University Hall; said also to have held a similar position for a time in the Tron Church, but of this there is no record; died before 1833. Published in 1801,

'First Collection of Psalm and Hymn Tunes, in four vocal parts.' Five volumes of this work were issued, the sixth being published in 1833, and edited by John Turnbull. He also edited 'Harmonia Sacra.' Steven's Collections are now of little value.

Surenne, John Thomas, a pupil of Henri Herz, was born in London, March 4, 1816. His father, Gabriel Surenne, a Frenchman, was a musician of ability, and is said to have been a good performer on the violin, viola, double bass, bassoon, and guitar. He removed to Edinburgh in 1817, in which city he is still remembered as being the author of a French-English Dictionary and other works.

In 1831 young Surenne was appointed organist of St Mark's Episcopal Chapel, Portobello, a post he held till about 1842, and two years later organist of St George's Episcopal Chapel, Edinburgh, resigning many years after on account of overwork. He died at Edinburgh, February 3, 1878. His compositions include several songs; an Overture in D, dedicated to the Leith Philharmonic Society; "Rondo de Concert," with accompaniments for two violins, viola, and 'cello, dedicated to J. M. Müller; "La Reconnaissance, Divertimento," dedicated to J. M. Wood; and many others. He will be best remembered by 'The Song and Dance Music of Scotland,' which he edited; also 'The Songs of Ireland.' In 1843 he edited, in conjunction with Henry E. Dibdin,

'A Collection of Church Music, consisting of Chants, Psalm and Hymn Tunes, principally original; arranged for four voices, with an accompaniment for the Organ or Pianoforte,' a supplement appearing in 1844. Also, 'The Scottish Episcopal Church Music Book,' Edinburgh. No date.

Thomson's, Rev. Dr Andrew, Collection. See page 278.

Thomson, James, "Teacher of Music, English, &c., Leith," is probably the same who led the psalmody in Lady Yester's Church, Edinburgh, for upwards of thirty years, and who retired from the office in 1830, receiving from the Town Council a pension of £15 yearly for the excellent manner in which he filled the office. Published

'The Rudiments of Music; To Which is Added a Collection Of The Best Church Tunes, Hymns, Canons, and Anthems. Dedicated to the Right Honourable the Earl of Haddington, . . . Governor of the Musical Society in Edinburgh,' Edinburgh, 1778. Thomson's work contains about forty-three tunes, the majority of which are still in use. A third edition, enlarged and improved, was printed in 1793.

Turnbull, John, son of John Turnbull; born at Paisley, January 12, 1804; music-seller at Ayr, and from 1827 precentor of the New Church there; settled in Glasgow on being appointed precentor of St George's Parish Church, July 19, 1833; died November 1, 1844. Turnbull was a musician of considerable local celebrity, and noted for his excellent knowledge of harmony. Edited

'A Selection of Original Sacred Music, in four vocal parts. . . . Intended to form the sixth volume of Steven's Sacred Music,' Glasgow, 1833. Second edition, October 1840. This contains sixteen originals by Turnbull, and has a preface written by C(harles) H(utchison). Also R. A. Smith's 'Devotional Music,' no date. Also, in conjunction with Robert Burns, music-seller, Glasgow, 'The Sacred Harp; A Selection of the most approved Sacred Melodies, with a variety of Original Tunes, Hymns, Anthems, &c., composed and arranged expressly for this work.' . . . Glasgow (1840). Second edition, no date. This contains Turnbull's "Torwood," which he composed extempore within the ruins of Torwood Castle, near Falkirk, September 1838. It was associated with Paraphrase xviii. verse 6, and is still occasionally heard.

Vale of Leven Tonic Sol-fa Association, one of the oldest musical societies in Scotland, was founded in 1862, and continues still in a flourishing condition.

'Selections Illustrative of the Psalmody of the Christian Centuries' was issued for the use of the members about 1870. It contains examples of Ancient, Medieval, Reformation, Post-Reformation, and Modern psalmody.

Walker, Charles, amateur musician; organist of St John's Episcopal Church, Aberdeen, for nearly twenty-six years; excellent flute-player and tenor vocalist; merchant and commission agent at Aberdeen, where he died, October 1875, aged fifty-eight years. Adapted and arranged

'The Music of the Hymnal as used in St John the Evangelist's, Aberdeen:' no date (about 1853).

Wilson's, John, Collection. See page 305.

PRINTED BY WILLIAM BLACKWOOD AND SONS.